The Bohemians

The Bohemians

American Adventures from Bret Harte's Overland Monthly

Edited by
Robert A. Bennett

Pioneer Press Books
Walla Walla, Washington
U.S.A.
1987

Library of Congress Catalog Number 87-062281

Pioneer Press Books
35 South Palouse
Walla Walla, WA 99362

Cover art by Norman Adams

Acknowledgments

A project such as this book is rarely a one person job, but rather is the result of the efforts of many people. It never fails to amaze me how much information is stored in our libraries, archives and museums. They are the repositories of our heritage, our unique history and the things that stamp us as Americans. I would like to extend my thanks for their help to the following people, most of whom either work in or with such institutions:

L.L. "Larry" Dodd, of Penrose Memorial Library at Whitman College; the staff of the Bancroft Library at Berkeley, California; David Thackery of the Newberry Library in Chicago; J. Bailes of the Library of Congress; Geraldine Davis of the California State Library in Sacramento; Nancy Pryor, Penrose Memorial Library, Whitman College; Lucille M. Patterson of Falls Church, Virginia; Bob Clark of the Montana Historical Society Library; Candace Pierce of Walla Walla, Washington; and Whitney Ellis of Walla Walla, Washington.

TABLE OF CONTENTS

Adventures in the South Seas

Adventures of the True Bohemian

Bohemianism

"Bohemianism" is of necessity opposed to "Podsnappery". It is sometimes opposed also to respectability, and always to conventionalism. Mr. John Podsnap, Charles Dickens' pompous British Philistine, protested anything likely to bring a blush into the cheek of a young lady, and *always* knew the exact designs of Providence! While Podsnappers concoct formulas, Bohemians forthwith swallow them. The chief cause of the antagonism which exists between Bohemianism and Podsnappery is the want of respect manifested by the former for the conventionalities of the latter.

The distinguishing features of a Bohemian are: antipathy for formulas, inherent restlessness and originality. Bohemians have no social creed, no tenets, no articles of faith in common. Attempt to pin Bohemianism down to a formula and you destroy its existence, which depends upon freedom from all conventional restraints.

In the old established societies of Europe with their well-defined social system, any departure from the clearly cut grooves of custom stood out. This is fortunate, because we are able to view many of them chronicled in the pages of history.

However, it wasn't to be from the closed monarchies of Europe that nineteenth century Bohemians would emerge. Freedom, so necessary to Bohemian existence, was found in the great republic, the United States. From the land of the farm and forest, from lake and prairie, from valley and mountains, the American Bohemians swarmed forth to replenish the earth and subdue it.

Their mission in the nineteenth century was one of progress and enlightenment. By weary travel in foreign lands, stubborn research amid the graves of buried theories, patient investigation, earnest thought, and ceaseless yearning after light and truth, they made their way. They were often wrong, and when wrong, as obstinate as when they were right. They were misled, and then as misleading to others. Often enthusiastic to the verge of fanaticism, they then exercised a similar influence upon their surroundings.

Yet, in the main, they were truth-seekers and expounders, light-seekers and diffusers, liberty-seekers and bestowers. After all is said and done, the Bohemians are the world's original men, bereft of whose energies and lacking whose onward struggles, our earth would be but a dull and stagnant planet!

Adventure
of
The Overland

Bohemianism flourished in nineteenth century America, especially in the unfettered West. Freedom, that ingredient so necessary for Bohemian existence, was at the heart of the new republic. The Constitution of 1787 and its subsequent Bill of Rights, ratified by 1791, opened the way for nineteenth century opportunities. With most of the good land in the East already taken, the West beckoned as the land of the future.

In the early 1840's, wagon trains began their transcontinental migration, following what became known as the Overland Trail. But it wasn't until the 1849 California gold discovery that the great onslaught of people descended on the West Coast. Tens of thousands came looking for their golden opportunity. San Francisco, with its wonderful bay and central location, both in proximity to the gold fields and as a coastal port, was destined to become the cultural and economic hub of the Far West.

To this city in December of 1851 came a young gold seeker named Anton Roman, fresh from his claim at the fabulously rich Scott's Bar, with over a hundred ounces of gold dust in his pack. At the bookstore of Burgess, Gilbert and Still he was persuaded to exchange some of his gold for books, which he intended to sell to the miners in their winter camps. The venture turned out to be so profitable that the lad abandoned his mining and went into the book business fulltime. By 1859 he had opened a permanent bookstore on Montgomery Street in San Francisco. From his position in the bookstore, Roman saw the need for books which

Anton Roman, first publisher of the Overland Monthly.

dealt with local concerns. One of the earliest books he published (1860) was a history of California from its discovery to 1849. Another was John S. Hittell's *The Resources of California* (1863), which passed through several editions. By 1868 Roman was considered one of the West Coast's major publishers. His successes brought him a personal acquaintanceship with most of the contributors to the current literature of the far West. Manuscripts were constantly submitted to him by these writers and he became convinced that enough was available to create a monthly magazine. A magazine, he said, "that would furnish information for the development of our new state and all this great territory (embracing the Pacific), to make itself of such value that it could not fail to impress the West, and the East also."

One writer who Anton Roman knew he could depend upon for contributions to the magazine was a young man named Francis Bret Harte. In fact, when Roman solicited advice as to who would edit the magazine, it was Harte who prominent people in the San Francisco literary community recommended.

The young man had a good background for the job. Raised in the sedate old city of Albany, New York, he was trained and educated by his father, a teacher and scholar with refined and distinctly literary tastes. To him Harte was indebted for his early acquaintance with the best literature and a familiarity with classical lore.

In 1857, when he turned eighteen, he was swept off his feet by the rising tide of migration to California, and he went there to visit his half-sister near Humbolt Bay. Harte was not averse to any kind of work, but his small physique made him unsuitable for hard manual labor. For a while he did odd jobs, acting occasionally as a messenger and tutoring the children of local farmers.

When a newspaper was started Harte got the job of "printer's devil". Apt and dexterous, he soon knew the typecases and had plenty of leisure time which he employed in writing bright locals and sketches. Soon, in addition to his other duties, he was made Assistant Editor.

Bret Harte c. 1870

-4-

A person who knew Harte in those days on Humboldt Bay remembered him as an interesting young man, well educated, with refined tastes and a keen sense of humor. "We saw a great deal of him socially at this time. He was fond of a game of *Whist*, and was genial and witty, but rather quiet and reserved. He was fond of a practical joke and something of a tease. A sensitive school teacher had married an Englishman who never failed to misplace his aspirates. One evening, Harte skillfully brought the conversation to songs and innocently mentioned *Kathleen Mavourneen*, saying with apparent candor, 'I don't remember the words. How does it begin?' The Englishman rose to the bait and exclaimed: 'The 'orn of the 'unter is 'eard on the 'ill,' whereupon the eyes of the schoolteacher flashed, while Harte's twinkled."

Craving greater opportunities, Harte moved to San Francisco in 1859. His first work was as a printer for a weekly newspaper, the *Golden Era*. During his idle time he wrote filler articles for the paper and his superiors quickly realized the young man's potential. Soon he was in the editorial chair. From the *Era* he went to *The Californian*, a literary weekly, but Harte wasn't the type of writer who could churn out columns of type very fast. As one of his associates reported, he worked slowly, looking at his desk awhile, and thinking it all out. He would write one paragraph, while others were pouring out columns; but, he added, "that paragraph was worth more than all our columns."

To Harte's rescue came one of his greatest admirers and supporters, the Unitarian minister Rev. Thomas Starr King. He predicted Harte's fame long before it happened. Early in 1864, King persuaded his friend J.B. Swain, Superintendent of the Mint, to hire Harte as his secretary. The new job at the mint was just the atmosphere the young writer needed.

During this period, he wrote some of the best known of his verses, including: *The Society Upon the Stanislaus*, *John Burns of Gettysburg*, and other gems which appeared in various San Francisco newspapers. To commemorate the death of his friend Thomas Starr King in March of 1864 he wrote *Relieving Guard*, in which a sentry, noting a falling star says to his comrade:

> "Somehow it seemed to me that God
> Somewhere had just relieved a picket."

The Lost Galleon, a collection of patriotic verse, was published in 1865, followed by *Condensed Novels*, and *Bohemian Papers*, a volume of prose in 1867. It was during this period that he wrote his famous California romance, *The Story of M'liss*, which was his first step towards his characteristic western American style that was to be copied by countless others who followed.

Part of the atmosphere at the mint included the visitors who dropped by on business and talked with the young secretary. One visitor to Swain's office tells of the following incident: "Upon entering the office I found Mr. Swain was engaged and while waiting for him, Samuel Clemens came into the room. Mr. Clemens had just arrived in San Francisco from Nevada City, where a few days before he had witnessed the most curious jumping frog contest. While Clemens was telling the story, Mr. Swain opened the door of his private office and asked me to step inside. "I remarked, 'Come out here, Swain, I want you to listen to this.' Mr. Swain accordingly joined our circle and Clemens began his story anew. The story was told in an inimitable manner, and its auditors were convulsed with laughter. When the story was completed, Bret Harte told Mr. Clemens that if he would write that account half as well as he told it, it would be the funniest story ever written." The story was put into manuscript form and printed in the *Golden Era* as *The Jumping Frog of Calaveras County*, gaining immediate attention as one of

Samuel L. Clemens, humorist

the best humorous short stories ever written.

In 1865 Anton Roman was familiar enough with Bret Harte to ask him to edit a packet of clippings which had been gathered together by a Mary Tingely. The resulting book of California verse was titled *Outcroppings* and proved to be an immediate success. In 1867 Harte edited for Roman the *Poems of Charles Warren Stoddard*. So Roman knew of Bret Harte's editorial skills when Charles Warren Stoddard recommended his friend for the job as editor of the new literary magazine in 1868. What worried the publisher, however, were his fears that Harte would make the magazine too literary, while Roman was also interested in helping develop the material interests of the region.

When Roman approached the young writer with the editorship, Harte raised doubts as to whether sufficient material of a proper character could be secured for a monthly magazine. He also wondered if there was a large enough market for the proposed plan. Roman assured him that he would procure half of the articles needed for the first six issues. He then showed Harte a map of the two hemispheres, pointing out San Francisco's central position. Finally, he showed the young writer the financial support he had enlisted from the business community. Harte only insisted on a few conditions before accepting the position. One was that he was to have absolute editorial control. The other was that all contributions would be published unsigned, as in the manner common to the periodicals of the Atlantic states. Thus assured, Harte agreed to tackle the new project, with Noah Brooks and W.C. Bartlett to serve as Associate Editors.

Facsimile of the cover of the first
Overland Monthly

The name, *Overland Monthly*, the cover, the bear logo, and the whole typographical appearance of the new magazine were selected by Harte. In the magazine's first issue he explained the name. "Turn your eyes to this map made but a few years ago. Do you see this vast interior basin of the continent, on which the boundaries of States and territories are less distinct than the names of wandering Indian tribes; do you see this broad zone reaching from Virginia City to St. Louis, as yet only dotted by telegraph stations, whose names are familiar, but of whose locality we are profoundly ignorant? Here creeps the railroad, each day drawing the West and East closer together." He went on to say that the new arrivals traveling the broad overland highway would settle this vast land. Coming across the overland highway would not only be people and merchandise but "the subtle inflowing of Eastern refinement, and shall we not, by the same channel, throw into Eastern exclusiveness something of our own breadth and liberality? What could be more appropriate for the title of a literary magazine, than to name it after this broad highway?" he asked.

Anton Roman had used a grizzly bear as his trademark in previous publications, but when Bret Harte became involved, he felt that the bear seemed to be floating in space. Drawing two parallel lines under the bear, he said, represented the new transcontinen-

tal railroad, then nearing completion. Harte said of his logo, "Take him if you please as the symbol of local primitive barbarism. He is crossing the tracks of the Pacific railroad, and has paused a moment to look at the coming engine of civilization and progress."

It was Anton Roman's desire to have Harte write a story for at least every other issue of the magazine. To that end, Roman kept close company with Harte for nearly three months prior to the first issue of the magazine, printed in July of 1868. During their time together, Roman provided the writer with sketches, tales and incidents depicting the life of the miners in the gold camps. Roman described those times as "delightful pleasure to me, and never can I forget his charming companionship." Bret Harte was charming to be with and, as Secretary of State John Hay once said of him, "Harte, you know, was not only one of the wittiest of men himself, but he was like a whetstone, the cause of wit in others."

The new editor and his two associates, Bartlett and Brooks, each agreed to write a short story for the first issue. While each of his associates finished their pieces on time, Harte finally confessed that he had not been able to complete his contribution. It was begun, he said, and at one time virtually finished. But dissatisfied with the work, he had thrown it aside and started out fresh. He promised the story would be ready for the August issue.

The Luck of Roaring Camp was finally written, although hindered for a few days in manufacture for the second issue. The hindrance came in the form of a "vestal virgin" from the printing office where the *Overland* was put into type. She declined to have her hand in the proof-reading or publication of a story in which one of the characters was a "soiled" dove and where another remarks: "He rastled with my finger, the d____d little cuss!" In telling of the incident, Harte said, "Believing only that I was the victim of some extraordinary typographical blunder, I at once set down and read proof. In its metamorphosis which every writer knows, seeing your story in type, changes his relations to it and makes it no longer seem a part of himself. As I read on, I found myself affected, even as I had been affected in the conception and writing of it — a feeling so incompatible with the charges against it that I could only lay it down and declare emphatically, that I could really see nothing objectionable in it." In fact, Harte threatened to resign if the story wasn't printed as written, and thus confronted, Roman agreed.

Although *The Luck of Roaring Camp* sounded the entry of a new writer into the field of American literature, a new note in modern fiction, and the employment of a new medium in literary art, it was not greeted with any enthusiasm by the public to which it had been primarily addressed — the California readers. "A few prurient prudes," to employ Harte's language, "frantically excommunicated it, and anathematized it as the offspring of evil." Actually, what made Californians reject the story was they felt it gave the wrong impression to the outside world of California life at the time. But the artistic quality of the tale, its original dissimilarity to current fiction, and its broad and generous humanity, made it warmly welcomed in the States beyond the mountains. Already the first issue of the *Overland Monthly* had secured a place and a cordial hearing in those States, and *Roaring Camp* fell into the hands of friendly readers and critics. It placed Bret Harte in great vogue at once.

Tangible evidence of the appreciation for the story speedily came to the then unknown and unnamed author in the shape of a letter from Fields, Osgood, and Co., the publishers of *The Atlantic Monthly*, making a request, upon the most flattering terms, for a story similar to the *"Luck."* Harte tried to write another story but his work failed to satisfy his own fastidious judgment. The wastebasket swallowed many sheets of his manuscript paper before he was willing to put into print his second tale, *"The Outcasts of Poker Flat,"* which appeared in the January issue. Thereafter the muse moved more swiftly, and *Miggles, Tennessee's Partner,* and other works appeared regularly in the magazine.

At the end of the first year of publication, Anton Roman was taken ill and advised by his physician to leave San Francisco for a rest. He sold the magazine to John H. Carmany for seventy-five hundred dollars. While Harte and Roman had gotten along fairly well, there was always a curious friction between the new publisher and his editor. When offers started arriving from the East, trying to induce Harte to leave California, Carmany made every effort to retain him. He was offered five thousand dollars a year for editing the magazine, one hundred dollars for every poem and story, and a quarter interest in the magazine. Carmany also offered to sponsor Harte on a lecture tour to be conducted under the auspices of the Mechanics Library Directors. Harte turned the offer down and, it is said, replied with quivering nostrils, "What, I to lecture before a lot of durned mechanics? Never!"

In September of 1870, Harte's poem, *Plain Language from Truthful James,* was published to almost universal acclaim. It soon acquired a shorter name and was extensively quoted as *The Heathen Chinee.* It's interesting to note that the poem very nearly missed being published at all.

It seems that Harte was short of copy for one issue of the magazine and needed a brief poem to fill the void. Nothing among the offerings of contributors satisfied his critical taste. When a colleague dropped by the office Harte revealed his quandary. After asking Harte why he did not write something himself, and receiving the reply that the writer was not in the mood, his friend sought permission to see Harte's manuscripts.

Upon discovering a poem entitled *On the Sinfulness of Ah Sin, as Reported by Truthful James,* he exclaimed "this is just the thing you want!" But Harte was not satisfied with the quality of the verse, and it required lengthy arguments to persuade him to send it to the printer.

After the type was set a number of revisions were made. Each alteration strengthened the thought and polished the form of expression. Some changes were suggested by the printer, the proof reader, and his friend, while others were original to Harte himself.

Strangely enough, Harte never became reconciled to publication of the final product, despite the fact that it was universally acclaimed as a great hit and added to his fame as much as anything he had written. If nothing else, the anecdote provides additional evidence that an author is frequently not the best judge of his own work!

Harte soon found that his literary efforts could command more than a California market. He had already given the *Overland Monthly* a national reputation; why should he not enter the larger world which was waiting for him? It came as no surprise to the friends who knew both Harte and the literary preferences of Eastern readers that he was soon asked to accept engagements in the older states of the Union. Accordingly, in the Spring of 1871, Harte resigned his office at the San Francisco Mint, his never-occupied professorship at University of California, and the editor's position at the *Overland Monthly*. He departed California, never to return.

Can Bret Harte be considered one of the Bohemians? The point is surely arguable in view of his aristocratic tendencies as well as his unwillingness to leave the security of a government position until his personal success made such a sinecure unnecessary. Yet Harte, like Twain, Cremony and many other writers who contributed to the *Overland*, did venture forth into a great unknown, seeking adventure, fame and fortune. Above all else, the characteristic which would qualify Harte as a Bohemian was his ability to be original. He was a pioneer in the interpretation of frontier life through the literary medium. He led an unconventional life, remaining always an artist who, with his bright pen, painted some of the finest word pictures in American Letters.

So much light has been shed on Bret Harte and his writings that it is easy to lose sight of the importance of the magazine he edited during his stay in San Francisco. This book is not designed to be Harte's definitive history, but is instead an anthology of some of the most interesting tales to appear in the *Overland*, the collection of which reflects to a great degree what the magazine was all about under Harte's editorial reign. As a reflection of the American spirit and the sense of adventure prevalent in its time, the *Overland Monthly* clearly had few rivals in the nation.

And it was Bret Harte's wisdom in his choice of contributors to the magazine which gave it license to such a claim. By selecting the stories of scientists, military persons, world travelers, professional writers and a host of other adventurers, it was he who gave the magazine its Bohemian flavor, for the Bohemianism of the last century was present not only in literature, but also in statesmanship, military affairs, art and commerce.

Harte included an editorial page reflecting his own keen wit and observations in every issue of the magazine. At the close of the editorial for the first issue of the *Overland* in July of 1868, he found it appropriate to end with a brief poem entitled *Returned*. We, too, find it apropos, and forthwith reprint that humorous sketch of nineteenth century life in the hopes that it will put the reader in the proper frame of mind to be transported back in time, to a day when sailing ships ruled the seas, and the horse was man's best friend.

It was a time when the American Bohemians were pouring forth to conquer the world. We hope, as you join them in their adventures, that you will agree it is a fascinating journey. After all, isn't there a little of the Bohemian left in each of us?

——————— Returned ———————

by Bret Harte

So you're back from your travels, old fellow
    And you left but a twelvemonth ago;
You've hobnobbed with Louis Napoleon,
    Eugenie, and kissed the Pope's toe.
By Jove, it is perfectly stunning,
    Astounding — and all that, you know,
Yes, things are about as you left them
    In Mud Flat a twelvemonth ago.

The boys! — They're all right — O, Dick
        Ashley,
    He's buried somewhere in the snow,
He was lost on the Summit, last winter,
    And Bob has a rough row to hoe.
You knew that he's got the consumption?
    You didn't! Well, come, that's a go;
I certainly wrote you at Baden,
    Dear me — that was six months ago.

I got all your outlandish letters,
    All stamped by some foreign P.O.,
I handed, myself, to Miss Mary
    That sketch of a famous chateau.
Tom Saunders is living at 'Frisco —
    They say that he cuts quite a show.
You didn't meet Euchre-deck Billy
    Anywhere on your road to Cairo?

So you thought of the rusty old cabin —
    The pines, and the valley below;
And heard the North Fork of the Yuba,
    As you stood on the banks of the Po?
'Twas just like your romance, old fellow;
    But now there is standing a row
Of stores on the site of the cabin
    That you lived in a twelvemonth ago.

But it's jolly to see you, old fellow —
    To think it's a twelvemonth ago!
And you have seen Louis Napoleon,
    And look like a Johnny Crapaud.
Come in. You will surely see Mary —
    You know we are married. What, no?
O, aye. I forgot there was something
    Between you a twelvemonth ago.

John C. Cremony, "king" of the Bohemians, led the most exciting of lives.

Charles M. Scammon, ship's captain, scientist and naturalist was a frequent contributor to *The Overland Monthly.*

Noah Brooks
Associate Editor of *The Overland Monthly*

Charles Warren Stoddard, one of Bret Harte's closest associates in San Francisco.

Miggles

by Bret Harte
June 1869

We were eight, including the driver. We had not spoken during the passage of the last six miles, since the jolting of the heavy vehicle over the roughening road had spoiled the Judge's last poetical quotation. The tall man beside the Judge was asleep, his arm passed through the swaying strap and his head resting upon it — altogether a limp, helpless-looking object, as if he had hanged himself and been cut down too late. The French lady on the back seat was asleep, too, yet in a half-conscious propriety of attitude, shown even in the disposition of the handkerchief which she held to her forehead and which partially veiled her face. The lady from Virginia City, traveling with her husband, had long since lost all individuality in a wild confusion of ribbons, veils, furs, and shawls. There was no sound but the rattling of the wheels and the dash of rain upon the roof. Suddenly the stage stopped and we became dimly aware of voices. The driver was evidently in the midst of an exciting colloquy with someone in the road — a colloquy of which such fragments as "bridge gone," "twenty feet of water," "can't pass," were occasionally distinguishable above the storm. Then came a lull, and the mysterious voice from the road shouted the parting adjuration:

"Try Miggles'."

We caught a glimpse of our leaders as the vehicle slowly turned, of a horseman vanishing through the rain, and we were evidently on our way to Miggles'.

Who and where was Miggles? The Judge, our authority, did not remember the name, and he knew the country thoroughly. The Washoe traveler thought Miggles must keep a hotel. We only knew that we were stopped by high water in front and rear, and that Miggles was our rock of refuge. A ten minutes' splashing through a tangled by-road, scarcely wide enough for the stage, and we drew up before a barred and boarded gate in a wide stone wall or fence about eight feet high. Evidently Miggles', and evidently Miggles did not keep a hotel.

The driver got down and tried the gate. It was securely locked.

"Miggles! O Miggles!"

No answer.

"Migg-ells! You Miggles!" continued the driver with rising wrath.

"Migglesy!" joined in the expression, persuasively. "O Miggy! Mig!"

But no reply came from the apparently insensate Miggles. The Judge, who had finally got the window down, put his head out and propounded a series of questions, which if answered categorically would have undoubtedly elucidated the whole mystery, but which the driver evaded by replying that "if we didn't want to sit in the coach all night we had better rise up and sing out for Miggles."

So we rose up and called on Miggles in chorus. Then separately. And when we had finished, a Hibernian fellow passenger from the roof called for "Maygells!" whereat we all laughed. While we were laughing the driver cried "Shoo!"

We listened. To our infinite amazement the chorus of "Miggles" was repeated from the other side of the wall, even to the final and supplemental "Maygells."

"Extraordinary echo," said the Judge.

"Extraordinary d—d skunk!" roared the driver, contemptuously. "Come out of that, Miggles, and show yourself! Be a man, Miggles! Don't hide in the dark; I wouldn't if I were you, Miggles," continued Yuba Bill, now dancing about in an excess of fury.

"Miggles!" continued the voice, "O Miggles!"

"My good man! Mr. Myghail!" said the Judge, softening the asperities of the name as much as possible. "Consider the inhospitality of refusing shelter from the inclemency of the weather to helpless females. Really, my dear sir—" but a succession of "Miggles," ending in a burst of laughter, drowned his voice.

Yuba Bill hesitated no longer. Taking a heavy stone from the road, he battered down the gate, and with the expressman entered the inclosure. We followed. Nobody was to be seen. In the gathering darkness all that we could distinguish was that we were in a garden—from the rose-bushes that scattered over us a minute spray from their dripping leaves—and before a long, rambling wooden building.

"Do you know this Miggles?" asked the Judge of Yuba Bill.

"No, nor don't want to." said Bill, shortly, who felt the Pioneer Stage Company insulted in his person by the contumacious Miggles.

"But, my dear sir," expostulated the Judge, as he thought of the barred gate.

"Lookee here," said Yuba Bill, with fine irony, "hadn't you better go back and sit in the coach till yer introduced? I'm going in," and he pushed open the door of the building.

A long room lighted only by the embers of a fire that was dying on the large hearth at its further extremity. The walls curiously papered, and the flickering firelight bringing out its grotesque pattern. Somebody sitting in a large arm-chair by the fire-place. All this we saw as we crowded together into the room, after the driver and expressman.

"Hello, be you Miggles?" said Yuba Bill to the solitary occupant.

The figure neither spoke nor stirred. Yuba Bill walked wrathfully toward it, and turned the eye of his coach lantern upon its face. It was a man's face, prematurely old and wrinkled, with very large eyes, in which there was that expression of perfectly gratuitous solemnity which I had sometimes seen in an owl's. The large eyes wandered from Bill's face to the lantern, and finally fixed their gaze on that luminous object, without further recognition.

Bill restrained himself with an effort.

"Miggles! Be you deaf? You ain't dumb anyhow, you know;" and Yuba Bill shook the insensate figure by the shoulder.

To our great dismay as Bill removed his hand, the venerable stranger apparently collapsed—sinking into half his size and an undistinguishable heap of clothing.

"Well, dern my skin," said Bill—looking appealingly at us, and hopelessly retiring from the contest.

The Judge now stepped forward, and we lifted the mysterious invertebrate back into his original position. Bill was dismissed with the lantern to reconnoitre outside, for it was evident that from the helplessness of this solitary man there must be attendants near at hand, and we all drew around the fire. The Judge, who had regained his authority and had never lost his conversational amiability—standing before us with his back to the hearth—charged us, as an imaginary jury, as follows:

"It is evident that either our distinguished friend here has reached that condition, described by Shakespeare as 'the sere and yellow leaf,' or has suffered some premature abatement of his mental and physical faculties. Whether he is really the Miggles—"

Here he was interrupted by "Miggles! O Miggles! Migglesy! Mig!" and, in fact, the whole chorus of Miggles in very much the same key as it had once before been delivered unto us.

We gazed at each other for a moment in some alarm. The Judge, in particular, vacated his position quickly, as the voice seemed to come directly over his shoulder. The cause, however, was soon discovered in a large magpie who was perched upon a shelf over the fireplace, and who immediately relapsed into a sepulchral silence, which contrasted singularly with his previous volubility. It was undoubtedly his voice which we had heard in the road, and our friend in the chair was not responsible for the discourtesy. Yuba Bill, who had reëntered the room after an unsuccessful search, was loth to accept the explanation, and still eyed the helpless sitter with suspicion. He had found a shed in which he had put up his horses—but he came back dripping and skeptical. "Thar ain't nobody but him within ten mile of the shanty, and that'ar d—d old skeesicks knows it."

But the faith of the majority proved to be securely based. Bill had scarcely ceased growling, before we heard a quick step upon the porch, the trailing of a wet skirt, the door was flung open, and with a flash of white teeth, a sparkle of dark eyes, and an utter absence of ceremony or diffidence, a young woman entered, shut the door, and panting leaned back against it.

"O, if you please, I'm Miggles!"

And this was Miggles! This bright-eyed, full-throated young woman, whose wet gown of coarse blue stuff could not hide the beauty of the feminine curves to which it clung; from the chestnut crown of whose head—topped by a man's oil-skin sou-wester—to the little feet and ankles—hidden somewhere in the recesses of her boy's brogans, all was grace—this was Miggles, laughing at us, too, in the most airy, frank, off-hand manner imaginable.

"You see, boys," said she—quite out of breath, and holding one little hand against her side, quite unheeding the speechless discomfiture of our party, or the complete demoralization of Yuba Bill, whose features had gradually relaxed into an expression of gratuitous and imbecile cheerfulness—"You see, boys, I was mor'n two miles away when you passed down the road. I thought you might pull up here, and so I ran the whole way, knowing nobody was home but Jim—and—and—I'm out of breath—and—that lets me out."

And here Miggles caught her dripping oil-skin hat from her head, with a mischievous swirl that scattered a shower of rain-drops over us; attempted to put back her hair; dropped two hairpins in the attempt; laughed and sat down beside Yuba Bill, with her hands crossed lightly on her lap.

The Judge recovered himself first, and essayed an extravagant compliment.

"I'll trouble you for that hair-pin," said Miggles, gravely. Half a dozen hands were eagerly stretched forward; the missing hair-pin was restored to its fair owner; and Miggles, crossing the room, looked keenly in the face of the invalid. The solemn eyes looked back at hers, with an expression we had never seen before. Life and intelligence seemed to struggle back into the rugged face. Miggles laughed again—it was a singularly eloquent laugh—and turned her black eyes and white teeth once more toward us.

"This afflicted person is"—hesitated the Judge.

"Jim," said Miggles.

"Your father?"

"No."

"Brother?"

"No."

"Husband?"

Miggles darted a quick, half-defiant glance at the two lady passengers who I had noticed did not participate in the general masculine admiration of Miggles, and said, gravely: "No—it's Jim."

There was an awkward pause. The lady passengers moved closer to each other. The Washoe husband looked abstractedly at the fire; and the tall man apparently turned his eyes inward for self-support at this emergency. But Miggles' laugh, which was very infectious, broke the silence. "Come," she said, briskly, "you must be hungry. Who'll bear a hand to help me get tea?"

She had no lack of volunteers. In a few moments Yuba Bill was engaged like Caliban in bearing logs for this Miranda; the expressman was grinding coffee on the veranda; to myself the arduous duty of slicing bacon was assigned; and the Judge lent each man his good-humored and voluble counsel. And when Miggles, assisted by the Judge and our Hibernian "deck passenger," set the table with all the available crockery, we had become quite joyous, in spite of the rain that beat against windows, the wind that whirled down the chimney, the two ladies who whispered together in the corner, or the magpie who uttered a satirical and croaking commentary on their conversation, from his perch above. In the now bright, blazing fire we could see that the walls were papered with illustrated journals, arranged with feminine taste and discrimination. The furniture was extemporized, and adapted from candle boxes and packing cases, and covered with gay calico, or the skin of some animal. The arm-chair of the helpless Jim was an ingenious variation of a flour-barrel. There was neatness and even a taste for the picturesque to be seen in the few details of the long low room.

The meal was a culinary success. But more, it was a social triumph — chiefly, I think, owing to the rare tact of Miggles in guiding the conversation, asking all the questions herself, yet bearing throughout a frankness that rejected the idea of any concealment on her own part. So that we talked of ourselves, of our prospects, of the journey, of the weather, of each other — of everything but our host and hostess. It must be confessed that Miggles's conversation was never elegant, rarely grammatical, and that at times she used expletives, the use of which had generally been yielded to our sex. But they were delivered with such a lighting up of teeth and eyes, and were usually followed by a laugh — a laugh peculiar to Miggles — so frank and honest that it seemed to clear the moral atmosphere.

Once, during the meal, we heard a noise like the rubbing of a heavy body against the outer walls of the house. This was shortly followed by a scratching and sniffling at the door. "That's Joaquin," said Miggles in reply to our questioning glances; "would you like to see him?" Before we could answer, she had opened the door, and disclosed a half-grown grizzly, who instantly raised himself on his haunches, with his forepaws hanging down in the popular attitude of mendicancy, and looked admiringly at Miggles, with a very singular resemblance in his manner to Yuba Bill. "That's my watch-dog," said Miggles in explanation. "O, he don't bite," she added, as the two lady passengers fluttered into a corner. "Does he, old Toppy!" — (the latter remark being addressed directly to the sagacious Joaquin). "I tell you what, boys," continued Miggles, after she had fed and closed the door on *Ursa Minor*, "you were in big luck that Joaquin wasn't hanging round when you dropped in to-night."

"Where was he?" asked the Judge. "With me," said Miggles. "Lord love you; he trots around with me nights like as if he was a man."

We were silent for a few moments, and listened to the wind. Perhaps we all had the same picture before us — of Miggles walking through the rainy woods, her savage guardian at her side. The Judge, I remember, said something about Una and her lion; but Miggles received it as she did other compliments, with quiet gravity. Whether she was altogether unconscious of the admiration she excited—she could hardly have been oblivious of Yuba Bill's adoration—I knew not; but her very frankness suggested a perfect sexual equality that was cruelly humiliating to the younger members of our party.

The incident of the bear did not add anything in Miggles's favor to the opinions of those of her own sex who were present. In fact, the repast over, a chillness radiated from the two lady passengers, that no pine boughs brought in by Yuba Bill and cast as a sacrifice upon the hearth could wholly overcome. Miggles felt it; and suddenly declaring that it was time to "turn in," offered to show the ladies to their bed in an adjoining room. "You, boys, will have to camp out here by the fire as well as you can," she added, "for thar ain't but the one room."

Our sex—by which, my dear sir, I allude of course to the stronger portion of humanity—has been generally relieved from the imputation of curiosity, or a fondness for gossip. Yet I am constrained to say, that hardly had the door closed on Miggles that we crowded together, whispering, snickering, smiling, and exchanging suspicions, surmises, and a thousand speculations in regard to our pretty hostess. I fear that we even hustled that imbecile paralytic, who sat like a voiceless Memnon in our midst, gazing, with the serene indifference of the Past in his passionless eyes, upon our wordy councils. In the midst of an exciting discussion the door opened again, and Miggles reëntered.

But not, apparently, the same Miggles who a few hours before had flashed upon us. Her eyes were downcast, and as she hesitated for a moment on the threshold, with a blanket on her arm, she seemed to have left behind her the frank fearlessness which had charmed us a moment before. Coming into the room, she drew a low stool beside the paralytic's chair, sat down, drew the blanket over her shoulders and saying, "If it's all the same to you, boys, as we're rather crowded, I'll stop here to-night," took the invalid's withered hand in her own and turned here eyes upon the dying fire. An instinctive feeling that this was only premonitory to more confidential relations, and perhaps some shame at our previous curiosity, kept us silent. The rain still beat upon the roof; wandering gusts of wind stirred the embers into momentary brightness, until, in a lull of the elements, Miggles suddenly lifted up her head and throwing her hair over her shoulder, turned her face upon the group and asked:

"Is there any of you that knows me?"

There was no reply.

"Think again! I lived at Marysville in '53. Everybody knew me there, and everybody had the right to know me. I kept the Polka Saloon until I came to live with Jim. That's six years ago. Perhaps I've changed some."

The absence of recognition may have disconcerted her. She turned her head to the fire again and it was some time before she again spoke, and then more rapidly:

"Well, you see I thought some of you must have known me. There's no great harm done, anyway. What I was going to say was this: Jim here"—she took his hand in both of hers as she spoke—"used to know me, if you didn't, and spent a heap of money upon me. I reckon he spent all he had. And one day—it's six years ago this winter—Jim came into my back room, sat down on my sofy, like as you see him in that chair, and never moved again without help. He was struck all of a heap, and never seemed to know what ailed him. The doctors came, and said as how it was caused all along of his way of life—for Jim was mighty free and wild like—and that he would never get better, and couldn't last long anyway. They advised me to send him to Frisco to the hospital, for he was no good to any one and would be a baby all his life. Perhaps it was something in Jim's eye, perhaps it was that I never had a baby, but I said 'No.' I was rich then, for I was popular with everybody—gentlemen like yourself, sir, came to see me—and I sold out my business and bought this yer place, because it was sort of out of the way of travel, you see, and I brought my baby here."

With a woman's intuitive tact and poetry, she had as she spoke slowly shifted her position so as to bring the mute figure of the ruined man between her and her audience—hiding in the shadow behind it—as if she offered it as a tacit apology for her actions. Silent and expressionless, it yet spoke for her; helpless, crushed, and smitten with the Divine thunderbolt, it still stretched an invisible arm around her.

Hidden in the darkness, but still holding his hand, she went on:

"It was a long time before I could get the hang of things about yer, for I was used to company and excitement. I couldn't get any woman to help me, and a man I dursent trust; but what with the Indians hereabout, who'd do odd jobs for me, and having everything sent from the North Fork, Jim and I managed to worry through. The Doctor would run up from Sacramento once in a while. He'd ask to see 'Miggles' baby,' as he called Jim, and when he'd go away, he'd say, 'Miggles; you're a trump—God bless you;' and it didn't seem so lonely after that. But the last time he was here he said, as he opened the door to go: 'Do you know, Miggles, your baby will grow up to be a man yet and an honor to his mother; but not here, Miggles, not here!' And I thought he went away sad—and—and"—and here Miggles' voice and head were somehow both lost completely in the shadow.

"The folks about here are very kind," said Miggles, after a pause, coming a little into the light again. "The men from the Fork used to hang around here, until they found they wasn't wanted, and the women are kind—and don't call. I was pretty lonely until I picked up Joaquin in the woods yonder one day, when he wasn't so high, and taught him to beg for his dinner; and then thar's Polly—that's the magpie—she knows no end of tricks, and makes it quite sociable of evenings with her talk, and so I don't feel like I was the only living being about the ranch. And Jim here," said Miggles, with her old laugh again, and coming out quite into the firelight, "Jim—why, boys, you would admire to see how much he knows for a man like him. Sometimes I bring him flowers, and he looks at 'em just as natural as if he knew 'em; and times, when we're sitting here alone, I read him those things on the wall. Why, Lord!" said Miggles, with her frank laugh, "I've read him that whole side of the house this winter. There never was such a man for reading as Jim."

"Why," asked the Judge, "do you not marry this man to whom you have devoted your youthful life?"

"Well, you see," said Miggles, "it would be playing it rather low down on Jim, to take advantage of his being so helpless. And then, too, if we were man and wife, now, we'd both know that I was *bound* to do what I do now of my own accord."

"But you are young yet and attractive—"

"It's getting late," said Miggles, gravely, "and you'd better all turn in. Good night, boys;" and throwing the blanket over her head, Miggles laid herself down beside Jim's chair, her head pillowed on the low stool that held his feet, and spoke no more. The fire slowly faded from the hearth; we each sought our blankets in silence; and, presently, there was no sound in the long room, but the pattering of the rain upon the roof, and the heavy breathing of the sleepers.

It was nearly morning when I awoke from a troubled dream. The storm had passed, the stars were shining, and through the shutterless window the full moon, lifting itself over the solemn pines without, looked into the room. It touched the lonely figure in the chair with an infinite compassion, and seemed to baptize with a shining flood the lowly head of the woman whose hair, as in the sweet old story, bathed the feet of him she loved. It even lent a kindly poetry to the rugged outline of Yuba Bill, half-reclining on his elbow between them and his passengers, with savagely patient eyes keeping watch and ward. And then I fell asleep and only woke at broad day, with Yuba Bill standing over me, and "All aboard" ringing in my ears.

Coffee was waiting for us on the table, but Miggles was gone. We wandered about the house and lingered long after the horses were harnessed, but she did not return. It was evident that she wished to avoid a formal leave-taking, and had so left us to depart as we had come. After we had helped the ladies into the coach, we returned to the house and solemnly shook hands with the paralytic Jim, as solemnly settling him back into position after each hand-shake. Then we looked for the last time around the long, low room, at the stool where Miggles had sat, and slowly took our seats in the waiting coach. The whip cracked, and we were off!

But as we reached the high road Bill's dexterous hand laid the six horses back on their haunches, and the stage stopped with a jerk. For there, on a little eminence beside the road, stood Miggles, her hair flying, her eyes sparkling, her white handkerchief waving, and her white teeth flashing a last "good bye." We waved our hats in return. And then Yuba Bill, as if fearful of further fascination, madly lashed his horse forward and we sank back in our seats. We exchanged not a word until we reached the North Fork and the stage drew up at the Independence House. Then, the Judge leading, we walked into the bar-room and took our places gravely at the bar.

"Are your glasses charged, gentlemen?" said the Judge, solemnly taking off his white hat.

They were.

"Well, then, here's to *Miggles*, God Bless Her!"

Perhaps He had. Who knows?

A Californian Abroad—
A Few Parisian Sights

by Mark Twain
August 1868

We went to see the Cathedral of Notre Dame. We had heard of it before. We recognized the brown old Gothic pile in a moment; it was like the pictures. We stood at a little distance, and changed from one point of observation to another, and gazed long at its lofty square towers and its rich front, clustered thick with stony, mutilated saints who had been looking calmly down from their perches for ages. The Patriarch of Jerusalem stood under them in the old days of chivalry and romance, and preached the third crusade, more than six hundred years ago; and since that day they have stood there and looked quietly down upon the most thrilling scenes, the grandest pageants, the most extraordinary spectacles that have grieved or delighted Paris. These battered and broken-nosed old fellows saw many and many a cavalcade of mail-clad knights come marching home from Holy Land; they heard the bells above them toll the signal for the St. Bartholomew's Massacre, and they saw the slaughter that followed; later, they saw the Reign of Terror, the carnage of the Revolution, the overthrow of a king, the coronation of two Napoleons, the christening of the young prince that lords it over a regiment of servants in the Tuilleries today; and they possibly continue to stand there until they see the Napoleonic dynasty swept away, and the banners of a great Republic floating above its ruins. I wish these old fellows could speak. They could tell a tale worth the listening to.

They say that a Pagan temple stood where Notre Dame now stands, in the old Roman days, eighteen or twenty centuries ago—remains of it are still preserved in Paris; and that a Christian church took its place about A.D. 300; another took the place of that in A.D. 500; and that the foundations of the present cathedral were laid about A.D. 1100. The ground ought to be measurably sacred by this time, one would think. One portion of this noble old edifice is suggestive of the quaint fashions of ancient times. It was built by Jean Sans-Peur, Duke of Burgundy, to set his conscience at rest—he had assassinated the Duke of Orleans. Alas! those good old times are gone, when a murderer could wipe the stain from his name and soothe his troubles to sleep, simply by getting out his bricks and mortar, and building an addition to a church.

The portals of the great western front are bisected by square pillars. They took the central one away, in 1852, on the occasion of thanksgivings for the re-institution of the Presidential power — but very soon they had occasion to reconsider that motion and put it back again!

We loitered through the grand aisles for an hour or two, staring up at the rich stained glass windows embellished with blue, and yellow, and crimson saints and martyrs, and trying to admire the numberless great pictures in the chapels; and then we were admitted to the sacristy, and shown the magnificent robes which the Pope wore when he crowned Napoleon I; a wagon-load of solid gold and silver utensils, used in the great public processions and ceremonies of the church; some nails of the true cross, a fragment of the cross itself, and part of the crown of thorns. We had already seen a large piece of the true cross in a church at the Azores, but no nails. They showed us likewise the bloody robe that the Archbishop of Paris wore who exposed his sacred person and braved the wrath of the insurgents of 1848 to mount the barricades and hold aloft the olive branch of peace in the hope of stopping the slaughter. His noble effort cost him his life. He was shot dead. They showed us a cast of his face taken after death, the bullet that killed him, and the two vertebrae in which it was lodged. These people have a somewhat singular taste in the matter of relics. Our guide told us that the silver cross which the good Archbishop wore at his girdle was seized and thrown into the Seine, where it lay imbedded in the mud for fifteen years, and then an angel appeared to a priest and told him where to dive for it; that he *did* dive for it, and got it, and now it is there on exhibition at Notre Dame, to be inspected by anybody who feels an interest in inanimate objects of miraculous intervention.

Next we went to visit the Morgue, that horrible receptacle for the dead who die mysteriously by violence, or by other unknown ways. We stood before a grating and looked through into a room which was hung all about with the clothing of dead men; coarse blouses water-soaked; the delicate garments of women and children; patrician vestments, hacked and stabbed, and stained with red; a hat that was crushed and bloody. On a slanting stone lay a drowned man, naked, swollen, purple; clasping the fragment of a broken bush with a grip which death had so petrified that human strength could not unloose it — mute witness of that last despairing effort to save the life that was doomed beyond all help. A stream of water trickled ceaselessly over the hideous face. We knew that the body and the clothing were there for identification by friends, but still we wondered if anybody could love that repulsive object or grieve for its loss. We grew meditative, and wondered if, some forty years ago, when the mother of that ghastly thing was dandling it upon her knee, and kissing it and petting it, and displaying it with satisfied pride to the passers-by, a prophetic vision of this dread ending ever flitted through her brain. I half-feared that the mother, or the wife, or a brother of the dead man might come while we stood there: but nothing of the kind occurred. Men and women came, and some looked eagerly in pressing their faces against the bars; others glanced carelessly at the body, and turned away with a disappointed look – people, I thought, who live upon strong excitements, and who attend the exhibitions of the Morgue regularly, just as other people go to see theatrical spectacles every night.

One night we went to the celebrated *Jardin Mabille*, but I only stayed a little while. I wanted to see some of this kind of Paris life, however, and therefore, the next night, we went to a similar place of entertainment in a great garden in the suburb of Asnieres. We went to the railroad depot toward evening, and our guide got tickets for a second-class carriage. Such a perfect jam of people I have not often seen – but there was no noise, no disorder, no rowdyism. Some of the women and young girls that entered the train I knew to be of the *demimonde*, but others we were not at all sure about.

The girls and women in our carriage behaved themselves modestly and becomingly all the way out, except that they smoked. When we arrived at the garden in Asnieres, we paid a franc or two admission, and entered a place which had flower-beds in it, and grass plots, and long, curving rows of ornamental shrubbery, with here and there a secluded bower convenient for eating ice-cream in. We moved along the sinuous gravel-walks, with the great concourse of girls and young men, and suddenly a domed and filagreed white temple, starred over and over and over again with brilliant gas-jets, burst upon us like a fallen sun. Near by was a large, handsome house, with its ample front illuminated in the same way, and above its roof floated the star-spangled banner of America!

"Well!" I said; "how is this?" It nearly took my breath away.

Our guide said an American – a New Yorker – kept the place, and was carrying on quite a stirring opposition to the *Jardin Mabille*.

Crowds, composed of both sexes and nearly all ages, were frisking about the garden or sitting in the open air in front of the flag-ship and the temple, drinking wine and coffee, or smoking. The dancing had not begun yet. Our guide said there was to be an exhibition. The famous Blondin was going to perform on a tight rope in another part of the garden. We went thither. Here the light was dim, and the masses of the people were pretty closely packed together. And now I made a mistake which any donkey might make, but a sensible man never. I committed an error which I find myself repeating every day of my life. Standing right before a young lady, I said,

"Oh, Dan, just look at this girl, how beautiful she is!"

"I thank you more for the evident sincerity of the compliment, sir, than for the extraordinary publicity you have given to it."

This in good, pure English.

We took a walk, but my spirits were very, very sadly dampened. I did not feel right comfortable for some time afterward. Why *will* people be so stupid as to suppose themselves the only foreigners among a crowd of ten thousand persons?

But Blondin came out shortly. He appeared on a stretched cable, far away above the sea of tossing hats and hankerchiefs, and in the glare of the hundreds of rockets that whizzed heavenward by him he looked like a mere insect. He balanced his pole and walked the length of his rope — two or three hundred feet; he came back and got a man and carried him across; he returned to the center and danced a jig; next he performed some gymnastic and balancing feats too perilous to afford a pleasant spectacle; and he finished by fastening to his person a thousand Roman candles, Catherine wheels, serpents and rockets of all manner of brilliant colors, setting them on fire all at once, and walking and waltzing across his rope again in a blinding blaze of glory that lit up the garden and the people's faces like a great conflagration at midnight.

The dance had begun, and we adjourned to the temple. Within it was a drinking saloon, and all around it was a broad, circular platform for the dancers. I backed up against the wall of the temple, and waited. Twenty sets formed, the music struck up, and then — they were dancing the renowned *Can-can!* A handsome girl in the set before me tripped forward lightly to meet the opposite gentleman — tripped back again, grasped her dress vigorously on both sides with her hands, raised them to a considerable elevation, danced an extraordinary jig that had more activity and exposure about it than any jig I ever saw before, and then, drawing her clothes still higher, she advanced gaily to the centre, and launched a vicious kick full at her *vis-a-vis* that must infallibly have removed his nose if he had been nine feet high. It was a mercy he was only six. That is the *Can-can*. The idea of it is to dance as wildly, as noisily, as furiously as you can; expose yourself as much as possible, if you are a woman; and kick as high as you can, no matter which sex you belong to. There is no word of exaggeration in this. Any of the staid, respectable, aged people who were there that night can testify to the truth of that statement. There were a good many such people present. I suppose French morality is not of that straight-laced description which is shocked at trifles.

I moved aside, and took a general view of the *Can-can*. Shouts, laughter, furious music, a bewildering chaos of darting and intermingling forms, stormy jerking and snatching of gay dresses, bobbing heads, flying arms, lightning flashes of white-stockinged calves and dainty slippers in the air, and then a grand final rush, riot, a terrific hubbub and a wild stampede! Heavens! Nothing like it has been seen on earth since trembling Tam O'Shanter saw the devil and the witches at their orgies that stormy night in "Alloway's auld haunted kirk."

We visited the *Louvre* at a time when we had no silk purchases in view, and looked at its miles of paintings by the old masters. Some of them were beautiful, but at the same time they carried such evidences about them of the cringing spirit of those great men that we found small pleasure in examining them. Their nauseous adulation of princely patrons was more prominent to me and chained my attention more surely than the charms of color and expression in the pictures. Gratitude for kindnesses is well, but it seems to me that some of those artists carried it so far that it ceased to be gratitude, and became worship. If there is a plausible excuse for the worship of men, then by all means let us forgive Rubens and his brethren.

But I will drop this subject, lest I say something about the old masters that might as well be left unsaid.

Of course, we drove in the *Bois de Boulogne,* that limitless park, with its forests, its lakes, its cascades, and its broad avenues. There were thousands upon thousands of vehicles abroad, and the scene was full of life and gaiety. There were very common hacks, with father and mother and all the children in them; conspicuous little open carriages with celebrated ladies of questionable reputation in them; there were Dukes and Duchesses abroad, with gorgeous footmen perched behind the carriage, and equally gorgeous outriders perched on each of the six horses; there were blue and silver, and green and gold, and pink and black, all sorts of descriptions of stunning and startling liveries out. But presently the Emperor came along, and he outshone them all. He was preceded by a body-guard of gentlemen on horseback in showy uniforms, his carriage horses (there appeared to be somewhere in the remote neighborhood of a thousand of them) were bestridden by gallant looking fellows, also in stylish uniforms, and after the carriage followed another detachment of body-guards. Everybody got out of the way; everybody bowed to the Emperor and his friend, the Sultan, and they went by on a swinging trot and disappeared.

I will not describe the *Bois de Boulogne.* I cannot do it. It is simply a beautiful, cultivated, endless, wonderful wilderness. It is an enchanting place. It is in Paris, now, one may say; but a crumbling old cross in one portion of it reminds one that it was not always so. The cross marks the spot where a celebrated troubadour was waylaid and murdered in the fourteenth century. It was in this park that the fellow with an unpronounceable name made the attempt upon the Russian Czar's life, last spring, with a pistol. The bullet struck a tree. Our guide showed us the place. Now in America that interesting tree would be chopped down or forgotten within the next five years, but it will be treasured here. The guides will point out that tree to visitors for the next eight hundred years, and when it decays and falls down they will put up another there, and go on with the same old story just the same.

I think we have lost but little time in Paris. We have gone to bed, every night, tired out. Of course we visited the renowned International Exposition. All the world did that. We went there on our third day in Paris — and we stayed there nearly two hours. That was our first and last visit. To tell the truth, we saw at a glance that one would have to spend weeks — yea, even months — in that monstrous establishment, to get an intelligible idea of it. It was a wonderful show, but the moving masses of people of all nations we saw were still a more wonderful show. I discovered that if I were to stay there a month, I would still find myself looking at the people instead of the inanimate objects on exhibition. I got a little interested in some curious old tapestries of the thirteenth century, but a party of Arabs came by, and their dusky faces and unfamiliar costumes called my attention away at once. I watched a silver swan, which had a living grace about his movements and a living intelligence in his eyes — watched him swimming about as comfortably and as unconcernedly as if he had been born in a morass instead of a jeweler's shop — watched him seize a silver fish from under the water, and hold up his head and go through all the customary and elaborate motions of swallowing it — but the moment it disappeared down his throat some tattooed South Sea Islanders approached, and I yielded to their attractions. Presently I found a revolving pistol several hundred years old, which looked strangely like a modern Colt, but just then I heard that the Empress of the French was in another part of the building, and hastened away to see what she might look like. We heard martial music — we saw an unusual number of soldiers walking hurriedly about — there was a general movement among the people. We inquired what it was all about, and learned that the Emperor and the Sultan of Turkey were about to review 25,000 troops at the *Arc de l' Etoile*. We immediately departed. I had a greater anxiety to see these men than I could have to see twenty Expositions. We drove away and took up a position in an open space opposite the American Minister's house. A speculator bridged a couple of barrels with a board, and we hired standing places on it. Presently there was a sound of distant music; in another minute a pillar of dust came moving slowly toward us; a moment more, and then, with colors flying and a grand crash of military music, a gallant array of cavalrymen emerged from the dust and came down the street on a gentle trot. After them came a long line of artillery; then more cavalry, in splendid uniforms, and then their Imperial Majesties, Napoleon III and Abdul Azis! The vast concourse of people swung their hats and shouted; the windows and house-tops in all the wide vicinity became a snow-storm of waving handkerchiefs, and the wavers of the same mingled their cheers with those of the masses below. It was a stirring spectacle.

But the two central figures claimed all my attention. Was ever such a contrast set up before a multitude before? Napoleon in military uniform — a long-bodied, short-legged man, fiercely moustached, old, wrinkled, with eyes half-closed, and *such* a deep, crafty, scheming expression about them! — Napoleon bowing ever so gently to the loud plaudits, and watching everything and everybody with his cat-eyes from under his depressed hat-brim, as if to discover any sign that those cheers were not heart-felt and cordial.

Abdul Azis, absolute lord of the Ottoman empire — clad in dark-green European clothes, almost without ornament or insignia of rank; a red Turkish fez on his head — a short, stout, dark man, black-bearded, black-eyed, stupid, unprepossessing — a man whose whole appearance somehow suggested that if he only had a cleaver in his hand and a white apron on, one would not be at all surprised to hear him say: "A mutton roast to-day, or will you have a nice porter-house steak?"

Napoleon III, the representative of the highest modern civilization, progress and refinement; Abdul-Azis the representative of a people by nature and training filthy, brutal, ignorant, lustful, unprogressive and superstitious—and a government whose three graces are Tyranny, Rapacity, Blood. Here in brilliant Paris, under this majestic arch of triumph, the first century greets the nineteenth!

Napoleon III, Emperor of France! surrounded by shouting thousands, by military pomp, by the splendors of his capital city, and companioned by kings and princes—this is the man who was sneered at and reviled, and called bastard—yet who was dreaming of a crown and an empire all the while; who was driven into exile—but carried his dreams with him; who associated with the common herd in America, and ran foot-races for a wager—but still sat upon a throne in fancy; who braved every danger to go to his dying mother, and grieved that she could not be spared to see him cast aside his plebeian vestments for the purple of royalty; who kept his faithful watch, and walked his weary beat a common policeman of London—but dreamed the while of a coming night when he should tread the long drawn corridors of the Tuilleries; who made the miserable *fiasco* of Strasbourg, and saw his poor, shabby eagle forgetful of its lesson, refuse to perch upon his shoulder; delivered his carefully-prepared, sententious burst of eloquence into unsympathetic ears; found himself a prisoner, the butt of small wits, a mark for the pitiless ridicule of all the world—yet went on dreaming of coronations and splendid pageants, as before; who lay a forgotten captive in the dungeons of Ham—and still schemed, and planned and pondered over future glory and future power; President of France at last! a *coup d'etat*, and surrounded by applauding armies, welcomed by the thunders of cannon, he mounts a throne and waves before an astounded world the sceptre of a mighty empire!

Who talks of the marvels of fiction? Who speaks of the wonders of romance? Who prates of the tame achievements of Aladdin and the Magii of Arabia?

Abdul-Azis, Sultan of Turkey, Lord of the Ottoman empire! Born to a throne; weak, stupid, ignorant as his meanest slave; chief of a vast royalty, yet the puppet of his Premier and the obedient child of a tyrannical mother; a man who sits upon a throne—the beck of whose finger moves navies and armies—who holds in his hands the power of life and death over millions—yet who sleeps and sleeps; eats and eats; and when he is surfeited with eating and sleeping and would rouse up and take the reins of government and threaten to *be* a sultan, is charmed from his purpose by wary Fuad Pacha with a pretty plan for a new palace or a new ship—charmed away with a new toy, like any other restless child; a man who sees his people robbed and oppressed by soulless tax-gatherers, but speaks no word to save them; who believes in gnomes and genii, and the wild fables of the Arabian Nights, but has small regard for the mighty magicians of to-day, and is nervous in the presence of their mysterious railroads, and steamboats, and telegraphs; who would see undone in Egypt all that Great Mehemet Ali did, and would prefer rather to forget than emulate him; a man who found his great empire a blot upon the earth—a degraded, filthy, poverty-stricken miserable, lecherous, infamous agglomeration of ignorance, crime and brutality, and will idle away the allotted days of his trivial life, and then pass to the dust and worms and leave it so!

An acquaintance of mine said, the other day, that he was doubtless the only American visitor to the Exposition who had had the high honor of being escorted by the Emperor's body-guard. I said with unobtrusive frankness that I was astonished that such a long-legged, lantern-jawed, unprepossessing looking spectre as he should be singled out for a distinction like that, and asked how it came about. He said he had attended a grand military review in the *Champ de Mars*, some time ago, and while the multitude about him was growing thicker and thicker every moment, he observed an open space inside the railing. He left his carriage and went into it. He was the only person there, and so he had plenty of room, and the situation being central, he could see all the preparations going on about the field. By-and-by there was a sound of music, and soon the Emperor of the French and the Emperor of Austria, escorted by the famous *Cent Gardes*, entered the enclosure. They seemed not to observe him, but directly, in response to a sign from the commander of the Guard, a young lieutenant rode toward him, with a file of his men following, checked his horse, raised his hand and gave the military salute, and then said in a low voice that he was sorry to have to disturb a stranger and a gentleman, but the place was sacred to royalty. Then this Reese River phantom rose up and bowed and begged pardon. The officer rode beside him, the file of men marched behind him, and thus, with every mark of respect, he was escorted to his carriage by the Imperial *Cent Gardes!* The officer saluted again, and fell back. The Reese River sprite bowed in return and had presence of mind enough to pretend that he had simply called on a matter of private business, and so waved them an adieu, and drove from the field!

Imagine a poor Frenchman ignorantly intruding upon a public rostrum sacred to some six-penny dignitary in America. The police would scare him to death first, with a storm of their elegant blasphemy, and then pull him to pieces getting him away from there. We are measurably superior to the French in some things, but they are immeasurably our betters in others.

Enough of Paris, for the present. We have done our whole duty by it. We have seen the Tuilleries, the Napoleon Column, the Madeleine, that wonder of wonders the tomb of Napoleon, all the great churches and museums, libraries, imperial palaces and sculpture and picture galleries, the Pantheon, the *Jardin des Plantes*, the opera, the circus, the Legislative Body, the billiard-rooms, the barbers, the *grisettes*—

Ah, the *grisettes!* I had almost forgotten. They are another romantic fraud. They were always so beautiful—so neat and trim, so graceful—so naive and trusting—so gentle, so winning—so faithful to their shop duties, so irresistible to buyers in their prattling importunity—so devoted to their poverty-stricken students of the Latin Quarter—so light-hearted and happy on their Sunday picnics in the suburbs—and Oh, so charmingly, so delightfully improper!

Stuff! For three or four days I was constantly saying to our guide, "Is that a *grisette*?" And he always said "No." He comprehended, at last, that I wanted to see a *grisette*. Then he showed me dozens of them. They were like nearly all the French women I ever saw—homely. They had large hands, large feet, large mouths; they had pug noses, as a general thing, and moustaches that not even good breeding could overlook; they combed their hair straight back, without parting; they were ill-shaped; they were not winning, not graceful; I knew by their looks that they ate garlic and onions; it would be base flattery to call them immoral.

Down with the imposters! I sorrow for the vagabond student of the Latin Quarter now, even more than formerly I envied him. Thus topples to earth another idol of my infancy.

We have seen everything, and tomorrow we go to Versailles. We shall see Paris only for a little while as we come back to take up our line of march for the ship, and so I may as well bid the beautiful city a regretful farewell.

THE HEATHEN CHINEE

BY BRET HARTE

[From the Overland Monthly, September, 1870.]

Which I wish to remark---
    And my language is plain---
    That for ways that are dark,
    And for tricks that are vain,
The heathen Chinee is peculiar.
    Which the same I would rise to explain.

Ah Sin was his name;
And I shall not deny
  In regard to the same
What that name might imply.
  But his smile it was pensive and childlike
As I frequent remarked to Bill Nye.

It was August the third;
And quite soft were the skies;
  Which it might be inferred
That Ah Sin was likewise;
  Yet he played it that day upon William
And me in a way I despise.

Which we had a small
    game,
  And Ah Sin took a hand;
It was euchre. The same
  He did not understand;
But he smiled as he sat by
    the table,
  With a smile that was
    childlike and bland.

Yet the cards they were stocked
In a way that I grieve.
And my feelings were shocked
At the state of Nye's sleeve,
Which was stuffed full of aces and bowers.
And the same with intent to deceive.

But the hands that were played
By the heathen Chinee,
And the points that he made,
Were quite frightful to see----
Till at last he put down a right bower,
Which the same Nye had dealt unto me.

Then I looked up at Nye,
And he gazed upon me;
And he rose with a sigh,
And said, "Can this be?
We are ruined by Chinese cheap labor"---
And he went for that heathen Chinee.

In the scene that ensued
  I did not take a hand;
But the floor it was strewed
  Like the leaves on the
     strand
With the cards that Ah
  Sin had been hiding,
In the game "he did not
    understand."

In his sleeves, which were long,
  He had twenty-one packs---
    Which was coming it strong,
  Yet I state but the facts;
And we found on his nails, which were taper,
  What is frequent in tapers---that's wax

Which is why I remark,
  And my language is plain,
That for ways that are dark,
  And for tricks that are vain,
The heathen Chinee is peculiar---
Which the same I am free to maintain.

THE END

Overland Monthly, September 1902

Adventures
in the
New America

A Run Overland

by Thomas Magee
December 1868

I had made what Carlyle terms the fearful discovery that I had a stomach, and with the discovery, under a doctor's advice, had made a drug shop of it for some months, lightening my pocket sensibly as I increased the frequency of each potion. I had taken bitters and tonics, iron and bismuth, morphine and other allayers of nervous excitement. I had for weeks steadily dosed myself three times daily with a tonic which my physician had repeatedly assured me was "splendid medicine." I did not doubt his assertion; but my stomach refused to be comforted by it or any other medicinal preparation; my nerves, too, were obdurate, refusing to be strung again, charm them as I might never so wisely. I had a chronic complaint, and some complicated nervous affection with it, which produced sleeplessness, slow circulation, and great depression of spirits. My last and best physician had advised me to make a long trip into the country, where I could have rest, and change of scene and air. He especially recommended a trip by steamer to New York, and back overland. I listened to this advice for nearly three months before I set about acting upon it.

The passage by sea to New York occupied twenty-two days. I spent ten bustling days in the great city, and left it at five o'clock upon a Saturday evening, tired and weary; so tired, indeed, that so soon as the cars whisked out of the Jersey City dépôt, I had a sleeping-car made ready, in which I was glad to stretch myself. The evening was beautiful, the month was May – the most promising and hopeful of the year; I lay with open window, enjoying the scenery of New Jersey. Lying in a sleeping car in this way is very pleasant amusement. The scenes presented to the eye change as rapidly as the shifting views of a panorama – with this difference, that in the one case we have art, and in the other, natural pictures. One can enjoy it so lazily, too, without stirring a finger. Farms, farm-houses, cattle, men, houses, towns, manufactories, and historical spots, were passed by with lightning rapidity by our express train – passed almost too quickly, indeed. I frequently wished that our rate of speed was slackened, so that more time might have been left for a contemplation of beautiful and interesting sights or objects. Those who cross the continent upon the Pacific Railroad will find this stretching in a sleeping-car, with open window, one of the most delightful of siestas.

The farms and farm-houses of New Jersey have an air of neatness and solid comfort that I wish were thought more essential to California rural life. They resemble those of England, in many places—a resemblance which is increased by the occasional existence of fat hedges, in place of the usual gaunt American rail-fence. New Jersey farmers have not the reputation of being very liberal, but they seem to enjoy life thoroughly and quietly. They cultivate their land upon the European system, bestowing great care upon it, and thus obtain the largest crops. The soil of New Jersey is generally thin and poor, yet proper cultivation has made it one of the most productive States in the Union.

At nine, P.M., we stopped for a few minutes at a small town in Pennsylvania, where, as usual, there was only about one-fourth the requisite seats and quantity of provisions for the passengers. When I reached the table a hungry crowd had already come down upon it like a wolf on the fold, and had effectually swept and devoured it of everything but doughnuts and milk—a supper of which is highly suggestive of nightmare and midnight misery. But possible nightmare had less terrors than existing hunger; and a hurried meal was made at the very reasonable cost of twenty cents. During the past seven years, which have been famine ones in New York, everything eatable has continued cheap in the interior of Pennsylvania. Board at the best country hotels has been but ten to twenty dollars per month.

I had never before spent a night in a sleeping-car. I found the beds wide enough for two, and extremely comfortable, and warm in every respect. There is, however, no suitable space given for undressing, which operation must be performed in the exposed passage-way that runs through the center of the car. Men can endure this, but it is very unpleasant for ladies, who have to resort to many quick-witted schemes to avoid publicity. The lateral motion of the cars aids rather than prevents sleep; there is something soothing in it. I slept well, and awoke much disappointed to hear that I had missed the best scenery of the Alleghanies in the night. Spring and Nature were in tears that the coming Summer might rejoice. The air was balmy and inspiring, however; everything green had been washed over Saturday night to appear with clean face on Sunday morning. We were passing one of the greatest sinews of strength possessed by the majestic State of Pennsylvania—the coal region. The country was not a rich agricultural one at all, comparatively little of the land we passed being under cultivation; but it was rich in wood on the surface and in coal underneath—twin possessions of the most valuable character, which have done much to place Pennsylvania where she now is, in the van of States.

Pittsburg at ten, A.M.,—a greasy mechanic among cities, the face of which is never clean. Even on a sunny Sunday morning, after rain, Pittsburg was still in its dirty, working clothes. Every house, in the vicinity of the railroad dépôt especially, had a most unpleasantly begrimed appearance, as if the air was constantly filled with soot and dust of ashes. Pittsburg is, however, the useful Vulcan which forges the iron thunderbolts that move the world of manufactories and commerce. It is one of the most old-fashioned cities of the Union. A great many of the houses are of the obsolete, red-brick style, a few relics of which are still left on Pearl street and in the vicinity of the Battery, New York. The streets, too, in nearly every case, are narrow and tortuous. Pittsburg is, perhaps, such a hard-working city, that it has no time to spend on outward adornment. It is the greasy but most useful mudsill. The beauty of the Monongahela, Alleghany, and Ohio rivers, which meet beside it, is almost destroyed by smoky manufactories, dust- and ash-heaps, coal-barges, dusky-looking steamboats, and general confusion. Pittsburg occupies a basin in which the god of Iron Manufactures has constantly a thousand smoking altars blazing to his honor.

At two, P.M. after five hours' delay in Pittsburg—amid a bedlam-like crowd and noise, in which everybody was asking questions about the arrival and departure of cars, etc., which nobody either seemed competent or desirous of answering—we moved off on the Pittsburg, Fort Wayne and Chicago road, toward the latter city. For a few miles the road ran through long lanes of manufactories; but these passed, we entered one of the most beautiful countries on the world. Nature and art have combined to make it delightful. The Ohio river runs through it. Long lines of beautiful lawns, carpeted with the brightest of green, stretch back from the river, rising into hill and mountain, the sides of which are covered with trees and shrubs. Cosy farm-houses nestle in among fruit and shade trees; and fat, contented cattle lazily stared at us as we passed. Some of the handsomest private villas I have ever seen in America, lie in this region. The Ohio river is frequently disturbed by steamers and barges, but they add to the beauty and variety of the scene, rather than detract from it.

A night of misery (there being no sleeping-cars) passed slowly. The morning found us in Indiana—in a country where the soil is good, but the timber, the houses, and the people, are poor. The fences were awkwardly constructed, and the farms were in slovenly order. Everything reminded one of many of the shiftless-looking farms and farm-houses of California. Green, stagnant pools near many of the houses were proof positive to the eye that "fever-n-ager," as the people call it, made many a man tremble in both body and spirit. That portion of Indiana through which we passed was in the strongest possible contrast with the country we had seen the evening before. The last seemed the Happy Valley of Rasselas; the other, a country in which frogs, misery and discontent reigned.

Toward noon the weather became cold, raw and foggy—one of those drear days of damp discomfort which San Franciscans are so well acquainted with. That portion of Illinois through which we passed, east of Chicago, disappointed me; it resembled Indiana too much.

Chicago was reached at noon, forty-three hours after leaving New York, from which it is distant nine hundred miles. Chicago—the young Giant of the West—with its 250,000 inhabitants, its streets lined with commercial palaces, and noisy as those of New York with the rattle of drays, wagons and other vehicles. Outside of New York there is no more bustling street in the United States than Lake street.

Lake Michigan looked cold and dreary, as seen from the top of the City Hall, very much like our bay when the wind is high and the weather foggy. Chicago is the pet city of railroads. Locomotives rush to it from all points of the compass, laden with every freight which is known to inland commerce. The ringing of the locomotive's bell and the whir of attendant cars are never out of the ears of some portion of the citizens. In enterprise and life, Chicago is what other cities talk of being. If its people had the opportunity that San Francisco has, our population would now be nearly double what it is. Chicago capitalists take the men who are building up the state by the hand, in every way, and help them along.

After a brief stay at Chicago, I found myself, at three o'clock one evening, in the dépôt of the Northwestern Railroad, among crowds of sturdy and gawky-looking German immigrants, who had been enticed away from "der Vaterland" to expand their lungs, ideas and muscle, in developing the grain-fields of Iowa and Nebraska.

Ah, yes! here is, indeed, a glorious prairie country—a land which autumn always finds fat in grain and good things. These are the prairies of which the West proudly boasts. Here the staff of life flourishes. A rich country generally makes well-clad people and comfortable homes, and here both are constantly seen. The soil is dark and rich all the way through Illinois and Iowa, to the Missouri river.

Council Bluffs and the Missouri river at two, P.M. Time, twenty-three hours from Chicago; distance four hundred and ninety-four miles. We do not pass through the flourishing town named, but are driven from the dépôt by stage down the river, through dust which in flour-like fineness would do no discredit to our Red Dog or Dutch Flat stage roads. A wheezy and disabled-looking old steamer, after a vast amount of labored puffing and blowing, lands us in Omaha, Nebraska.

The Missouri river at Council Bluffs and Omaha is one of the meanest, most tortuous, shallow, shifting and unreliable of rivers to be found anywhere. Its bed is at one point to-day, and has shifted half a mile off by to-morrow. It is more uncertain in all things than even the proverbially "on-sartin" white man. The west bank, where the railroad shops and dépôt now are, was at one time the bed of the river. Regular lines of steamboats run on the Missouri, between St. Louis and Omaha, and also up to Fort Benton— some 3,000 miles of corkscrew river navigation.

Omaha is the chief town of Nebraska, and is the initial point of the Union Pacific Railroad. It has one of the handsomest possible sites, on the easterly slope of a wooded and grassy hill. Its population is about 15,000.

Nebraska has a population of about 50,000 persons. It was then suffering from an invasion of grasshoppers. They were everywhere, and were busily engaged in devouring everything. These pests and locusts are the curse of agriculture in all of the territory lying between the Missouri and Nevada.

Nebraska is a great grain country. Indeed, if its newspapers are to be believed, it is far ahead, in this and other respects, of all other places in the world. Of its climate, its resources, the chances it offers to new-comers, let a writer whose style is very florid, and whose business is advertising for the Union Pacific Railroad, say a few words:

"The new State of Nebraska presents many inducements to immigrants who are seeking a home, whether they come as laborers, farmers, mechanics, or as capitalists. It is between the fortieth and forty-third parallels of north latitude, north of Kansas and west of the Missouri river; bounded by it for about three hundred miles, and extending westward about four hundred miles.

"No finer land for agricultural purposes than this can be found. The soil is from three to ten feet deep, and wholly inexhaustible, so bountiful has nature been in her gifts. Land which has been cultivated for thirteen years produces just as fine crops, without manure, as when first broken.

"The trip from Omaha to the mountains is one of great interest. Towns, cities and villages are literally springing up in a night along the whole line of the road. No finer trip can be taken by the tourist who would see nature as she is, than to visit these hunting-grounds of the red man, now so fast disappearing, and enjoy the pleasures of the chase for the buffalo, elk, deer, antelope, etc., who yet roam in thousands over these plains. The scenery at the mountains cannot be surpassed. Italy has no more gorgeous sunsets; and the rising sun, bursting forth in all its splendor, with the pale moon, still empress of the deep cañons, retiring slowly—both seen at the same moment—present a scene of grandeur and sublimity which nowhere else exists in such perfection; and then in the distance rise to the clouds the snow-clad mountains, bearing almost continually the hoary cover of winter."

A little air is recommended to those who read this quotation. The truth is about as much inflated in it as a balloon previous to ascension. Nebraska has nothing to boast of. Long droughts, grasshoppers, locusts, and distance from markets, make the immigrant's lot anything but what it is above represented.

I left Omaha at five, P.M., after a day and a half stay in it. Seventy miles west of Omaha we struck the plains proper, and from that point on to Cheyenne the trip was a very monotonous one, much resembling a trip by sea. The country was almost entirely a dead level, having nothing but prairie-grass and sagebrush growing upon it. The atmosphere was as clear as a mirror; so clear indeed that distances are rendered very deceptive. Low, distant hills, which appear to be but five miles away, are twenty to twenty-four distant. The air of the plains is notedly dry and healthy, and a trip out upon them is one of the most strengthening and inspiriting possible. But the eye is wearied with the unending sameness and want of scenery, not only east of Cheyenne but out to Laramie, across the Rocky Mountains. These mountains, on the present overland route, are a delusion. There is no elevation deserving the name of mountain from Omaha to Fort Bridger, although you stand, at the summit of the Black Hills, 8,250 feet above the sea. This height is crept up to so gradually by low hills, however, that the ascent is made almost imperceptibly to the senses. There is not a railroad in the world, except perhaps some in Russia, that runs through such an uninteresting country as the Union Pacific Road. The great Valley of the Platte is a desert, except for grazing purposes. Want of water makes it so. It has also one of the most erratic climates in the world. Rain, hail, snow and sunshine are often seen at once. Northers frequently blow, accompanied by hail, against which it is very difficult for anything living to stand up. Hail has been known to cut the prairie-grass close to the roots, and the wind to blow it away, leaving not a stem for a distance of over fifty miles. The horizon darkens, and the air changes to wintry sharpness in a few minutes; while sunshine and balmy air succeed just as quickly. Rain is absorbed by the thirsty soil, and lost as quickly as it falls.

Except for unreliable grazing purposes, as I have said, the Platte Valley is a wide expanse of desert: yet a hundred writers have found it more pleasing, when out on the Union Pacific Road, to represent it as the very opposite. One writer, who indulges in the most extravagant hyperbole about the railroad and everything connected with it, furnishes the following:

"There is nothing connected with the Union Pacific Railroad that is not wonderful.

"Long before the Platte Valley is reached, it spreads before the eye like a vast bay opening out onto an ocean, whither the track appears to lead. The grain fields of Europe are mere garden-patches beside the green oceans which roll from Colorado to Indiana. The valley widens with the advance; the hills behind sink into the plain until the horizon there is perfect.

"There is really little known by the people of the character of the railroad enterprise. Most think that a company of capitalists are hastily putting down a rude track, over which cars can be moved with care, for the purpose of securing lands and money from the Government. But the fact is, that one of the most complete roads of which the country can boast is being laid. Fictions of the East must be re-written to match the realities of the West."

After reading such productions, one is almost compelled, against reason and truth, to worship at the gilded shrine of unmitigated humbug. Those who think, as the writer just quoted tells us most people do, that the Union Pacific Road is a rude track that is being hastily put down by a company of capitalists to secure Government lands and money, think precisely in accordance with the facts of the case; the road being probably the most hastily and slightly constructed one over which passenger-cars run in the world. Between Cheyenne and Laramie, a distance of nearly thirty miles, we passed four trains of cars which had run off the track and been smashed up, owing to the sharpness of the curves and the hastily-constructed track. Upon my asking the conductor of the train in Cheyenne at what time we would reach Laramie, his reply was: "About seven o'clock this evening, if we don't get off the track and be smashed up, which is just as like to occur as not."

The first writer I have quoted, in speaking of the cities and towns along the road, says:

"Almost all the stations have a considerable village, flanked with a farming population; and Fremont, Columbus, Grand Island, North Platte, Julesburg, Cheyenne, and many others, have more than doubled their population during the past year, or grown to be cities, where before was nothing but the wild waste, and no sound but that of the beasts of prey, or the whoop of the wilder savage; and each does an extensive business with the surrounding country."

The strength of imagination of these Western writers is something terrible. The towns spoken of were called into a hurried existence by the railroad, and when it moved on, their sites — except in one or two instances where machine-shops have been located — were as completely deserted and almost as much given up to beasts of prey and the whoop of the savage as they were one hundred years ago. Cheyenne was the chief town when I passed over the road, and a wickeder, more harum-scarum, or for any good purpose, useless town, never probably existed. It was made up entirely of saloons, eating, dance and gambling houses of the lowest and most rascally description. The railroad *employés* were the flies around which all these spiders had spread their nets.

A ride of twenty miles on the Union Pacific Road gives one almost as good an idea of the country through which it runs, as a continuation of the ride out to Cheyenne. At each station there are three or four railroad employés, whose duties are nominal, because the road has no local traffic at all, except what it derives from the supplying of government posts. Ten soldiers were located at each station as a protection — but they are an utterly inadequate one — against Indian raids. They always stood shouldering arms on the platform during the stoppage of the train. They were badly dressed, and were cold, miserable and half-starved looking. Attached to each station was a subterranean passage-way leading from the ticket office to a beaver-like underground structure with rounded top. These buildings were sunken stockades, with sod-covered roofs, each having loop-holes for musketry, thus making convenient the insertion of leaden deposits into attacking Indian bodies. A more wretched or lonely life cannot be imagined that that of these soldiers and station keepers. Their scalps are in constant danger. The excitement connected with expected Indian attacks is the only stir, if not solace, which their monotonous existence has. Almost anything is preferable to the inertia of the plains.

The trip between Omaha and Laramie City, a distance of five hundred and seventy-five miles, was made in thirty hours, or at the rate of nineteen miles per hour.

None of the Laramie City hotels had sleeping accomodations while I remained in the town. I slept in a spare sleeping car which was there. The best hotel was a large tent, with rough and dirty pine-board table and seats. The proprietor and his wife and child lived, and had their household furniture and bed, in one corner of this tent. There was no screen set up for privacy. While eating my breakfast on Sunday morning, the proprietor's wife sat, with her child upon her knee, on the dirty and disordered bed. She was surrounded by laborers, gamblers, a bar, barber-shop, general dirt and grease, and most admired disorder. She looked as if she had not a soul to sympathize with her in the world, and as if she had not a comfort in life. Women have a terrible life of it in these frontier towns, and I do not wonder that many of them become unsexed by their isolation among the roughest possible specimens of men.

After a delay of some five days in Laramie, I took the overland stage for Salt Lake. There were five other passengers in the coach. There was, therefore, no opportunity to recline, and sleep, for the first night at least, was out of the question. Between enforced wakefulness and the bumping of the stage in and out of "chuck-holes," and other miseries, I spent one of the most wretched nights of my life. The early morning found us at Rattlesnake Station, one of the most beautiful places that we had yet seen on the overland trip. We stopped at Rattlesnake for breakfast. I rode outside all that day, and the healthy, dry air soon made me feel almost as fresh as though I had slept on a bed of down. The day was most pleasantly spent in social conversation with the drivers. Tales of Indian horrors, and of hairbreadth escapes from their murderous hands formed the staple of our conversations. The stage-drivers, and all with whom I talked on the entire trip, agreed in saying that there was but one cure for Indian deception and Indian massacres. Whip the Indians well and they will behave. They know no sentiment but that of fear. About two years ago, Gen. Connor, the only competent Indian-fighter that has for years been in command on the plains, cornered the Shoshone and Bannock Indians, then two of the most troublesome tribes on the plains. He did not indulge them in that most unmitigated of all humbugs, a "big talk" about their great father in Washington and his red children, and all that. They had been fighting white men, and he caught them and fought them, killing over fifteen hundred, and so completely routing them that they all begged for mercy. It was freely granted, but before it was they complied with his every demand. These Indians have never since molested a white man. They still continue to fight with other tribes; indeed, when I was at Fort Bridger they were indulging in a spreadeagle pow-wow over a few scalps which they had "raised" from the heads of some of their enemies. But they let white men alone, although they have just as much excuse as newspapers say other Indians have for committing outrages. The press of the Pacific and the Atlantic States have shed oceans of sympathetic tears over Indian wrongs committed "by thieving Indian agents and bad white men." This is another bubble of bosh, which no amount of truthful testimony to the contrary seems capable of pricking. For one outrage or case of dishonesty practiced against an Indian by an Indian agent or white men, fifty cases of Indian outrages against innocent white men can readily be found. Feeding, pow-wowing with, and above all, arming Indians, only result in increasing their already large stock of impudence and laziness, and in increasing their belief that they are feared. The tables must be turned. One good whipping will do it, and prove the most friendly thing that can be done for our "red brethren." This is not one of a thousand theoretical panaceas for Indian troubles with which newspapers now-a-days overflow, but is based upon successful trial. Let Gen. Connor, or some other such man, be given command on the plains, and he will accomplish the task named, and thus save hundred of valuable lives and millions of dollars yearly. The Indian is, from the skin to the marrow, a mean, cowardly, blood-thirsty sneak, of the most despicable kind. He never takes a risk except when there are twenty to one hundred chances in his favor. A tiger may as easily be tamed. Fear is the only monarch to which he can be made to bow.

After the first night's ride it was easy to sleep — yea, and to snore right sonorously — despite the terrible jolting and incessant clatter of the wheels. Appetite, too, was a monster which despoiled the tables of the stations at an astonishing rate. The charge of one dollar and a half per meal was reasonable, in view of the appetites with which overland travellers sit down to table.

The most of the ride east of Salt Lake is made in Wyoming Territory, all of which, that I have seen, was a desert. But in the Bitter Creek Mountain region, the desert rose from common barrenness into a desolation that was almost grand in its loneliness and hopeless poverty. Grass almost totally disappeared, and even sage-brush was not plenty. Alkali and sand were monarchs. There were no mountains; only low hills, and sand in the early stages of petrifaction. The wind blows with terrible fury sometimes, and combined with the rain it had scarped the hills into the most fantastic shapes. Here, the face of a hill was cut to resemble the flutes of an organ — there, like the battlements of a castle; here, it resembled an animal crouching — there, it was honeycombed like a torpedo-pierced wood-pile. Death and desolation perched everywhere; yet Wyoming is rich in gold and coal, and the last is a most valuable resource in a treeless region.

The drive through Bridger's Pass was grand and beautiful, and when the welcome announcement was made that we had passed the water-shed of the continent — that all water now ran Pacific-wards — we were all delighted. After we passed Fort Bridger, the scenery began to mend, and the country to be valuable for agriculture. The lofty Wasatch and Uintah ranges of mountains, with snowy tops, delighted our eyes. They *were* mountains, and the first elevations deserving the name that we had seen. High mountains, with snow on their peaks in summer, are an almost infallible proof that there is a good country below. The snow will feed streams in spring and summer, and deserts cannot be where streams are plentiful. The interior of our continent is a desert only because it is waterless and treeless. The value of water — life-giving water — precious and all-powerful to the fruitfulness and beauty of a country — can nowhere be more plainly illustrated than on the overland trip.

Echo and Weber Cañons lie east of Salt Lake. They are passed by a forty miles' ride. The scenery in these cañons is grand as it is peculiar, and is ample recompense for all the previous experience of the desert. The cañons are long and deep clefts through high mountains, and are generally only wide enough to admit of the passage of a brawling river and the stage. Every variety of scenery, and all of it startling and novel, is seen in these cañons.

Salt Lake at six P.M., five days and a half from Laramie. The distance between the two is four hundred and seventy-five miles. The beauties of the Mormon city, like everything else which has been written of between the Missouri River and Nevada, are exaggerated. Nature has done more for the place in giving it a beautiful site and rich soil, than the Mormons have done in beautifying it.

I remained four days in Utah, which in many places is a garden. Then westward again. The country between Salt Lake and Austin is not so poor as that between the Missouri River and Utah, because it is constantly intersected by mountains. It is mountain and valley nearly all the way. But from Austin to Virginia we have hopeless desert and alkali again. On the trip from Mormondom we have balmier air, purer and clearer atmosphere, than ever before, and life is luxury.

Virginia at one, A.M. Sound asleep that night — satisfying and refreshing! Off for the railroad and the Sierras at ten, Reno at one. I rode up to the summit of the Sierras that night, and at three the next morning we started down the mountains for Sacramento. Nothing that is seen on the transcontinental trip makes any show of comparison in grandeur with our snow-capped Sierras. In elevated peaks, in deep cañons, in noble woods, in crystal waterfalls and lakes, the Sierras are unsurpassed. After the trip across the desert, the sharp, life-giving air of the mountains was a luxury of which one could not have a surfeit.

In the Central Pacific Railroad, man has graven his name upon the nineteenth century in characters so full of energy and triumph that time will never be able to efface them. It is a great and enduring causeway for the travel of all people, and for the breaking down of all barriers of isolation which ignorance, barbarism or exclusiveness have set up.

Sacramento at one, P.M., San Francisco at nine. And the circle is complete.

The total expenses of the round trip I have treated of, in my case, were about as follows: to New York per steamer, say $125; ten days in New York, say $100; outfit for overland trip, $50; expenses of overland trip, $280; total, $555 in gold. I was only fifty-six days absent from San Francisco. After crossing the Continent, it is a matter of great wonder to me that so many persons travel by steamer. The overland trip is in every respect infinitely superior, especially on the score of health. All who have made it agree in saying that a few days' shaking up in one of Wells, Fargo & Co.'s coaches is, for the most of diseases, worth all of the medicine that ever doctor prescribed or unwilling patient swallowed. The stage ride only occupies about five days now, which is well divided by a night's rest at Salt Lake City.

I have endeavored to speak impartially of everything I saw upon the overland journey. Many of my conclusions differ greatly, I am aware, from those of many other writers who have preceded me. Wholesale puffery and rose-tinted pictures have been the rule. Each writer seems to have thought it necessary to follow the example of his predecessor; afraid, apparently, to utter his own opinions about what he saw. I have had no such fear. I have endeavored to give facts and not fancies; to paint with the sober colors of truth, rather than with the brighter but less durable ones of error.

I cannot close this article without expressing the opinion that there is not a people or a land from the Atlantic to the Pacific more favored than the people and the State of California. One county, such as Nevada, Placer, Sacramento, or Solano County, is worth all the territory from the Missouri river to Nevada. Colorado is very rich in minerals, but not more so than California and Nevada, while its mines can probably never be profitably worked at home, on account of the high price of fuel, and because of other prohibitory expenses. Again, the precious metal in the ores of Colorado is so firmly locked in the embrace of base, stubborn metals, that even most approved and expensive processes only partially succeed in saving the gold.

A round trip such as I have described, while it serves to make the Californian more contented with his own State, conduces also to erase local prejudices. There are fair skies, rich fields, and well-to-do people outside of our State, although we occasionally talk as if we had a monopoly of all these and many other desirable things. In our yet crude life we lack many things, too, which the older Atlantic States possess, and which we should perhaps aim more strongly to secure.

After passing over an entire country, from ocean to ocean, one feels strongly that, while it may be a good thing to be a Californian, and it may also be good to be a Democrat or a Republican, it is immeasurably best of all to be an American! We have inherited the fair and great land of the West. Our domain literally extends from sea to sea, and almost as literally "from the river unto the ends of the earth." This, however, is not so much subject for boasting, as matter for remembrance that to whom much is given, from them much also will be required. That we should not bury our great gift in petty struggles for sectional supremacy, is the lesson taught by A Run Overland.

Thomas Magee *has proven to be a rather elusive contributor to the* Overland Monthly. *Little reference is made to him in researched historical and literary works. We know only that he was a recognized leader in San*

Francisco's realty profession in the latter 1800's, and that he was one of the few who correctly forecast the revitalization of Market Street after the city's 1906 earthquake.

His interests were apparently broad, giving rise to the publication of short books and essays on such diverse topics as China's Menace to the World, the immortality of the Sequoia tree, the Chicago Exposition of 1893, and a review of a few great authors and their works. One publication of passing interest to San Franciscans might be his Greater San Francisco Pictorial Souvenir, a twenty-four page gem issued through the Royal Publishing Company in 1907.

Eight Months at Sitka
by C. Delavan Bloodgood, U.S.N.
February 1869

The cession of the Russian possessions in North America to the United States by the Emperor of all the Russias—devised for the purpose of strengthening, if possible, the good understanding existing between the two nations, gratified the great American heart. The sympathies of the large majority of the natives of the great Republic clung to the cause of Russia during the Crimean war, and that sympathy was reciprocated in the time of their own distress. There existed no recollections save of international congruity, official courtesies, and personal friendliness. The eagerness with which our people sought every scrap of intelligence pertaining to the new domain, revealed an interest exceeding that which might attend an achievement merely of the prehensory proclivity, charged as a national habit; it was rather of satisfaction that some tangible evidence appeared of an alliance, cherished for years, with so friendly, so progressive, so potent an empire.

Concerning all Alaska it is not purposed in this writing to attempt at a description, but simply to give an account of a trip to Sitka, or New Archangel, its capital, at the time of the official transferrence, and to note some observations and impressions which obtained during the first eight months after their advent and under the *régime* of the Americans.

In compliance with a provision of the treaty, appointing agents for the formal delivery and reception of the territory, Captain Alexis Pestchouroff, of the Imperial navy, was happily designated on the part of his Majesty the Emperor—the President selecting the late General L.H. Rousseau, of the United States army. Those officers and others connected with the specific duty assembled at San Francisco, where the United States sloop-of-war *Ossipee* was awaiting to convey them to Sitka. Friday, September 27th, 1867, despite the superstition of mariners, was the day of departure, and that fairest and balmiest of mornings the *Ossipee* was under way, bound upon the interesting expedition. Steaming by the flag-ship *Pensacola*, her band saluted with the Russian national hymn and our own familiar airs—the officers and crew manifesting an enthusiastic interest in our mission, which was echoed along the wharves and among the shipping throughout the harbor's extent. Passing through the Golden Gate out by the Farallones, our course was shaped direct for Sitka. Though fresh from the passage from New York in a paddle-steamer, the soldiers and civilians of our party found that aboard a screw with heavy armament, breasting the long and grand swell of the Pacific, they had to endure a new motion compounded from a roll, a pitch, and a wallow, and to suffer a relapse of the *mal de mer:* and so distressingly prostrating was its effect, that the medical officers seconded their entreaties to put in for Victoria. Accordingly the course was changed, as much to the gratification of the advisers, desirous of enjoying the scenery within the islands, as to the satisfaction of the sufferers.

The sixth morning from departure the ship entered the Juan de Fuca Strait, which separates by twelve miles the kelp-fringed shore of Vancouver's Island from our Washington Territory, where from the water's edge high up the majestic Olympian range grow stately firs and pine sufficient to spar the shipping of the world. At evening we were at anchor amid the English fleet in that gem of a harbor, Esquimalt — shut in by rocks covered with mosses and foliage, then gaudily tinted by the frosts, while over against them were pretty groves, within which, half hidden, are the tasteful residences of the officers, whence winding roads and paths lead out by the goverment buildings, to which dockyard paint and primness could not impart an official aspect — it all seemed better befitting an oriental than boreal clime. Besides serving as the depot and rendezvous for the English squadron, Esquimalt is the principal port for Victoria, four miles distant, to which a fine hard road leads between fragrant hedges, by well-tilled farms with fruitful orchards, and snug cottages with their lawns "like we 'ave at ome," and over the long bridges spanning the estuaries, and into the *city* — once the western seat of power of the Hudson Bay Company. But the quiet of their immense warehouses and long wharves betokens that the dynasty of that consummate monopoly, which had ruled a region equal in extent with the United States, is ending. Tenantless and shabby-appearing buildings in unfrequented streets, stand as monuments to the Cariboo delusion; but there are some elegant residences. The churches and government buildings are of agreeable aspect, and the natural surroundings and vistas of the loveliest. Our unusual presence and mission was sufficient to excite a fresh discussion of the political future of British Columbia; indeed, it would be difficult for an American to suppress expression of his "views," after personal observation of the topography and resources of Vancouver's Island — the key to Puget Sound, the harbors of Washington Territory for hundreds of miles, and interposed as an irritating geographic wedge in our extending coast line.

Two days sufficed for coaling and interchanging the usual ceremonious visits, when our voyage was resumed, and by the inside passage — nature's safe highway through these tempestuous seas. A drizzling autumn rain had set in, but it was disregarded for the enjoyment of the novel and marvelous scenery — in some places the channels leading under bases of mountains rising abruptly out of the deep waters, till their silvered tops mingled with the mist and clouds; at others, winding among islets with every variety and fashion of leafy and mossy covering, through strange haunts of wild fowl, until night closed in upon us in a snug cove at Active Pass. The next day, Sunday, running through the Gulf of Georgia, the service was read on deck amid scenes of grandeur which seemed hushed in reverant observance, and while the icy peaks were still glowing in the sunlight, our anchor was let go in Duncan's Bay, within Vancouver's Island. We had next morning to pass a strait, through which the flowing tides run nine knots per hour. Waiting for the favorable moving of the waters, a party landed to try their new guns upon the game which alone possesses the locality. After a few hours un-skillfully employed, a gun and the cornet recalled all persons and boats, and the perilous passage was essayed. But the pilot had started a little too early; the eddying waters were still madly rushing through the narrows, on which our ship was whirled and tossed, unheeding rudder and propeller, as if she had been a toy of cork. Nearly three hours were consumed in making as many miles, through the successive whirlpools and rapids, then the way became smooth, though torturous, to the night's anchorage in Alert Bay, Cormorant Island. All next day the rain poured down and fogs drew close about, rendering it unsafe to proceed. The Indians found us out, as they had at other stopping places, and came alongside clamoring for whiskey and tobacco — most stultified, unhealthy-appearing wretches, and in uncouth and untidy garbs; one with a fur cap and a pelt about his shoulders, the rest of the body bare; another in high boots and an old bit of carpeting — red and black paint completing the covering; the squaws attired even more fan-tastically — some in the cast-off garments left them by miners the spring before; one crumpling around her, in the canoe, the largest size tilting hoop-skirt — the necks of all shingled in with beads. The distortion of their heads was the most repulsive. Lower down among the islands were the *flat-heads;* here, the standard of beauty is the *sugar-loaf* — produced by tightly bandag-ing the head in pappoosehood — and the height of squawish loveliness, about twenty-one inches from chin to apex of cranium. Rubber-cladding ourselves, we landed to visit a burial-place near. Some years since, many of the tribe were swept off by small-pox. Where the victim was seized, there, supplied with food and water, but unattended, he was left to live or die. After the abatement of the epidemic the corpses were burned and the ashes collected in little boxes covered with blanketing, and lashed up among the branches of the trees. Besides this species of sepulture, their favorite chief was placed in a mausoleum of hewn logs, about twelve feet square, with blankets nailed over roof and sides, which, now mouldy and worm-eaten, were dropping off. In the center, upon a trestle, was the rude box in which the body was closely doubled, and around it were deposited such personal effects as hunting, fishing, and culinary apparatus, clothing, trinkets, etc. The trees surrounding had been cut away, save one, from which the branch-es were lopped; from its top the remnant of a pennant was flying; at its mid-dle was fastened a board bearing his "crest," and lower down another, inscribed with hieroglyphics, possibly a flattering epitaph. In front of this sepulchral wigwam, and driven into the ground about three paces apart, were slabs hewn to resemble sentinels, with blazings for features, and about, as it were, the shoulders, pieces of blanketing were wrapped. A number of canoes of different sizes and fashions, drawn up in line, were rotting near.

After the storm had ceased we crossed over a portion of Queen Charlotte's Sound, an unsheltered stretch of thirty-five miles, and the anchorage at night was in Safety Cove, around the points of Calvert Island. Surfeited as we were with magnificent scenery, the beauty of this spot exacted lively expression from every beholder. A deep nook scooped out, as it were, from the mountain's side as a hostelry for benighted ships; the waters of the little basin teeming with fish and fowl, and the thick woods with game, while down the mountain's sides noisy cascades descended — never could have been found more superb a wild. Our next harbor, Carter's Bay, was also a beautiful one, but less secure. The night was wild, and through the gorges the "willi-waws" would come swooping down, straining our cables and lashing the little bay into foam. Through Finlson's Strait and Grenville Sound, next day, the panorama on either hand surpassed all heretofore enjoyed — it was the region of mists and rainbows and waterfalls. Starting amid mountain-peaks elevated from 1,500 to 2,000 feet, or, as it seemed, from the clouds themselves, hundreds of silvery and ribbon-like rivulets wound down over rocks, through mosses and trees; lower down, from rocky reservoirs, larger streams rushed foaming forth, took a Niagara-like leap, then roaring on over lesser falls, plunged seething into the tide. By scores and hundreds could these cascades be enumerated. For two days we were weather-bound at Fort Simpson, the northernmost post of the Hudson Bay Company, and questionably proximate to the parallel fifty-four degrees forty minutes. Surrounding the fort is the village of the Chimpseans, whose lodges present a most novel heraldic system and style of ornamentation. Above and around the oval hole of entrance to each is rudely carved a grotesque representation of some animal or animals — the "crest" — and in this manner is expressed all the family and tribal crossings — the "bar" sinister predominating. In addition, before each chief's or first family's lodge is erected a huge spar covered from top to bottom with figures of men, beasts, birds, fishes, reptiles — all conglomerated into one grand *chef d'oeuvre*. Compared with those met below, the Indians of this tribe seemed vastly superior; a process of *enlightenment* has unquestionably been going on among them, dating from the establishment of the post. Their squaws do not distort the head; but the fashion is to make a slit through the under lip, parallel with the mouth, in which, in early years, a silver stylet is worn, but the aperture gradually dilating the old dames come to sport a plug of bone or wood (technically, *labret*), of an inch or two in width, and of half that thickness. In their employment of cosmetics, red paint is streaked on the scalp at the parting of the hair, and smeared over eyebrows, nose, and chin—a few radiating lines of black from the eyes consummating their irresistibility.

From Fort Simpson our course led for two hundred and fifty miles through a labyrinth of channels in the Princes of Wales Archipelago and Clarence Strait, containing numerous snug retreats, one of which afforded us refuge for thirty hours while a storm raged. Passing by Cape Ommaney into the broad ocean still bounding under the pressure of the late gale, our destination was seventy miles distant; but the *Ossipee*, washing her own decks and striking her own bell, was twenty-four hours in reaching it. The morning was clear and mild, as heading toward the concave line of bright, snow-crested mountains we entered Sitka Sound—passing in under that most distinctive of landmarks: the extinct volcano Edgecombe, with its cone 2,800 feet, crater, 280 feet deep, three miles in circumfrence, and nearly filled with snow. From its rim, radiating downward with almost geometric regularity, are the deep gorges scored by the lava less than a hundred years ago. From the base, till meeting the snow half-way up, evergreens grow evenly as if cropped by gardening rule. The Sound is eleven miles wide at this entrance, and Sitka fourteen miles distant. Slowly working our way in between lines of breakers, and in such deep waters that lead and anchors are alike useless, we glided through a gateway left in the maze of islets which form a perfect breakwater—and there, nestled under the beetling mountains which circumscribe three-fourths of the vista, on marshy lowlands (comprising, perhaps, one thousands acres), was Sitka.

And what a wonderful prospect was opened—the amphitheatre of mountains, surmounted by masses of ice and snow, with striated sides, suggestive of avalanches; the chains of symmetric cones of volcanic type; the lesser and graduated spurs, with vestures toned from the gray moss that pushes out under the glary ice, through the different depths of perennial green, to the neutral hues of the annual leaves still clinging to the gigantic trees at their bases. And tumbling down through rocky passes, and rushing on between banks thickly hedged with alder, the Indian River pours its cold and sparkling water out into that pebbly bay, as peculiar in outlines and intricacies as it is unequalled in beauty by an port of which tourists write, or sailors sing. The harbor is marked out and maintained by triple rows of islets lappingly interspersed, which stretch before the town, leaving a channel about three hundred yards wide, within which all vessels must moor, with anchors from each bow and quarter. Here, intricately tied up, we found the United States ships, *Jamestown* and *Resaca*, sent thither for climactic purification, after their scathing by yellow fever at Panama; the transports with our troops aboard; and not an inconsiderable fleet of merchantmen flying the bunting of many different nations. After many tedious evolutions, the *Ossipee* was finally secured, Friday, October 18th, three weeks from day of departure from San Francisco. That same afternoon our troops were disembarked and drawn up alongside the Russian garrison, on the little plaza, left upon the table-rock on which is the Governor's residence. The Commissioners, attended by officers of the services of their respective countries, advanced to the flag-staff; Captain Pestchouroff ordered the Russian flag hauled down, and thereby and with brief declaration transferred and delivered the territory of Alaska to the United States; the garrisons presented arms, and the Russian batteries and our men-of-war fired the international salute; a brief reply of acceptance was made, as the stars and stripes were run up and similarly saluted — and we stood upon the soil of the United States.

The town of Sitka, founded in 1799, contained at the time of transfer less than a thousand inhabitants, and, in its every appearance and arrangement, was totally un-American. There was this uniformity and appearance of order only — that the government buildings, which comprise the Governor's residence, See-house, club-house, hospital, barracks, and warehouses, were very large and constructed of ponderous hewn logs, painted yellowish and roofed with red metal. The other buildings and residences are also of logs, and small, but unpainted, and straggled along one street or thoroughfare. Adding to the general incongruity of arrangement, there was commenced, when the fact of the cession became public, a sandwiching in, *ad libitum*, of rough board shanties for Jewish traffic, numerous flaring saloons, and other structures for congruous purposes. In the center of the town, the one street bifurcated around it, stands St. Michael's, the Cathedral of the Oriental or Russo-Greek Church, built also of logs, painted white, with bright-green roofings; dome and spire surmounted by the distinctive triple cross; the tower containing a chime of bells; on the northern and head wall is hung a large and weather-beaten painting of St. Michael and the Dragon. At the palisades is a chapel for Indians, and a Lutheran meeting-house is used by the post chaplain, or serves for general assemblies. There is a square enclosure containing willows and firs, and upon a high rock in the center is a sort of pagoda — this is known as the Princess' Garden. A few buildings in by-ways, and some venerable hulks drawn up on the beach, complete the general features of the settlement. There is a beacon atop of the Governor's house, and there are numerous workshops, and a strong wharf, with stone steps, suited for the tide which rises some sixteen feet; but the foregoing enumeration will suffice for a description to which more minuteness cannot add interest.

Russian America, so isolated from the Empire, had been swayed almost as a separate monarchy: its potentate — the Fur Company — whose Court was at Sitka — any policy or interest at variance with its rule — rank treason. Emigration and enterprise, other than for its established purposes, were restrained. The Imperial Governor was salaried by it; his administration subject to the Company's approval; tenure of office, positions, and all but life, subservient to it. Still, to all appearance, the reign was grateful to the inhabitants, and the change of dominion distrusted. The Prince Maksoutoff, for gallant services in the Imperial navy, had succeeded to the governorship, and possessed the confidence and affection of all classes. Among the subalterns and in the church establishments were persons of rank and refinement. Many speak the English language, nearly all either French or German, and a well-selected library was accessible to all. In their domestic establishments were observed the elegancies of society, and the comforts and luxuries abundantly possessed. Pleading guilty to a solecism upon their hospitality, most cordially exercised, I will note some few peculiarities. One or more antechambers interpose between the domiciliary apartments and the dreaded external air; instead of stoves, one or more cylindrical brick furnaces heat and encumber each room. Mats, pieces of thick carpeting, or robes of fur, are disposed in places, but not entirely covering the floor; the furniture, of rich material though cumbersome; the piano, an indispensable article; numerous mirrors and pictures panel the walls. Across an upper corner of each apartment is placed a small painting of our Saviour, the Virgin, or heads of Saints, surrounded by gold or silver filigree; and no Russian home but presents this token of their faith. The upper part of the Governor's house was arranged for a theatre, and, at their numerous gatherings, plays, music, dancing, cards, and billiards, relieved the monotony of the hyperborean nights. At such times the varieties and quantities of substantial refreshments and choice wines and liquors would astonish dyspeptic Americans. Tea of delicious flavor seems constantly prepared, and a tumbler of it, placed in a saucer, is presented to the caller, and to the visitor, repeatedly; the cheroot, which follows, is enjoyed alike by both sexes. The transition from this society to the condition of the lower order is very abrupt. The employés comprised Russians, creoles, and a large class with bloods interminably mixed. Their pay was small, and requirements few; small rooms, proportioned to the numbers in the families, were alloted, free of rent, in the untidy barracks; medical attendance was provided, and schools, and an asylum for orphans. Their rations were issued daily; whatever else was required could be purchased at low rates—established at St. Petersburg, and paid for with the sheep-skin money: their only circulation medium. The common winter garb for the men is a long sheep-skin coat worn

"With the skinny side out and the woolly side in;"
for the women, robes of cheap and mixed furs, though on festivals there are as struggling attempts at finery as may be elsewhere observed. The church calendar provides over a hundred holidays, which they honor and enjoy proportionate to the amount of *vodki* procurable; but whether from temperament or discipline, it seems to excite in them suavity and subordination, rather than incivility or riotous conduct. But, though passing their simple lives in such a secluded place, it does not follow necessarily that innocence and modesty are their especial characteristics. A large bathing establishment is kept for the employés (all classes must enjoy their bath every week or alternate ones), to which it is not uncommon for parties to resort regardless of sexual distinctions. That super-heated, steamy, sudsy, birch-twig-flagellating process called a Russian bath, must be too generally

understood to warrant a description of the torture submitted to by the writer in fully acquainting himself with the institution.

The Oriental Church, integral in the authority of the Empire, maintained an establishment at each of the Fur Company's posts. It is represented here by a bishop, three priests and two deacons, who, with numerous acolytes, serve in the cathedral church. Those in the two lower orders of priesthood may marry — but for *once*; celibacy, however, is required of a bishop — that he has never married or is a widower. From its exterior, one is unprepared for the richness of decoration within St. Michael's; vessels of gold, inlaid with precious stones; candelabra and other implements of silver; rich paintings within embossings of silver and gold. The sanctuary, occupying the head of the cruciform edifice, is shut off at times during the service by curiously ornate and latticed folding doors — in either arm a chapel — within the dome, silver bas-relief representations of the principal events in the life of our Saviour. The vestments in richness and design are in perfect keeping; and the flowing locks and beards of all holding holy office impart a fitting feature in the ceremonials. A service continues seldom less than two hours, and is almost entirely antiphonal; instruments of music are never employed, but often the chiming of the bells adds consonance to the responses of the choristers and the impressive ritual. If a sermon is given, it is very brief and read by an acolyte from a printed book — none "for the times" are issued by the sacred synod. There are no seats in the church; the men stand in one part, the women in the other, side by side, prince and fisherman, officers with sailors and soldiers, Russian and half-breed, factor's wife and servant, all earnest and devoutly rendering worship and honor to the Holy Trinity. On special festivals, the floor is strewn with evergreens, and wreaths and banners and ribbons are additional decorations; the profusion of candles floods the building with light, and at all services the air is heavy with incense. The genuflections are frequent and extend to touching the forehead to the floor. In Lenten time when the lights were dimmed and all was expressive of woe, and night and day the services scarcely intermitted, priests and congregation would remain for many minutes with faces to the dust murmuring their penitential supplications. The service is essentially symbolic, and though rendered in the Slavonic tongue, its significance cannot be misunderstood nor its gorgeous richness unappreciated. What if there may have been gathered "accretions during the Dark Ages, from its contact with ignorance and heathenism," reverence cannot be withheld from the Eastern Church, most venerable for its antiquity in the world, and which has kept up a succession of bishops in the same sees from the time of the Apostles till now. Holding to the Julian calendar, the Russian dates are twelve days later than ours of the Gregorian, and their Sunday commences at sunset on our Friday; but on both holy days full services are rendered. Christmas was observed with magnificent church ceremonials and merry domestic festivities, when from the laden Christmas trees the orphans and children of the poor exacted cheerful tribute. Till Ash-Wednesday was a continuous holiday and carnival amusement. But their gladdest festival was Easter, at which they enthusiastically portrayed their emotional and religious transition from penitential grief to hope and joy. Easter-even, at midnight, the bells chimed forth their liveliest, and the church, so long, dark, and funereal, blazed forth in dazzling light; the congregation in gayest attire, each one bearing a lighted candle, seemed in the greatest exhilaration. "Christos vaskrasce!" "Christos vaskrasce!" Christ is risen! was the inspiring refrain repeated and echoed over and over throughout their triumphal celebration which continued three hours, terminating with the ceremony in which, after the clergy, each of the laity exchanged with the bishop the salutation Christos vaskrasce! and a kiss upon each cheek and the chin; after which the same was interchanged generally among the congregation, promptly and cordially, uninfluenced by station or condition. All Easter-week the bells seemed never to cease chiming, and, as the days were sunny and balmy, the populace would stroll down by the river, and, with the inseparable tea-apparatus, arrange a picnic and follow with sylvan sports, quite irreconcilable with ideas of an hyperborean clime. Of the peculiarities in the sacraments and rites, baptism is celebrated at home to avoid exposure to cold, as the child is stripped and three times immersed. The name is then bestowed by the priest, and is supposed not to have been before revealed even to the parents. At funerals the corpse is borne in an open coffin over evergreen boughs, strewn from the residence to the church, and thence to the cemetery; and there is carried with it, in resemblance to the old classic custom, a dish of rice cooked with raisins, which, after the interment, is returned to the home and partaken of daily by the mourning relations while it lasts. A wedding is an elaborate affair, and decidedly a trying ordeal, for the ceremony requires nearly an hour for its performance. The pair, followed by proper attendants, and all bearing lighted candles, are met at the church door by a priest, who leads them to an altar beneath the dome, where, after many genuflections and responses, an elegant crown is placed on the head of each and they are then led slowly three times around the altar, reciting the obligations they are about assuming. It is the bride's privilege at any time before completing the third and last circuit, to withdraw from the engagement; that Rubicon passed, the plighting of troth is completed by exchanging rings, drinking from a goblet wine three times in alternation, and then, after repeating their vows, they kiss the Bible, the cross, and their crowns; the bride furthermore kneels, and thrice crossing herself before the image of the Virgin, kisses the feet. The ceremony terminates with a general embracing of the couple by their respective friends. On board every Russian vessel before sailing, high mass was celebrated, but though in general very interesting and unusual, the festivals and ceremonials are too numerous to warrant in this space even enumerating.

Outside a line of palisades, and straggled along the water front, are about fifty square log huts or lodges comprising the Indian village. Within them, for the most part of the time, the population of about 1,000 are squatted, and in all stages of dress and undress, from verminous blankets to a coating of soot; while without a corresponding number of wolfish-faced dogs doze in day-time, and dolefully howl in concert throughout the night. A disgusting and distinctive stench pervades the locality and all pertaining to it. A descriptive summary (which would apply to and include representatives of numerous other tribes, which from curiosity or for traffic thronged to the capital) must specify that they are indolent, besotted, diseased, thieving, and offensively impotent. When other means for procuring liquor fail, they may work. As a shag or gull is eaten with as much relish as venison, their hunting is graduated by convenience. They do not possess sufficient ingenuity to manufacture curious trinkets. Laws and regulations concerning the sales of spirits yet lack efficient stringency, for never a day or night passed but were seen drunken Indians, or their disgusting orgies disturbed the night. The Governor had been compelled, from prudential sanitary considerations, to separate and immure the sexes. Their thieving extends from adroit shop-lifting to stripping copper from ships' bottoms. It is most extraordinary how their prowess and importance have been over-rated; they live on the coast or by rivers where fish abound, with no means of transportation save their rude canoes hollowed from logs; to retreat from the coast would be but to starve; they have no stock of supplies or ammunition, and possess but a few guns, and those ill-conditioned and of obsolete pattern. Distinct and dwindled tribes, all unallied and generally tamely warring with each other, occupy the insignificant villages referred to. The Russians were first astonished at our force sent to occupy the territory, so much larger than they had ever maintained, and then drolly amused that reën-forcements should follow! The language of the Sitkans differs from the Chinook, and is a succession of unpleasant gutturals; they make no stint in paint or ornaments for their tawny bodies, though many went through the winter barelegged and barefooted. The bodies of their dead are burned and the ashes preserved in small hive-like structures at the rear of the lodges, adorned with paganish art; some of the ashes, however, are mixed with soot, which the relatives smear over their faces (to wear, not to be washed off), and this, with closely-cropped hair, constitutes their garb of mourning. The medicine-men possess perquisites superior to the chiefs; the ceremony of constituting their office is termed *tomanoss*, and was witnessed at the coldest period in the year. The aspirants, some thirty young bucks, had been kept fasting and practicing incantations for two days, until wrought up to an almost frenzied condition, when they were brought out, and in the presence of the entire population, stripped and plunged into the harbor; after remaining in the chilling water ten or fifteen minutes, they were called out and set to whipping each other, which they did vigorously and com-petitively; then into the water and out again for "a course" at the hands of the "Board." This process continued an hour, and resulted in the "plucking" of about two-thirds; the others returned to resume their heathenish charms and maintain the fast. Next day the water and whipping tests were repeated and continued until one-half of the remainder of the "class" "bilged"; then the enduring ones, conducted to the principal chief's lodge with great clamor and rejoicing, were admitted to a grand hoo-doo, which signaled and completed the conferring, *secundum artem*, of the degree of medicine-men and bestowal of the power of sorcery. Some certain animal is held sacred by every tribe; this "emblem," with the Sitkans, is the crow, and consequently those confident and garrulous birds sit at ease and caw in door-ways and on window-sills. Their vocation of scavengers now protects them rather than the superstitious indulgence sanctioned by the Russians. Slaves are held among the tribes — captives and their descendants — and the Dahomey custom of sacrificing them, at the deaths of their owners or chiefs, still prevails. During the past few years the Russians had been accustomed to ransom the victims by ample outlays of stores and ammunition; since the advent of the Americans, one selected for the pyre took refuge and obtained protection within the garrison.

It requires an extensive stretch of the commonly accepted opinions concerning climactic characters, to appreciate the pecular conditions at Sitka, so usual is it to fancy isothermal lines united and continued with those of latitude. Following the parallel fifty-seven degrees thirty-five minutes (that of Sitka) eastward, it crosses the floes in Hudson's Bay, the northern part of frigid Labrador, and passes within less than two degrees of Greenland's icy shore; but the isothermal line extended, emerges at, or below, the capes of Virginia; as well might Chesapeake Bay be cited as the region of icebergs and the habitat of the walrus and polar bear, as Sitka Sound. A great stream of aqueous vapor perpetually rising from the western waters, and borne over that part of the Alaskan coast, maintains a high mean temperature and of moderate range. Striking the vast mountain barriers, condensation as constantly results, and that its product, rain, does not continuously descend, is but from meteorologic accidents, which deflect the currents and vary the susception of the condensing surfaces. Those "little accidents," however, are not of frequent occurrence. Statistics may show that in other localities a greater amount of water falls during the year, but at none could be recorded more frequent showers. In winter, even, the fall of rain greatly exceeds that of snow. Nor is there any considerable product of ice; upon the artifical lake but seven inches formed, and that porous and unmarketable. Glenboke (deep) Lake, beyond the first eastern range, remains open except about the shores. In the harbor once only was noticed a few thin patches of ice, not sufficient, however, to retard a boat's progress. Beyond gardening, no agricultural attempts had been made, and it is yet to be demonstrated if they are unadvisable. In that alluvial soil trees attain tropical dimensions, and the thickets are almost inpenetrable; and to meet the most distant advance of spring, the grasses and wild flowers spring forth with astonishing forwardness.

Before the ships which transported our expedition had discharged their cargoes, there occurred a storm unprecedented in the memory and traditions of the inhabitants, reports of which were ominously mingled in the accounts of the inauguration of the new domain. It was terrific; bursting forth suddenly in the full fury of a northern storm—stranding ships, razing buildings, besoming the coast. After that, and until the vernal equinoctial, winds were not more violent than at lower latitudes on the Pacific. In mid-winter the daylight was diminished to six hours and a few minutes' dura-tion. For weeks neither sun, moon, nor other heavenly body would be visi-ble. In best weathers the diurnal light, for a good portion of its continuance, but faintly streamed forth from behind the mountains, where the mists drift and dull clouds hang. Lacking the stimulus of light; the dampness affecting animal spirits barometrically; intercourse with the outer world almost cut off; restricted necessarily, in exercise; even gustatory sense palled by un-changing diets of game—through such an hibernation "the contented mind" might brave nostalgia, but the sensitive body scarcely hyperaemia!

Exhibitions of the aurora borealis were less frequent than we had infer-red, but on one occasion, late in spring, occured a display exceeding our excited expectations. Brilliant and symmetrical arches first spanned the heavens; then, rows of perpendicular flaming columns extended up from the horizon as if in support; then, again, all would dissolve, glide off, or sink down among the side scenes the mountains provided. Next, from a glowing spot at the zenith, concentric discs diverged, rapidly revolving, ex-panding, contracting, intermingling, some whisking away from the nucleus and waltzing off across the sky, and all displaying lustrous variations of the prismatic spectrum, from faintest amber to deepest, softest violet. The morning's advancing light dimmed those gorgeous pyrotechnics of nature ere our enjoyment approached satiety.

The change of season from damp and darkness to light and warmth, seemed more marked and genial in influence than that which in lower latitudes tardily dispels the snow and frosts, and difficulty lures spring from the lap of winter—the daylight expanded so rapidly; the foliage so promptly and gratefully responded to the warmer showers; the animating industry of the fisherman preparing their tackle for a harvest scarcely short of the miraculous; the incessant clanging of the augmenting swarms of sea-fowl; the long lines of wild geese (dwindled to faintest trace on the southern sky), returning to their native fastnesses—all, were not less exhilarating than diverting. By the last of May there was no night; the evening and morning twilights intermingled and merged into the day, and all through the twenty-four hours were heard the cheerful chirpings of the migratory singing birds.

Concerning the products and resources of our new possessions outside Baranoff and adjacent islands, the writer obtained no more reliable infor-mation than that which has been collated and extensively circulated by cor-respondents and pamphleteers, from the marvellous recitals of voyagers, hunters, and Indian traders; but with such tangible evidence as the fisheries afford, and the packages of valuable furs which fill warehouses and laden ships, and such a vastness of forest surrounding, one is at a loss as to what is not credible.

Nimrodian excursions, necessarily undertaken in boats and often conducted for leagues, beyond the usual successes, discovered to us many rare, and some unrecognized, ornithological specimens, and afforded wonderful varieties of scenery. In one mazy region we landed and visited the (to the Russians) famous Klutchy — a series of hot mineral springs issuing from the rocks at least fifty feet above tide mark, and with a temperature of one hundred and forty-eight degrees, Fahrenheit. Suitable buildings were erected there by the Fur Company, whither were sent intractable cases of rheumatism, scorbutic and other diseases common to the climate, and the report is unvarying of benefits experienced.

To this changed dominion flocked in amplest proportion, a herd of all sorts and conditions of men — Alaskan pioneers, aspirants for colonial emoluments and honors. Before our first sunset gun was fired, their preëmpting stakes dotted the ground, and ere long they had framed a city charter, devised laws and remunerative offices, and by an election, at which less than one hundred votes were mustered, gave publicity to, and inaugurated their schemes. Their squatter claims were confirmed and recorded; next cropped out a judiciary. Though first confined to disputes among themselves, it soon extended to passing final judgment in cases involving life and liberty, and even in matters of nice international complexity, utterly ignoring in act and appearance the military presence and only legally constituted and competent authority. Some such a course, perhaps, is unavoidable in the incipiency of colonization, though it reflects humiliatingly upon the nationality of those concerned. Speculation became rife and unreasonable, and suspicion rested upon the commonest commercial transactions — while the prices for the veriest necessities of life were so inflated, that actual distress threatened the poorer classes and the unwisely venturesome. Whether influenced by these conditions or not, the large majority of the employees did not accept the beneficient provision of Article III of the Treaty — admitting them "to the enjoyments of all the rights, advantages, and immunities of citizens of the United Staes" — but returned within the Empire as transportation could be provided for them.

C. Delavan Bloodgood *(1831-1903) began his long naval career in 1857 after graduation from Colgate University and Philadelphia's Jefferson Medical College. Following service in the Civil War, the doctor was part of the expedition sent to Alaska to receive the new territory from the Russians. In 1884 Bloodgood was appointed Medical Director of the U.S. Navy, a position he held until his retirement in 1893. He died at his home in Brooklyn, New York, in 1903.*

In Whirlwind Valley

by Albert S. Evans

February 1869

On the morning of Monday, November 9, 1868, we looked forth from the door of the comfortable bed-room car in the camp train of the Central Pacific Railroad, in Lander County, Nevada, four hundred and twenty miles east of Sacramento, and eighteen miles east of Argenti. It was a clear, frosty winter morning, and the scene before us was romantic and stirring in the extreme—such a scene as we may not look upon again on the American continent. Eastward, the upper valley of the Humboldt—a broad, level prairie—stretched away to a point where the bald, rugged, snow-capped mountain chains from the north and south, abutting sharply on the river like lesser pillars of Hercules, form the magnificent Pass, made forever hideous by the abominable appelation of the Beaowawe Gate. To the north-eastward beyond the Gate, the Humboldt Mountains, with jagged outlines, clad in winter costume, loomed like giant Arctic icebergs, white, cold and sharp against the deep blue sky. Parallel lines of treeless mountains, red, rock-ribbed, barren and naked, save where Winter had in mercy thrown over them his mantle of snow to hide their natural deformity, bordered on either side the valley, stretching away to the westward for a hundred miles or more. Behind us the long lines of the railroad track and telegraph stretched out to the bank of the Sacramento more than four hundred miles away. Around us was the advancing and triumphant Army of Civilization; before us the dim, mysterious heart of the North American continent, toward which the track was crawling like a mighty serpent even while we slept. Before us, far up the valley, and for many miles beyond the gate, curled the blue smoke from the camp-fires of the thousand Chinese laborers—the real pathfinders of empire here—engaged in grading the track. On either side stretched long lines of horses and mules drawing heavy wagons freighted with materials and supplies for the road and laborers ahead. Behind us came train after train loaded with iron and timber, and swarming with blue-coated Asiatics, the rear-guard of the army, engaged in finishing up the work the vanguard had begun. Orderlies and foremen of gangs were gallop-ing back and forth on the prairie, carrying orders to those under them, or receiving them from the commander of the forces, the Superintendent of Construction. The track had been pushed forward three-fourths of a mile that morning before we arose, and a swarm of men were then constructing a permanent bridge of stout, square timbers, just brought from the Sierra Nevada, three hundred miles away, across a deep bayou or arm of the Humboldt still further on — a work which they would complete long before noon. A tall Shoshone Indian, wrapped in his tattered blanket, stood looking on in solemn silence, as the workmen added joint to joint on the lengthening iron track, and unwound coil after coil of the telegraph wire, affixing it to the insulators, lifting the tall crosses upright and planting their feet firmly in the soil — his soil and the soil of his ancestors, for ages past.

Did he see in the advancing army of white and yellow faces, the brace of iron bars and the lengthening line of wire, over which the lightning was to pass on the errand of civilization, the proof of the greatness of Uncle Sam, and the hopelessness of any further effort to stem the tide which is sweeping away the last remnant of his race? Was he musing on the history of the past, and bitterly contrasting it with the present and so much of the future as shall be shared by him and his? Was he dreaming of the Happy Hunting Grounds beyond the western horizon, where his race shall rove amid green fields and broad forests, steal stock, and scalp their enemies in peace, with no white man to molest them in their innocent amusements, or make them afraid; or was he debating the question, whether it was best for him to start at once for White Pine, and chance it, or wait until spring? What, in short, were his thoughts?

Guileless reader, trust me that I know him better than the young ladies who have studied him only in Cooper's novels. "Lo" is a practical man to the extent of the capacity which God has given him. He was calculating the amount of barley he could probably pick out of the dirt after the mules had done feeding, and keeping his weather-eye open for any old clothes which might be cast off by the owners and left by the wayside when the train moved on.

Breakfast over, saddle-horses were led up for us, and we mounted and galloped away to the southeastward on a trip to the great Volcano Springs, in Whirlwind Valley, which had been graphically described to us by a Spanish lady, who had visited them on the day previous. The sun, rising over the snowy mountain-tops, poured his flood of light down from an unclouded sky upon the broad, brown valley. The ugly deformity of sage-brush which covered the ground, and the nakedness of the straggling tufts of bunch grass, were concealed beneath a coating of bright hoar-frost, which sparkled in the sunlight like one vast spray of diamonds in silver settings. Rose-hued and coralline glowed the snow-fields on the upper mountains; soft as the velvet cheek of the plum, seemed the rugged outlines of the bare, red hills, as the sunlight filtered through the dim, blue haze, which, rising from the river and the thousand camp-fires along its banks, filled all the lower air and beautified the whole desert landscape. The mountain air, keen with the touch of coming winter, sent the blood coursing through our veins with accelerated speed, creating an exhiliration of spirit, such as creaming champagne or sparkling Moselle never yet produced.

Our horses, accustomed to the country, bounded forward at a steady gallop, heedless of rocks, sage-brush, and the narrow arroyos, which at short intervals crossed the trail, never stumbling or hesitating for a moment, and evidently enjoying the trip as heartily as ourselves. A covey of sage-hens rose from the grass and flew away unharmed; we had no guns to kill or frighten them with. A wolf sprang out of a clump of bushes, gave a quick, short cry, and turned to see what audacious intruder upon his domains had disturbed his morning slumbers. With a shout we charged upon him at the height of our horses' speed, and gave him a race of a mile or more; but the wolf came out a little ahead at the end, and we did not make game of him.

Turning around Shoshone Point, we emerged into open ground, and the Whirlwind Valley stretched away before us to the southward, skirted by bare, red hills on either side for miles. Across the Valley, some six miles to the southeastward, half-way up the western slope of a hill, perhaps six hundred feet in height, we saw a long table-land or *mesa*, white upon the top, and with long ribbon-like streaks of blue and white running down from thence to the plain below. This had been designated as the locality of the Volcano Springs; but beyond the discolorations mentioned, there was nothing to attract the mention of the traveller, and one might pass the point a dozen times without being made aware of their existence. "There she blows!" exclaimed my companion, after we had ridden on in sight of the place for some minutes. Looking up I saw a long jet of white steam shoot far up into the air from the top of the *mesa*. Another and another followed, and in a few minutes a dozen or more were rising from different parts of the hillside, and one or two from the plain at its foot. Half an hour's gallop brought us to the foot of the hill. Some time before we reached it we heard a noise as of many steam engines working away in some huge factory, and as we forced our horses up the steep acclivity over ground which resounded beneath their tread, hollow and cavernous, we heard other sounds emanating from the deep bosom of the mountain. Dismounting, we hitched our panting, half-frightened horses to a huge, honeycombed rock, and approached the opening in the earth from which the steam was escaping. The orifice might have been ten inches in diameter, and from it poured a stream of scalding water, clear as crystal, while a column of steam rose forty or fifty feet in to the air. The whole *mesa* appeared to be composed of lime, soda and sulphur deposits, the gradual accretion of years, and was blistering with a fierce heat from the undying fires below. It was as if we were walking over the surface of a fresh-burned lime-kiln on which rain had just been falling. The orifice was round, and had the appearance of having been artificially lined with coarse white porcelain. It was higher than the hill around it — showing clearly that it was gradually rising steadily from below by the accumulation of its own deposits, as a brick chimney increases in height as brick after brick is added to it by the mason. A kind of basin, several feet in width, surrounded the orifice, and in this basin were many curious lime formations, some resembling coral—others, round and polished as if by the wheel of the lapidary—others still, polished on one side, and on the other presenting the appearance of a basket of wax-flowers. We went on to another and still larger spring. There was a low, humming sound accompanying the action of the first; the second worked exactly like a steam pump, with a steady, regular stroke—the water being thrown out not in a continuous stream, but in jets corresponding with the regular strokes of the piston. As we stood over it, we could hardly divest ourselves of the impression that we were standing above a well-regulated steam engine in full operation, as, in fact, we were. We timed the pulsations with our watches, and counted just one hundred in a minute. From many small orifices, some not larger than one's finger, all around us steam was escaping, and the whole *mesa* seemed a mere crust, perforated like a cullender. We stamped with our boot-heels on the crumbling shell, and broke through it in one place. Below we found a mass of soft, coarse, granulated matter—red, white, and yellow, resembling in appearance rice-pudding, well intermixed with red-wine sauce, blistering hot, as if fresh from the oven, and emitting a nauseating odor of which a few sniffs were all-sufficient. We dug down into the mass with our hands, as long as we could stand the heat, and found it growing softer in proportion to its depth.

Passing on to the southward over a small divide, we saw a number of springs which had been running at intervals during the night, but were then inactive; long ribbons of ice, running out from them over the side of the *mesa* and down into the plain three hundred feet below, where all the water sinks and disappears. Others projecting in some cases three or four feet above the surface of the hill, appeared to have completely choked themselves up with their own deposits, and ceased to operate entirely, the water finding an escape elsewhere.

Looking southward along the height extending over half a mile of space, we saw dozens of these hot-water volcanoes—if we may be permitted the expression—in full operation, and an immense number of others quiet for the moment, but bearing evidence of being in working order, and liable to resume operations at any moment. The largest of those quiet at the moment had an orifice as large as a sugar hogshead, and was filled to the surface with clear, sparkling water. The sun was now well up in the heavens, and the air, especially where affected by the clouds of steam, warm enough to make the temptation to indulge in a tepid bath almost irresistible. The water in the basin, though not boiling, was not quite cold enough for bathing purposes, and we concluded to wander on a little farther and wait for it to cool. In the basin of another spring we found what appeared to be a large branch of the most delicate white coral, and determined to secure it. With two sticks cut from the hillside above, we fished it out at last, only to find, to our intense disgust, that it was merely a piece of sage-brush, which had fallen or been thrown into the water, and had become coated all over with the fine white lime deposits, not a trace of the vegetable fibre being left exposed to tell the true character of the curious object. Another formation of similar appearance promised better, and we fished that out also; it proved to be the ragged fragment of a blue woollen blanket, coated in like manner, and regarding it as a great curiosity in its way, we carried it off with us when leaving this place. But what became of the man who wore the blanket? That question worried us. Had we dug deeper we might have found a marble statue which would have answered the question. Finding at last a shallow pool of water, which had run down from a spring then quiet, we sat down, and stripping our heated feet gave them a soaking while we waited for the cooling of that in the basin of the great spring above us, and looked around on the strange scene about us.

There appeared to be at least one hundred of the larger springs which were more or less active daily, and hundreds of smaller openings in the hillside from whence steam and nauseating gases escaped. The hill, against the side of which the *mesa* on which the springs are located has been raised up, rises above this *mesa* or bench some three hundred feet quite abruptly, and further back to the eastward were peaks some hundreds of feet higher still. Red igneous rock, lying in layers pitching westward toward the valley, crops out on the whole face of the hill, and lava mixed with broken quartzite and vitrified rock strews the whole plain below. It appears as if these springs had originally flowed from the edge of the plain at the foot of the hill some three hundred feet below, where they now find vent, and had built up the whole *mesa* from their own deposits little by little; the pipes by which the water escapes growing longer and longer day by day as the altitude of the hill increased. Possibly there may have been a volcanic crater at this point, and the cold water, from between the layers of rock in the hill above, pouring down into it and coming into contact with the fire or heated rock may produce the steam, which, having no other means of escape, throws all the water above it out through the long pipes to the surface, the action being repeated in quick succession as long as the supply of water continues. This theory is plausible enough, but how about the cessation of action for fifteen minutes and hours in duration? And what about the origin of the lime, soda and sulphur deposited in such vast quantities by the sparkling water? The springs may, after all, owe their origin to chemical action entirely. One theory may be just as good as another, and probably more so.

While we were sitting with our feet in the tepid water, discussing the question of the formation of the place, a low, droning, moaning sound came up from the deep bosom of the hill, followed by a sharp "clap! clap! clap!" as if a pair of giant hands had been struck together three times with force, then, with a tremendous swash, a torrent of scalding water flew into the air, scattering in all directions from the great spring in which we had just been proposing to bathe, and poured in a stream ten feet wide down the hill. Had we remained by the side of that spring a few minutes longer, the chances are that some subsequent visitor would have discovered two beautiful statues, each the impersonation of manly beauty, and long discussions would doubtless have ensued in art circles as to the nationality of the sculptor — to whose immortal genius the world was indebted for such masterly conceptions, such matchless execution, etc., etc. It pleases us to have been able to save the world from doubt on that point. The torrent poured out incessantly for perhaps fifteen minutes, then began to subside. A low, gurgling sound came up as from the throat of a dying Cyclops, the water fell still lower; then came a long death-rattle; there was a perceptible shudder extending along the mesa for many rods; then all was still.

We went back to where our horses had been left, and prepared to leave the accursed region. A pool of clear water which had been thoroughly cooled, attracted our attention, and we took a drink. Just at that moment it occurred to us that the lime deposits quickly covered everything with which the water came in contact — that we might become porcelain lined, and forever incapable of enjoying the pleasures of taste and touch. What would signify a champagne lunch, or a claret punch with strawberries in it, to a man in that fix. This idea and the minerals in combination contained in the water acting together, induced us to suddenly put it — the water — back where we found it, and we felt more like leaving than before.

Leading our impatient horses down the steep hillside to the plain, we mounted and galloped away. Looking back without the fear of the fate of Lot's wife on our mind, from a distance of a mile or more, we saw that the springs along the whole hillside and in the plain at its foot, which had been acting independently thus far, were all apparently in operation at once, and a great cloud of steam was swaying and swirling in the wind, which had sprung up from the southward. Half an hour later we looked back again, and no steam at all was visible. Looking forward into the valley of the Humboldt, we saw the line of tracklayers miles advanced up toward the Beaowawe Gate, and the camp-train moving forward to a new position. Another link had been added to the great chain; the hands stretching out from the shores of the Atlantic and the Pacific had approached one degree nearer the point at which they shall ultimately unite in friendly grasp. The cinders, ashes and smouldering embers of the burned-up world of the dead Past, were behind us; before us the life, action, energy of the living Present — the abundant promise of a glorious Future.

The telegraph lines hummed as the news of the burning of the Atlantic Mail Line steamship, Missouri, *reached San Francisco. The ship burned on October 22, 1872 enroute to Havana and the well-known journalist Albert S. Evans lost his life in the tragedy.*

As a correspondent for the Chicago Tribune, **Albert S. Evans** (1831-1872) *had come to California and the Southwest to report on the mining districts* under the pen name "Allamonte." Mark Twain, a contemporary of Evans' in the gold fields, satirized him as the immortal "Fitz Smythe", the journalist who, in order to get rid of his newspapers, had to feed them to his horses.

Evans later wrote for the Alta California in San Francisco and served as its City Editor for a time. During the Civil War he served as a Colonel on the staff of the governor of California. Following the war Evans traveled extensively throughout the Southwest and was a frequent contributor to the Overland Monthly with sketches of the sights he encountered.

In 1870 his book on Mexico, Our Sister Republic, was published. His only other book, A La California, which contained a collection of articles written on life in the Golden State, was published posthumously in 1873 following the voyage which cost him his life.

⸻ A Cloud-Burst on the Desert ⸻
by Albert S. Evans
August 1869

There is an undefinable, indescribable charm — a kind of weird attraction — which becomes most powerful and absorbing in traversing the burning deserts of the far South-west. To the wearied dwellers in cities, the silence and utter desolation of the red, sun-scorched desert, the naked, rock-ribbed mountains, the long, tortuous passes and cañons, the wide, treeless plains, strewn with volcanic ashes, and the slag and cinders of a burned-up world of the past, possess a charm which is lacking in the crowded streets, the rush the roar and tumult of the town. Danger passed is something to look back on with a feeling of pleasure; danger yet to be met comes in time to possess a charm of itself, and throw around the journey on the desert more of attraction than can be found in any trip through civilized and thickly peopled lands. Those who have never felt and enjoyed this sensation could gain no idea of it from a written description; those who have felt it always look back to it with pleasure, and experience at intervals an almost irresistible longing to return to the scene and go through it all again.

The dangers of desert travel have often been described, and recounted in a thousand ways by as many pens and tongues. Many a traveler has told us of his conflicts with the Apache, the Comanche and the Sioux, and that branch of the subject has been fairly exhausted; but one of the most common dangers, one which ever hangs suspended over the head of the traveler in the desert lands along our south-western border, seems never to have been touched upon to any extent. That danger is found in the terrible "cloud-burst" which in arid, treeless lands sometimes changes in an instant the whole surface of a wide landscape, and sweeps away in a moment objects which have served as landmarks for ages. The huge clouds which come up from the Pacific, and are borne over the Coast Range Mountains by the air-currents born of desert heat and ocean cold, entering some peculiar stratum of air, are operated upon in a manner which we are unable to describe — perhaps because we do not know any thing about it — and all the moisture contained in them becomes suddenly condensed and precipitated in overwhelming volume on the desert. Torrents roll forth from the barren mountains, tearing wide channels, many feet in depth, in the loose, gravelly sands of the plains, sweeping even great rocks before them in their irresistible fury, and disappear from the sight of the astonished traveler so suddenly as to leave him forever after in doubt as to the evidence of his senses: whether the terrible convulsions he has witnessed were in fact real or imaginary — actual occurrences, or the fantastic creation of a disordered fancy.

All who have crossed the upper arms of the Colorado Desert, from San Bernardino *via* San Gorgonio Pass, Toros, Dos Palmas and Chucolwalla, to the Colorado River, will remember the ragged-edged volcanic rift in the southern side of the Glacier Mountains, twelves miles east of Dos Palmas, knowns as Cañon Springs — a villainous locality, affording a very little water, which at times is poisonous to man and beast from the impregnation of copper and other minerals, and always distasteful — with no grass, no wood, and millions of rattlesnakes, whose rank odor at times fills the whole place to such an extent that it is almost impossible to force a horse to remain there after his burning thirst has been slaked at the water-hole under the rocks. This is a common camping-place for travelers between Los Angeles and La Paz. Three years ago — in the month of March, 1866 — a Government train, consisting of a number of large army wagons, heavily laden with supplies, forage, etc., etc., accompanied by a large detachment of United States troops, bound for Arizona, was suddenly overwhelmed while camping here in fancied security by one of these irresistible torrents from a cloud-burst, swept out of the cañon, borne forth into the rocky desert, and scattered far and wide in the pitchy darkness of a starless night. One officer, while being borne down the torrent, was recognized by a Mexican *vaquero* as he swept past the camp-fire, lassoed and pulled by the neck out upon the rocky edge of the cañon. Others, less fortunate, were carried miles away and left among the black lava rocks, bruised, exhausted, and half dead, as the roaring waters subsided among the desert sands. Passing there a few days later, we found Indians digging barley out of the sand among the wrecks of the wagons, miles below the camping ground; and saw one poor soldier dying at Dos Palmas from the injuries he received while being rolled over the jagged rocks by the torrent, from which he vainly sought to escape. His ribs were crushed in by the rocks; and when the falling waters left him on the desert, three miles from the cañon, he lay all night in his clothing, exposed to the cold wind, helpless, and even unable to cry out for assistance, had any been within hearing of his voice.

At another time, while lost on the eastern side of Cabezon Valley, in the blazing heat of summer, the writer and a companion rode their horses at a gallop for at least fifteen miles along the dry bed of such a torrent, which had poured out of the San Bernadino Mountain on the day before; and though we sought diligently all that day and the succeeding one for water, a only a lucky accident, or a miracle, saved us at last from perishing with thirst, so suddenly had every drop sunk down into the desert sands and disappeared.

It was in March, 1866, that the writer, having ridden through the wild and almost impassable defiles of the Red Mountain, on the eastern shore of the Colorado, and with infinite toil and trouble picked his way on foot down the pass on the north, dragging his weary horse after him into the valley of Bill Williams Fork, found himself at last safely on the northern bank of that accursed stream at "Aubrey City," awaiting the arrival of a friend from "up the creek," and enjoying the first "square meals" and comfortable bed which had fallen his way for weeks.

We were bound for the Great Central Copper Mine, on the south bank of Williams Fork, twelve miles from its mouth, and expected to reach there in a couple of hours' ride, having sent word to William Thompson, the Superintendent, in advance, to meet us at Aubrey. The Fork had been up, and as the road to the mines leads along the stream, which it crosses and recrosses a dozen times in as many miles, it was not safe for a stranger to attempt passing up alone, on account of the quicksands which form in shifting bars all along its course, and are liable to engulf in an instant horse and rider. When the stream falls for a short time, the sand packs down solid, and loaded teams can pass up and down with perfect safety; but at high water the road is dangerous to the last degree. Thompson did not arrive that evening, and before morning the creek, swollen by a passing shower, went up to a impassable point again. Two days more, and an Indian swam the Fork with a "paper" in his hair, informing us that Thompson would be with us the next day. He came at last, worn down with the trip, covered with mud, and not in the best of humor, having been down twice in the quicksands, and having nearly drowned old Blanco, the faithful mustang, which he had led down for me to ride back upon. At sunrise next morning we were off. For three miles the road ran along a hard *mesa*, and admitted of fast riding, then followed around the base of a range of precipitous hills, just above the water's edge, for some distance. We determined to keep the northern bank as long as possible, then ford the creek and take to the hills on the southern side. Soon the trail ran into the creek, and we were compelled to work our way along the bank, over loose rocks and under precipices, as best we might. At last we reached a point beyond which it appeared doubtful if we could force our animals; and dismounting, I left Thompson, with the horses, standing on a narrow ledge of rocks, and worked my way along on foot around a bold, projecting point to see if there was foothold for horses to be obtained. When just turning back to report the possibility of a passage I heard a cry; and running with all speed to the place where Thompson and the horses had stopped, saw him holding old Moro by the bit, and looking ruefully over the rock toward the bed of the creek. A glance was enough to reveal the situation. Blanco, having tired of standing still, had attempted to turn around, in doing which he slipped and went heels over head off the rock, into the water and quicksand below. His head alone projected above the water, his body having disappeared beneath the quicksand. We got old Moro to a place of safety and tied him; then went back and set to work with all haste to rescue poor Blanco from death. Thompson wore, strapped on his thigh, a bowie-knife as large as a butcher's cleaver, made from a huge saw-mill file, and so heavy that he could cut through a sapling as thick as a man's wrist at every blow. With this he cut down willows almost as a man cuts grass with a scythe, and in a few minutes we had a wide bed of them laid carefully by the side of the poor, struggling brute. The surface of the sand was tolerably hard; but as we walked over it, it quivered like jelly. The light sand and water beneath are of unknown depth, and liable to engulf one at any moment. The sensation in traveling over it was such as one experiences sometimes in a nightmare, but never in waking life, save in an Arizona quicksand. A Mexican came up on horseback—bound like ourselves to the mines—and lent a hand. With many a weary tug and strain we succeeded at last in getting the horse out on his side on the willows, and stripping him of his saddle and bridle, allowed him a few minutes to breathe; then, with yells and blows, forced him to scramble to his feet, and ran him out upon a little island, where there was hard ground. The horses were now all brought together, and saddles and blankets arranged for a new start. Thompson walked out upon a sand flat which led to another little island, and, though it shook and quivered under him like jelly, pronounced it possible to run our horses over it. The Mexican started ahead, and his horse crossed in safety to the island in the middle of the stream. The crust of hard sand, weakened by the passage of his horse, began to yield under the feet of poor old Blanco; and in spite of yells and blows, he stopped for an instant, then went down like a plummet, and only his head was to be seen. His fall frightened Moro, and he halted, only to go down like Blanco, in the twinkling of an eye. Then Thompson, like one possessed, threw off everything but his shirt and pants, and the air grew blue with curses. The first proceeding was repeated, and we soon had willows piled by the sides of the horses, as before. The dumb animals, with an instinct more than human, folded their legs under them and remained as quiet as if asleep, fully conscious that the least struggling would engulf them beyond the chance of a resurrection. Doubting our ability to lift the horses from the quicksands by our strength alone, we attempted to wade over the Fork to get assistance from a Mexican camp a little distance away. The stream, though rapid, was fordable, but the wide flat of quicksand on the other side was impassable. I fell through once, and was only saved from being engulfed and drowned in the treacherous sands by a pole which I carried horizontally in my hands, which sustained my weight, and enabled me to pull myself out and regain firmer footing. Floundering about in the mud and water, losing our spurs and falling over and over again, we succeeded at last in getting our horses out upon their sides on the piles of willows, and finally ran them at full speed to a gravelly bar, on which they could stand in safety until they were rested, and we had cleaned up our saddles and equipments, and made ready for a new start. It was now 10 A.M., and the sun, shining from an unclouded sky, made the air in the narrow valley oppressively hot. Thompson looked uneasily up the Fork, from time to time, and the horses appeared to fret and look apprehensively in the same direction; but I saw nothing of danger, and nothing was said about it. "Well, we are over the worst of it, and in fifteen minutes more we will reach the upper crossing and be out of trouble," said Thompson, with evident relief.

We were riding along the flat gravelly bar, congratulating ourselves on the escape from the loss of our animals in the quicksands, when a dull, roaring sound, like the passing of a distant hurricane over the country, coming from the eastward, broke on our ears. "We must hurry, for the creek is going to rise—I saw a black cloud up toward the head of the creek at daylight, and have been fearing a freshet all the morning," said Thompson; and we urged our horses into a rapid trot to reach the crossing. Suddenly the roar increased to a volume like distant thunder, and the Mexican, throwing up his hand, with the exclamation, "Mother of God, protect us!" wheeled his horse for the *mesa* on the north side of the stream, and dashed away at full gallop. One glance up the stream was enough—I shall never forget the sight! Around the bend ahead, and perhaps half a mile distant, was coming a solid wall of water at least ten feet in height, filling the whole valley of the Fork, and bearing every thing before it. We ran our horses at their utmost speed for the *mesa*; and just as we reached its foot, the water, driven out of the bed of the creek by the pressure of the coming flood, ran around us. We reached the top of the *mesa*, some thirty feet in height, and looked down upon a scene which beggars tongue and pen. The valley of the Fork along which we had ridden but a moment before dry-shod, was filled with a roaring flood from bank to bank. The purling stream, which a man could ford on foot ten minutes before, was now fully a thousand yards in width, from ten to thirty feet in depth, and with a current with which no race-horse could compete for speed. The whole face of the flood was covered with drift-wood; great cotton-woods were lifted out of the earth and borne away like straws: nothing could stand before the tremendous rush of waters. The air was filled with the rank odor of alkali and fresh earth carried down by the raging waters; and the surface of the flood was covered with a cream-like foam, showing how violent had been the action of the torrent above. Near where we reached the *mesa*, a party of Mexicans were at work cultivating a small ranch, and as the flood approached them, attempted to run for the heights. A minute later, we saw them swimming for their lives in the edge of the torrent, while their house was going down the Fork bodily with the speed of a high-pressure steamboat. Their crops were already washed away, and they were reduced to beggary, even before they touched the shore and were assured of their lives.

The deafening roar of the surging waters made it almost impossible for us to make ourselves heard by each other, even when a few feet apart; and words were idle even if they could be heard. We lay an hour in silence on the *mesa*, gazing at the wild waste of waters before us, and then turned our horses' heads for the black hills to the northward, knowing full well that we could not cross the flood with a steamboat, if we had one, and that we must seek a new road to the place we had left in the morning. Hour after hour we toiled on, dragging our almost worn-out horses up and down shelving hill-sides, and over loose, jagged rocks, which cut our boots to pieces and tore the shoes from the feet of the animals; and, just as night set in, we arrived once more at Aubrey, utterly exhausted with our fruitless day's labor.

All that long, dreary night, we lay in our blankets in our friend's hospitable cabin, and listened to the roar of the waters and the splashing of trees in the flood, as the banks on the opposite side of the stream were undermined and went crashing down, to be swallowed up in the hungry torrent. Next morning we found that the flood, pouring into the Colorado from Williams Fork, had set back the waters of the river like a dam, and raised it bankful for miles to the northward.

That day the Fork fell rapidly, and next morning we determined to once more attempt to get up to the mine. Our horses had just been saddled and made ready for the trip, when a man came down from a ranch about a mile distant, in breathless haste, to tell us that the hostile Apaches, or Hualapais, had made a raid upon him and run off his entire stock of horses and mules, seven or eight in number, toward the mountains. Irataba, the old desert giant, head chieftain of the Mojaves, had arrived on the evening with José, one of his young captains, and five young warriors, from La Paz, *en route* for Fort Mojave, where half his tribe reside. The old fellow at once ran up to the ranch, and soon returned to tell us that there were but five Indians in the band which had made the raid; and if we would make all possible haste we might overtake them before they were joined by another party, clean them out, recover the plunder, and ornament the pommels of our saddles with very elegant top-knots as souvenirs of a pleasure trip in Arizona. I have not space to tell the story of the hastily gathered Falstaffian army, which an hour later rode forth into the unexplored desert mountains to the north-east; of the long day's toil in the burning heat, the chase at night-fall, the ambuscade which we escaped, the bitter cold which nipped us as we lay hid all night in the chaparral, the pursuit next day, and the temporary escape of the Hualapais with their plunder, the exasperation of Irataba, who with his young braves had tracked the flying enemy like so many bloodhounds on the scent—and on foot kept up with our horses, which were going at a swinging trot, or even at a gallop; of the second and third expeditions, the burning of the Hualapai villages, and the bloody reprisals on either side which followed in quick succession. Suffice it, that just a week after we made our first attempt to go up the creek twelve miles, we emerged from the desert on the northern bank of that delectable stream, opposite the mining camp, and were met beneath the wide-spreading alamos by an old Mexican, in ragged trowsers and wide, slouched *sombrero*, whose odd rig and huge American beard had earned for him the *sobriquet* of Robinson Crusoe. Angel—such was his patronymic—received us with outstretched arms, and welcomed us to the camp. He had been out on a little *paseo* that day—it was Sunday, and he was not obliged to work at the mine—but had not been very lucky. It is true that he had run across two Apache-Mojaves, a buck and a squaw, in a cañon in the hills, and got them both with one shot from his dilapidated old musket; but he had seen no other game, and was a little discouraged. It was not a good day for sport! He piloted us from island to island, until we were at last safely across the stream; and, as we went on up to camp, showed us obligingly where two men mounted on mules had been caught by the cloud-burst in a narrow cañon and overwhelmed in an instant. Both mules and one of the riders perished in the flood, but the other man climbed the rocks to a point where the water just touched his beard, and there clung, like a young chimney swallow to a brick, until the subsiding flood fell below his waist, and he knew that the worst was over.

These are some of the well attested effects of the "cloud-burst" on the desert, and of such are the "moving adventures by flood and field" which the traveler encounters on the American southwestern frontier.

The Ice-Caves of Washington Territory

by R.W. Raymond

November 1869

No ice! — Disconsolate drinkers hung about their bar-rooms, sipping insipid cocktails and cobblers, or playing "freeze out" in grim irony, to decide who should have the first lump out of that refrigerant cargo daily expected from the north. Butter pathetically swam about on the platters; cucumbers visibly wilted for disappointed hope; fresh meat grew prematurely old with sorrow; the ice-cream shebangs shut up their business, and all over town might be heard the diabolical chuckle and supercilious snuffle of the tea-kettles, celebrating the triumph of hot water over cold. Even the Templars couldn't stand it. That worthy association had no scruples about appropriating the convivial songs of all ages, and, skillfully injecting "cold water" into the place originally occupied by "ruby wine," to adapt them for the uses of reform; but the strongest stomach in the fraternity rebelled at the Bacchanalian choruses: *"Warm* water for me," "Tepid and bright, in its liquid light," "In the simmering stream our brows we lave, and parboil our lips in the crystal wave." For once the all-transforming wand of the Muse of Temperance was powerless; and the melodeon of the Lodge "dried up." This was the situation at Portland, Oregon; and it was, to borrow the most expressive word in the Chinook jargon — that ripest fruit of time, product of all languages, essence of concentrated speech — it was, I say, *cultus:* yes, *hyas cultus,* or, in feeble Saxon, highly inconvenient, disgusting, demoralizing.

Happy Dalles City, meanwhile, reveled in ice. The living were content, the unburied dead were comfortable, topers were saved the additional sin of profanity, and the seductive song of "Run, cold water, for you and me" was not a disconsolate voice crying in the sagebrush. The philosophic observer, inquiring as to the cause of this strange contrast, was informed that a mysterious ice-cave in Washington Territory constituted a reserve upon which the Dalles fell back in seasons when the improvidence of the Oregonians, and some unusual irregularity in climate, combined, exhausted the supply of the great necessity of civilized life.

Moved by various individual motives, but united in the desire to render thanks at head-quarters for this blessed relief, a small party of us formed the plan of an excursion to the cave. There was a keen and portly Portlander, who cherished a secret intention of building a hotel, constructing a wagon-road, and creating out of the cave a fashionable ice watering-place. There was a young, enthusiastic Tourist from the Mississippi Valley, who, having lived out West till the West was East, had come to explore the veritable Occident, beyond which there is none. There was a Veteran Inhabitant, who goes out every spring on snow-shoes and "claims" the cave, under an ingenious application of mining law, as a mineral deposit, so as to obtain a monopoly of the ice-packing business. And finally, there was the present writer—a person habitually animated by the purest impulses known to reconstructed humanity—who joined the party because he wished to do so: than which no reason could be more conclusive or free from base motives.

As we disembarked from the handsome steamer of the Oregon Steam Navigation Company, near the mouth of the White Salmon, we found ourselves assembled upon the sandy bank, as follows: four men, four horses, and a huge quantity of bacon, crackers, etc., together with a pair of blankets apiece. The work of distributing the baggage and packing it behind our saddles so that it would not pound on a trot, nor rattle on a gallop, nor quietly slip off on a walk; so that the matches would not ignite upon the coffee-pot, nor the bacon flavor the sugar, nor the sardines burst among the crackers, nor the candles (for exploring the cave) be mangled by the knives and spoons, (for exploring the victuals) was not accomplished without some difficulty. But at length all was adjusted except the frying-pan, which would not pack, and was accepted by the Veteran with some profane grumbling, as a very unnecessary evil, which ought by rights to be "slung to thunder," but was unjustly slung to him instead. That frying-pan owes its safety throughout our trip to the fact that it was borrowed and must be returned. The Veteran rode ahead, brandishing it sullenly, like some new instrument of warfare, and we followed in single file.

It was a ride of some forty miles to the cave, through the bewildering beauty and grandeur of the Cascade Mountains. We galloped over high, breezy table-lands; we looked down on Josselin's nestling ranch, alive with cattle and lovely with fruit-laden orchards; we followed the narrow trail along the steep mountain-side, the deep misty cañon of the White Salmon below us, and beyond it the leafy mountains rising, ridge above ridge, until they were veiled in the smoke of burning forests far away. We threaded our way through thick wildernesses of undergrowth, parting the branches with our hands, and scarcely able to see before us the path, well worn for the feet by patient pack-mules, but not yet quite ready for a rider taller than a bundle of ice. Anon, we emerged into beautiful openings, carpeted with bunch-grass or wild oats, and dotted with stately oaks and pines—the ground kept smooth and lawny by woodland fires, that creep silently from tuft to tuft of grass or dry leaves, or smolder along the course of fallen trunks, and kiss, with burning, deceitful passion, as they pass, the feet of the giants of the forest, that disdain to notice such trifles while they can look abroad upon a measureless world and sky. But now and then, favored by drought and wind, the creeping fires grow bold and spring like tigers upon some feeble, dry old tree, wrapping it in flame from root to crown; or they gnaw at a sturdy trunk till its strength is undermined, and then, some fair, quiet day, like that on which we rode through these solitudes, the overstrained column gives way suddenly, and—with a groan, a rustling of unavailing resistance, a vain wringing of leafy hands and a wild tossing of rugged arms, a crack-ling, a crashing, a great rush and sweep, and a final heavy boom as of far ar-tillery, waking the echoes of the pitying hills—a tree falls! Beautiful, but ah! how sad were the belief, that imprisoned within it was a conscious Dryad—conscious, but not immortal: to feel her life carried downward in that mighty fall, into the hopeless abyss of annihilation; or, sadder yet, to lie thereafter prone in the forest, and wait the deliverance even of utter destruction at the merciful hands of Time and Decay!

But now we stand upon the crest of a high, steep ridge, adown which, with slow and careful steps, we must lead our horses. At the bottom rushes the swift White Salmon, which we cross upon a frail, swaying bridge to climb the rocky height upon the other side, and mount again to gallop through the woods. West of the river, the surface rises in irregular terraces, the results of successive basaltic overflows. The rocky ridges, peeping through the soil, cross our path at intervals; and the fine dust rising from the trail beneath our horses' feet is the same in character as that which daily chases the wagons on the roads over the vast volcanic highlands between the Columbia and the Snake. These rugged outcrops are the haunts of the graceful rattlesnake and the vivacious yellow-jacket. My acquaintance with one individual of the latter, though brief, was long enough to be fatal to him and memorable to me. Our party was quietly jogging through the forest, and my eyes were fixed, with mild lack of interest upon the crupper of the steady beast that bore the Tourist, when suddenly that respectable charger stopped, tried to kick with all his feet at once, reared, plunged, bucked, and revolved his tail with furious rapidity in a plane at right angles with the axis of his body. A moment after, my own steed began a similar series of antics, under the attacks of a host of little bandits in golden mail, whose retreat we had invaded. I laughed aloud at the novel situation, but the insult was ter-ribly avenged. Straight out of the empty air came a raging cavalier to answer the challenge, and we fought it out in half a second. He insisted on his right to choose ground, weapons, and distance, to wit: my hand, his sting, and considerably less than nothing. His arrangements were so well made that he was well "into" me before I got "onto" him. Result: one small, dead yellow-jacket, of no account whatever, and a hand and arm nearly as useless. I "gained flesh" for an hour with astonishing speed; I lost sight of my knuckles and sinews; and, had I that day presented my hand to an aged, purblind father, he would have had cause to say, "The voice is the voice of Jacob; but the hand is the hand of the Boy in Pickwick." Some good whisky was wasted (as the Veteran opined) in external lotions; but for a day or two I could only hang up the useless member, and make believe I had lost an arm at Gettysburg, and deserved well of a grateful Republic. Since that time, I have had opportunity to study the yellow-jacket; and I know that, like other desperate characters who hold life cheap, he is to be respected and feared. He who would merely kill you may be a coward after all, and you need not leave the country on his account; but he who hates you, and in comparison with that passion cares not whether you kill him or no, is dangerous. Avoid him if you can, treat him kindly when you may, smash him when you must; but be sure that, nine times out of ten, he will first put dagger into you.

We strike into the well trodden trail of the Indians, and frequently meet cavalcades of them returning, heavy-laden, from the great huckleberry patches, where they collect their winter store. Others of them are spearing or netting salmon at the cascades of the Columbia and DesChutes; and with dried fish and fruit galore, they will pass a merry winter in their squalid manner. These fragmentary tribes of the upper Columbia — Klikitats, and what not — are not so handsome as the Nez Perces, farther to the north-east; but there are now and then fine faces among them — laughing-eyed young squaws, old men with judicial brows, straight, strong athletes — and the children all promise a future beauty which privation, hardship, and disease too surely erases as they grow up. Was there a time when the Red Man roamed, etc., etc., contented and happy, valiant and handsome — the perfect and worthy child of Nature? Show us the relics of former decent habitation, and good victuals, and we may, perchance, answer in the affirmative; but perpetually living out of doors, without clothes to speak of, and subsisting upon food in precarious supply, and frequently of inferior quality, is not calculated to develop a high type of physical, any more than of mental manhood. If this doctrine be held to cast a slur upon Adam, who represents to us the state of savage innocence to which some people think we ought to return, I can only say that Adam's career was a disgraceful one. He had a better chance than the rest of us, and he ruined himself and his descendants by a piece of real Indian laziness and folly. Lolling about and eating the spontaneous fruits of the earth, instead of tilling the garden with industry, is just his sin, and theirs. This copper-colored Adam, who was placed in the Eden of the New World, has mismanaged it in the same way. He and his dusky Eve have loitered and idled away the centuries, living carelessly upon the bounty of the passing time. Verily, by reason of family resemblance to Adam, (and, for that matter, to Cain, also) the Indians should be set down as a very early offshoot from the Eden stock, transplanted before the parent tree had begun its better growth.

Too much preaching and philosophizing, says the Tourist, who is interested in the squaws and babies, and not at all in Adams. In deference to his wishes, I subside into silence and a trot. These Indians all talk Chinook, which is the most fascinating of tongues. Being the product of a deliberate agreement of men — a compromise, it is said, between the Hudson's Bay Company's agents, the Jesuit missionaries, and the once powerful Chinook tribe — it is, of course, superior to those misshapen dialects that spring up of themselves, no one knows how. From the French, Spanish, English, Indian, and Hawaiian these wise etymologists took what was best in each, and the result comprises melody, force, and wondrous laconic expressiveness. It is none of your tame tongues, that can be spoken of without gesture. Little boys, declaiming in jargon, could not possibly retain in nervous grasp the seams of their trowser-legs. One of the most frequent words is *kahkwa*, meaning "thus," or "like this," and invariably accompanied with pictorial illustration of movement or feature. Let us address this ancient chieftain, solemnly riding at the head of a long train of "cayuse" horses, laden with his household, his "traps," and his huckleberries: *Klahowya sikhs?* (How dost thou venerable sir?) *kah mika klatawa?* (and whither journeyest?) *Nika klatawa kopa Simcoe; mika King George tilikum, Boston tilikum?* (I travel to the Simcoe Reservation; are ye of King George's men — that is to say, Englishmen, or of the Boston tribe — that is to say, Yankees?) *Nesika Boston tilikum, King George cultus.* (We are Americans all, and regard King George with loathing and contempt.) *Okook mika klootchman?* (Is yon beauteous being thy bride?) *Siah kopa lamonti?* (Far to the mountains? — *lamonti*, from the French, *la montagne*.) To the first, *Nawitka* (Yes); to the latter, *Wake siah, wayhut hyas kloshe okook sun, kah chilchil kahkwa tomolla keekwillie kahkwa, tomolla moosum kopa lamonti.* (Not far; good road, to-day; steep, to-morrow, low and level, thus and thus; to-morrow night a camp at the mountain). A very commonplace conversation, but full of music, if you read it aloud, Mademoiselle, with your sweet voice. But the Veteran is loping far ahead. Jargon has no charms for him; he has prattled too many years with these Babes of the Wood.

It is thirty-five miles from the mouth of the White Salmon to the ice-cave; and over this trail by which we travel, the ice is "packed" upon the backs of mules and horses. We meet upon the road the loaded train. On each beast two sacks, each of which contained, at starting, a block of ice weighing, perhaps, two hundred pounds, but destined to melt away to half its original dimensions before it reaches the steamboat landing. By this simple device, as the toilsome day wears on, the burden diminishes; and while it grows lighter, distills refreshing coolness on the bearer. The dividends of the business would be larger, however, as the Portlander acutely remarks, if the ice were better packed at the cave. But this is a fair sample of the mining industry of the coast. Happy that enterprise, whereof the drippings *only* equal the savings!

The sun drops into the hazy west, as we ride into a forest glade, and the Veteran exclaims, "Here she is!" We resolve upon an immediate preliminary examination of the cave, and subsequent supper and sleep. All that presented itself was an opening in the ground a dozen feet square, formed by the fall of a portion of the roof. We had passed within a few hours, numerous openings of this kind, the mention of which I have omitted for artistic reasons. I would not fritter away the reader's interest in minor caverns on the way. The examination of several, however, qualifies me to give wise explanation of their nature.

These caves are channels in the basalt, through which the latest flows of melted matter passed. The phenomenon of a stream of lava, walled and roofed with congealed material of the same character, may be observed at almost any active volcano. I have seen it on the sides of Vesuvius during a quiet eruption. If the source of such a stream is suddenly choked, the lava will continue to flow for some distance, protected from rapid cooling by the crust above, and thus a portion of the channel will be left empty. It is not difficult to recognize this process in the basalt caves of Washington Territory. Their walls are covered with traces of the departing fluid matter, and on their floors may be found masses of the congealed lava, still fibrous from its last vain effort to follow the current. It looks, Mademoiselle, like that piece of abortive molasses candy which you threw away in despair, because it got so stiff and would not "pull." But whence the ice — that strange dweller in these homes of fire?

Only a few of these caverns contain ice, and they are connected at both ends with the open air, by means of passages formed by the falling in of the crust, or the fissuring of the rocks by frost, or, finally, by the gradual denudation of the surface, exposing the ancient channels themselves. The intense, refrigerating airs of winter are thus allowed free passage. Alternately with these the percolating waters of the surface find their way into the caves in such small quantities that they freeze, layer upon layer, solid from the bottom; and the store of ice thus accumulated thaws slowly during the summer. This summer thaw is retarded, not only by the covering which protects the ice from the direct rays of the sun, but also by the fact that the melting ice at one end of the cave, through which the summer draught enters, itself refrigerates the air, and maintains a freezing temperature at the other end. We noted in the main ice-cave, which we explored, a decided difference in the degrees of thaw at different points. This difference was due to the cause above mentioned; and I had the honor to determine it by sliding unintentionally down a glacial stalagmite and observing practically the degree of moisture upon its surface. The popular report, that as fast as ice is removed from the cave it continually and at all seasons forms again, is without foundation. The amount of it in the cave is not very great, though as yet undetermined; and what there is, perpetually, though slowly, wastes away. The main body of ice has a level surface, indicating subterranean drainage at a certain point, above which water does not remain in the cave. There are a few stalactites, and still more numerous stalagmites, here and there. One of these is a superb, transparent hillock, rising nearly to the roof, and christened the Iceberg. Here I took my slide.

The entrance used by the ice-miners is the opening in the roof already alluded to. At this point the channel turns at right angles, and this sharp turn left the roof with less support, so that it fell in. We followed the cave more than two hundred feet in one direction from this entrance, and perhaps five hundred in the other. The short arm of it contains most of the ice, and the long arm simply reaches out through fallen rocks and rubbish to daylight. The terminus of the cave in the other direction was reached by the Tourist, who, being a small man and an ambitious, hatcheted his way over the iceburg and crawled out of sight into a fissure beyond, from the depths of which his voice was presently heard, announcing that it was "too tight a fit" for him to go farther. *Tableau:* Tourist in the hole, triumphant; writer perched on the Iceberg, curious, but cautious; portly Portlander, half-way to the entrance, resolving to have that hole made bigger when the hotel is built; and Veteran at the entrance, not caring a straw. This is the way in which such explorations are usually conducted.

The dimensions of the cavern are not large. It does not exceed thirty feet in width, nor (at present, with the bottom full of ice and fallen fragments of basalt) twenty in height. Others in the neighborhood are larger, but do not contain so much ice. From the nature of their origin, it is not likely that any of them possess extraordinary dimensions, except in length. In this direction they extend for miles, though they can seldom be followed underground without labor in removing rocks, etc., for more than a few hundred feet. It was in the present instance the indefatigable Tourist, who, with the docile writer in his wake, made a second visit to Hades after supper; and, entering by the familiar chasm, found the new exit far to the south, and emerged thereby, to the great amazement of the party by the camp-fire, under whose unconscious feet he had passed, to re-appear in an unexpected quarter.

If you ever visit the cave, don't let the Veteran persuade you that it is necessary to ride two miles farther to camp, on account of water. There are pools of clear ice-water within it; and behind a tall pine, not far away, you will find two wooden troughs, half sunk in the earth. One of them is very leaky; the other not so much. Let one of you stand at the bottom of the cave, and another lower from above the coffee-pot, made fast to a lariat. A third can run to and fro with the precious liquid; and in a few minutes you will have water for your horses in the trough. The Veteran will sit on a log, scornfully at first, but finally snort his approbation.

The joys of camping out I do not undertake to describe. In this effeminate day, when people sit in their parlors and read about things instead of doing them, thank goodness there is something left which can not be put into words. There is a period of perfect peace, when, rising at midnight and putting a fresh log on the fire, one gazes placidly about upon his sleeping comrades, lights a pipe, and communes with himself, the dancing flame, and the solemn, silent forest. Interjected between the jollity of the evening meal, and the business-like activity of breakfast, packing and mounting, this midnight pipe of peace is like a whiff from another world. How ridiculously different from sitting up in bed and lighting the gas.

Another thing which I omit is a description of fair St. Helen's and grand Mt. Adams. How they accompany us with their eternal beauty, all the way! How delightful is the change from the gloomy caves to the paradise that lies just beneath the edge of the melting snows on Mt. Adams. There innumerable varieties of flowers bloom, even at this late season — the whole Flora of the coast — but dwarfed by their Alpine locality into forms of infinite delicacy, and, hovering among them, multitudes of humming-birds, who have gathered here to find again the blossoms of June, vanished long since from the South. Streams alive with trout — *hyiu tenas salmon* — and white goats on the snowy fields above, to tax the skill and daring of the more ambitious sportsman. I could give you a fine description of all these things, but I must stop here; and morally it is quite as well, for the smoke in the air prevented us from seeing Adams, or visiting the Paradise of Humming-birds — but which is, nevertheless, there; and so you will find out, when, next July, you add to your summer trip along the grand Columbia, a charming three-days' excursion to the region I have faintly depicted.

Rossiter Worthington Raymond *(1840-1918) was appointed United States Commissioner of Mining Statistics in 1868. His work required long trips to the Far West and much writing. His literary ability made his reports models of clarity and technical excellence.* (Statistics of Mines and Mining in the States and Territories West of the Rocky Mountains, eight reports, 1869-77).

The young man was ideally suited for the job. As a boy he had lived in a cultivated atmosphere and graduated at the head of his class at Brooklyn Polytechnic where his father taught'English. Following graduation he spent three years in Germany as a student at the Royal Mining Academy. Returning home in 1861 he served as aide-de-camp on the staff of Major-General John C. Frémont. Resigning his commission in 1864 he went into partnership with a consulting mining engineer in New York. In 1867, he became editor of the American Journal of Mining. *When his articles attracted attention in Washington, D.C. he was soon appointed commissioner.*

The role in which he achieved his greatest experience was that of Secretary of the American Institute of Mining Engineers, a post he held from 1884 to 1911. His position as editor of the Institutes' publications gave him marked influence throughout the profession, and he helped many struggling young men express their ideas. On his seventieth birthday he was presented the Gold Medal of the Institution of Mining & Metallurgy of London. A year later in Japan, the Mikado presented him the Order of the Rising Sun, Fourth Class.

A Glimpse of Montana

by E.W. Carpenter

April 1869

Montana! The name struck pleasantly upon my ear as I first heard it on the seventeenth of March, 1864, in connection with the announcement that on that day the eastern portion of the Territory of Idaho had suffered Congressional amputation and been formed into a new body politic bearing the above title. Whether it was the harmonious ring of the name, or a vague feeling that destiny was to link my fate with the new Territory, I knew not; but I was so far impressed with an interest in it that I at once marked its outlines upon the map, thus unwittingly tracing the boundaries of my future home, and in a trifle over one year thereafter I was pursuing my winding way, by means of three thousand miles of crooked Missouri river-navigation, from St. Louis to Montana Territory.

An account of that trip I will not transcribe upon these pages. Two months of life on a "mountain steamer," with cracked roofs and warped decks, especially adapted to the broiling of passengers in fair weather and drenching of them in foul; two months of life between a double wall of muddy bluffs bounding the river on either side and cutting off whatever scenery might lie beyond, was naught but tedious in the experience and could not prove entertaining in the description. The Indian camps which we passed at numerous points upon the river soon ceased to have any novelty connected with them, and certainly they possessed no other qualities of an interesting character which could recommend them to our consideration. Frequently as the boat stopped to wood up we would be visited by mass delegations of Indians, a precious set of "bucks," ringed, streaked, and striped in visage, and equally spotted in their morals; talented in stealing and duplicity, in begging and loafing — emblems, according to some Eastern notions, of American liberty. With their mouths watering for such luxuries as brown sugar and second quality tobacco, these large owners of sore-backed horses and husbanders of two or three slavishly treated squaws apiece, would swarm around the boat, and despite all trade regulations, effect sundry exchanges of robes for blankets and other articles especially coveted by the red men. One of the most ridiculous sights I have ever seen was when, upon one of these occasions, Rotten Tail, chief of the Crows, with all the dignity of a Roman emperor, marched upon the boat clad in a blue military coat and moccasins, with a long stretch of bare legs between, and carrying in his hand a carpet-bag. Whether this latter contained his spare pants, I know not, but I immediately thought of the Mexican uniform, said to consist of a shirt and pair of spurs, and surmised that Rotten Tail might have imitated our neighbors of the unhappy republic. But despite the numerous enthusiastic receptions given us by the natives, our contemplation of the Indian race was quickly lost in contempt, and the journey became utterly barren of interest. It shall therefore be passed over in silence, If, however, any of my readers consider the failure to describe it a fatal omission, they are referred to the narrative of Lewis and Clark, the explorers, who, under the direction of the United States Government, ascended this river in advance of all other whites in the years 1804-5, and who so far entered into the details of their journey as to chronicle in each day's history the character of the weather and other equally interesting items.

Dophan's Rapids are situated two hundred and fifty miles by river below Fort Benton, the nominal head of navigation on the Missouri, but which, unfortunately for myself and ninety-nine fellow-travellers, proved to be just two hundred and fifty miles above it, in the spring of 1865. The Rocky Mountains, popularly supposed to be the abiding-places of perpetual snows, had dared to so far contradict the prevailing idea during the previous winter as to almost entirely dispense with their fleecy coverings. Consequently there had been stored up in drifts and deposited in banks none of those crystal supplies upon which the Missouri so much depends for its successful navigation. Governor Johnson, a massive specimen of a wag, exceeding dry both in speech and appetite, the butt of many a joke, and in compliment to his ponderosity, styled by his fellow-voyagers the chief ruler of all the "bad lands" along the river, assigned another cause for our troubles, in the statement that the bar-keeper had taken so much water from the river for the dilution of his whiskey, that our boat, "only drawing two feet," could not proceed further. However this may have been, certain it is that our steamer was not equal, as it is claimed some of the Mississippi boats are, to the task of running on a light dew, and we were compelled to exchange the river for the land as an avenue of travel.

If any one wishes that his first impressions of Montana should be favorable, he should not land, where did the passengers of the *Deer Lodge*, in the "bad lands" — a section of country giving an air of desolation to much of the eastern portion of Montana, and aptly described by General Sully as looking like "hell with the fires put out." Particularly near the river banks does the surface of the ground assume the appearance of uncouth ash heaps. Cut and gullied by the spring torrents which come pouring down from the table lands elevated several hundred feet above the level of the stream, utterly destitute of all vegetation save straggling bunches of sage-brush, cracked by the sun and white with alkali; here and there a pool of stagnant water, green in color, and sufficiently purgative in quality to make the reputation of a thousand Brandreths — such was the desert of dry mud hills in which we landed and through which the wheels of our wagons half ploughed and half rolled for several days before we reached the more level and less infernal plateaus in the vicinity of Fort Benton.

But because of what we missed, not less than on account of our unpleasant experiences, was our compulsory land journey to be regretted. While sweltering in the "bad lands," we were leaving behind us some of the most beautiful scenery in Montana—the Citadel Rocks, which excited the admiration of Lewis and Clark over sixty years Ago. These curious formations of nature are of soft white sandstone, worn into a thousand grotesque shapes by the waters which have come down from the table lands during countless ages. As the traveller now looks upon them, towering up from the bank of the Missouri River to the height of two and three hundred feet, his fancy pictures elegant ranges of palaces, long and magnificent galleries, supported by columns variously carved out, and the whole ornamented with a profusion of statuary. A nearer approach ruins the structures which fancy has built, but the picture of departed magnificence which still remains is not less imposing than the first impression. Spires, battlements, and columns, niches, monuments, and pedestals, some prostrate and broken, others erect and entire, but all as far above the works of art in beauty as nature is above art itself, and all seeming like the stone embodiment of a poet's dream, are presented to view. And all this we missed.

Arrived at Fort Benton, we found the trading post of the great American Fur Company, a dozen uncouth houses of logs and adobes, lemonade made with syrup, at thirty-eight cents per glass, full-breed squaws, suggestive half-breed children in abundance, and a village, considered in all its parts, about as picturesque as a hole in the ground. In fact its situation in a bend of the river and at the foot of the high bluffs, gave it the appearance of having been sunk several hundred feet below the general surface of the earth; and my convictions were, before I left the town, that it ought to have been sunk still further. But although the wind blew a perfect hurricane, as it is very apt to do at that point, and although a combination of untoward circumstances made my stay at the nominal head of navigation anything but agreeable, still I must do it the justice to say that it has much improved since those days, and now sustains with considerable dignity its position as *entrepôt* for the general bulk of goods which find their way to the Territory of Montana. The year 1865 was an unfortunate one for steamboat men, and Fort Benton was therefore much depressed commercially as well as physically during that season; but since then it has been demonstrated that with proper management the Missouri is easily navigable to that point, and a busy town has supplanted the straggling village of four years ago. In 1868 thirty-five steamers, bringing nearly five thousand tons of goods, arrived at Fort Benton.

One hundred and forty miles southwest of Benton lies the present metropolis of Montana, the city of Helena. A number of us provided ourselves with horses and were, therefore, enabled to modify our route of travel as our fancy might dictate. Hence it was that we turned to the left of the usual route pursued, in order that we might visit the Great Falls of the Missouri. This name is given collectively to a succession of rapids and cataracts with which the Missouri River is filled for a distance of about twelve miles, and which have an aggregate descent of 383 feet. This river of cascades commences at a point about thirty miles above Fort Benton, and presents the appearance of a giant torrent, from two to four hundred yards in width, as it pours down its swollen floods toward the sea. But the name "Great Falls" is applied more especially to a magnificent cataract having a descent of eighty-seven feet and a width of three hundred yards. These falls combine, in the most pleasing manner, the grand and the picturesque, being for about one-third of their width of a perpendicular character, and for the other two-thirds broken into numerous beautiful cascades by the sharp and projecting rocks which here and there force their heads above the torrents, as if still determined to continue the unequal contest with that element which has already crushed the flinty hearts of their fallen brethren around them. Along the base of these falls, and seeming to connect the two banks of the river by means of its airy arches, extends a bridge of light foam and spray, upon which, crossing and recrossing ever, dance all the colors of the rainbow — fairy spirits of the flood, which, clothed in their habiliments of mist, a raiment varying as the winds, have for ages, even before the sun shone upon the face of man, held high carnival in this most hidden portion of nature's solitudes. Upon either side of these falls the banks of the river consist of perpendicular, rocky cliffs, one hundred feet in height, grim-looking fortresses, which year by year tower still more majestically above the stream by reason of the constant abrasion of the river's bed at their base.

About six miles above the falls is another, which, on account of the rough character of the ground — the country for several miles back from the river being broken by deep and impassable ravines — we did not visit, but the following description of this companion piece to the Great Falls, as given by Lewis and Clark, will prove interesting: "The whole Missouri is suddenly stopped by one shelving rock, which, without a single niche, and with an edge as straight and regular as if formed by art, stretches itself from one side of the river to the other for at least a quarter of a mile. Over this it precipitates itself in an even, uninterrupted sheet to the perpendicular depth of fifty feet, whence, dashing against the rocky bottom, it rushes rapidly down, leaving behind it a spray of the purest foam across the river. The scene which it presented was indeed singularly beautiful, since, without any of the wild, irregular sublimity of the lower falls, it combined all the regular elegancies which the fancy of a painter would select to form a beautiful waterfall."

Leaving the Great Falls and resuming travel on the usual route from Benton to Helena, we found but little interest. The prairie dog villages, with their myriads of diminutive inhabitants, formed into perfect borough organizations, as was shown by the little mounds dotting the plains, and the ranges of the Rocky Mountains in the distance, gave the mind food for temporary contemplation; but the eyes soon tired of gazing upon these objects, and we soon found our thoughts all concentrated on the possibilities and probabilities of the future in the land of gold, into the heart of which we were hastening. All of us had heard of the snug fortunes which had been acquired in California in a few months' time, and I presume there was not one of our horseback party that did not believe himself to be the identical individual whom Fortune had selected for the bestowal of her favors. And thus, each occupied with his own speculations, we galloped over the approximately level and grassy plains and easy gradients pursued by the Helena and Fort Benton road.

We arrived at Helena in a drenching shower, and splashed up through a narrow street between double files of straggling log-cabins. We were 5,000 feet nearer heaven than when we left home, but the surroundings incline the "tender foot," fresh from the States, to the belief that he has travelled many times that distance toward the other place. Although Last Chance Gulch, upon which Helena is situated, had been discovered barely six months, still the town, containing five hundred buildings and ten times that number of inhabitants, was well supplied with its hurdy-gurdy and gambling houses, Sunday street auctions, an active "Vigilance Committee," and various other attributes of a mining camp, all in complete running order. We had hardly put up our horses when a pistol-shot, quickly followed by a second, gave us notice that a murder had been committed in broad daylight and in cold blood. The murderer, almost instantly arrested, was not allowed to remain long in the hands of the sheriff, but was taken in custody by the Vigilance Committee, which proceeded to his trial in a neighboring lumber-yard. During the remainder of that day and a portion of the next the committee was engaged in the examination of witnesses. A verdict, "guilty of murder," was given and the death penalty pronounced. The prisoner, placed in a wagon and surrounded by a well-armed guard of fifty men, was taken to the Hangman's Tree on the borders of the town, the fatal noose placed about his neck, the wagon withdrawn from under his feet, and in less than twenty-four hours from the time that he committed his crime he was a lifeless corpse swaying in the wind. A few more days elapsed and the Hangman's Tree bore a second time its lifeless fruit. Crime was rampant, the Courts were powerless, and it therefore became necessary that harsh measures should be resorted to in order that the lives and property of the people should be protected. Thus it happened that seven men were eventually executed on this one Hangman's Tree, and in the Territory at large five times that number, all by the Vigilance Committee, no person having yet suffered the death penalty in Montana at the hands of the civil authorities.

But the Helena of 1865, and which at that time filled me with disgust, is not the Helena of 1869. Low log-cabins with their dirt-roofs have been replaced by substantial stone buildings and frame structures, the streets have been graded and supplied with plank walks, the Courts are regularly organized, the Vigilance Committee is no more, and the city boasts its eight thousand inhabitants. Property on Main Street, which four years ago could be had for the taking, is now worth from one hundred to two hundred dollars to the front foot according to the location, and real estate in all portions of the city is held at high figures. Whether well founded or not, certain it is that the denizens of this mountain metropolis and territorial capital that is to be have an abiding faith in the permanency of their city, and scout the idea that any White Pine excitement, or Kootenai stampedes, can work injury to it. Helena is no longer a mining camp. True it is that it still has an intermittent hurdy-gurdy house, street auctions on Sunday, gold-dust for a circulating medium, and other characteristics of those temporary abiding-places connected with newly-discovered diggings; but as opposed to these, as a "stand off," in the slang of the section, there are now represented in the city four religious societies, a moral life-preserver in the shape of an excellent public library and reading-room, and other similar institutions, such as receive but little encouragement or support in such towns as never get beyond the dignity of camps. The Masonic fraternity is represented by three Lodges, one Royal Arch Chapter, and a Commandery of Knights Templar; the Odd Fellows and Good Templars by one Lodge each; and the Fenian Brotherhood by one Circle. The form of government adopted by the town is, in an eminent degree, Republican, although the executors of the law are, to a man, Democratic in politics. There is no city or town organization — the county officers being found amply sufficient to collect all the taxes the people feel willing to pay. Each property owner fixes the grade of his own sidewalk, every merchant can pay his own night watchman, and every disciple of Bacchus can worship his god in the gutter, nightly for a week, without being once provided with more comfortable lodgings by gentlemen in blue. The people, like those of most mining countries, are generous and cordial. The majority of them, like their brethren in California, have seen much of the fortunes and misfortunes of this life, and know how to sympathize with such as may have been deserted by the fickle goddess and left "out of luck."

The great line of division between the people of Montana is politics, and this line is more distinctly drawn than I ever before saw it in any community. A large number of the inhabitants, among whom are some of the first settlers of the country, emigrated to the Territory, from Missouri, during the war, for the purpose of avoiding the troubles there. Many of these, being ruined at the outset and always endowed with strong Southern sentiments, brought with them from their old home a marked aversion for all holding opinions similar to those of their aggressors. Hence it is that they have, up to the present time, kept almost entirely aloof, not only in their social intercourse, but, to a great extent, in their business relations, from those of Northern birth. A sorrowful picture is indeed presented when we find the people of a community so divided that they must needs attend different churches solely on account of politics — and yet such has been the case here. Signs of a more liberal spirit are now evinced, and it is hoped that the much-needed reform may soon be completed.

The situation of Helena, determined by the accidental discovery of the Last Chance mines as it was, is nevertheless of a highly advantageous character, in a commercial point of view. Situated within one hundred and forty miles of Benton, as before stated, it is also within twelve miles of the Mullan Pass of the Rocky Mountains, furnishing one of the best roads in the country by means of which to reach the mining camps and towns of Montana's Pacific slope. To the south and east of Helena lie the most thickly-settled portions of the Territory, connected with the metropolis by excellent natural roads, and provided with numerous stage lines. Helena is in fact the commercial center of Montana and the natural supply points for its settlements.

In this connection I will remark that the trade of Montana with the Pacific coast, which was quite extensive three years ago, has now dwindled to insignificant proportions, and in place of the long trains of pack animals, loaded with clothing, saddlery, and merchandise of every description, which once reached the Territory from the "other side," there is now received almost nothing save a few sacks of flour and boxes of apples. This change has been produced by the very rapid and extraordinary reduction of freights on the Missouri River — the rates from Chicago to Helena being now only seven and eight cents per pound in lieu of the twenty and twenty-five cents of three years ago. This has effectually put an end to the occupation of the packer, who cannot deliver goods from Walla Walla to Helena for less than twelve cents. The advantages of river communication which Montana possesses will always prevent San Francisco from competing successfully with Chicago for the annual ten million dollars' worth of trade of this Territory. It is true that San Francisco will be, on the completion of the Pacific Railroad, nearly twice as near Montana as Chicago, and it is probable that California may do a fair business with this Territory in fruits, wines, teas, and other light articles of Asiatic production. After the close of navigation on the Missouri it may also do a light fall trade in flour, blankets, saddlery, and other such articles as may be found to be scarce in the market. The great bulk of goods which find their way to the Territory will, however, avail themselves of the low freights attendant on river navigation.

Montana is prosperous. What makes it so? First of all — its mines. And here let me call the reader's attention to a few historical and statistical paragraphs.

The first discovery of gold in what is now the Territory of Montana was made in the year 1852, on Gold Creek — one of the head-waters of Clark's Fork of the Columbia — by François Finlay, a French half-breed, who was passing through the country on his way from California to the Red River of the North. Being unprepared to thoroughly prosecute any prospecting, he found merely light particles of float-gold, but nothing in paying quantities.

His discovery was not, therefore, made immediately available, but became the foundation for the surmises and sage conjectures of the trappers, who at that time were the sole white inhabitants of the country. Six years after, as James and Granville Stuart and Reese Anderson were on the way from California to the States, they fell in with a party who told them of Finlay's discovery—and to Gold Creek our returning Californians repaired. They found gold everywhere—in some cases as high as ten cents to the pan; but provisions being scarce, and troublesome Indians plentiful, the party was compelled to leave the country for the time being. In 1860 Henry Thomas, or "Tom Gold-Digger," so called on account of his persistent, and, by many, thought to be foolish, search for gold, set up on Gold Creek a few rough sluice-boxes hewn from logs, by means of which he realized from one to two dollars per day, in coarse gold. It was not, however, until two years later, in 1862, or just ten years after the first discovery of float-gold, that the precious metal was found in paying quantities. At that time the Stuart brothers, previously mentioned, set up the first regular string of sluices in Montana, and from that date the reputation of this Territory as a gold-bearing country was to continually increase. Prospecting was the order of the day, and stampeding the order of the night, in all portions of the Territory.

The Bannock mines and the immensely rich deposits of Alder Gulch, which gave birth to Virginia City, and from which it is estimated that twenty-five million dollars' worth of gold have been taken, were soon after discovered, and the excitement was at its height.

From that time until the present new diggings have been constantly rewarding the prospector for his searching, until it is now estimated that there are in the Territory one hundred and fifty distinct gold-bearing gulches, having an aggregate length of five hundred miles, and theoretically capable of giving employment to seventy thousand men. Practically, however, there is not to exceed one-fourth of this number engaged in working the ground mentioned, much of which has been for the present mined out, and which is doomed to lie idle until increased facilities of communication and the further development of the agricultural resources of the country shall cause wages to fall below five and seven dollars per day, in gold-dust—their present rate. The total yield of the Montana placer mines is estimated at one hundred million dollars, although it may have been a few million either more or less than this.

Perhaps the most remarkable diggings in the Territory are those at Diamond City, on Confederate Gulch. From these mines, situated in a deep ravine, and consequently long unopened, one thousand dollars in gold have been obtained from a pan of dirt, and "clean ups" of from three thousand to eight thousand dollars per day to the claim have been made in common sluices. These mines are at present yielding more largely than any others in the Territory, and bid fair to continue in their productiveness for several years to come.

But even should the placer deposits of Montana to-day cease to yield further of their golden sands to the industry of man, still would they have performed their mission in opening up to civilization one of the most beautiful regions of America — a country with a delightful climate, pure and healthful air, rich agricultural valleys, broad pastures covered with nutritious grasses, such scenery as can only be found in the Rocky Mountains, facilities for water communication superior to those of any other inland Territory, and with permanent mineral wealth still bound up in its ribs of rock, still but faintly revealed in the backbone of the continent.

The quartz mines of Montana are gradually attaining to prominence. If the county records are to be taken as evidence, 8,000 ledges put in an appearance upon the books. These names are each supposed to represent 2,200 feet of valuable quartz, making, in the aggregate, a gold mine 4,000 miles in length. If, however, the ledges which have been developed are taken as evidence in the case, it will be found that our 4,000 miles dwindle to not over four.

Montana is not rich in gold alone. Her silver mines, particularly those of Phillipsburg, have been proven to be rich and extensive, and her copper ledges on the Muscleshell will yet add greatly to her resources. The abundant supply of wood with which the Territory is favored has caused the coal deposits of Montana to lie comparatively idle; but numerous mines have already been discovered on the Missouri and its tributaries to the north and east of Helena. This coal is of a bituminous character, and is already commencing to be used for fuel.

Although seldom regarded as an agricultural country, Montana has greater reason to be considered one than some others making more pretension. With a climate which calls for the wild flowers in March and gives pasturage to stock during the entire winter, with extensive valleys favorably situtated for irrigation, and with deep, rich soil, the Territory, in the short time which has elapsed since its settlement, has already become self-supporting, and with a plenty of good farms still to be had for the taking, promises to yield abundantly for exportation so soon as a reduction in wages will warrant it. In the Statistical Almanac of the Montana Publishing Company it is stated that there were last year produced in the Territory 850,000 bushels of wheat, 540,000 bushels of barley, 650,000 bushels of oats, 770,000 bushels of potatoes and 30,000 tons of hay, the total value of the crop for the season being $5,913,000, and the total number of acres cultivated being 87,473. As high as sixty bushels of wheat and five hundred bushels of potatoes have been produced to the acre. Seven flouring mills are kept in operation.

Manufactures are represented to but a small extent, the high price of labor rendering it expedient to purchase in the States those goods which would support this branch of industry.

The population of Montana is not far from 30,000 souls, not including in the estimate the wretched remnants of Indian tribes not supposed to be endowed with a conscience or an immortal spirit. This population is very extensively of the masculine gender, and, unlike that of polygamatic Utah, of the singular number. They have come to the mountains to hew out their fortunes, or, as they express it, their "home stake," and are content to work in a single harness until such time as they can set up a double team with first-class equipments.

A few glimpses of Montana have been given, and they are only glimpses. If they have served to interest or amuse, to show the reader that what was once thought to be the least valuable of the public domain is the site of a powerful State that is to be, then the purpose of the writer is accomplished. Had it been intended to do Montana full justice, a volume, rather than a magazine article, would have been employed. That great hobby of all Montanians, the North Pacific Railroad, would have been duly discussed, a deserved tribute paid to the character of the "honest miner," the various routes of travel, the Dutchman's "plains across" and "river up" considered, and the mining laws of the Territory would have been briefly placed before the reader. All these omissions the writer is conscious of. If the reader regrets them as much as himself he is content.

Edwin Wallace Carpenter, *(1841-1909), was born in Foxboro, Massachusetts, April 20, 1841. The first literary work for which he received pay was an illustrated article descriptive of the manufacture of straw bonnets, which was given the first page of* Harper's Magazine *for October, 1867. He located at Helena, Montana, in July, 1865, and furnished occasional paid correspondence to the* Chicago Tribune, New York Tribune, *and* Boston Advertiser. *His first connection with the press of Montana was as Helena correspondent of the* Montana Post *in the fall and winter of 1865 and the spring of 1866. Helena was then a new mining camp, and the* Post *was published at Virginia City, then the capital. About July 17th, 1866, Messrs. Tilton & Dittes, publishers of the* Post, *began the publication of the* Tri-Weekly Republican *at Helena. This was the first paper other than a weekly published in the territory up to that time, and Mr. Carpenter was named the Editor. After leaving the Montana press in 1869, Mr. Carpenter furnished an article on Montana to the* Overland Monthly *of San Francisco; and later a story entitled "Dips, Spurs and Angles," which was given the leading place in that magazine for February, 1873. Mr. Carpenter was fondly remembered by the old-time editors and publishers, and on his occasional visits to the territory was heartily greeted by them, they using their persuasive powers to induce him to come back to Montana and to the profession - but without success.*

In and Around Astoria

Capt. C.M. Scammon

December 1869

It was a clear June morning when we "made" Cape Disappointment, to the northward, and a brisk breeze soon brought us to the mouth of the Columbia. This grand river, the main commercial artery of Oregon, fed by the mountain torrents of the interior, runs far into the ocean before losing itself in the salter water. As you look up its valley, the scenery full equals the anticipations of the traveler. On the right, among the broken ranges, peers Saddle Mountain, with its peculiar, jagged summit — a landmark which often gladdens the eye of the tempest-tossed seaman. Farther inland are seen the heavy-timbered highlands, and, towering in the distance, the snow-clad peak of St. Helen's, rising to the height of 11,225 feet. To the left is Cape Disappointment, its brown cliffs capped with a growth of tall firs and a white tower light-house. Nearby are Chinook Point and Scarborough's Hill, which bound the eastern extremity of Baker's Bay. Farther up, Point Ellis is seen, wooded to the water's edge, like many others along the river banks. To the northward extends a diversified country, clothed in the ever-green foliage of the fir and hemlock.

Crossing the bar, we were soon anchored off Astoria. The principal part of the town is built a little to the west of the old trading-post, but some of the best dwellings are situated near. All that remain of the old establishment are the rock foundations of the chimneys, and the cellars and embankments. The rising ground immediately back, for the distance of long musket-range, was cleared of trees by the fur-traders, to prevent the Indians attacking them in ambush. In going over the ground now, it is difficult to realize the fact, for, at the present time, is found a growth of trees, some of which measure three feet in diameter at the base. On a hill-side, intervening between the old trading grounds and the farther limits of the former clearings, is the cemetery of the town. (New grounds are now enclosed in a valley beyond.) The first head-stone erected here was wrought out of the brown sandstone found along the shores of the river; and the workmanship, evidently, was that of some ingenious *employé* of the Hudson's Bay Company, who, with the rude tools at hand, managed to erect a comely monument to the officer whose remains lie beneath it. The cemetery is not enclosed by wall or pickets, but nearly every grave has a neat fence of wood or iron around it, fashioned according to the taste of the one who has paid the last tribute of affection to the departed. Several were adorned with moss-roses and wild flowers in full bloom.

When we first visited this place, the luxuriant verdure of a moist climate covered the land; but after the frosts of winter came, turning the velvet hedge to leafless twigs, it exposed the rough stones marking the graves of two men who met a fate similar to that of their officer, and who, for some reason, were buried on lower ground, near the bank of the river. The memorial cut upon their humble monuments was nearly effaced; but what remained read as follows: "*Ni M— of - John I- Aged — Seam— Todd— In Cross— River M— 1814.*"

The view from the cemetery is full of interest. The distant Cape Disappointment is plainly seen, which is fortified with the heaviest ordnance of late invention. One discharge of the battery might do more execution than a hundred rounds from a line-of-battle ship in the days when the Columbia was first visited by vessels of war.

On the swift tide, drifting to the ocean, are seen green trees, with their waving tops, appearing as if uprooted from the river banks by rapid currents and the blasts that sweep through the valley. On the opposite shore, near Chinook Point, once curled the smoke from the lodges of a numerous tribe of the aborigines; but they, with their inhabitants, have passed away. The camp-fires have ceased to burn, and already have sprung up the new dwellings of the immigrants and their children, showing that an ancient race has passed away, and a superior one has taken its place.

Near the native village, a *numclose* ground was set apart and regarded as sacred, where the Great Spirit made its nightly visits. Perched upon stakes in the canoe, the Indian found a sepulchre—the warrior, with his bow and quiver of arrows, his fishing-tackle, and other necessary articles about him, ready, as tradition says, to begin life in the other world. But facts entirely destroy the romance of the Indian burial, when we find, on visiting the grounds, that all the personal effects of the deceased have in some manner been made usless, to prevent them from being appropriated to the benefit of the living; so the hunter and fisher who has gone to the spirit-land will find all his implements sadly out of order: the tin-ware perforated, the crockery broken, the bow cracked, and arrows destitute of point or feather; and all, like their former owner, have ceased to be useful in this world. The foaming breakers, prowling at the margin of the ocean, run over the treacherous quicksands which cover many a gallant ship that has sailed around the world, triumphing over storm and wave, till buried deep beneath the Columbia's sands. All around is full of interest; and in this home of the dead lie people from almost every clime, who have passed a life of adventure, and whose true biographies would make a volume of thrilling incidents.

Astoria has a population of about five hundred. All the buildings are wooden structures, generally painted white, giving the town a neat, pleasant appearance. It is the shire-town of Clatsop County. The court-house is located near the center of the place. The custom-house is at the foot of one of the principal streets, near the beach. The Episcopal church, whose spire is ornamented with a gilt cross, rises above the surrounding dwellings; and for this neat structure much credit is due the ladies of the "society," who have given entertainments, where refreshments were sold at such prices as were sure to pay a good profit. To provide a bell, they hit upon the plan to raise the purchase-money by giving notice to the Sunday-school children that by putting a "bit" into the "bell fund" every Sabbath, their contributions would soon amount to a dollar, and that sum would entitle each one to a share in the bell; and every shareholder is to have the bell rung five minutes on the day of his or her wedding. It is needless to say that the bell fund was completed, the bell purchased; and, doubtless, the question has puzzled the brain of many a fair Astorian, who would receive the first compliment from the silver-tongued orator that holds so elevated a position above them.

Another new church has been erected on a sightly spot in the suburbs, which adds much to the beauty of the place. The community liked to see tasteful public buildings, and all have subscribed liberally toward their erection.

The place where the custom-house now stands is known as Shark Point. It derived its name from being the site chosen for the temporary dwelling-place of the officers and crew of the United States schooner *Shark*, wrecked on the bar at the mouth of the Columbia, in 1846. They built substantial quarters out of drift-logs, which were in abundance along the beach, forming the walls of round timber, and covering the rough with planks split from the straight-grained fir and cedar. The building took the name of "The Shark House," and was, up to the day of its destruction, turned to any purpose that occasion required. It sheltered many an immigrant who had passed through all the hardships of "crossing the plains;" at one time it was converted into a cooper's shop; an early settler, with his wife, at another period, made it their dwelling-place. A pile of staves served them for a bedstead for the first week, and here they lived in comparative comfort, after the toils of their long overland journey from the East, and recorded that "one of the bright spots in their lives was the time they lived in the Shark House." At another time, it was turned into a store, where a variety of goods suited to the trade were to be had at three hundred per cent above the original cost. Characteristic of frontier life — ready for adventure or frolic — the Shark House, on the Fourth of July, 1849, was turned into a ballroom, where a general gathering of choice spirits assembled, who, forgetting past troubles, made the day and night a time of jubilee. One of the guests, in dilating upon the festivities, remarked: "Old nigger Saul, one of the *Peacock's* crew, was the fiddler. When we began to dance, the floor was a little wavy; but it was all on a level afore morning, though!"

There were no good roads leading from Astoria. One was opened at the expense of the Government, several years since, as far as Salem, the capital of the State; but there is little need of roads at present, as water communication to all places adjacent is much more convenient: hence have sprung up a large fleet of river-craft, from common row-boats up to plungers, sloops, and schooners. The Astorians, in lieu of "driving out," go boat-sailing, or boat-rowing, as may best suit their fancy: some of the ladies being skilled in the use of light-pulling oars, or "sculls," as well as the management of a boat under sail. Frequently may be seen parties embarked on the large, convenient "plungers," for a pleasure excursion on the broad Columbia or its tributaries, and sloops and schooners plying to and fro with loads of produce. One of the latter passed us, drifting lazily with the tide: the Dutch skipper was hoisting sail, while his Indian *frau* was at the helm. From appearances, he and his companion made up the crew—a unity of aquatic characters as much in imitation of good old Holland life on board the galiot, as a scow-schooner and a squaw on the Columbia could make it.

On the right bank of the Columbia, ten miles from its mouth, projects a rounding elevation of land, thickly wooded, called Tongue Point; midway between this and the old Fort Astoria is a cluster of dwellings, and the first custom-house building, erected at the time Columbia River was made a port of entry. The founder of this settlement was General Adair, the first Collector of Customs, and who filled the office for many years. He still holds to his first choice of residence in the country, living in a commodious cottage, with his fruit trees on one side and the forest firs on the other.

In the bay formed by Tongue Point, the hulk of the old ship *Silva de Grace* rests on a reef of rocks. She was wrecked in 1849, with a cargo of lumber on board, bound to San Francisco, where rough boards were selling at sixty cents a foot. The vessel now appears as if clinging like a mammoth *aulone* to its slimy bed, listed a little to starboard, with her bow slightly elevated. The full figure of a headless woman surmounts the cutwater, indicating that this noble ship was once one of the finest afloat. Her bulwarks are now gone, and the forecastle, where the active crew trod the deck, is now overgrown with moss and waving grass. The starboard side of the quarter-deck—that post of honor, where the care-worn captain took his promenade—is marked by a luxuriant bunch of alders just peering above the taffrail. It has been frequently said by the inhabitants along the river, that "if the old *Silvie* could only talk, wouldn't she spin a yarn?"

The two headlands forming the mouth of the Columbia are Point Adams, and Cape Disappointment, or Hancock. The former is a sandy flat, covered with trees, and the last mentioned a picturesque landmark rising to the height of about three hundred feet. In view of accounts given by the early explorers, Disappointment seems a fitting name for it. Mention has been made of its being a promontory, on which the light-house stands; and on the brink of the cliffs, facing Point Adams and Baker's Bay, are batteries of heavy guns that fortify the northern bank of the river. The quarters for the officers, as well as the barracks for the troops, and other necessary buildings, are situated behind the cape, along the western border of Baker's Bay. The light-keeper's house is also there. A military air of neatness and good order pervades the whole establishment.

The scene from the cape, seaward, is an expanse of rolling ocean; in the mouth of the Columbia, boiling breakers, sand-spits, and winding channels. On visiting the cape, we were reminded that "the cave," a little to the northward, was worth seeing, and we visited it. In form, it is not peculiar. Its length is about two hundred feet; width and height, at its mouth, one-fourth of its length. It is a mere air-hole, left by some fiery eruption of past ages; but once within its labyrinths, facing toward the sea, the sights and sounds are interesting. On the left are the breakers, rolling up their foaming tops along the channel of the Columbia, where the mariners of olden times had threaded the treacherous passage. Before you the heavy surge of the Pacific is tumbling in with deafening sounds, and the distant edge of the blue sea undulates toward the clouds. After watching the restless waters for a few moments, one feels as though the basaltic foundation beneath his feet was still in motion.

Near the head of Baker's Bay, in 1850, stood a wooden hotel and a few houses, that boasted the name of "Pacific City." Although it has been represented on paper as a coming metropolis, the hotel was all that gave significance to the place, and the last known of it was that a rank alder had forced its way through and above the roof.

On our arrival, we passed the mouths of the rivers Skippernon, Young's, and Lewis and Clark's. Of these rivers, Young's is the most eastern, and is about twelve miles in its windings; Lewis and Clark's — of about the same extent — is only remarkable for its name; and the Skippernon, about three miles long, is navigable two-thirds of its length. On the coast, thirty miles south of the Columbia, is a small river, called the Nehalem, whose source is in the hilly country about ten miles to the eastward. Along its northern banks rises Mount Ne-a-kah'-ne, which is shorn of trees on the side facing the sea, and may be seen when passing near the coast.

Numerous conflicting reports have for a long time been in circulation among the whites, concerning treasure that is said to have been buried by either Japanese, Chinese, or Spanish sailors, or freebooters, at a date anterior to the discovery of the Columbia by Heceta. The most authentic account, drawn from the principal chiefs of the Nehalem tribe, is, that many years ago a vessel, with a great number of men on board, armed with guns and swords, was wrecked near the mouth of the Nehalem; the personal effects of those on board, some chests of money or treasure, and the boats, being all that was saved. A large excavation having been made, the treasure was deposited, with great care and ceremony, and two swords were laid in the form of a cross upon it, before the earth was replaced. The Indians were made to understand that they must never attempt to approach or molest what was there deposited, on penalty of offending the Great Spirit. At the time of depositing that treasure, two men from among the shipwrecked crew were interred. Soon after, all of the remaining survivors embarked in their boats and steered southward.

It is generally believed that the vessel in question must have been one of the old Spanish *galleons*, or some one of the buccaneers who formerly visited the Spanish coast on the Pacific. Whatever may have been the character of the vessel and her numerous crew, the ceremony performed at the time made such an impression on the minds of the savages that to this day the tradition is held in the greatest sincerity; no Indian, it is said, can be induced to approach nearer the supposed locality than is necessary to point out the approximate place.

Another tradition among them is, that many years ago a Japanese or Chinese vessel came ashore between the Nehalem and the Columbia, laden with beeswax, that in this vessel there were only two or three men, all of whom took Indian wives, and adopted Indian life.

Up to the present time, large square cakes of wax are occasionally found along the adjacent shores; one piece we have seen had the imprints of beach stones upon it, and the surface had turned nearly white, except where covered with black sand, but in no other respect had it deteriorated by age, or by being submerged in sea-water. No relics, however, remain of those ancient vessels to indicate the spot where they became wrecks, although several visionary money-diggers have made fruitless search for the treasure supposed to have been hidden at the foot of Ne-a-kah'-ne, on the banks of the Nehalem.

Captain Charles Melville Scammon *(1825-1911) at the age of seventeen went to sea despite the misgivings of his father who wanted to see the lad attend college. A close attention to details and study of navigation secured his rapid promotion, and by the age of twenty-three he was a master in his profession.*

The first vessel he commanded was the schooner Phoenix, *a trader in the Carolinas. In 1849 he was placed in command of the bark* Sarah Moers *of Bath, Maine, from which port he sailed for San Francisco, where he arrived in February of 1850. Upon his arrival he found the gold fever at its height, but the allure failed to attract the young captain away from his calling. Until 1861 he was engaged in trading, freighting, whaling, and sealing - always as a master of his ship. Among the ships he commanded were: barks,* Emma, *1850;* J.A. Thompson, *1850-51; brig* Mary Helen, *1852; bark* Rio Grande, *1853; schooner,* Mary Taylor, *1854; ship* Lenore, *1855-56. In 1857 he commanded the brig* Boston *on a whaling voyage and continued whaling for the next 3 years.*

In 1861 he received an appointment from the United States Secretary of the Treasury as a Lieutenant in the United States Revenue Marine Service. He was soon in charge of the U.S. Revenue marine steamer, Shubrick. *In the winter of 1865 the Captain and his vessel were transferred to the U.S.*

navy for ninety days so that the Shubrick could transport Colonel Charles S. Buckley, Chief of the Western Union telegraph expedition, to Sitka, Alaska. It had been proposed to run a line through Siberia and Western Russia before the Atlantic Cable was laid. Captain Scammon was offered command of the Western Union Telegraph fleet which comprised eight vessels. When the success of the Atlantic cable was assured, the Captain returned with the fleet to San Francisco and resumed his position in the Revenue Marine Service.

Through 1874 he was in command of the cutter Joe Lane, steamer Wayanda, steamer Lincoln and finally the steamer Oliver Walcott, the first Revenue Marine Steamer built on the Pacific Coast. Due to his many years at sea, his naturally strong constitution had weakened and he was advised by his physicians to retire. He then settled down on a farm in Sonoma County, California.

During the years he had been at sea, Captain Scammon had been a close observer of nature and a student of natural history. He wrote of his observations and contributed many articles to the Alta California and Overland Monthly. In 1874 his book, Marine Mammals of the Northwestern Coast of North America, was published to widespread acclaim. The book and the Captain were for years the recognized authorities upon the subjects they treated, which included the American Whaling industry.

Old Texan Days

by J. Ross Browne
October 1868

Many years ago, at the close of a dreary day's journey, during which a norther blew without cessation, we reached the town of Bastrop, on the Colorado. The situation is good, and there seemed to be no lack of that sort of improvement which marks the progress of Texan civilization — a church, a jail, a court-house, and the usual accompaniment of bar-rooms and billiard saloons. The least important object, as in all the towns I had yet seen, was a decent inn, where we could get even tolerable accommodations. Rooms with six or eight beds, and every bed "double shotted," were the nearest approach to comfort to be had anywhere. We drove up to a frame shanty, with a swinging sign in front promising entertainment for man and horse; and upon asking for the "gentleman" who kept the house, were answered by a sharp-faced, spunky-looking little man — "Here he is — what will you have, gentlemen?"

One of our party — a Texan — acted as spokesman.

"Well, guv'ner — if you can give us beds for ourselves and feed for our horses, that's about all we'll ask of you at present."

"Don't know about that, sir — don't know about that. My house is pretty full. Take your horses round thar and put them in the stable, and we'll see about it."

Having performed this service, under the direction of our landlord, we returned to the house.

Upon entering the bar-room, we found it well packed with customers. There was an open wood fire, around which some dozen men of very rough and fierce appearance were crowded, smoking cigars, and talking in rather an excited manner. There appeared to be some difficulty under discussion — a fight, or series of fights — which had occurred during the day. From what I could gather, a man by the name of Jones had been killed by another man named Brown. In the course of the affray, the relatives of each party took sides, and had a free fight, in which several were stabbed. Such an occurrence was not uncommon in this part of the country; but the present affair derived a peculiar interest from the fact that it was not likely to end for some time. These affrays in Texas were about as clannish as the old Scottish feuds, in which whole tribes took part. Not unfrequently they involved entire neighborhoods, and extended over a period of several years. The bitter blood must be all shed before they came to an end.

Whilst standing by the fire listening to the details of the affray, and the comments of the crowd, I gathered this much: that the persons present were no way related to the hostile parties, but merely spoke of the killing and subsequent free fight as artists; that a relation of the man killed, one Tom Jones, was looking about town in search of one Jack Brown, the man who had committed the act; that both were armed to the teeth, and were very desperate men, and if they came together somebody would get hurt.

During the conversation, the door opened, and a tall, powerful man of dark complexion, prominent features scarred with old cuts, and very deep-set, wicked eyes, stalked into the room, and looked around fiercely at the group of talkers. His belt was garnished with pistols and bowie-knives, and he carried his right hand in the bosom of his waistcoat. There was a dead silence.

"Has anybody seen Brown?" said the man, with a searching glance at each face. "Say, have you seen Brown here?"

The tone of the new-comer was somewhat insolent. Nobody thought proper to answer the question.

With an impatient oath, he walked up towards the fire-place, edging his way through the crowd, and scrutinizing every face keenly, as if to find out whether there was among them even one who sympathized with Brown. It would have been difficult for the keenest physiognomist to ascertain this fact, for there was not one who manifested the slightest emotion either of fear or interest. Every man continued to puff his cigar quietly, looking coolly in the face of Mr. Tom Jones, as if neither he nor his affairs afforded them any concern. I could see, however, that there were some unconscious movements of the hands towards certain private armories; and that they were well prepared to resent any infringement upon their rights.

I stood leaning against the wall by the fire, and was somewhat surprised when the blood-thirsty Mr. Jones approached, and looking steadfastly at me for a moment, asked:

"Have *you* seen Brown?"

"What Brown?" I ventured to inquire.

"Jack Brown!"

"No, sir! I don't know Jack Brown, sir: never heard of him before to-night to my knowledge."

The answer appeared to be satisfactory; the man turned and strode out of the room, banging the door after him. I was very glad not to be Jack Brown, and felt no disposition to claim relationship with him; for, besides being a man of peaceable nature, I was not prepared with suitable arms for a bloody fray of this kind. Doubtless Jack Brown was quite able to take care of himself. I never heard the result of the difficulty.

Upon the departure of Mr. Jones, the company were about to renew the discussion, when the supper bell rang. With one accord they broke for the eating-room, forgetting all about the feud and its various points of interest.

I observed among the number of eager candidates for supper, a half-drunken fellow of very seedy appearance, who had been asleep in the corner of the bar-room, but who, now thoroughly aroused, was rapidly following up the crowd. The landlord met him in the passage and ordered him back. An altercation ensued. The fellow drew a knife, and declared he would have his "supper or blood!" Upon this, the landlord struck him on the head with the bell, a very heavy weapon, knocking him down senseless. Snatching up the knife which had fallen from the man's hand, he pitched it out into the street; then dragged the prostrate body of his antagonist to the door, and pitched that out also. Two or three of the boarders jumped up from the supper table to see the fight, but there being no prospect of sport after the man was cast out senseless, they hurried back to secure their places at the supper-table. The landlord very coolly picked up his broken bell, rubbed his foot over some ugly spots of blood upon the floor, and turning to me observed—"When a fellow won't pay his board, he must expect to be roughly handled. No man shall loaf on me, sir: no sir, it shan't be done! I've boarded such chaps long enough, sir."

"And now it seems you intend to floor them," I remarked.

"Yes, sir—just so. Walk into supper, sir; you'll find a vacant seat near the head of the table."

I went in and sat down near the landlord's wife, a very showy lady, who presided at the head of the table. She had what might be called good strong features; that is to say, she seemed to be a lady perfectly able to take care of herself and several others in any emergency requiring physical or mental energy. Her dress and head-gear were fine enough for any ball-room. Altogether she was a very formidable looking lady. During the progress of the meal, I observed to her:

"Your husband, madam, seems to have no easy time of it."

"No," said she, laughing; "I heard him scufflin' with someone in the passage just now. Which whipped?"

"Well, madam, I don't know exactly when a man is considered whipped in Texas; but I saw your husband knock his opponent down with a bell and then pitch him into the street as limber as a bag of meal."

"Yes," said the landlady, still rather amused; "the Major has to do these things sometimes. He's not slow in a tussle when his dander's up. Won't you have some more tea, sir?"

I inferred from all the signs that there was at least one person in the house who was not at all afraid of the Major. I was certainly justified in believing that I had not witnessed anything unusual. Further, I was satisfied the landlady had been a widow at least once in her life.

It is not my purpose to enter into a detail of the petty vexations of my journey, but this night in Bastrop was fraught with more than ordinary discomfort, to say nothing of the excitement. The landlord said he was very much crowded, and could not let me have a single bed. He would give me a small room with a double-bed, (which was about two feet and a-half wide, as I soon discovered) and if nobody else came, I stood the chance of getting through the night without a bed-fellow. There was certainly one class of bed-fellows omitted by the Major in his estimate of the chances.

To provide against accident, I braced the door with a table and bureau, there being no lock. The confused noise of voices, the clinking of glasses and rattling of dice down below, and the heavy tramp of booted feet along the passage, kept me awake to a late hour, when in spite of noise and vermin, I fell into a doze. A knock at the door aroused me.

"Hello thar, stranger!" It was the dread voice of the landlord!

"Hello!"

"Open the door, if you please. Here's a lodger wants to get in."

"Can't do it, sir — he must find another room."

"Sir!" cried the spunky little landlord, "if you don't open the door, I'll have to *bust it in!*"

I remonstrated; the Major insisted upon his right to put another man in my bed. I denied the principle that two-feet-six was a double bed; the major contended often it was a treble bed in Texas. Finally, I offered to compromise by paying for two places.

"That's not the thing, sir — that's not the thing!" roared the Major in a high state of excitement; "the man must have a bed to sleep in, and there's no other!"

"Well, sir, he can't sleep with me!" was my reply, and I began to look around for some weapon of defense. There was nothing in the room, save the bureau, table and bed, not one of which seemed an available instrument of death. So I thought it best to add — "Or, if he does, he must be prepared for the consequences. I'm troubled with fits!" which was true in some senses, for I often had fits of melancholy, and was subject at times to fits of abstraction.

"Never mind," said the stray lodger, "let him be. I don't hanker after a bed-fellow with fits. Let's try it on somewhere else." The rest of the night I was left to my slumbers.

Between Bastrop and San Antonio we stopped at mid-day at a ranch. The proprietor, a polite but rather stern looking man, came out to meet us as we approached. He was followed by a pack of young dogs, of very fierce aspect, which he could hardly restrain from jumping upon us. In the course of conversation, he informed us that this was an excellent breed of "nigger-dogs," which he was training to hunt runaway negroes. By way of practice, he was in the habit of starting off a negro boy with directions to go down into the brush, a few miles distant, and climb a tree. Allowing a little time to elapse, he would then start the dogs on the trail, and follow them on his horse. He laughingly added, that upon reaching the brush, he "generally found the little nigger tree'd." It was certainly rather an amusing pastime — to the dogs and their master. I did not deem it prudent to question the little negro on the subject, but doubtless he enjoyed the sport as well as could be expected.

While in San Antonio, I stopped at a small Mexican cabin near the outskirts of the town, to see a man who had been scalped a few days before, on the trail to Eagle Pass. It seemed that he was a noted horse-thief, whose depredations had caused the settlers a good deal of trouble, but who had long succeeded in evading punishment. The last horse he stole was in the neighborhood of San Antonio. It was a fine animal, worth over two hundred dollars. He was trying to escape with it to the Rio Grande, and had nearly reached the *Agua Frio*, when he was attacked by a band of Camanches, who took the horse from him and then scalped him.

I went to see him in company with the physician who was attending him. The poor fellow was lying on a rough bed in the corner of the room. He suffered great pain, as I judged, for he seldom stopped groaning. He must have been originally a man of great muscular strength, but was now emaciated, and presented a very cadaverous appearance; his dark beard and moustache contrasting fearfully with the death-like pallor of his skin. His mind seemed quite unsettled. Sometimes in the midst of his groans, he would stop suddenly and utter the most horrid imprecations. When the doctor approached, he wept like a child, and begged him for God's sake to put an end to his sufferings at once. A bandage was on his head. The doctor removed it, and displayed a spectacle from which I could not but shrink aghast — a round, raw spot about the size of the palm of the hand, puffed up and swollen at the edges, where the scalp had been torn from the skull after the circular incision by the knife. The poor man shrieked with pain when the dressing commenced, and it required all the power of two stout Mexicans to hold him upright in the bed. This had to be done frequently, so that it did not surprise me that he should beg to be put to death.

The doctor told me that this was the third or fourth case he had attended. In speaking of the effects generally, he said it was rarely the patient recovered. The brain was always affected by the least irritation; and it was only when there was great insensibility of the nervous system, and the recuperative powers of youth were in great vigor, that there was much hope. He gave me a very interesting story of a case which had occurred many years ago, in one of the frontier wars with the Camanches. The victim was a man well known in San Antonio, and was now residing there in the full enjoyment of health. A thin skin had grown over the scalped part, but it was destitute of hair, and was so sensitive to atmospheric influences, that he could tell the approaching changes of the weather almost with the accuracy of a barometer. Indeed, it was a common thing for the neighbors to go to him in order to find out when a norther might be expected. He seldom failed to give a correct prophecy, though it might be a day or two in advance. He greatly prides himself on his powers of divination, and was familiarly known as "Old Weather-gauge." The loss of his scalp was a standing subject of jest to himself and his friends. He used often to maintain good humoredly that it was a great advantage to be scalped, for whilst other men had only their eyes to see with, he could keep a look-out from the top of his head.

John Ross Browne *(1821-1875) emigrated in 1832 with his family from Dublin where his father had been a newspaper editor. Displaying an early flair for writing, Browne was contributing to local Louisville, Kentucky papers by the time he was sixteen years old.*

At eighteen years, he had already determined that he wanted to travel the world and write about his experiences. As a first step towards this goal he left Kentucky for Washington, D.C. and immediately obtained a position as reporter for the U.S. Senate.

Thoroughly disillusioned with Congress within a period of six months, Browne left for New Bedford, Massachusetts and shipped out as a common seaman aboard a whaler. For three years he lived before the mast, and wrote his first book, Etchings of a Whaling Cruise, *based upon this experience.*

A seasoned traveler by 1849, Browne sailed around the Horn to California and soon became the official reporter for California's first Constitutional Convention.

Leaving California in 1853, he journeyed through Europe and the Holy Lands, an experience which led to his best known work, Yusef. *In its preface Browne wrote: "If there be any moral in this book, therefore, it is this: that there is no great difficulty in traveling all over the world when one sets about it with determination...".*

Returning to California in 1855 as a confidential agent for the government, he investigated Indian Affairs and Customs Houses, leaving this post in 1860 to again travel through Europe as a correspondent for Harper's *and the* Sacramento Union.

In 1864 he returned to California and his exotic home in Oakland known as "Pagoda Hill," where he and his wife raised eight children. Browne served the federal government in many capacities culminating in his final post as Minister to China (1868).

J. Ross Browne's other books are "Crusoe's Island *(1864);* An American Family in Germany *(1866);* The Land of Thor *(1867); and* Adventures in the Apache Country *(1869). Browne also wrote many reports while working for the government, among which* Resources of the Pacific Coast *(1869) has been the most widely used.*

The Last Tie

by Dr. J.D.B. Stillman
July 1869

When we stood for the first time on the iron-bound shores of the Pacific a generation ago and looked upon their desolate mountains, after a voyage of more than half a year, we thought in our forlorn hearts that the last tie that bound us to our native land was broken. We did not dream that the tie that was to reunite us, and make this our native land forever, was then flourishing as a green bay tree in our woods; but even so it was, and here, in the month of May, it lay before us, a polished shaft, and in whose alternate veins of light and shade we saw symbolized the varied experience of our California life.

Would I accept an invitation to go to the "front" and see the last spike driven? Old veterans and companions in frontier life would be there — men with whom I had hunted grizzlies in the river jungles. We had hungered and feasted together on the Plains, slept with our feet to the same fire, and fevered side by side when the miasma had shrunk the blood in our veins. Could I refuse to share in this triumph on the great day, long prayed for, that was to witness the finishing blow to the greatest enterprise of the age? California would be there with her bridal gift of gold; Nevada and Arizona were coming with their silver dowers, and a telegram from Sacramento informed me that a place would be reserved for me in the special car that was to convey the high contracting parties of the first part to the scene of the memorable event.

With one lingering look at the fireside where my children played, a cheerful word to my exhausted patients, and a hope that they might improve the opportunity of my absence to recuperate their wasted strength — I was off.

The regular passenger train from Sacramento starts at about six o'clock in the morning, and we moved off soon after in a special one, consisting of the superintendent's car and a tender. The car was arranged with a kitchen, dining, bedroom, and parlor, with sleeping accommodation for ten persons; the tender was provided with water-tanks, for the greater part of our way was over regions where good water could not be obtained, refrigerator and stores for a protracted sojourn in the desert. A careless glance around was enough to lull any apprehensions that might have been felt from past experience, that we might be compelled to eat our stock on the road, or search for manna in the land of the "Diggers."

Stretching myself out on a sumptuous lounge, I looked out on the brimming, turbid river and breathed the morning air laden with the perfume of a city full of roses. The pulse of life beat high, the town was on tip-toe of expectation, and gushing with the enthusiasm of triumph. The crowds cheered as we passed, and President Stanford on the platform bowed his thanks. Besides the President there were the three Government Commissioners, Sherman, Haines, and Tritle, Chief Justice Sanderson, Governor Safford of Arizona, Collector Gage of Nevada, and a few others who, like myself, were not particularly distinguished but born to good luck.

Across the bridge and out upon the plain we flew, alternate flashes of wheat fields and flowery pastures, and ghosts of trees went by; the rumble and clatter of car wheels filled my ears and soon lulled me into a drowsy reverie, and I "dreamed a dream that was not all a dream."

I stood as a child in my father's door-yard and saw the rippling flood as it flowed for the first time over the sandy floor of that stream—small as it seemed when measured by the line, but mighty in its results—that immortalized the name of Clinton, and opened the great lakes and prairies of the west to the commerce of the Atlantic. A troop of boys, barelegged, were frolicking in the frothy current; one stoops down and catches a fish struggling half smothered, and bears him away in exultation; the booming of cannon rolls their paeans of victory from the Hudson to Erie, and back again through a wilderness, startling the black bear from its covert and awakening the lands of the Iroquois with the march of a mighty people.

Again I stood amidst a group of curious, skeptical men on "Albany Hill," when a ponderous steamer on wheels was about to test the practicability of making steam a motive power on railways. They had been successful in England, and why not here? A line of road had been constructed for fifteen miles as straight as a beam of light from the sun and at a water level. I heard again the fizzing of the steam and the gush of water as the machine vainly essayed to a start. More fuel was supplied, the fizzing grew louder and sharper—slowly the wheels began to revolve but slipped on the track—sand was thrown on, when, with a cheer from the hopeful, the enormous black mass began to move off. The crowd grew excited and followed on, men on horseback led the way, determined to be in at the death and see how far the joke would go. Faster the iron horse moved on, faster the horsemen rode, and as the dreadful sounds redoubled, their steeds bolted the course, with starting eyeballs, terror-stricken. The locomotive was the victor; one dog alone contested the race, bounding and barking on till lost in the distance, and on the long vista, where the parallel lines met, the black speck disappeared, leaving a film of smoke to float away among the pines. One man—I could call his name—laughed outright; another shook his head: "Somebody would get hurt yet." Mr. Van Epps, my schoolmaster, said that he "never had any doubt that so much was possible, but he had many reasons for believing that steam could not be successfully introduced to the propulsion of carriages. It was a very pretty philosophical apparatus."

And still I dreamed; the air grew momentarily cooler, the pines grew larger and darker, deeper and darker yawned the cañons, the train seemed poised in mid-air, now flying through tree-tops, and now circling like an eagle the beetling cliffs they call Cape Horn. Far below, rivers flowed like silken threads, and as silent; above us, the snowy peaks kept creeping down, and sombre shadows of giant pines, whose vast trunks had withstood the storms for a thousand years, oppressed us with their gloom. We plunge into the bowels of the mountain and out at once into the sunlight and past the cheerful dwellings of men. We are cribbed in by timbers, snow-sheds they call them; but how strong! Every timber is a tree trunk, braced and bolted to withstand the snow-slide that starts in midwinter from the great heights above, and gathering volume as it descends, sweeps desolation in its path; the air is cold around us; snow is on every hand; it looks down upon us from the cliffs, up to us from the ravines, drips from overhead and is frozen into stalactites from the rocky wall along which our road is blasted, midway of the granite mountain. We are in pitchy darkness in the heart of the mountain—the summit of the grade; out again into the light; on, on through wooden galleries mile after mile; a sylvan lake flashes out from its emerald setting among the mountains—a well-dressed gentleman touches me on the arm, and taking a cigar from his lips, asks me if I will not take luncheon. "Where are we?" I respond. "There is Donner Lake and we will soon be at Truckee." "Two by honor and the odd card, that gives you the rubber—Jake says 'lunch,' and we will get our revenge in the dining-room."

I was on earth again.

Truckee was the first place that I could realize. It is worth a trip over the mountains to see that city alone. The whole place is "bran-new"; every board in every house, and there are many of them, looks as if just from the saw-mills, so fresh and bright; such crowds of great, healthy-looking, bearded men. The enormous amount of lumber in and around this place creates a wonder in the mind of one coming from the west—What will be done with it? But one approaching from the east will exult more than wonder. Down the valley of the Truckee River winds the great highway, crossing the river several times. Just before entering a tunnel, when the road slips in between the mountain and the river, we came near driving our last spike. Some Chinamen on the mountain side were cutting trees, and seeing the regular train pass, and knowing nothing of a special one, they probably thought it a fit time to run a log down the mountain. But whatever may have been their intention, the log landed on the railroad just before us—its length fifty feet and its greatest diameter three and a half feet—the smaller end rested on the track midway between the rails, and the other rested on the bank at angle of about forty-five degrees. The short turns of the road prevented the threatening danger from being discovered until we were almost upon it; but the promptness of the engineer, and the lightness of the train, saved us from a catastrophe. The pilot picked up the log, or did its best to do it, and went through bankruptcy; but the force of the blow was not lost, for the heavy frame of the engine tripped the log and landed it where there was just room for it, yet did not prevent it from clearing away the steps of the starboard side of the train from stem to stern. The only person injured—and he but slightly—was one of our party who was on the engine, who, seeing what seemed an inevitable crash, jumped from the train. The force of the blow can be conceived from the fact that the log was broken through the middle, where it was at least three feet in diameter.

It was near sundown when we reached the last crossing of the Truckee, where our crippled locomotive was sent into the hospital, and our cars were made fast to the regular train. Here the desert proper begins; here for five hundred miles we lose sight of sweet running water, and the attention of the traveller is arrested by the water trains—numerous tanks mounted on trucks, used to supply the grand army of laborers and animals while the work was going on, with all the water they used. The worst part of the overland route was always represented by the early emigrants as this forty miles from the Truckee River to the Sink of the Humboldt, or Humboldt Lake as it is now more generally called. There is absolutely no water that is not hot and poisonous, and the low shrubs that abound everywhere are bitter and unwholesome to animals. The bunch grass on which the animals support life thus far, here gives out entirely, and it was this last forty miles that broke the hearts of so many faithful animals in the memorable emigration of 1849, and their bones still lie at every rod in the sands where they fell, to witness for years to come the terrible sufferings they endured. The nearer they came to the life-giving waters of the Truckee the more abundant these sad memorials are strewn. Several of our party were among the overland emigrants of that year, and they pointed out where, one by one, their animals perished, where they abandoned their wagons, and where their guns—the last article they could afford to part with—were planted, muzzle downward, into the hillocks in the desperate struggle for water and life. The coniferous trees we left far back on the slopes of the Sierras, and a few cottonwoods or poplars only flourished here and there along the banks of the lower part of the river. But there is no spot so desolate that does not teach some thrilling lesson inhe world's history. If you would study the anatomy of the human form you must strip it naked; the region before us required no such denuding process; in the economy of Nature it was bare enough, and its very bones were everywhere exposed to the eye. The stunted growth of pale, green, bitter shrubs did not conceal the earthy salts that covered the ground with their frostwork, and the swift wheels of the train raised a cloud of ash-colored dust that settled over everything. Yet no man would have had the speed slackened on that account. It was a country that one could not travel over too fast.

The lessons taught in Physical Geography in that one day's travel were deeply interesting. To pass from the extremes of fertility through Alpine snows between sunrise and sunset of the same day cannot be done every-where, or anywhere else as far as I know. Why this contrast? In what age of the world was this "great basin," through which the Pacific Railroad runs for hundreds of miles, drained of the mighty flood that filled it and which has left its water lines hundreds of feet above us as distinctly legible as those that are washed to-day? From the great Mud Lake on the north, away south where the Pyramid drinks up the Truckee, and the Humboldt and Carson sink in the alkaline sedge and Walker's River finds its grave, and eastward to the palisades of the Humboldt is the bed of what was once an inland sea larger than any body of fresh water now known upon the globe. If the water had disappeared by evaporation the change would have been gradual; but the appearances indicate distinct periods of subsidence. In the valley of the Great Salt Lake there are five well-marked ancient beaches, or benches as they are there called; the highest is best defined, and is eight hundred feet above the present level of the lake; there is no outlet in all its borders, and if the water should return to its old level it would cover every habitable spot on its shores.

The novelty of a spring-bed in a railroad car was too great to allow of sound sleep; it was too much like being tossed in a blanket all night; and with the first light of morning I was up. The air was cold, and snowy moun-tains were in sight — one is never out of sight of them. A volume of steam in the distance indicated hot springs.

At Elko we parted with the most of our passengers, who were bound for the White Pine country a hundred miles south of the railroad. Another night brought us to the front, where we saw the novel sight of a town on wheels. Houses built on cars to be moved up as the work progressed. Here were the Chinamen who had built more railroad in a given time than was ever done before by any people. The Central Pacific Company had been battling for years with the formidable difficulties of the Sierra Nevadas; and when at length they descended from the mountains they passed like a hur-ricane across the open country. All the material except the lumber was transported around the continent; and yet with such vigor was the work pushed forward, that three hundred miles of the road was constructed in nine months. Ten miles of track were laid in one day; and it is worthy of note, that all rails were taken from the trucks and deposited in their places by eight men, four on a side. These rails weigh on an average five hundred and sixty pounds; and allowing fifty feet to each rail, the amount of iron borne by each man during the day of eleven hours was seventy-four tons! This was without relay. The names of the men who performed this feat are justly a part of this record. They were: Michael Shay, Patrick Joyce, Thomas Dailey, Michael Kennedy, Frederick McNamara, Edward Killeen, Michael Sullivan, and George Wyatt.

We arrived at Promontory Summit on Friday, under the information that the connection of the two roads would be made on the following day. The morning was rainy and dreary; two or three tents were pitched in the vicinity for the rendezvous of those ruffians who hang about on the march of industry, and flourish on the vices of men. The telegraph operators at the end of the respective lines were then within a few rods of each other, and communication was opened with the officers of the Union line to the eastward of us. We were informed, after some delay, that it would be impossible for them to arrive before Monday. The delay seems to have been an unavoidable one; but it was to cause a great disappointment to the people of California, whose arrangements for a celebration the next day were completed. The intelligence was sent back to Sacramento and San Francisco; and messages were returned that the celebration must take place according to the published programme; that it could not be delayed without defeating its object altogether. We all felt the embarrassment of our position keenly; but we tried to make the best of circumstances we could not control. To spend three days in this desolate spot, surrounded with sage-brush, with only such neighbors as would make it dangerous to venture away from the car, lest we have our throats cut on the suspicion that we might have a spare quarter in our pockets, was not charming. The camps of the construction parties of each road had fallen back from the summit to the low ground near the lake, after the close of one of the most celebrated contests of engineering skill and energy on both sides ever known, and were resting on their arms.

One-half of our party procured a conveyance to the camps of the Union Pacific, where General Casement, their Superintendent of Construction, generously dispatched a train to convey them to Ogden. On the following day the same gallant officer came up to the end of his track, with a special train which he put at the disposal of Governor Stanford to take the rest of us over their road. The offer was accepted, and we ran down to Weber Creek station, and an opportunity was enjoyed of viewing some of the finest mountain scenery in the world. The Wasatch Mountains rise from the plain on the west shore of the lake to the height of six thousand feet above its surface, or ten thousand feet above the level of the sea. They are the very ideal of inaccessible snow-covered mountains, set off by the green fields and blushing tints of the peach orchards just coming into flower. Mr. Hart, the Central Pacific artist, who accompanied us, took some fine views of this mountain from the railway overlooking the town of Ogden. The tide-rip is well marked where the currents of traffic from East and West meet — where the barley from the West greets the corn from Illinois, where paper is currency, and coal takes the place of Juniper trees as fuel. We feel while looking about, that we have met half way. A genuine thunder storm seemed to have been got up for the occasion and drove us all indoors, while we were at Ogden, and cooled the air. Here we found plants common at the East, but unknown in California — as the old familiar *Taraxicum* or Dandelion; and *Rhus toxicodendron* or Poison Ivy takes the place of the *Rhus diversiloba* or Poison Oak.

On the following day we ran our own train back, about thirty miles, to Monument Point at the north end of the lake — the only point where the railroad touches it; and we spent several hours upon its shore. A beautiful sea is Salt Lake when seen from an elevation — its color varying from brilliant blue to green; but a study of its briny shore reveals it as a dead sea in which no living thing is found. The waves cast up masses of the remains of insects which have perished on its surface, and which are known as the "grasshopper line" — the high-water mark. A few fish in the lake would allow no grasshopper line along the shore; but here the insects are pickled when they perish, and are finally blown ashore. Its islands, when visited by Fremont and Stansbury, were inhabited by myriads of birds, where undisturbed they bred in security; but we saw no living thing within or above its waters. Our steward with his gun procured a mess of snipe from a marsh where a fresh water brook lost itself in the sedge at a distance from the lake — among them was a rufus-headed Avoset!

On the morning of the tenth, as we looked out of the car, we saw a force of Union Pacific men at work closing up the gap that had been left at their end of the road, and the construction trains brought up large numbers of men to witness the laying of the last rail. About ten o'clock the whistle announced the long-expected officers from the other side. We went over at once to meet them. In a superb piece of cabinet-work, they call a "Pullman car," we met Vice President Durant, of whom we have heard so much, with a black velvet coat and gay neck-tie, that seemed to have been the "last tie" to which he had been giving his mind, gorgeously gotten up. General Dodge was there, and he looked like business. The veterans Dillon and Duff were there to give away the bridge. General Dodge on the part of the Union Pacific, and Edgar Mills on the part of the Central Pacific, were appointed to arrange the preliminaries.

The munificence of private citizens of San Francisco had contributed two gold spikes, each designed to be the last one driven. Gentlemen from Nevada had contributed a silver one, at whose forging a hundred men had each struck a blow. The Governor of Arizona, also on behalf of his Territory, had one of silver. The Laurel tie that we brought with us was adjusted to its place; and in order that each gold spike should be the *last*, one was presented by Governor Stanford, President of the Central Pacific, to Vice President Durant, of the Union Pacific, who should drive it as the last on the latter road, while the other was to be the last on the Central road, and be driven last of all by Governor Stanford, who had thrown the first shovelful of earth at the opening of the road.

It had been arranged with Mr. Gamble, superintendent of the telegraph lines, that throughout the cities of the United States, wherever fire-alarm telegraphs were established, connection should be made with the last spike and the hammer that drove it, so that the blow should announce itself and fire cannon on the shores of both oceans at the same instant. Preparations having been completed, the operator sent notice to all stations throughout the country to be ready, and the whole nation held its breath. A reverend gentleman present was invited to invoke the blessing of Almighty God upon the work. The operator announced: "Hats off, prayer is being said;" and as we uncovered our heads, the crowds that were gathered at the various telegraph offices in the land uncovered theirs. It was a sublime moment, and we realized it. The prayer ended, the silver spikes were driven. Durant drove his of gold. Stanford stood with the silver sledge gleaming in the air, whose blow was to be heard farther, without metaphor, than any blow struck by mortal man; the realization of the ancient myth of Jupiter with the thunderbolt in his hand. The blow fell, and simultaneously the roar of cannon on both shores of the continent announced the tidings: *It is done!* The alarm bells of the principal cities struck, one — two — three — synchronous with the strokes of the hammer; and people rushed from their houses, thinking a general alarm of fire was being rung. The cause soon became known, and banners everywhere were flung to the breeze; other bells joined in the cry of joy and of trimph. *Te Deum Laudamus* was sung in the churches, and the chimes rung out the national anthems. The nation made a day of it.

But I set out to tell what we did there among the sage-brush, away there in the heart of the wilderness. We Californians were too few to make much noise. We did the best we knew; but we were swallowed up in the multitude that came up from the East.

The officers of a detachment of the Twenty-first regiment, with their wives, on their way to California, arrived in time to witness the ceremony; and soon after the detachment itself came up under arms, accompanied by the regimental band playing national airs. The locomotives from each side rolled over the place of junction as if to weld the union, touched pilots and screamed their best. The only women from California were Mrs. Ryan, wife of Governor Stanford's agent at Ogden, and Mrs. Strowbridge, the wife of the superintendent of construction for the Central Pacific, who had been with her husband at the front during the whole time of the building of the road; and a post of honor was assigned her as the "Heroine of the Central." The preärranged telegrams to the President of the United States, the Associated Press, and others, were sent off; and after cheering the companies and everybody interested, we adjourned to the car of Mr. Durant, when answers to our messages began to pour in from Chicago, New York, and Washington, announcing that the lines worked as intended, and that the country was in a blaze everywhere at the East.

Governor Stanford threw open his car, and the officers of the Eastern company returned his visit. And then the trains bound east and west went their respective ways; the troops who travel only by day went into camp; and after an ineffectual attempt to capture the officers of the Union Pacific Company and bring them prisoners to California, we steamed away from that spot which will be distinguishable until the sawed ties from the Sierras and the hewn ones from the Laramie are rotted away.

Years to come, the traveller as he passes the place will look out for the laurel tie and the gold and silver spikes that garnished the last rail that connected the two oceans with a continuous band of iron. Could they hope to see them there? Why, even before the officials left the spot they were removed and their places supplied with those of the ordinary material, and when the throng rushed up, the coveted prize was not there. What their fate would have been we can judge by that of their successors, which had to be replaced by the new ones even before we left the spot. They were broken to pieces for relics; and the unfortunate rail itself was failing beneath the blows of hammers and stones, to be borne away in fragments as heirlooms.

Dr. Jacob Davis Babcock Stillman *(1819-1888) journeyed to the California goldfields in 1849 and helped to establish Sacramento's first hospital. Returning to New York City and the wife he had married shortly before his California trip, Stillman resumed his medical practice. Following her untimely death, he made a trip to Europe and returned to marry again in 1854.*

Unhappy with life in New York, Stillman traveled to Texas looking for greener pastures where he wrote of his adventures for the Crayon, *a magazine edited by his brother. A collection of the stories,* Wanderings in the Southwest, *was later published.*

In 1856 he returned with his second wife to Sacramento, California, where he practiced medicine until the flood of 1861-62. Moving thence to San Francisco, Stillman became involved in public affairs as well as California history. He contributed many articles to local newspapers as well as the Overland Monthly, *and was invited to ride Leland Stanford's train to "the last tie" ceremony at Promontory Point.*

Their acquaintance with each other led to Stillman's later involvement in elaborate studies of one of Stanford's racing horses, the results of which accompanied the series of E.J. Muybridge photographs which proved for the first time that all four hooves of the race horse left the ground at once.It also earned Muybridge the title of father of the motion picture. Their joint findings were published in Stillman's book, Horse in Motion, *in 1882 under the auspices of Senator Stanford.*

Dr. Stillman's only other book was an account of his experiences during the gold rush, Seeking the Golden Fleece, *which was published in 1877.*

Adventures
in
California

——— Restaurant Life in San Francisco ———
by Noah Brooks
November 1868

A broken pauper lay a-dying in a San Francisco hospital. For weeks his only fare had been the meager and coarse diet of the eleemosynary institution in which he found himself drawing near to the end of an improvident life. He was surrounded by the bare and comfortless scenes of a county hospital; yet, looking back over his checkered career in the country, filled with vicissitudes and exciting situations, he drew one single comforting conclusion. He had nothing to say about his usefulness as a man and citizen, nor of any ennobling or virtuous action of his own; but, looking greedily over the past, he consoled himself with the emphatic remark: "Well, I have had a good living, anyhow."

The reader need not suppose I have introduced the sombre figure of the dying pauper into the foreground of this sketch that his doleful story may point a moral or adorn a tale. But the unctuous consummation of the life of this poor Lazarus, whom I have brought out into the warm light from the plenteous restaurants of San Francisco, is that which has been, and shall yet be all that thousands of Californians can say truly of themselves, when they take in the final retrospect of a busy life. If there is a country upon the face of the earth where the comforts and delicacies of the table are of absolutely paramount importance, it is certainly California. Leaving out the abjectly and squalidly poor, it is nevertheless true, that the lowest and most moneyless classes of society have more daintiness of palate and contempt for coarse or homely fare than the same sort of people living anywhere else. Love of good living is one of the peculiarities of the nation, possibly, but in California the national weakness is a ruling passion. The butchers complain that they cannot find customers for the coarser cuts of meats; there are no people whose fastidiousness is so blunted by hunger that they will take the profuse waste of hotel tables, and though grinding poverty is more common in San Francisco than in the old flush times, a disdain for the lower grades of flour, and beefsteaks "off the round," seem to pervade all ranks of life. If a few pieces of coin stand between the San Franciscan and beggary, he must have his sirloin and *café noir* to-day; to-morrow may be leanness and abstinence; to-day he must have the best that the market yields.

So the restaurants of San Francisco are numerous, plenteous, inviting and even cheap. There is abundant provision made for him whose purse is slender or whose conscience forbids him to "sponge" the landlord out of a costly refection; but even the cheap must be good and appetizing, for he who has money to pay for anything will only pay it for one of the numerous grades of "the best." The stranger from other shores may consent to dull the edge of appetite with what keepers of cheap boarding houses call "filling" food, but your old stager takes refuge in crime or suicide when all other resources fail, and his dinner is not rounded into completeness without some tolerable likeness of a dessert. Where, but in San Francisco, would a sturdy beggar ask alms with a cigar between his lips?

The number of gentlemanly Arabs in San Francisco is quite surprising. Their tents are furnished lodgings and their hunting-grounds are the restaurants and hotels of the city. They are respectably connected in the directories with business houses, banks, offices, or other establishments; but their place of abode no man knoweth; they do not themselves always know. Here to-day and gone to-morrow. Seen on 'Change or in their other places of resort for business or pleasure, they melt away in the sleeping hours as their wild prototypes of the desert disappear in the sand or reappear as if from out of the sky. The gentlemanly Arab is not long satisfied with one place of eating, nor with one place for sleeping. Here and there is a reformed member of the tribe, of whom his landlady remarks, with pride and wonder: "He has been with me nigh on to three years, come Christmas;" but the race is generally nomadic, changeful, and a burden of grief to respectable old ladies who let furnished lodgings. These are the chief patrons of the San Francisco restaurants. And when we consider how many homes are unbuilt and unborn, how many lives are comfortlessly passed in the unsatisfying and artifical eating-places and keeping-places of this metropolis, one may be justified in once more bringing to the foreground the forlorn figure of the dying pauper, to match his faded colors with the sombre hues of the picture. Were all the now single men in San Francisco, between the ages of twenty-one and forty-five years, to be married this month, and set up their own household gods, the restaurants would be insolvent, and half of the hotels would be compelled to close their doors.

But the single men are not the only customers to the restaurants. Not a few childless couples live in lodgings, and have their food brought to them by servants from the eating-houses, in that advanced stage of staleness which justifies the epithet of "cold victuals." These are they who fancy that crisp muffins and juicy beefsteaks, erewhile hot from the coals, are fit food for the civilized man after being carried half a mile on the head of an unwholesome servant. For such persons the "filling" food above referred to were just as good and vastly more economical. Other families prefer to partake of these streams nearer to the fountain head, and go to the restaurants as health-seekers go to medicinal springs—to be filled. There may be women with the graces and attractions of home life about them, in the habitations of people who live thus; they avoid the fuss and fumes of cooking about the house, and have no fear of that terrible tyrant — the cook. But the reader who cons these pages amidst the refining blandishments of a well-ordered home, may well give a sigh of commiseration for the unhappy mortals who never know the dear delights of a family table, spread with the home dishes which loving hands and tender thoughtfulness have prepared. A mistaken notion of economy may drive husband and wife to the restaurants, or induce them to submit to the indignity of being fed by errand boys, but the apparent saving is secured at an alarming sacrifice. Even large families have tried the experiment of restaurant life in San Francisco, and I have seen the head of such a family marshal his partner and seven children from lodgings to restaurant twice a day, to the great admiration of numerous beholding neighbors. These frequent such places for repast as have private rooms for families and ladies, where they secure such partial seclusion as is attainable under the circumstances; but not unfrequently one sees in the great restaurants of San Francisco the unaccustomed garb of women gleaming out with startling effect in the long lines of feeding men. There are women at some of the most expensive restaurants, or *rôtisseries*, habitual customers, whose gay attire marks where they are grouped apart in the long saloon, taking their dinner with great self-possession. These persons have no better name than "Boston Sal" or the "Girl in Green." They constitute almost the only female element in restaurant life in San Francisco, as the great eating public sees it.

One of the numerous book-writers, whose observations on California have come back to us from the East in printed form, has said that the three primal necessities of a newly-built town in California were as follows:

1st — A whisky saloon.

2d — Billiards.

3d — A French restaurant.

That French cookery is cosmopolitan as well as national is tolerably well illustrated by the fact that in the cosmopolitan city of the republic it has the predominance over that of all other peoples. We miss here that genius which makes ambrosial bouquets from nothing. In the vulgar profusion of California larders and markets, the *delicatesse* of French gastronomic art is lost. In the astonishing luxuriance of the raw material for Titanic feasts, the keen taste and refined elegance of our Gallic cooks is quite demoralized; and the pitying dismay of such a genius as Ude or Brillat-Savarin, in the midst of our coarse profuseness, would be akin to that of the worthy alderman, who, at a civic feast, remonstrated with a healthy young gentleman from the country, who was throwing away a magnificent appetite on a leg of mutton when turtle-steaks and venison were to come. But with all these drawbacks, the French framework of dinner, from soup to fruit, *café noir* and cordial, is adopted in San Francisco; and the majority of the restaurants are those which give French cookery and French wines to their guests. It may be that there is something in the dry, exhilarating climate of San Francisco, and in the artificial, unhomelike manner of life, that is favorable to the growth of semi-French habits and tastes. It is certain that our perennial season of fruit and flowers, our wealth of game and profusion of rich meats, are not at all suggestive of the frugal or substantial dinners of the older states of the Union. Baked beans garnished with crispy pork, brown bread, Indian-meal pudding, and the homely dainties of New England are counted as beyond all price by her wandering sons, and feeble imitations of those local feasts exist in San Francisco restaurants and homes; but they do not thrive after transplanting any better than do the corn pone of Virginia, the chicken-gumbo of New Orleans, and the "side-meat" of Missouri. There may be an attempt to reproduce these cates in California, but the endeavor is a sickly one. As there is no cooking like "mother's," so there can be no successful appreciation of national or local American dishes, except they be partaken on the soil that gave them birth. A New York chicken-pie is not to be despised wherever we meet its delicate and melting contents entombed in flaky, odorous pastry, moistened with rich juices; nor can we sneer at her who brings to the table light-brown masses of the baked Indian-meal pudding, gemmed all over with amber-hued blocks of jelly: but there is something incongruous in associating these dainties with the lavish profusion of California fruits, flowers and game. We may have the roast "spare-rib," pumpkin-pie and baked beans of New England in a San Francisco December; but San Francisco December strawberries, roses and mushrooms will impertinently intrude on these offspring of a colder clime; and a reckless wealth of melons, grapes, oranges, undried figs, and Christmas roses and daisies will somehow put to the blush the sturdy viands. At any rate, they are not sought for.

With French cookery come French hours of breakfasting and dining. Leaving out the large class of persons whose vocation compels a certain hour — generally an early one — the time for a perfect restaurant breakfast in San Francisco is between ten and twelve o'clock in the morning. There are persons, whose case is one worthy of consideration, who breakfast at seven or eight o'clock; nay, there are some who surprise their stomachs with a meal (call it not breakfast!) bolted by early gaslight in the morning dews and damps. These people feed, only; your true gentleman takes his cup of coffee and boiled milk on rising; gives his best brain to reading, writing or business; and has a light breakfast of fruit, a chop and bordeaux at twelve o'clock. Others, late risers, take a substantial breakfast with tea or coffee between ten o'clock and noon, and shunning such gastronomic insults as luncheons, (which "gents" call "lunch") dine at six. However our people may skirmish in detachments during the earlier part of the day, they generally mass in their attack upon the six-o'clock dinner. At this hour a first-rate French restaurant presents a lively and cheerful spectacle. The spotless linen, glittering glass, bright lights, brisk waiters, and deftly changing courses, present a glamour to the unaccustomed eye which conceals the fearful lack of zest, which sicklies o'er the whole, to the weary eye of the habitual diner-out. In the genuine French restaurant, however, there is an air of comfort which few American establishments have, or keep long. There is an absolute neatness about the table service, and a certain air of tastefulness about the simplest dishes served up, which some families, who think highly of themselves, would do well to imitate. The sprightly garniture of an inexpensive *entrée*, the crispy perfection of the bit of broiled fish, the thoughtful arrangement of the viands on the table—all serve to recommend the repast to the unwilling appetite; and one pardons the self-gratulatory flourish of the waiter, and his little air of triumph as he says: "*Voila, Messieurs.*"

There are a few early diners who drop in about five o'clock, and some delay their appearance until later; but the supreme hour all over San Francisco is at six. Here you will see a few French bachelors; generally they are gray but "chipper," as the Yankees say; and they come in as briskly as though not turned thirty; a rose in the buttonhole, a smile and sally for the flower-girl and the waiter, and a jaunty air generally, distinguish them from the heavy feeders and heavy drinkers of other nationalities. Then there are your old Californians; they come in twos, and threes, drinking a great deal of claret, requiring much waiting upon, talking only of bonds, stocks, dividends, first and second mortgages, and such appetizing themes. They bloom hugely at each other over the little round table where they sit, and occasionally gurgle an apoplectic laugh; but for the most part they are solid, substantial and solemn. Their business for the day is done, and they address themselves seriously to the business of the evening, sitting late over their black coffee, cordial and cigars, and finally, steadying their uncertain footsteps, they silently nudge each other away from the pay counter. Then there is the group of gay young men, who prefer *sauterne* to the *vin ordinaire* of the restaurant, and occasionally indulge in the extravagance of a bottle of champagne. These are not the regular visitants of the house, but drop in from cheaper establishments, or from suburban homes on opera nights, or when they have an evening engagement. They may be known by the dreadful fascination which the prevalent language of the place has upon them; inspired by the fluency of the waiters (and the champagne) they wildly break out into desperate and unintelligible French, to the complete bewilderment of the well-bred servant, who listens to their jargon with a countenance of lively concern, and hastens to have out his quiet laugh in the kitchen. These gay young gentlemen have a prodigal way of ordering "the best you've got," which is quite captivating, and marks them as fit subjects for a heavy reckoning in the practiced eye of the cash-taker. As they are making the most of it, they insist upon a rigorous service of all the courses, and a liberal display of fireworks when black coffee and burnt brandy are in order. They chaffer gaily with the flower-girls who pass among the tables, joking these ready-witted young persons with the air of "sad dogs," who have their little follies which they might tell. In striking contrast to these airy youths, are the sedate frequenters of the house, who take their pleasures quietly and solitarily, or in low-voiced couples plod conscientiously through the regular five courses, red wine, soup, dessert and appurtenances. To them this sort of thing is a burden, and they read the evening paper between the courses, as though its damp folds were a relief from the dreary monotony before them. The waiter, who speaks French to the American and English to the Frenchman, cannot cajole these out of their *blasé* moodiness; even the harmless little trick of pretending that your regular boarder speaks French does not deceive him any more, and he refuses to be beguiled. He has all the little arts of the restaurant frequenters at his fingers' ends. No man better than he can perform the cunning little tricks in the table preparation of the small adjuncts of dinner which are found only at such a house as this. The wary *garcon* attempts not to abuse him with stale dishes or rejected desserts. He knows his rights and dares maintain them. He has a British disgust for French fashions, but manages to worry along with the best French cookery, and contemptuously classes all other restaurants than French, as "hash-houses."

At some of these French houses, especially designated as *rôtisseries*, the kitchen is nominally open to inspection; one apartment of the department being on a line with the principal eating room. Here one may see fowls slowly revolving before a cheery wood fire, and an occasional stew-pan sending forth its appetizing odors. The windows are garnished with displays of marbled beef, preternaturally bloated turkeys, live frogs in glass globes, and a succulent vegetable show. But this is all a sham. It is a "company" kitchen, a gilded mockery, and an unreal imitation of the real place of cookery which lies beyond. Into the steamy mysteries we only cast a glance; into its dreadful secrets enter not, O, my soul! Let us who are condemned to spend our lives at restaurant tables take the goods the gods provide, nor seek to know aught of that seeming chaos from which they are evoked. What wots it if we suspect, or even know, that the cleanliness and neatness of our maternal home is a stranger to the restaurant kitchen? Let us shut our eyes and ears to any dreadful revelations, lest we be condemned to starve in the midst of plenty. The viands look clean upon the table; why should one rashly seek to know more of the processes which gave them form, shape, taste and color.

But if there is something to excite the apprehensions of the fastidious in the occult doings of the better class of restaurants, what shall be said of those where a substantial dinner may be bought for a sum which would only pay for a cup of coffee in New York? Let us charitably believe that all is well behind the gaudily-papered wooden partition whence we hear the ceaseless boiling, broiling, frying and frizzling of multitudinous dinners, served up at ten cents per plate and, in the language of the advertisement, "no charge for the third dish." Here we find a very different class of customers from those we meet at the up-town restaurant. The din of plates and waiters' calls is fearful; the flies are like unto the flies of Egypt; the tables are marble and uncovered, or if covered are not spotless. Those who eat here are in a hurry to be gone, and they seem to think that one cannot afford to waste much time on a dinner that costs only fifteen cents. Here is the laborer, the unlucky miner, the man seeking employment, and the penniless adventurer who has not fully concluded whether he will shuffle off this mortal coil or try for a light sentence in the county-jail. Yet, here is a certain sort of comfort. The huge piles of cakes and pies in the window are inviting; the plate of roasted meat, vegetables and bread has its flanking dessert of pastry or pudding; every customer gets his honest money's worth, and he knows it and is satisfied. If his appetite is discursive, he has a wide variety in which to range; if it is clamorous, he may satisfy it without exhausting a slender purse.

Above this grade of eating-houses is another, a sort of superimposed layer, as the geologist would say, yet overlying a more costly stratum. In these there is a varying line of luxury and cost. But all of them are plenteous and filled at the dinner hour with hungry men. Nowhere in the world, perhaps, is there so great variety of comestibles as in these restaurants. For six months in the year strawberries are common, and at all seasons there is an abundance of fresh fruits of some sort. Grapes and pears that grace only the tables of the very wealthy in Atlantic cities, are lavished here in unstinted profusion. Reed-birds, quail and wild ducks in their season, and domestic fowls, are almost as common as beef-steaks and chops in other lands. The Californian love of good living is as prominent in these middle-class restaurants as anywhere. Respectable citizens and well-to-do businessmen dine luxuriantly for fifty or seventy-five cents, though, of course, they do not have a bottle of table claret with their roast, nor cognac with their coffee.

The difference in the cost of restaurant living in San Francisco and eastern cities is very marked. To dine well in New York, Boston or Washington costs one very dear, as our cheaply-fed Californian counts dearness. Few French restaurants in California serve their dinner *a la carte;* usually the attentive servants allow you to exercise some election of soup; but that gentle provocative of appetite being disposed of, the silent attendant places before you, fish, salad, two or three *entrées*, vegetables, roast, dessert, fruit and coffee, in their proper order and succession. The fish is hot and crisp from the fire; the *entrées* are those Frenchy side-dishes, hot and spicy, which you find nowhere outside the restaurants that follow the Parisian mode. The vegetables have the flavor of nature, and are not sodden in water as those of American hotels always are. You may have them with your *entrées:* but it is not *en réglé* to take vegetables with the roast. Such a dinner as this, with a bottle of sound claret and an *omelette au rhum* or other trifle with a fruit-dessert, costs in the best San Francisco restaurants a dollar and a half. The same repast would cost four times as much in any of the Atlantic cities.

It is possible that this cheapness and convenience of living, added to the harrowing reflections which most young men have upon the extravagance of women, has something to do with keeping the ranks of bachelors so full. Timkins, for instance, pays forty or fifty dollars a month for a handsomely-furnished *suite* of rooms, and about as much more for his board at a good restaurant: what wonder that he asks why he should break up his comfortable and inexpensive manner of life, while a single silk dress may cost more than his housing and subsistence for one entire month? Selfishness may keep many of the gentlemanly Arabs in their much-abused habits of living; but there is some reasonable excuse for the bachelors, so long as French dinners are so very cheap, and dry-goods are so excessively dear.

But the distant reader must not think that the French is the only foreign cookery transplanted to this soil. The flavors of many nationalities are pronounced instances of their several national schools of the art. Germany has several restaurants — not especially distinctive, but essentially Germanesque in their customers. In the lower part of the city are numerous Italian restaurants, a few of which are really first-class, if prices indicate such grades. Here we meet the red-shirted Masaniellos of San Francisco; the ill-mannered louts who bellow their applause or disfavor from the opera gallery, and furnish the cue oftentimes to the less demonstrative fashionables in the glittering circles below. The fishing business of the bay of San Francisco is exclusively in the hands of these brave and hardy men; and at six o'clock you shall find them congregated about the little tables of their favorite resorts, talking loudly, pouring continuous streams of red wine under their huge dark mustachios, emphasizing their speech with table-thumps and smelling dreadfully of fish and the salt, salt sea. Like the ancient wassailer, they eat but little meat; they chiefly affect the croquettes, macaroni and rice preparations which these restaurants serve up in great perfection.

One of these Italian houses is famed for being the place in which (it is said) the best macaroni outside of Italy is set before the guests. This nourishing dish is here cooked in a great variety of ways; and travelled people, gourmands and *blasé* diners-out go to the obscure little house to enjoy a new sensation. The lower rooms and the public eating-hall are carpeted with sawdust, and the resinous smell of the same penetrates the house; even the private apartments are barely furnished. But for a truly Apician banquet, give an infrequent guest the six courses of macaroni served in six different styles, with one course of mushrooms, and a red wine *a discretion* — and he may truly say: "I have dined to-day." The Italian restaurants, however, are more exclusively patronized by the people of their own nationality than is true of any other class.

Nor should the Chinese houses of refection be overlooked in any sketch of restaurant life in San Francisco. The Chinese are social and cheerful in their habits. They seize every possible occasion for a feast, and the restaurants of the race in this city are almost constantly lighted up with the banquets of their numerous customers. Generally the restaurants are cheap and even meagre in their furniture and fare; but they, too, offer a wide range of prices for their patrons. One house has a *carte* of viands which aggregates a dinner all the way from fifty cents to fifteen dollars to each person. The Chinese restaurant is a rambling series of rooms, to which the in-genious fancy of the imported carpenter has given an oriental appearance, by cutting large circular openings for exit and entrances, dispensing with doors, hanging gaudy scrolls of gilded, painted and lettered paper about the rooms, and fitting up a carpeted platform whereon he who is so disposed may smoke during his intervals of repast, or from which musicians discourse most execrable sounds during the progress of a dinner of ceremony. The hour of six o'clock is too early for the Chinese. They come to take their ease, and when they have money to spend, they spend it liberally in the same way that Timkins does at the San Francisco "*Trois Frères*," insisting always on "the best." They wait until the day is fairly over, and the last customer departs before they abandon themselves to their slowly-eaten repast. Nine o'clock is the hour for a formal or festive dinner. They cook chickens and ducks nicely, though queerly, the bird being first split clean in two; but almost everything has the same taste of nut oil sicklied over all, and few western palates can endure even the most delicate of their dishes. Shark's fins, stewed bamboo, duck's eggs boiled, baked and stewed in oil, pork disguised in hot sauces, and other things like these, are the standard dishes of a Chinese bill of fare, though they have an infinite variety of sweetmeats which are really palatable, and of sweetcakes, which are inviting in their quaint, odd forms and decorations, but are ashes and wormwood to the taste. The Chinaman is liberal and bountiful to his guest; champagne flows freely; the skill and taste of the cook is exhausted to tickle his palate and gratify his eye, and a more changeful variety of courses pro-longs the banquet than is ever found on the tables of any other people.

California has not in all her restaurants and houses produced one distinc-tive local dish. The fare is cosmopolitan, and the *cuisine* is a strange mosaic of bits from many people; but there are no California dishes, unless the fiery compounds of Chili peppers and other burning things which we captured with the country are ours. Nor are they Californian peculiarly; they burn the palate of him who travels in Mexico or South America, whence they came. Russian caviar, Italian macaroni, German pretzels, Swiss cheese, Yankee codfish-balls, English roast beef, Spanish omelettes, French kickshaws and Mexican ollas and Asiatic nameless things, all blend in the banquet which San Francisco restaurants daily set before their thousands of captious, hungry and exacting guests. Among them all there is nothing that is specially Californian. But it is a Californian specialty that here is daily set a repast, rich, varied and inexpensive, and to form which contributions of nature and art have been brought from every land beneath the sun.

Noah Brooks *(1830-1930) was an intimate friend of Abraham Lincoln during the Civil War, and it was only due to an acute cold that he wasn't* with Lincoln the evening the President was assassinated.

The two men had first met back in Illinois during Lincoln's early political career when Brooks was a correspondent covering the elections for various newspapers. Brooks' first impressions of Lincoln were unfavorable, based on the lanky man's appearance. But once he heard the future president speak, he was instantly converted and became a life-long supporter.

Brooks had started his newspaper career in Boston after deciding that an intended art career might leave him hungry. He quit in 1854 to move to Illinois to join a close friend in a business venture. While in Illinois he also worked as a freelance correspondent and it was at this time that he met Lincoln. The business venture failed and Brooks tried farming in Kansas.

Hearing of a rich Colorado gold strike, he became one of the thousands of '59ers. When he arrived in California, he had no money and "scarcely a rag to my back." He fell back on his art career and did quite well by selling sketches of Goldcamp life. In 1860 he had the means to buy with B.P. Avery the Marysville Daily Appeal, a Republican paper in a predominantly pro-slavery neighborhood. But Avery and Brooks touted the Republican cause and Lincoln carried their district by a slim margin.

Brooks' wife, Caroline, died in May of 1862. By November, Brooks was sailing through the Golden Gate enroute to Washington, D.C. as a correspondent for the powerful Sacramento Daily Union.

It was during this time that Lincoln reestablished their relationship. Weekly visits to the Lincoln household soon became daily and Brooks was seen coming and going at the Lincolns' both night and day. What attracted the older Lincoln to the young reporter? One of Brooks' biographers suggests that although he was witty and congenial, perhaps he was one of those rare birds, the good listener. In any case Lincoln respected Brooks' views and soon asked him if he was interested in replacing the departing John Nicolay as his personal secretary. John Wilkes Booth eliminated that possibility.

Depressed over Lincoln's death, Brooks accepted a government position back in San Francisco, but was soon back into newspaper work. He served as Managing Editor of the Alta California from 1867-1871. During his Alta years, Brooks was also involved in the founding of The Overland Monthly. He was one of Bret Harte's early supporters, contributing many articles and serving as an associate editor.   In 1871, Brooks left California to work in New York City. Until his retirement in 1894 he worked for The Tribune, The Times, and as Editor of the Newark Daily Advertiser. In retirement he returned to his birthplace in Castine, Maine, to a home he dubbed, "The Ark", and here wrote five more books while traveling extensively.

By the turn of the century Brooks had become seriously ill and returned to California for his health. His decline continued, and in August of 1903 the end came quietly at his home in Pasadena.

Lost in the Fog

by Noah Brooks

December 1868

"Down with your helm! you'll have us hard and fast aground!"

My acquaintance with Captain Booden was at that time somewhat limited, and if possible, I knew less of the difficult and narrow exit from Bolinas Bay than I did of Captain Booden. So with great trepidation I jammed the helm hard down, and the obedient little *Lively Polly* fell off easily and we were over the bar and gliding gently along under the steep bluff of the Mesa, whose rocky edge, rising sheer from the beach and crowned with dry grass, rose far above the pennon of the little schooner. I did not intend to deceive Captain Booden, but being anxious to work my way down to San Francisco, I had shipped as "able seaman" on the *Lively Polly*, though it was a long day since I had handled a foresheet or anything bigger than the little plungers which hover about Bolinas Bay; and latterly I had been ranching it at Point Reyes, so what could I know about the bar and the shoals of the harbor, I would like to know? We had glided out of the narrow channel which is skirted on one side by a wide, long sand-spit that curves around and makes the southern and western shelter of the bay, and on the other side by a huge elevated tongue of table land, called by the inhabitants thereabouts, the Mesa. High, precipitous, perpedicular, level, and dotted with farm-houses, this singular bit of land stretches several miles out southward to sea, bordered with a rocky beach, and tapered off into the wide ocean with Duxbury Reef — a dangerous rocky reef, curving down to the southward and almost always white with foam, save when the sea is calm, and then the great lazy green waves eddy noiselessly over the half hidden rocks, or slip like oil over the dreadful dangers which they hide.

Behind us was the lovely bay of Bolinas, blue and sparkling in the summer afternoon sun, its borders dotted with thrifty ranches, and the woody ravines and bristling Tamalpais Range rising over all. The tide was running out, and only a peaceful swash whispered along the level sandy beach on our left, where the busy sandpiper chased the playful wave as it softly rose and fell along the shore. On the higher centre of the sand-spit which shuts in the bay on that side, a row of ashy-colored gulls sunned themselves, and blinked at us sleepily as we drifted slowly out of the channel, our breeze cut off by the Mesa that hemmed us in on the right. I have told you that I did not much pretend to seamanship, but I was not sorry that I had taken passage on the *Lively Polly*, for there is always something novel and fascinating to me in coasting a region which I have heretofore known only its hills, cañons and sea-beaches. The trip is usually made from Bolinas Bay to San Francisco in five or six hours, when wind and tide favor; and I could bear being knocked about by Captain Booden for that length of time, especially as there was one other hand on board — "Lanky" he was called — but whether a foremast hand or landsman, I do not know. He had been teaching school at Jaybird Cañon, and was a little more awkward with the running rigging of the *Lively Polly* than I was. Captain Booden was, therefore, the main reliance of the little twenty-ton schooner, and if her deck-load of firewood and cargo of butter and eggs ever reached a market, the skillful and profane skipper should have all the credit thereof.

The wind died away, and the sea, before ruffled with a wholesale breeze, grew as calm as a sheet of billowy glass, heaving only in long, gentle undulations on which the sinking sun bestowed a green and golden glory, dimmed only by the white fog-bank that came drifting slowly up from the Farralones, now shut out from view by the lovely haze. Captain Booden gazed morosely on the western horizon, and swore by a big round oath that we should not have a capful of wind if that fog-bank did not lift. But we were fairly out of the bay; the Mesa was lessening in the distance, and as we drifted slowly southward the red-roofed buildings on its level rim grew to look like toy-houses, and we heard the dull moan of the ebb-tide on Duxbury Reef on our starboard bow. The sea grew dead calm and the wind fell quite away, but still we drifted southward, passing Rocky Point and peering curiously into Pilot Boat Cove, which looked so strangely unfamiliar to me from the sea, though I had fished in its trout-brooks many a day, and had hauled drift-wood from the rocky beach to Johnson's ranch in times gone by. The tide turned after sundown, and Captain Booden thought we ought to get a bit of wind then; but it did not come, and the fog crept up and up the glassy sea, rolling in huge wreaths of mist, shutting out the surface of the water, and finally, the gray rocks of North Heads were hidden, and little by little, the shore was curtained from our view and we were becalmed in the fog.

To say that the skipper swore would hardly describe his case. He cursed his luck, his stars, his foretop, his main hatch, his blasted foolishness, his lubberly crew — Lanky and I — and a variety of other persons and things; but all to no avail. Night came on, and the light on North Heads gleamed at us with a sickly eye through the deepening fog. We had a bit of luncheon with us, but no fire, and were fain to content ourselves with cold meat, bread and water, hoping that a warm breakfast in San Francisco would make some amends for our present short rations. But the night wore on, and we were still tumbling about in the rising sea without wind enough to fill our sails, a rayless sky overhead, and with breakers continually under our lee. Once we saw lights on shore, and heard the sullen thud of rollers that smote against the rocks; it was aggravating, as the fog lifted for a space, to see the cheerful windows of the Cliff House, and almost hear the merry calls of pleasure-seekers as they muffled themselves in their wraps and drove gaily up the hill, reckless of the poor homeless mariners who were drifting comfortlessly about so near the shore they could not reach. We got out the sweeps and rowed lustily for several hours, steering by the compass and taking our bearings from the cliff.

But we lost our bearings in the maze of currents in which we soon found ourselves, and the dim shore melted away in the thickening fog. To add to our difficulties, Captain Booden put his head most frequently into the cuddy; and when it emerged, he smelt dreadfully of gin. Lanky and I held a secret council, in which we agreed in case he became intoxicated, we would rise up in mutiny, and work the vessel on our own account. He shortly "lost his head," as Lanky phrased it; and slipping down on the deck, went quietly into the sleep of the gin-drunken. At four o'clock in the morning the gray fog grew grayer with the early dawning; and as I gazed with weary eyes into the vague unknown that shut us in, Booden roused himself from his booze, and seizing the tiller from my hand, bawled: " 'Bout ship, you swab! We're on the Farralones!" And sure enough, there loomed right under our starboard quarter a group of conical rocks, steeply rising from the restless blue sea. Their wild white sides were crowded with chattering sea-fowl; and far above, like a faint nimbus in the sky, shone the feeble rays of the lighthouse lantern, now almost quenched by the dull gleam of day that crept up from the water. The helm was jammed hard down. There was no time to get out sweeps; but still drifting helplessly, we barely grazed the bare rocks of the islet, and swung clear, slinking once more into the gloom.

Our scanty stock of provisions and water was gone; but there was no danger of starvation, for the generous product of the henneries and dairies of Bolinas filled the vessel's hold—albeit, raw eggs and butter without bread might only serve as a barrier against famine. So we drifted and tumbled about—still no wind and no sign of the lifting of the fog. Once in a while it would roll upward and show a long, flat expanse of water, tempting us to believe that the blessed sky was coming out at last; but soon the veil fell again, and we aimlessly wondered where we were and whither we were drifting. There is something awful and mysterious in the shadowy nothingness that surrounds one in a fog at sea. You fancy that out of that impenetrable mist may suddenly burst some great disaster or danger. Strange shapes appear to be forming themselves in the obscurity out of which they emerge; and the eye is wearied beyond expression with looking into a vacuity which continually promises to evolve into something, but never does.

Thus idly drifting, we heard, first, the creaking of a block; then, a faint wash of sea; and out of the white depths of the fog came the bulky hull of a full-rigged ship. Her sails were set, but she made scarcely steerage-way. Her rusty sides and general look bespoke a long voyage just concluding; and we found on hailing her that she was the British ship *Marathon*, from Calcutta, for San Francisco. We boarded the *Marathon*, though almost in sight of our own port, with something of the feeling that shipwrecked seamen may have when they reach land. It was odd that we, lost and wandering as we were, should be thus encountered in the vast unknown where we were drifting by a strange ship; and though scarcely two hours' sail from home, should be supplied with bread and water by a Britisher from the Indies. We gave them all the information we had about the pilots, whom we wanted so much to meet ourselves; and after following slowly for a few hours by the huge side of our strange friend, parted company — the black hull and huge spars of the Indiaman gradually lessening in the mist that shut her from our view. We had touched a chord that bound us to our fellow men; but it was drawn from our hands, and the unfathomable abyss in which we floated had swallowed up each human trace, except what was comprised on the contracted deck of the *Lively Polly*, where Captain Booden sat glumly whittling, and Lanky meditatively peered after the disappeared *Marathon*, as though his soul and all its hopes had gone with her. The deck, with its load of cordwood; the sails and rigging; the sliding hutch of the little cuddy; and all the features of the *Lively Polly*, but yesterday so unfamiliar — were now as odiously wearisome, as though I had known them for a century. It seemed as if I had never known any other place.

All that day we floated aimlessly along, moved only by the sluggish currents, which shifted occasionally, but generally bore us westward and southward; not a breath of wind arose, and our sails were as useless as though we had been on dry land. Night came on again, and found us still entirely without reckoning and as completely "at sea" as ever before. To add to our discomfort, a drizzling rain, unusual for the season of the year, set in, and we cowered on the wet deck-load, more than ever disgusted with each other and the world. During the night, a big ocean steamer came plunging and crashing through the darkness, her lights gleaming redly through the dense medium as she cautiously felt her way past us, falling off a few points as she heard our hail. We lay right in her path, but with tin horns and a wild Indian yell from the versatile Lanky, managed to make ourselves heard, and the mysterious stranger disappeared in the fog as suddenly as she had come, and we were once more alone in the darkness.

The night wore slowly away and we made out to catch a few hours' sleep, standing "watch and watch" with each other of our slender crew. Day dawned again, and we broke our fast with the last of the *Marathon's* biscuit, having "broken cargo" to eke out our cold repast with some of the Bolinas butter and eggs which we were taking to a most unexpected market.

Suddenly, about six o'clock in the morning, we heard the sound of breakers ahead, and above the sullen road of the surf I distinctly heard the tinklings of a bell. We got out our sweeps and had commenced to row wearily once more, when the fog lifted and before us lay the blessed land. A high range of sparsely wooded hills, crowded with rocky ledges, and with

-134-

abrupt slopes, covered with brown dry grass, running to the water's edge, formed the background of the picture. Nearer, a tongue of high land, brushy and rocky, made out from the main shore, and curving southward, formed a shelter to what seemed a harbor within. Against this precipitous point the sea broke with a heavy blow, and a few ugly peaks of rock lifted their heads above the heaving green of the sea. High up above the sky-line rose one tall, sharp, blue peak, yet veiled in the floating mist, but its base melted away into a mass of verdure that stretched from the shore far up the mountain side.

Our sweeps were now used to bring us around the point, and cautiously pulling in, we opened into a lovely bay, bordered with orchards and vineyards, in the midst of which was a neat village, glittering white in the sunshine, and clustered around an old-fashioned mission church, whose quaint gable and tower reminded us of the buildings of the early Spanish settlers of the country. As we neared the shore (there was no landing-place) we could see an unwonted commotion in the clean streets, and a flag was run up to the top of a white staff that stood in the midst of a plaza. Captain Booden returned the compliment by hoisting the stars and stripes at our mainmast head, but was sorely bothered with the mingled dyes of the flag on shore. A puff of air blew out its folds, and to our surprise, disclosed that Mexican national standard.

"Blast them greasers," said the patriotic skipper, "if they ain't gone and histed a Mexican cactus flag, then I'm blowed." He seriously thought of hauling down his beloved national colors again, resenting the insult of hoisting a foreign flag on American soil. He pocketed the affront however, remarking that "they probably knew that a Bolinas butter-boat was not much of a fightist anyway."

We dropped anchor gladly, Captain Booden being wholly at a loss as to our whereabouts. We judged that we were somewhere south of the Golden Gate, but what town this was that slept so tranquilly in the summer sun, and what hills were these that walled in the peaceful scene from the rest of the world, we could not tell. The village seemed awakening from its serene sleepiness, and one by one the windows of the adobe cottages swung open as if the people rubbed their long-closed eyes at some unwonted sight; and the doors gradually opened as though their dumb lips would hail us and ask who were these strangers that vexed the quiet waters of their bay. But two small fishing-boats lay at anchor, and these Booden said reminded him of Christopher Columbus or Noah's Ark, they were so clumsy and antique in build.

We hauled our boat up alongside and all hands got in and went ashore. As we landed, a little shudder seemed to go through the sleepy old place, as if it had been rudely disturbed from its comfortable nap, and a sudden sob of sea air swept through the quiet streets as though the insensate houses had actually breathed the weary sigh of awaking. The buildings were low and white, with dark-skinned children basking in the doors, and grass hammocks swinging beneath open verandas. There were no stores, no sign of business, and no sound of vehicles or labor; all was decorous and quiet, to use the skipper's description, "as if the people had slicked up their door-yards, whitewashed their houses, and gone to bed." It was just like a New English Sabbath in a Mexican village.

And this fancy was further colored by a strange procession which now met us as we went up from the narrow beach, having first made fast our boat. A lean Mexican priest, with an enormous shovel hat and particularly shabby cassock, came toward us, followed by a motley crowd of Mexicans, prominent among whom was a pompous old man, clad in a seedy Mexican uniform, and wearing a trailing rapier at his side. The rest of the procession was brought up with a crowd of shy women, dark-eyed and tawny and all poorly clad, though otherwise comfortable enough in condition. These hung back and wonderingly looked at the strange faces, as though they had never seen the like before. The old padre lifted his skinny hands, and said something in Spanish which I did not understand.

"Why, the old mummy is slinging his popish blessings at us!" This was Lanky's interpretation of the kindly priest's paternal salutation. And, sure enough, he was welcoming us to the shore of San Ildefonso with holy fervor and religious phrase.

"I say," said Booden, a little testily, "what did you say was the name of this place, and where away does it lay from 'Frisco?" In very choice Castilian, as Lanky declared, the priest rejoined that he did not understand the language in which Booden was speaking. "Then bring on somebody that does," rejoined that irreverent mariner, when due interpretation had been made. The padre protested that no one in the village understood the English tongue. The skipper gave a long low whistle of suppressed astonishment, and wondered if we had drifted down to Lower California in two days and nights, and had struck a Mexican settlement. The colors on the flag-staff and the absence of any Americans gave some show of reason to this star-tling conclusion, and Lanky, who was now the interpreter of the party, asked the name of the place and was again told it was San Ildefonso; but when he asked what country it was in and how far it was to San Francisco, he was met with a polite "I do not understand you, Señor." Here was a puz-zle; becalmed in a strange port only two days drift from the city of San Francisco; a town which the schoolmaster declared was not laid down on any map; a population that spoke only Spanish and did not know English when they heard it; a Mexican flag flying over the town, and an educated priest who did not know what we meant when we asked how far it was to San Francisco. Were we bewitched?

Accepting a hospitable invitation from the padre, we sauntered up to the plaza, where we were ushered into a long, low room, which might once have been a military barrack-room; it was neatly white-washed and had a hard clay floor, and along the walls were a few ancient firelocks and a venerable picture of "His Excellency, General Santa Aña, President of the

Republic of Mexico," as a legend beneath it set forth. Breakfast of chickens, vegetables, bread, and an excellent sort of country wine (this last being served in a big earthen bottle) was served up to us on the long unpainted table that stood in the middle of the room. During the repast our host, the priest, sat with folded hands intently regarding us, while the rest of the people clustered around the door and open windows, eyeing us with indescribable and incomprehensible curiosity. If we had been visitors from the moon, we could not have attracted more attention. Even the stolid Indians, a few of whom strolled lazily about, came and gazed at us until the pompous old man in faded Mexican uniform drove them noisily away from the window, where they shut out the light and the pleasant morning air, perfumed with heliotropes, verbenas and sweet herbs that grew luxuriantly about the houses.

The padre had restrained his curiosity out of rigid politeness until we had eaten, when he began by asking, Did our galleon come from Manila? We told him that we only came from Bolinas: whereat he said once more with a puzzled look of pain, "I do not understand you, Señor." Then pointing through the open doorway to where the *Lively Polly* peacefully floated at anchor, he asked what ensign was that which floated at her masthead. Lanky proudly, but with some astonishment, replied: "That's the American flag, Señor." At this the seedy old man in uniform eagerly said: "Americaños! Americaños! why, I saw some of those people and that flag at Monterey." Lanky asked him if Monterey was not full of Americans and did not have plenty of flags. The Ancient replied that he did not know; it was a long time since he had been there. Lanky observed that perhaps he had never been there. "I was there in 1835" said the Ancient. This curious speech being interpreted to Captain Booden, that worthy remarked that he did not believe that he had seen a white man since.

After an ineffectual effort to explain to the company where Bolinas was, we rose and went out for a view of the town. It was beautifully situated on a gentle rise which swelled up from the water's edge and fell rapidly off in the rear of the town into a deep ravine, where a brawling mountain stream supplied a little flouring mill with motive power. Beyond the ravine were small fields of grain, beans, and lentils on the rolling slopes, and back of these rose the dark, dense vegetation of low hills, while over all were the rough and ragged ridges of mountains closing in all the scene. The town itself, as I have said, was white and clean; the houses were low-browed, with windows secured by wooden shutters; only a few glazed sashes being seen anywhere. Out of these openings in the thick adobe walls of the humble homes of the villagers flashed the curious, the abashed glances of many a dark-eyed señorita, who fled, laughing, as we approached. The old church was on the plaza, and in its odd-shaped turret tinkled the little bell whose notes had sounded the morning angelus, when we were knocking about in the fog outside. High up on its quaintly arched gable was inscribed in antique letters "1796." In reply to a skeptical remark from Lanky, Booden declared that "the old shell looked as though it might have been built in the time of Ferdinand and Isabella, for that matter." The worthy skipper had a misty idea that all old Spanish buildings were built in the days of these famous sovereigns.

Hearing the names of Ferdinand and Isabella, the padre gravely and reverentially asked: "And is the health of His Excellency, Gen. Santa Aña, whom God protects, still continued to him?"

With great amazement, Lanky replied: "Santa Aña, why, the last heard of him was that he was keeping a cockpit in Havana; some of the newspapers published an obituary of him about six months ago, but I believe he is alive yet somewhere."

A little flush of indignation mantled the old man's cheek, and with a tinge of severity in his voice, he said: "I have heard that shameful scandal about our noble President once before, but you must excuse me if I ask you not to repeat it. It is true he took away our Pious Fund some years since, but he is still our revered President, and I would not hear him ill-spoken of any more than our puissant and mighty Ferdinand, of whom you just spoke — may he rest in glory!" and here the good priest crossed himself devoutly.

"What is the old priest jabbering about?" asked Captain Booden, impatiently; for he was in haste to "get his bearings" and be off. When Lanky replied, he burst out: "Tell him that Santa Aña is not President of Mexico any more than I am, and that he hasn't amounted to a row of pins since California was a part of the United States."

Lanky faithfully interpreted his fling at the ex-President, whereupon the padre, motioning to the Ancient to put up his rapier, which had leaped out of its rusty scabbard, said: "Nay, Señor, you would insult an old man. We have never been told yet by our government that the Province of California was alienated from the great Republic of Mexico, and we owe allegiance to none save the nation whose flag we love so well;" and the old man turned his tear-dimmed eyes toward the ragged standard of Mexico that drooped from the staff in the plaza. Continuing, he said: "Our noble country has strangely forgotten us, and though we watch the harbor-entrance year after year, no tidings ever comes. The galleon that was to bring us stores has never been seen on the horizon yet, and we seem lost in the fog."

The schoolmaster of Jaybird Cañon managed to tell us what the priest had said, and then asked when he had last heard of the outside world. "It was in 1837," said he, sadly, "when we sent a courier to the Mission del Carmelo, at Monterey, for tidings from New Spain. He never came back, and the great earthquake which shook the country hereabout opened a huge chasm across the country just back of the Sierra yonder, and none dared to cross over to the main land. The saints have defended us in peace, and it is the will of Heaven that we shall stay here by ourselves until the Holy Virgin, in answer to our prayers, shall send us deliverance."

Here was a new revelation. This was an old Spanish Catholic mission, settled in 1796, called San Ildefonso, which had evidently been overlooked for nearly forty years, and had quietly slept in an unknown solitude while the country had been transferred to the United States from the flag that still idly waved over it. Lost in the fog! Here was a whole town lost in the fog of years. Empires and dynasties had risen and fallen; the world had repeatedly been shaken to its centre, and this people had heeded it not; a great civil war had ravaged the country to which they now belonged and they knew not of it; poor Mexico herself had been torn with dissensions and had been insulted with an empire, and these peaceful and weary watchers for tidings from "New Spain" had recked nothing of all these things. All around them the busy State of California was scarred with the eager pick of gold-seekers, or the shining share of the husbandman; towns and cities had sprung up where these patriarchs had only known of vast cattle ranges, or sleepy missions of the Roman Catholic Fathers. They knew nothing of the great city of San Francisco, with its busy marts and crowded harbor; and thought of its broad bay—if they thought of it at all—as the lovely shore of Yerba Buena, bounded by bleak hills and almost unvexed by any keel. The political storms of forty years had gone hurtless over their heads, and in a certain sort of dreamless sleep, San Ildefonso had still remained true to the red, white and green flag that had long since disappeared from every part of the State save here, where it was still loved and revered as the banner of the soil.

The social and political framework of the town had been kept up through all these years. There had been no connection with the fountain of political power, but the town was ruled by the legally elected Ayuntamiento, or Common Council, of which the Ancient, Señor Apolonario Maldonado, was President or Alcalde. They were daily looking for advices from Don José Castro, Governor of the loyal province of California; and so they had been looking daily for forty years. We asked if they had not heard from any of the prying Yankees who crowd the country? Father Ignacio—for that as the padre's name—replied: "Yes; five years ago, when the winter rains had just set in, a tall, spare man, who talked some French and some Spanish, came down over the mountains with a pack containing pocket-knives, razors, soap, perfumery, laces, and other curious wares, and besought our people to purchase. We have not much coin, but were disposed to treat him Christianly, until he did declare that President General Santa Aña, whom may the Saints defend! was a thief and gambler, and had gambled away the Province of California to the United States; whereupon we drove him hence, the Ayuntamiento sending a trusty guard to see him two leagues from the borders of the pueblo. But, months after, we discovered his pack and such of his poor bones as the wild beasts of prey had not carried off, at the base of a precipice where he had fallen. His few remains and his goods were together buried on the mountainside, and I lamented that we had been so hard with him. But the Saints forbade that he should go back and tell where the people of San Ildefonso were waiting to hear from their own neglectful country, which may Heaven defend, bless and prosper!"

The little town took on a new interest to us cold outsiders after hearing its strange and almost improbable story. We could have scarcely believed that San Ildefonso had actually been overlooked in the transfer of the country from Mexico to the United States, and had for nearly forty years been hidden away between the Sierra and the sea; but, if we were disposed to doubt the word of the good father, here was intrinsic evidence of the truth of his narrative. There were no Americans here; only the remnants of the old Mexican occupation and the civilized Indians. No traces of later civilization could be found; but the simple dresses, tools, implements of husbandry and household utensils were such as I have seen in the half-civilized wilds of Central America. The old mill in the cañon behind the town was a curiosity of clumsiness, and nine-tenths of the water-power of the arroya that supplied it were wasted. Besides, until now, who ever heard of such a town in California as San Ildefonso? Upon what map can any such headland and bay be traced; and where are the historic records of the pueblo whose well defined boundaries lay palpably before us? I have dwelt upon this point, about which I naturally have some feeling, because of the skeptical criticism which my narrative has since provoked. There are some people in the world who never will believe anything that they have not seen, touched, or tasted for themselves; California has her share of such.

Captain Booden was disposed to reject Father Ignacio's story, until I called his attention to the fact that this was a tolerable harbor for small craft, and yet had never before been heard of; that he never knew of such a town, and that if any of his numerous associates in the marine profession knew of the town or harbor of San Ildefonso, he surely would have heard of it from them. He restrained his impatience to off long enough to allow Father Ignacio to gather from us a few chapters of the world's history for forty years past. The discovery of gold in California, the settlement of the country and the Pacific Railroad were not so much account to him, somehow, as the condition of Europe, the Church in Mexico, and what had become of the Pious Fund; this last I discovered had been a worrisome subject to the good Father. I did not know what it was myself, but I believe it was the alienation from the church of certain moneys and incomes which were transferred to speculators by the Mexican Congress, years and years ago.

I was glad to find that we were more readily believed by Father Ignacio and the old Don than our Yankee predecessor had been; perhaps, we were believed more on his corroborative evidence. The priest, however, politely declined to accept all we said; that was evident; and the Don steadily refused to believe that California had been transferred to the United States. It was a little touching to see Father Ignacio's doubt and hopes struggle in his withered face as he heard in a few brief sentences the history of his beloved land and Church for forty years past. His eye kindled, or it was bedewed with tears, as he listened, and an occasional flash of resentment flushed his cheek when he heard something that shook his ancient faith in the established order of things. To a proposition to take passage with us to San Francisco, he replied warmly that he would on no account leave his flock, nor attempt to thwart the manifest will of Heaven that the town should remain unheard of until delivered from its long sleep by the same agencies that had cut it off from the rest of the world. Neither would he allow any of the people to come with us.

And so we parted. We went out with the turn of the tide, Father Ignacio and the Ancient accompanying us to the beach, followed by a crowd of the townsfolk who carried our water and provisions for a longer voyage than ours promised to be. The venerable priest raised his hands in parting blessing as we shoved off, and I saw two big tears roll down the furrowed face of Señor Maldonado, who looked after us as a stalwart old warrior might look at the departure of a band of hopeful comrades leaving him to fret in monkish solitude while they were off to the wars again. Wind and tide served, and in a few minutes the *Lively Polly* rounded the point, and looking back, I saw the yellow haze of the afternoon sun sifted sleepily over all the place; the knots of white-clad people standing statuesque and motionless as they gazed; the flag of Mexico faintly waving in the air; and with a sigh of relief a slumberous veil seemed to fall over all the scene; and as our bow met the roll of the current outside the headland, the gray rocks of the point shut out the fading view, and we saw the last of San Ildefonso.

Captain Booden had gathered enough from the people to know that we were somewhere south of San Francisco, (the *Lively Polly* had no chart or nautical instruments on board, of course) and so he determined to coast cautiously along northward, marking the shore line in order to be able to guide other navigators to the harbor. But a light mist crept down the coast, shutting out the view of the headlands, and by midnight we had stretched out to sea again, and were once more out of our reckoning. At daybreak, however, the fog lifted, and we found ourselves in sight of land, and a brisk breeze blowing, we soon made Pigeon Point, and before noon were inside the Golden Gate, and ended our long and adventurous cruise from Bolinas Bay by hauling into the wharf at San Francisco.

I have little left to tell. Of the shameful way in which our report was received, every newspaper reader knows. At first there were some persons, men of science and reading, who were disposed to believe what we said. I printed in one of the daily newspapers an account of what we had discovered, giving a full history of San Ildefonso as Father Ignacio had given it to us. Of course, the other newspapers, as I find is usual in such cases, pooh-poohed the story their contemporary had published to their exclusion, and made themselves very merry over what they were pleased to term, "The great San Ildefonso Sell." I prevailed on Captain Booden to make a short voyage down the coast in search of the lost port. But we never saw the headland, the ridge beyond the town, nor anything that looked like these landmarks, though we went down as far as San Pedro Bay and back twice or three times. It actually did seem that the whole locality had been swallowed up, or had vanished into air. In vain did I bring the matter to the notice of the merchants and scientific men of San Francisco. Nobody would fit out an exploring expedition by land or sea; those who listened at first, finally inquired "if there was money in it?" I could not give an affirmative answer, and they turned away with the discouraging remark, that the California Academy of Natural Sciences or the Society of Pioneers were the only bodies interested in the fate of our lost city. Even Captain Booden somehow lost all interest in the enterprise, and returned to his Bolinas coasting with the most stolid indifference. I combatted the attacks of the newspapers with facts and depositions of my fellow voyagers as long as I could, until one day the editor of the *Daily Trumpeter* (I suppress the real name of the sheet) coldly told me that the public were tired of the story of San Ildefonso. It was plain that his mind had been soured by the sarcasms of his contemporaries, and he no longer believed in me.

The newspaper controversy died away and was forgotten, but I have never relinquished the hope of proving the verity of my statements. At one time I expected to establish the truth, having heard that one Zedekiah Murch had known a Yankee peddler who had gone over the mountains of Santa Cruz and never was heard of more. But Zedekiah's memory was feeble, and he only knew that such a story prevailed long ago; so that clue was soon lost again, and the little fire of enthusiasm which it kindled among a few persons died out. I have not yet lost all hope; and when I think of the regretful conviction that will force itself upon the mind of good Father Ignacio, that we were, after all, imposters, I cannot bear to reflect that I may die and visit the lost town of San Ildefonso no more.

California Culinary Experiences

by Prentice Mulford

June 1869

I am a survivor of all the different eras of California amateur cookery. The human avalanche precipitated on these shores in the rush of "49" and "50" was a mass of culinary ignorance. Cooking had always by us been deemed a part of woman's kingdom. We knew that bread was made of flour, and for the most part so made by woman. It was as natural that it should be made by them as that the sun should shine. Of the knowledge, skill, patience and experience required to conduct this and other culinary operations, we realized nothing. So when the first — the pork, bean and flapjack — era commenced, thousands of us boiled our pork and beans together an equal period of time, and then wondered at the mysterious hardness of the nutritious vegetable. In the fall of "50" a useful scrap of wisdom was disseminated from Siskiyou to Fresno. It was that beans must be soaked over night and boiled at least two hours before the insertion of the pork. And many a man of mark to-day never experienced a more cheerful thrill of combined pride and pleasure, than when first he successfully accomplished the feat of turning a flap-jack.

We soon tired of wheat cakes. Then commenced the bread era; the heavy bread era, which tried the stomach of California. That organ sustained a daily attack of leaden flour and doubtful pork. The climate was censured for a mortality which then prevailed, due, in great measure, to this dreadful diet. With the large majority of our amateur cooks, bread-making proved but a series of disastrous failures. Good bread makers, male or female, are born, not made. In flour we floundered from the extreme of lightness to that of heaviness. We produced in our loaves every shade of sourness and every tint of orange, from excess of salaeratus. Our crust, in varying degrees of hardness and thickness, well illustrated the stratifications of the earth. Our loaves "did" in spots. Much prospecting was often necessary to develop pay-bread.

In the early portion of "51," just preceding the pie period, came an epoch of stewed dried apples. Even now, my stomachic soul shudders as I recall that trying time. After we had apple-sauced ourselves to satiety, with diabolical ingenuity we served it up to each other, hidden in thick, heavy ramparts of flour. It was a desperate struggle with duff and dumplings. Like

Ney returning alone to Paris after the dreadful Russian campaign, I can now recall no living comrade of the dried apple era.

But those who first ventured on pies were men possessed in some degree of taste and refinement. No coarser nature ever troubled itself with pie-making. The preparation and seasoning of the mince meat, the rolling out and manipulation of the crusts, their proper adjustment to the plate, the ornamental scollops around the edge, (made with the thumb) and the regulation of the oven's heat to secure that rich shade of brown, required patience and artistic skill.

The early pie-makers of our State were men who as soon as possible slept in sheets instead of blankets, who were skilled in washing linen, who went in clean attire on Sundays, and who subscribed for magazines and newspapers. On remote bars and gulches such men have kept households of incredible neatness, their cabins sheltered under the evergreen oak, with clear rivulets from the mountain gorges running past the door, with clothes-line precisely hung with shirts and sheets, with gauze covered meat safe hoisted high in the branches of the overshadowing trees, protecting those pies from intruding and omniverous ground squirrels and inquisitive yellow-jackets; while about their door-way the hard, clean-swept red earth resembled a well-worn brick pavement. There is morality in pies.

There was a canned provision era, fruitful in sardines and oysters. The canned oysters of those days were as destructive as cannister shot. They penetrated everywhere. In remote and seldom-visited valleys of the Sierras, I have grown solemn over the supposition that mine were the first footsteps which had ever indented the soil. And then I have turned but to behold the gaping, ripped and jagged mouth of one of those inevitable tin cylinders scattered like dew over the land, and labelled "Cove Oysters." One of our prominent officials, giving evidence in a suit relative to the disputed possession of a mining claim in a remote district, when asked what, in the absence of a house or shaft, he would consider to be indications of the former presence of miners, answered: "Empty oyster cans and empty bottles."

California has furnished many a focus for the combined operations of cooks from foreign lands and from the various sections of our own Union. I recall now such a focus. The Polyglot House at Hangville, kept by an Italian who had been so badly Anglicised as to wantonly apply or neglect his H's. He had an Irish wife and employed a Chinese clerk *de cuisine*. These three being employed in the kitchen, the cooking was wretchedly cosmopolite, having all the defects of the different nationalities and but few of their virtues. Indeed, the preparation of food with this trio was a mere mechanical operation. The landlord entertained a theory that while the American deemed potatoes indispensable to a meal, the condition of this vegetable when brought to the table was a matter of complete indifference, so that it had at some period been boiled. It was the American eye, not palate, to be gratified. For year after year at the Polyglot House potatoes were regularly brought on and as regularly taken off the table untouched. Few cared to taste these sodden, puttified tubers a second time. But the landlord was content. The American had seen his potatoes. That was all he wanted. There are many other cooks in whose world a properly boiled potato as yet has never entered. A depraved, yet common, taste caused the Polyglot House steak to be fried in lard. In view of meat so outraged, could the belligerent character of the Hangville people be wondered at? The sanguinary disposition so prevalent in the early days was not entirely owing to unaccustomed excitement and freedom from restraint. Such cookery, and consequent bad indigestion, had something to do with it.

The composition of the Polyglot House coffee was ever a mystery. While drinking it we whistled "down brakes" on our imaginations. An imprudent investigatory taste might in it have recognized the particular aroma of every roast, every stew, every frying, every baking, broiling, boiling and brewing, which had transpired in that kitchen for a month. I always wondered at such times if I really had a correct idea of the flavor of a boiled dish-towel. A Texan became indignant with it one morning, walked in to the kitchen, beat the unfortunate Chinese assistant with a club, and then tendered him this recipe for making coffee: "John, no good coffee. You no makee better coffee to-morrow, you catchee more club." The act was brutal, but the Texan had been too long under the influence of the Polyglot House diet to be entirely responsible for his actions. Indeed, I hold that pork, badly baked bread, and beef hardened but not cooked in hot grease, had much to do in the generation of the spirit which would have sundered our Union.

Our Chinese cooks imitate the American style with a painful accuracy. The Celestial member of the Polyglot House trio knew that a certain amount of meat, flour and vegetables were to be daily prepared after the fashion taught him by his employer. He knew that at noon the white flag being hoisted as a signal that dinner was ready, a crowd of hungry men, all the morning toiling in the turned river-bed a quarter of a mile below, would rush up, and first putting a hair edge on their appetites by draughts of that corn whisky which rasped the throat as it went down like a shower of powdered glass, would, in the shortest possible time after being seated, hurry down quantities of his mechanically prepared food. It was to them merely the fuel for generating motive power to run six hours longer, as are wood and water to the engine. He exposed it to heat on the principle that you season your wood, to burn the easier. American humanity to this Celestial was merely a collection of high pressure flesh and blood machines, for whom he prepared fuel.

"John's" day's work over, he betook himself to a mushroom-looking Chinese village, hard by, improvised out of boards, canvas, gunny sacks, mats, sheets of tin and bushes. Here, with his comrades over their summer evening meal, he would linger for hours, and I suspect that some of their hilarity might have had its rise at certain queer aspects in which the life of the lordly American seemed to these sociable Mongolians.

Different mining partners have afforded me a rich and varied experience in cooks. I once lived near a slovenly, and, of course, literary cook. His was a good, easy disposition, but it bore a frequent thorn of such natures — intense laziness. He had never more than a day's fuel prepared in advance. He depended mainly on a few old, chipped and battered stumps, near his cabin. The inexhaustibility of such stumps is wonderful. Coming home from work, he would snatch at the dried, dead weeds and twigs in his path. These furnished sufficient fuel to boil the kettle and warm his meat, by a culinary fiction deemed cooked. This man was human; he had a soul; yet he regarded eating as a mere animal necessity, and cooking one of the evils entailed upon man by the miserable weakness of Adam for an apple — possibly a dried apple. One-third of his table was ever set. It held a plate, a knife and fork, tin cup and spoon, two yeast-powder boxes containing pepper and salt, an oyster-can holding sugar, a tea-cup lined with dried mustard, a snuffy candlestick, a coffee pot, and a bottle of molasses. In addition to its legitimate office, the frying pan did the platter's duty. Its area was coated with a dark, unctuous substance, the accumulation resulting from an entire absence of soap, hot water and towels. The crockery was quite immovable. The remaining space of table area was covered with a chaos of of books and papers. For he was not a mere bookworm. He was the literary anaconda of the Southern mines. Most of the older settlers leaving, to him by a sort of natural inheritance had fallen the library purchased in the palmy days of Hangville. And in this library, quite filling his cabin, did he eat, read, live, move, and have his being. He devoured together beef, bread, apple sauce, and Humboldt's Cosmos. His private mark was in every book and on every paper, the imprint of a greasy thumb or a dash of molasses. This simultaneous employment of brain and stomach resulted to him injuriously. He lost his memory. He forgot a book's contents a week after reading it. And so he revolved from year to year through the Hangville library in an endless circuit. He may be reading and eating yet. There are people who should reflect on this.

Leaving the literary eater I endured for a few months a cook of ungovernable temper. The extremes met. He always lost his temper while preparing breakfast, and anger being an infectious madness, both of us usually partook of that meal in a condition of antagonism with everything and everybody. At first we had one of those little stoves which consume so many eight-inch sticks; whose fires demand so much nursing to be kept alive; at one moment roaring like an angry bull, and the stove as red as a turkey's comb — the next, suddenly relapsing into a cold and cheerless silence. The combustible cook, annoyed at such tricks on the part of the little stove while glancing at the weekly paper, or holding converse with a neighbor, would in revenge kick it and smash our diminishing crockery. One morning he gave it a fatal blow with the axe. Then we secured a large, a very large, but also a very old stove, whose maximum of usefulness had been passed in a boarding house. Its constitution was undermined. The expansion of its proportions under the stimulus of a hotter fire than usual would cause the entire area of top, and with the superimposed array of culinary furniture, to fall into the blazing furnace. Consequent on the snatchings in the fire with rag-wrapped hands for the pots, pans, and kettles, or fishing for the same with sticks, were painfully scorched and burned fingers. The combustible cook, blazing with curses, would then kick that stove, which received such action with heavy and stolid unconcern. No injury was done save to the combustible cook's toes. He would diverge into forcible projections of cups about the kitchen. Ultimately his rage concentrated itself wholly upon a harmless little tin pepper box, shaken from its shelf by the combustible cook's tremors, and then invariably kicked from corner to corner of the room, and at last out of the back door, to be regularly brought in again when the storm had subsided. I was obliged to leave this man. My sympathy with these extreme nervous moods was too great, and I saw dyspepsia in the distance.

I spent one winter with a fickle and unmethodical cook. He oscillated from the extremes of method and neatness to those of neglect and slovenliness. There was a place for everything and everything in its place — about once a month. His coffee was too weak or too strong; his steaks of extreme rareness or burned to a crisp; his potatoes boiled to pieces or impervious to the fork; his bread subject to varying moods of heaviness. He had no patience for measuring quantities. In salting a dish for instance, he did but institute a wild guess as to the proper quantity. Hence came days of extreme saltness. There were also days of extreme dish-washings. There were days of no dish-washing at all. There were periods of total culinary riot and demoralization, when old and new coffee were boiled together; when the tea-pot refused to pour a drop from the accumulation of tea-leaves; when no warm meals were prepared, and when old stews, trembling on the verge of sourness, were thrust upon our meek and suffering stomachs. Such things are outrages and insults unpardonable to the digestive organs.

I once prospected together an upper ledge and a mechanical and abstracted eater. This man's whole soul was at the time concentrated on a series of ledges that we had taken up. We were encamped well up the slope of Table Mountain, a wide expanse of country being spread out before us. Over this, while seated at breakfast under a tree, would the mechanical eater's eye wander. He was planning new mineral discoveries on those distant hills. Up and down silently oscillated his fork, conveying morsels of something from plate to mouth. The tines occasionally missed and fastened themselves in the table. Gastronomically considered, he was an unfeathered ostrich. He would swallow everything I placed before him. He confided his stomach to my care with the unthinking trustfulness of a child. There was merely a body brought by animal instinct to a table at certain regular intervals to be supplied with a few more hours' propelling force. As for the mechanical eater's soul, part of it was left behind at the bottom of our shaft fifty-two feet underground, and the remainder was skimming along the range of hills holding the line of claims we had taken on the extension.

Then a fussy cook came into my life. He deemed himself, and falsely too, a great executive culinary power. He was always planning more dishes than his mind could grasp or his hands could handle. He could set and would set, were they at hand, any number of people at work in the preparation of a single meal. The house was always in a chronic condition of bustle. His mind, while he was engaged in cooking, would wander outside of culinary operations, and so in preparing a great dinner he would interpolate shaving and shirt-button sewing. He often suffered temporary aberration of mind, by having too many dishes on the fire at the same time, and in this condition would rush distractedly about the premises with a carving knife in one hand and a tormentor fork in the other, looking for a stove cover, a pot lid, or whatever his hands might have last laid hold of. These articles were found in the strangest places; sometimes in the hen-coop; sometimes in the fork of the tree which shaded our cabin. It required one person to keep run of these things, dripping as it were constantly from him. He was lengthy and elaborate in the preparation of food. I incurred his contempt by hinting disapproval of so many hours of preliminary bustle to so few minutes of mastication. The reverse regarding time suited me better. I argued the table sociability of a company of French miners nearby, over their soup, bread, and claret. They ate and cooked to live. We lived principally to cook. I was bold enough to attack the laboriously-prepared Christmas dinners of my ancestors. This touched the tenderest article of faith in the fussy cook's creed. For he worshipped the recollection of those New England holiday dinners, involving so much preparatory mince-pie making, turkey and pig stuffing, as utterly to exhaust the mental and physical energies of "our folks," so that when at last they sat at the feast all capacity for its enjoyment had been baked and roasted out of them.

The fussy cook was very trying. He raved even though the tin drinking cup was not hung up on the right nail; he criticised sarcastically my irregular manner of cutting bread; he insisted on daily polishings of the tin-ware; he read me many lectures on my careless habits, and, worse than all, he would inveigle me into chopping hash on a flat board. This idiosyncracy came on when his mind and the stove were already overburdened with dishes, and when we had neither chopping-knife nor chopping-tray. I never could conveniently nor agreeably chop a mass of meat and potatoes on a flat board. It was always inclined to spread and fly about in all directions. He argued that it could be done correctly in that way. He grappled with the theory: I with the practice. He succeeded in his demonstrations: I failed in mine. I was obliged to leave him. I suffered too many martyrdoms endeavoring to chop hash with a hatchet on a flat board.

Fate then placed me with an experimental cook. He was always essaying new dishes, the result of his ponderings over a coverless old cook-book by some chance left in our cabin. And besides, he entertained culinary plans of his own invention which, when carried out, resulted in strange mixtures. The *debris* left over from several meals, on the score of economy, was tortured, simmered, stewed, and concentrated into hybrid conglomerates regardless of the assimilation of flavors. During the week the venerable cook-book's pudding recipes were intently studied. On Sundays these studies were practically carried out. So our Sabbath roast was slighted and cast in the shade through the excessive attention bestowed on that pudding, which generally turned out a wretched failure; a heavy, sodden, unassimilated, watery lump of flour, eggs, and suet, with a defected mass meeting of plums on the "lower level." Where the experimental cook accomplished one success, he made ten failures. But he never flagged. Neither had he any hesitation during these investigations in risking his own stomach and that of his best friend. Science would be naught without experiment, yet it is often accompanied with danger. So it was here. I left him.

My own individual culinary experiences have been varied, and at times exciting. The rudimentary period commenced on a whaling schooner, cruising in the waters of Lower California. On this vessel, without a moment's consideration as to fitness or ability, did I ship as cook and steward. The *Henry* being small, her decks were lumbered up with whaling gear, boats, casks, try-pots, etc. My galley was not amid-ships, where the thrones of all sea-cooks are or should be, but jammed up against the starboard bulwarks. In rough weather, the *Henry* was always aspiring to a perpendicular position by the head or stern, and seemingly disappointed at not attaining it, indulged in such fearful lee lurches as to shock my pots, pans, and kettles out of that galley on an Indian file rush across the deck into the lee scuppers, myself bringing up the rear. My stove was not a marine stove. It had no guard about the outer edge to secure the loose apparatus on top from rolling off. This defect I endeavored to remedy by a system of wires, attaching the pots to the galley ceiling. The effect in heavy weather was extraordinary; my kettles swinging on and off like a complicated system of pendulums. My first two months' performance gave no satisfaction. There was a general and daily howl of execration from cabin to forecastle against the cook — the literary cook. It had been whispered aboard that I had "written for a paper." It needed but this to confirm and intensify the prejudice against me, first started by such misdeeds as coffee boiled in salt water, and duffs of such barbarous preparation as to be laid in silent indignation at the cabin door for the Captain's inspection. Misfortunes fell on me thick and fast. I tumbled down those cabin stairs overwhelmed in the ruins of wearily-prepared dinners. I left faucets running, drenching the store-room with molasses. I flung overboard spoon after spoon, hidden in the cloudy water of the washtub. When "cutting in" whales, the decks were filled with blubber, and I cooked in a sea of grease. Worse, the try-pots fed by blubber scraps sent forth day and night an unceasing shower of sooty flakes, which covered and permeated everything. A greasy, dismal and blackened cook performed greasy, dismal, and black cookery. Even my bread was cloudy with atomic particles of the leviathan resolved by heat into lamp black. There were mutterings heard among the crew as to "what sent that quill-driver to sea to spoil grub for poor sailors." Once it was intimated to me that I had better resign. I would not. I was resolved to weather the tempest. I did. My bread improved. The mutterings diminished. I shipped pies surreptitiously into the forecastle. They covered a multitude of culinary sins. I bribed the stomach of the entire crew, and before the voyage was up I became a favorite.

A solitary eight months' prospecting tour on the head waters of the Tuolumne and Walker rivers graduated me as a mountain cook. In doors, we are ever increasing the number of culinary conveniences. Out of doors, culinary science lies in diminishing them. A green willow stick is far better than a frying pan. Transfixed thereon, and held for a few moments over a bed of live coals, your steak acquires a flavor not to be lured inside of any kitchen. It incorporates in itself the freshness of the mountain air, and the sublimated essence of wild green leaves. It is not deadened by the myriad stenches of the town. Locating mountain kitchens is an art. They must be where wood and water are in sight, and the soil free from dampness. Not under dead trees, or dead limbs, which have a strange propensity to fall in the calmest weather. Not in the midst of dry dead grass, which enkindled from your fire will burn you out of your migratory house and home. Devoid of wood ants, so prompt in five minutes after you are seated to institute exploring expeditions up your pantaloons. Your provisions and apparatus is carried in a series of bags. These, after picketing your horses, you arrange in a certain regular order on the windward side of the fire. Of the saddle and blankets is made a sort of couch. The fire burns five minutes. This brings the blaze into solidity; then on goes your coffee pot; *ad interim* you arrange on the cloth your plate, knife, fork, bread, sugar, and butter cans, cut your willow stick, and sharpen it; the water boiling, you pour in the "making" of coffee, and set it where it may only simmer; the fire is raked open, coals are disclosed, over these your steak is suspended, the stick being at one end set in the ground and the heat graduated by bending to or from the fire, two minutes and it is done; a dash of cold water settles the coffee. "Supper's ready." Time, twelve minutes.

And these were royal suppers and breakfasts, partaken high upon on mountain sides, in little depressions, offering a bush for shelter, with a cool spring, and for the eye a grand drop curtain, covered with a confusion of mountains, valleys, lakes, plateaus, and snow-clad summits, each day changing the picture, and each hour painting its own tints and shades. True, there was regret that no sympathizing soul was by to enjoy with me the spectacle; still in loneliness there was compensation that, the meal past, I could linger long over the scene unmolested. No fussy cook was at hand to disturb the sacredness of such grand and quiet hours with vexatious hunts after dish-rags. And while in the morning those great preparations went on, a saucy sneak of a coyote has often for me mingled a dash of comedy in the sublimity of the spectacle, by the inquisitive look with which at one moment he regarded me, as seated on a crag near by, he seemed to wonder what should tempt a man into his domain, and the next yelped impatiently for my departure, intent only on the remnants of food left by the amateur cook.

Prentice Mulford *(1834-1891) first wrote for publication under the name "Dogberry" for* The Union Democrat *in Tuolumne County, California. For three years he mined, prospected, taught school, ran for office, lectured and "organized gigantic mining enterprises." He had no ambition to become a writer. His highest aspiration was to own a gold claim paying four dollars a day. But as his aspirations increased, his gold claim earnings diminished. In the fall of 1866 Mulford claims, "All my worldly goods were an old gun, a saddle, a pair of blankets, an enfeebled suit of clothes and a trunk, with abundant room for many things not in it."*

It was then that he received a letter from Joseph Lawrence offering him a job at The Golden Era, *one of the leading literary papers of San Francisco. At the* Era *he frequently met Bret Harte, Mark Twain, Charles Warren Stoddard, Artemus Ward and Adah Menken. He remained at the* Era *for about a year then sustained himself on a meager income writing for various newspapers and magazines, including the new* San Francisco Chronicle, *founded by Charles DeYoung. Mulford used to relate the story that, "De Young was always predicting that he would start a great morning paper. Almost everyone laughed at the idea. But one morning he did it. Then they stopped laughing."*

In 1872 he got the idea of going to Europe, "to advance by writing and talking the good and glory of California." For this purpose he raised five hundred dollars from local businesses. While there, he reported on the Vienna World's Fair for the San Francisco Bulletin. *Mulford returned to America in 1873 with nine dollars in his pocket and a new wife. For a time he lectured and supported himself with freelance work. His marriage failed and in the middle 70's he went to work for the* New York Graphic *as "head boiler down and condensor of news." He left the* Graphic *because he said he "was sick and tired of chronicling in short meter day after day the eternal round of murders, scandals, burglaries, fires, accidents, and other events which people seem to want to know. I became so thoroughly saturated with the horrors consequent on civilization that I wanted to go for a dose of arsenic, a razor, a pistol, or Paris Green myself. I retired on a very small fortune and built a ramshackle shanty in a New Jersey wilderness seventeen miles from New York. It cost forty dollars and was not an elegant piece of architecture."*

While in the New Jersey wilderness, Mulford began to write his philosophical essays known as the White Cross Library. *The first of the series was put out in May of 1886 and was published once a month in pam-*

phlet form. In his philosophy he maintained that a person's thoughts were the controlling factors in health and success. He also believed in reincarnation as leading to perfection of the spirit. The quality of his thought brought a tribute from Whittier who spoke of him as "a sage and seer." Prentiss Mulford was found dead in the bottom of his small boat on Long Island Sound in 1891.

Knapsack and Blanket

by Prentice Mulford
October 1869

One day, while passing along Battery Street, I saw, within one of those rough curiosity shops known as junk-stores, a quantity of old Army knapsacks. I entered, ascertained the price, became appalled at their cheapness — being twenty-five cents apiece — left a quarter, and emerged with one, the back of which, in white letters, informed me that it had formerly been borne by an armed man in Co. B, Sixth Infantry, C.V.

A knapsack, when first you inspect it, appears to be a hopeless tangle of straps, bag, and buckles. It is not to be put on properly without study and patience. I was three days learning the mystery of its proper adjustment. I had planned a tour on foot to my old home in the Southern Mines. The knapsack was filled with clothing and provisions; on its top was snugly buckled a heavy pair of blankets; yet, everything being in readiness for the start, I discovered, on a preparatory trial, that I could not get the thing on properly. It hung too far forward; it hung too far backward; it hung sideways. Straps, meant apparently to buckle somewhere, flapped about in dismal idleness, seeming to say, that when their place was found for them, they were ready to do their duty; but a masterly inaction was all to be expected at present. I perspired and lost patience over what seemed to me this diabolical military invention. I threw it on the floor, sat on a chair, and gazed upon it in a despairing study. At last, by accident, I mastered it. Do you know the exultant sensation which came over you when first you were able to swim four consecutive strokes, or skate as many yards? I felt thus glorified. It was too great an achievement to go unmentioned. Coggins was in his room. I visited him, commenced a conversation on traveling, drew it along to travel on foot — thence it flowed naturally to knapsacks. I divulged the possession of such an article. I expatiated on its carrying qualities for the foot traveler, and on the ingenious arrangement of straps, belts, and buckles, by which a weight of thirty or forty pounds was equally distributed on the shoulders and spinal column. Secretly exulting in my newly acquired skill, and eagerly desiring to display it somewhere, I invited Coggins to my room, that he might behold a practical exemplification of the beauties and uses of knapsacks.

And when all this was accomplished I had forgotten the knack, and the thing proved as contrary as at first. I put it on a dozen times in every way but the right one; and worse than all, Coggins, who was to be the admiring witness of my skill in buckling on a knapsack, took me in hand and showed me my art, so recently found and lost.

The Stockton boat, as I went on board, was fretting, fuming, smoking, and churning the muddy waters, with that mixture of fuss, impatience, and importance assumed by all steamboats half an hour before starting. It was a period of very low fares. Already the steamer was crowded, and every berth taken. Every available space on the lower deck was piled with boxes, barrels, bundles of long-handled shovels, bundles of pick-handles, and agricultural implements, for they had not yet finished torturing the earth's surface in the interior. The cracks and crannies of this collection were filled with Chinamen, with more bundles, shovels, mats, boxes, and their round, shallow, funnel-shaped hats. They had spread their blankets even in the few inches of space between the top of this pile of freight and the upper flooring. They were dimly seen in cracks far away in its interior. There was a cheerful circle perched on a crate of hardware; another couple had concentrated persons, mats, and opium-pipes on two flour-barrel heads, and very happy and contented they were withal. Down the gangway rattled and crashed the trucks, rushing on board more bales, barrels, and boxes, the deck-hands aiming carefully, with the view of running over every man who stood within a foot of their course. This is the only amusement these poor, hard-worked fellows have. At last — bearing on his face and person the marks of the "Barbary Coast," bad liquor, an empty pocket, and a prolonged spree — a drunken miner was trundled on board, and deposited with steamboat haste and unceremoniousness in a chaos of household furniture. Then came the slowly widening chasm between the boat and the pier; the final starings, farewells, shoutings, and handkerchief-wavings between those departing and the loungers on Broadway Wharf; and the *Julia* betook herself, steadily and resolutely, to her night's work. The pulsations of the engines became less labored and more regular; past long, clean clipper-ships at anchor we glided, gathering speed at each revolution. We gaze down upon the trim and orderly decks of a man-of-war; we note the flashing of the sentinel's bayonet, the gold bands of the officers' caps, the heads of neat and clean man-of-war's men thrust over bulwark and through port-holes; and then the city recedes and grows indistinct in its own afternoon cloud of dust and smoke. The barkeeper clears his deck for action. About him, as a common center, gather well dressed men, leaving their wives and families in the cabin, and broken down deck-passengers proffer their last quarters for a few more swallows of that damaging and deceitful comforter, whisky. For we must drink when we travel. "More steam," tinkles that little bell, rung from the pilot-house. "More steam!" We take the hint, grope our way to the lower deck, and along dark, freight-laden passages, pitch the inflammable compound into our already corroded stomachs, and our quarters into the prospering barkeeper's drawer. There seems to be no such thing as natural repose for the American soul. We pace the deck forward and aft with impatient steps. Below is heard the fierce hiss and tremendous sigh of steam rushing with explosive and terrific power through the hidden arteries of iron. Boiler, bolts, bars, cranks, and wheels are worked to their utmost tension in forcing the steamer's hull through the waters. Our paddles tap mockingly, and laugh at the resistance of the billows, as they come fresh from the Golden Gate. Yet it is not half fast enough. We are impatient that the Red Rock is so long being approached; when passed, we wish it would sooner fade in the distance.

Space for one's person now commences to grow less in the upper cabin. The waiters, in some mysterious manner, suddenly evoke a long dinner table, stretching from end to end of the apartment. Those having staterooms flee to them for shelter. Unfortunate people having none are, by degrees, dispossessed of their chairs. The important black waiters commence a system of rushing, jostling, toe-treading, and momentarily threaten personal collision, until the unfortunates lingering in the cabin are fought out, conquered, subdued, and finally driven into a narrow reservation on the forward deck. There are no seats. They stand awaiting the sound of the dinner-bell. The black men, thoroughly masters of the situation, occupy much time in arranging the table. The tantalizing smell of the viands lingers in the nostrils of the chairless beings occupying the reservation forward, and arouses them to a hungry and impatient fury. In secret, the lordly black man rejoices at this collective stomachic misery. I believe it is his daily bread. But his countenance betrays no expression of joy or exultation. All over it is written the all-absorbing, all-important business of dinner-getting. At last the bell rings. We rush; we bolt our nutriment hot and solid. The agony is over.

Two or three hours having elapsed—the rulers of the situation having leisurely supped—we may, at last, again sit. We watch and eagerly occupy vacated chairs. Benicia, with its little fuss of stoppage, loungers, and hacks, is passed. In the gathering darkness, the great bulk of the Sacramento boat, gleaming with fires below, with lights above, and, still higher, red and green signal lanterns—bearing its hundreds from the Northern Mines, or fresh by railway from the East—swells grandly by. The night wears on. The San Joaquin is entered. The air grows warmer. The hum of the mosquito—the lively resident of this vast marsh of *tule*—is heard. The cabin grows more and more quiet. That poker game at yonder table—a decaying relic of former and flusher days, with its attendant orders, per waiter from the bar, for drinks—at last ceases. At first, we sleep in our hard-won chairs, with head reclining on the table. Our foot, our leg, our arm, enters into a condition of prickly numbness. A few reckless spirits slide prone upon the floor. We despise, at first, such conduct. Then we gaze upon them enviously. Upon our ears fall their tantalizing snores. We become at once sleepily reckless and resolute, pull off coat and boots, arrange them *á la* pillow, and go under the table. So does everybody. The thick, sultry atmosphere of the cabin trembles with snores — snores gruff, snores abrupt, snores shrill, snores piping, snores apoplectic, snores asthmatic. By and by commence the stoppages, the bell ringings, the gong soundings, the engine signals, consequent on the doublings, and turnings, and twistings of the boat in the now crooked and narrow channel of the San Joaquin. We hear the brush of the *tules* on the guards. We can feel the muffled concussions of the hull against the low, muddy bank. And, at last, all of this ceases; we stop; the droning of steam through the escape-pipe is heard, and the boat is tied up at the "Head of the Slough."

Mounting my pack, I stole from Stockton in the edge of the evening. A few promenaders regarded me with surprise; and more than once after I had passed, I overheard the remark: "Looks like '49." Previously, a few acquaintances — their incredulity as to my intention of making the trip "across the plains" being overcome — suspected me of slight tendencies to insanity. It is almost a sin, in these days, for a man to walk when he can ride; and, not only to walk, but to pack "grub and blankets" on a traveled route, is a combination of sin, disgrace, and shame. This idea so extensively prevails that but comparatively few are equal to the exertion of a day's moderate travel. The national leg is weak and shrunken, for lack of training.

I slept in a stubble-field the first night. The next, I secured a fresh haycock. Meals on the first day were cold. There was no fuel. On the second, I picked up on the wagon-track enough bits of board to boil my coffee. I expected heat, dust, perspiration, misery, aching limbs, and lame back, until I should be "broken in." All this, and even more, were realized. I sat down to rest under every convenient bush or tree, and when they gave out, I gnashed my teeth in the summer glare of a California sun. I lost the road — took that leading to Mariposa, when I should have gone toward Sonora — and when corrected, blundered across the Sonora route into that leading to Copperopolis. A rancher, at whose house I stopped to fill my canteen, asked me if "the small-pox was worse in San Francisco." He saw a victim fleeing from pestilence.

The main trouble lay in that my hours of traveling and domestic economy were not properly regulated. Four hours' walking in the early morning with a rest in the middle of the day, and three or four hours when the afternoon sun has a very decided declination, is far better for bodily ease and benefit, than a ceaseless all-day plodding, with strength and endurance strained to their utmost. Then I had at first no system in managing my traveling kitchen. I did not, in cooking a meal, take out my bags of coffee, sugar, bread, salt, pepper, and meat, and arrange them in a row near the fire, so as readily to find each. I did not, before kindling a fire, see that water and fuel were on hand in sufficient quantities to last, without further trouble as to their provision. No, a blaze was started with a few twigs; then I would travel several hundred yards to fill the camp kettle with water; find the fire quite burnt out on my return; rekindle it, set thereon the coffee-pot;

hunt about for more fuel; return, warned by a fizz and cloud of steam, smoke and ashes; find the coffee-pot upset: hence, swearing; internal and external, general and extreme irritation, which, just before a meal, is conducive to very imperfect action of the digestive organs. And when I sat down to my coffee and broiled meat, there was no arrangement of blanket to sit down upon. Food swallowed in an uncomfortable position loses half its savor. That effect, and the meal commenced, bread was wanting. Rummage the knapsack. No sugar in the coffee. Another interruption, and rummaging of knapsack. A little salt. Another rummaging. All these interruptions interfere greatly with the comfort of eating. Besides, my larder for such a trip had been too extensively planned. I had erred in imagining that the pleasure of appetite in this out-of-door life depended so much on a variety of viands. I would have broiled steak, bread and butter, stewed apple, and canned tomato, at the same meal. But the weight — the dreadful weight — of all this, was grievous to be borne, with the thermometer at ninety-five degrees, no shade, water of disgusting warmness, and legs comparatively unused to exercise. The trouble of cooking robbed the eating of all its pleasure. Better is a cup of coffee and a crust of bread by a little fire on the plains, than turkey and cranberry sauce, if that turkey and cranberry sauce must be prepared when every step costs a grunt, and the backbone, bent over the smoky evening camp-fire, feels as if a ramrod was run through it.

Everybody in "'49," on their way to the Southern Mines, packed their blankets at least once across the plains. And nearly everyone having such experience remembers it with a savage growl for its apparently interminable length, its heat, and those warm, muddy drinks of water found only at long intervals in the deeper depressions of the sloughs. Yet I like these plains. I like them for their ever blowing breeze — the same raw sea-breeze of San Francisco, warmed and softened by its passage over the country. I love them as surveyed in the gray of the morning from the summit of the higher rolls, as billow after billow of land, yellowed by the summer's sun, stretches north and south, far as one may see, walled on the east by the Coast Range, while there shoots up in the west, a hundred miles away, those sharp, white triangles — the snow-clad summit peaks of the Sierras. I love them at evening, when the sun — his long day's work nearly completed — descends into that line of haze bordering the western horizon, and exchanges his noonday suit of dazzling, scorching brilliancy for an evening dress of yellow, unburnished gold, while your shadow stalks along after you in grotesque and unearthly length; and that bullet-headed, burrowing owl, from his hillock by the road-side, stupidly gazes and blinks at you with his great eyes, his head turning as on a pivot as you pass, until, giving a weird screech, he tips over into his hole along with his companions, the ground-squirrel and rattlesnake.

So, passing from plain to gently inclining, wooded hills, from them to steeper ascents, clothed with the dark-green *chaparral*, I came at last to the mountains bordering the Tuolumne. I pitched my camp one evening, over-looking Hawkins' Bar and a long stretch of the river below.

In "'49," Hawkins' Bar was "a place." It was a sort of central dépôt for the Southern Mines. Hither, first came the newly arrived immigrant from the Eastern States. He found at Hawkins' Bar rich diggings, but he found them all taken up. From the top of this hill, catching his first view of the Tuolumne, he beheld its banks lined with men, shaking cradles, turning over big boulders, and toiling with pick, pan and shovel. The united crash of pebbles on hundreds of quickly agitated rocker sieves, sounded in his ear like the roar of a cotton factory. Far below, was the straggling, irregular camp of tents, and canvas, log, and brush houses. Among them, like ants, crept the black dots of men. Blanket-bearing travelers were continually coming — hopeful, expectant, and wondering, like himself, or wearily toil-ing up the hill, either going back to Stockton, or off in search of new dig-gings. For there were discouragements, and curses, and revilings of the country, then. Long files of pack-mules were coming in, laden with flour, pork, shovels, and whisky. Up and down the river, as far as he could see, were still men and their roughly built log, brush, and canvas houses. Or, a few years later — mining being then conducted in a more extensive and systematic manner — he might have seen the river's rocky bed laid bare on riffle, bar, and cañon. Water-wheels were revolving and flashing in the morning sun, while through long lines of clean, white pine fluming flowed the reduce volume of the Tuolumne. There was the clank of machinery working by day and night the never tiring pumps; men were rolling up in barrows from those deep, wet holes the rich gray gravel snatched from the grasp of the river — its volume reduced and power weakened by the torrid heats of August. And when he went down into "camp," he found men bear-ing home from work their pans, the bottoms covered with golden scales — their rich, heavy, yellow metal standing out in strong and tantaliz-ing relief against the bright tin bottoms. Within walls of illuminated canvas, shining out in the darkness of the night like blotches of smothered fire, there was rough and disgusting revelry, and gambling by wild and senseless miners, and gambling by cool, careful, and desperate vultures, graduates of the boats ploughing the broad and muddy Mississippi. There were a few gayly, lightly dressed women; and oaths, laughter, drunkenness, and little holes through the canvas made by flying pistol bullets, and shots and bullets already flying; and a crowd without the door of the tent, bending over, jostling each other, and almost trampling on a prostrate, speechless body, whose white shirt-bosom was splashed and soaked with something black, which a sudden glare of light shows to be warm, flowing blood.

The river still flowed on and fretted over rock and riffle. The everlasting hills — their dark-green sides of *chaparral* wrought almost to blackness in their evening shadow — looked down upon it as they have looked for cen-turies. But men, tents, labor, revelry, and murder; the arriving and depart-ing travelers and the strings of mules; the long array of wheels, pumps, and flumes winding with the river's course—all have gone. Through the still, soft evening air, laden with the balsamic odor of dried herbage, comes no sound save the eternal roar of the river, as it was heard ere men vexed and tortured its channel.

Two unoccupied, rotting cabins are all that remain of the once famous Bar; there are trenches, furrows, deep pits, and tunnel mouths in the face of the red banks; raceways cut in the solid ledge, now forever useless; great piles of dirt and boulders, already overgrown with weeds and bushes; around are seen the rough stone, mud-plastered chimneys of former cabins; the gaping fire-place, black with the smoke of its last back-log; the home-made wire pot-hooks still hanging. Among the tall, rank weeds you kick up the old tin-pots, old shoes, pieces of earthenware, and other *débris* of civilization; you stumble over long disused home-made chairs and benches, broken cots, fallen shelves, and shattered tables. The gold has been quite all dug out, melted, coined, spent and re-spent; the diggers long since went away; they are either home, "up north" at Cariboo, "down south" in Arizona, or in the recesses of the Rocky Mountains; they are dead, diseased, dissipated. A few have permanently remained. They lie on the hillside yonder.

On Hawkins' Bar hill that night I crept into my blankets, and in a very few minutes crept rapidly out again. In the interior of California, the sluggard has not to go to the ant; the ant comes to the sluggard. I had camped near the residence of a colony of these industrious and overpraised insects. An exploring party had entered my blankets, and when I would compose my limbs to rest, they explored me—crawled over me, and bit my body.

The ant is one of the nuisances of the interior. They live in holes, the full depth of which no man has ever probed. People imprudently building their houses near these holes, suffer an incessant invasion of ants. Vainly, do they pour down hot water and scald them by myriads. Vainly, do they seek to dig them up. Ants ever come. There may be a partial stoppage, but more ants seem evolved from the bowels of the earth. Day after day, they march on and in your house; death has no terrors for them, and despairing housekeepers lost at last all faith in the efficacy of their destruction.

I was obliged to move camp after dark, and trust to chance for finding a location free from ants. I bore away a colony in my blankets and clothes. They were gradually killed off during the night, while groping dismally about various portions of my person. After being killed, they pass about half an hour in sending forth a strong and disagreeable smell. Then the ant's mission seems accomplished.

Occasionally, a spiteful scorpion will, half a dozen times during a second, stab you with what seems a red-hot barb, and cause you to emerge from your blankets faster than the ant. Fortunately, they are not so plentiful. The yellow-jacket stings at dinner, while disputing with you the possession of your steak. He stings as well as the wasp. Mosquitoes swarm just after sundown. Fleas become chronic traveling companions. These are the little crosses of a life under the sun and stars.

I traveled down the river toward a certain Bar, where I expected to find some of the "boys." All along were marks of decay, desolation, and loneliness. In many places, the trail had been washed away by the great freshet of " '61." Faint foot-marks only were visible on the rough, jagged surface of the bare ledge. It was, also, thickly overgrown; and I forced my passage through the heavy, fragrant white clusters of the buckeye blossom. Where once stood Swett's Bar — a lively camp of the flush times — was a great bank of fine, white sand, and on this an enormous heap of drift-wood. Not a house, not a chimney, not a vestige of man's occupancy in former days, was visible. Well had the Tuolumne, calling to its aid the mountain snows, performed its work of obliteration. But for a few scars on the red hill-sides, from whence dirt had been taken to fill in dams, fast growing over with weeds, the landscape seemed as when the first excited gold-seeker viewed it from the top of yonder hill.

I found the few remaining "boys" at Indian Bar. These "boys" came out in " '49," and, for the most part, have been resident on this very Bar ever since. Some had, for a season, left for Cariboo, Washoe, or the scene of some new mining excitement; yet, invariably did they return to the old spot. True, it was quite worked out; but they liked it for the good old wicked, free-and-easy, flush times' sake. It was free, too, from the harsh, changeable climate of Nevada, or the excessive cold of Cariboo. Its mining history was rich in gold and vicissitude. In early years, the "Point" had been worked, and paid well. At last it was worked away back into the mountain, and worked out, leaving only on the bare ledge great heaps of cobble-stones. Back, a hundred feet in height, rose a bank of unprofitable red dirt. The "Point" miners left, after selling the remains of their claim to Chinamen; yet they left the richest of that claim behind them. Finally, the "Point" diggings became unprofitable, even to the Chinamen. Indian Bar went down. Years after, some of the "boys" were working on the bank for "grub and whisky." Thirty feet above the level of the Tuolumne, they found a thin streak of river-washed gravel, prospecting a few cents to the pan. Following it in farther, it prospected a "bit;" then two, three, and four "bits;" then as many dollars — "ledge blue and pitching backward." The astounding truth was revealed: it was a back channel of some distant era, rich in gold! Indian Bar came up. Once more the "boys" realized " '49." They were rich. Old Jones sold out for eight thousand dollars — went home — in six months came back "broke," and went once more to work with his cradle, "rocking" a dollar per day from the tailings of his former rich claim, now realizing for its proprietor thousands weekly. "Scotty," another proprietor, went mad with *delirium tremens,* and, with the devils after him, ran, a madman, over the *chaparral* hills, pursued, like a wild beast, by horsemen, until he dropped dead. The remainder freed themselves from their money as fast as it came out, without killing themselves. The back channel finally came into possession of sober, hard-working men, who worked it out. All of it now left is a great gap in the foot of the mountain, and a vast deposit of cobble-stones. Again, Indian Bar went down. A few of the "boys" only were left, delving in a few overlooked spots for "grub and whisky."

Then came the copper excitement. Some Chinamen, working hard by, found in the ledge a deposit of glistening, yellow ore. They brought it to the storekeeper: "Was it gold, John?" A wandering copper prospector came along one evening. He saw the lumps of pure sulphuret. He said no word to anyone; ascertained from whence it was taken; and shortly the whole country blazed with the elaborate notices of the "San Francisco," "North Star," "Old Dominion," "Young America," "Stars and Stripes" Copper Companies, claiming "this ground, with all its dips, spurs, angles, side and cross veins." The "boys" woke up to find the very ledges under their cabins teeming with copper ore — and claimed. They awoke the "day after the fair," and posted a few notices, claiming copper veins on the more remote hill-sides. What next? Agents came from "below" in business suits and white linen, horses and buggies; scientific men, who talked oxydes, carbonates, gangue, rock, sulphates, and phosphates; superintendents, plucked direct from behind counters and counting-rooms, who knew more about mining than the oldest man in the mines. Towns were laid out, ferry privileges claimed, drifts were run, shafts were sunk. Blasts boomed along the solemn hills, drill and hammer tinkled, men fell down shafts and were blown up again. Everybody was rich — in prospective. To-day the tunnels and shafts still remain, but the windlasses are rotting, the dirt-buckets falling to pieces, the towns unbuilt, the air unvexed by explosions; the maimed, powder-blackened, blown-up men are resting on the seared, yellow hill-side; and the "second Copperopolis" is extinct. Indian Bar went down. It has never come up again. The "boys" still remain.

Some of these boys were now gray and grizzled. In their cabins I found the inevitable sack of flour, of potatoes, the hanging piece of pork, the little, rough table with its scanty array of crockery, the blanket spread out, the India-rubber and leather boots, the canvas and mud-stained mining clothes, the cracked and battered stove, the walls plastered with prints from pictorials, whereon, year after year, Federals and Confederates stand in unchanging hostile attitude — loading, firing, and charging, while heroic Generals still command — veiled in a sort of dirty obscurity, the accumulation of years of smoke, dust, and flies. Outside, we have the rheumatic dog, doubly dear to the "boys" by reason of the memory of his former master, long ago drowned on yonder foaming riffle; a few bold and intrusive hens, constantly making forays, inside the cabin, after the table crumbs; and, perhaps, the little garden enclosure of old sluice-lumber, growing potatoes, onions, and radishes.

The boys still hung their hopes on some rich and unworked spot in the river-bed. Year before last they "got in," but the river rose just as they had taken out enough to pay expenses. Last year they had barely "got in" ere the river came down, and they took out — nothing. This year they will "play for a home stake." "No whisky or poker games this season, sir."

So, in the long twilight — the supper cooked and eaten — did the boys talk over their pipes and tobacco. Then, after the inevitable fashion, they recited the golden glories of "'49:" Down there, by that jutting mass of rocks, Sam Holden took out his pound per day. Had a barrel of brandy always on tap in his tent. Pete Wilkins was found murdered in his cabin in yonder gulch. He was known to have buried a pickle jarful of dust somewhere on the hill-side yonder, a few days before. And, how we did make money, and gamble, and drink, and shoot, then!

That was twenty years ago. Twenty years! And these men talk of going home, East, just as they talked five years ago; yes, and ten years ago. They hardly realize that for them, in their long-forsaken native towns and villages in the States, there is no home; that faces, to their mental vision, fresh and blooming, are seamed and wrinkled as their own; that in their birth-places they would be as strangers in a strange land.

Here is their real home. Here, where the dashing river sings the same evening lullaby as it sang ere robbed of its treasure: here, where the air is so soft and balmy; where the rude changes of the Northern clime are unknown; where, with the least caress, the generous earth pours forth vegetables, fruit, milk, and wine in profusion; where, still, metallic treasure lies locked in the hills, to be revealed by time and accident. This is their home; but they know it not.

The California Gray

by Prentice Mulford

July 1869

In August, 1854, the schooner *Henry*, two hundred tons burden, ten Sandwich Islanders, one great negro forward, and a captain, two mates, one cooper, one cook, and one passenger aft—sailed out of the Golden Gate bound on a "pick up" voyage along the coast of Lower California. We went forth to "pick up" whales, seals, aulones, (*Haliotis*, a shell-fish in great repute among the Chinese) and anything else which might come in our way. Just abaft the foremast was a sort of brick altar, in which were set two immense try-pots; still further aft came a collection of spars, booms, cordage, and barrels. Two whale-boats hung by the davits over the quarter, a yawl at the stern, and the entire deck was crowded with all manner of articles, lashed and stowed away, whose names are discouragingly maritime.

At the end of a week the *Henry* sailed through a low cleft of rocks and anchored in a mill-pond of a bay nearly surrounded by bare, treeless, shrubless, clinky-looking volcanic crags, with here and there a stalk of the uncomfortable, prickly giant cactus, standing out like an immovable sentinel in relief against the sky. On the rocky reef separating this miniature bay from the ocean, the Pacific incessantly beat, pounded and thundered, wasting its strength in the endeavor to pulverize the low barrier, sending sheets of spray quite to the opposite side of the beach and through the narrow entrance, pulsating great, silent throbs of waves, which fell with a subdued and muffled crash on the shore of St. Bartholomew's, or, as the whalemen would call it, "Turkle Bay." Here the *Henry* stayed two months. At five in the morning all, save one man, manned the boats and left the vessel. They were absent all day, and the solitary being left on board read, cooked, smoked, washed dishes, sang, wondered what might be going on in the world he had left behind, and threw billets of wood, belaying-pins and table-cloths at the voracious gulls, who were continually pirating about the quarters of turtle meat, hung up in the rigging, and with amazing impudence at times descending into the cabin to investigate the breakfast-table crumbs. All this while the remainder of the crew were drenched with spray, clinging to surf-washed rocks, and awaiting the opportunity given them by the retiring surges to pry off with iron chisels the snails of shell-fish, whose outside shell, with its variegated interior of pearly color, so often ornaments your parlors.

With these the boats at night, laden to the water's edge, returned. Next day, they were taken on shore, the fish cut from the shell, freed from a string of entrails, plunged for a couple of hours into a try-pot of boiling water, then taken out and spread on boards to dry in the sun; all this being performed under the eye and direction of Mr. Sam Wee, a literary Chinaman, who, during the entire passage down, laid in his berth reading bundles of his native hieroglyphics, and who was brought to this remote spot to teach us how to prepare aulones for the Chinese stomach.

Along this coast, some near, some afar off, are sundry lone, uninhabited islands. No man has ever dwelt permanently on them. Some are mountainous and well-wooded. Such a one was Cerros, whose cedar-clad peaks were seen one morning hanging high in the air above the *Henry*, their bases concealed by a dense fogs. Its shore was the resort of the great seal-elephant for which we were then cruising. The aulone gathering was varied by short excursions for this purpose. A boat was lowered and at about noon returned without seal, but bringing two melancholy, ragged, strange white men. Two months before the vessel of which they were part owners had left them on the island to hunt seal. It then sailed away, ostensibly to cruise for a similar purpose about the coast and other islands, but never returned. The couple left on Cerros began at last to look anxiously for her, and finally to wonder why she did not come back. Just before we took them off they had reached their last biscuit and were living entirely on shell-fish, turtle, and venison. There are deer and rattlesnakes on Cerros. How they came there is a mystery. The island is full forty miles from the mainland. The hermit sealers were glad to join our crew. There ought, they said, to be of seal oil nineteen barrels stored in a cave on the island of Natividad. Thither we sailed and found a low, bare rock, white with bird lime, and covered with solemn pelicans, but no oil. The rascally partners of the Cerros hermits, as was afterwards ascertained, had carried it off, steered for a South American port, sold vessel and cargo, divided the gains, and then, if they possessed consciences, been ever after tormented with the recollections of their two companions willfully abandoned on lone Cerros.

Then we headed for Guadalupe, a large and still more lonely island, two hundred miles from the mainland. Three days' sail and we sighted what seemed a bare, brown ridge of mountains, forty miles in length, rising from the ocean. Off the headland around which we sailed at dusk perpendicular columns of granite shot straight out of the waves, a thousand feet in height. Their summits seemed level plateaus, covered with some kind of vegetation. The sea-birds' nests are still safe there. No man will ever tread those level tops, some of them acres in extent, until ballooning is made practically useful. Thousands of the smaller seal about their bases were enjoying the effect of a general bellowing previous to retiring for the night. This combined with the dashing and thundering of the waves among the worn and hollowed rock, the cries of thousands of gulls, shags, and pelicans, coming home to roost, the wind whistling through the rigging, and the horizon in the fading evening light gathering its vapory and indistinct boundaries closer and closer around us, had an effect so strange as to silence even the tongues of our eternally-talking Sandwich Islanders. Next morning a boat's crew was sent to ascertain if any elephant-seal had "hauled up" on the beach. These animals during certain winter months drag their huge gray bodies out of the ocean, slowly and laboriously up the sandy beach. The experienced eye of the seal hunter may discern them in this situation miles away. A boat is sent on shore. Perhaps four or five of these creatures are thus found. They are helpless. The party armed with long sharp lances approach. The seals awkwardly dig in the yielding sand with their flippers, but a snail rivals their pace back to their element. The hunters approach still nearer. The seal gnashes his great tusks at them in helpless rage and fear. They tap him lightly on the head with the lance-point. He throws it angrily back. This motion uncovers his breast, and instantly the sharp edge is driven deep into his heart. But without the premonitory tap he seizes the iron lance in those powerful jaws and bends and twists it as though it were a holiday tin sword.

Two weeks later, the *Henry* might have been lying nearly high and dry almost on her beam-ends in a very narrow and tortuous channel of salt water, a couple of feet in depth and running through a vast flat of light sand, left bare by the tide for miles. A jump from the bulwarks and you were on dry land. On one side, a mile away, was seen a fringe of green bushes; on the other a range of low sand-hills, behind which the surf could be heard tumbling and roaring. This was Margarita Bay lagoon at low tide. At high water it was covered seven feet in depth. The *Henry* resumed her proper position, and commenced moving, towed by the united force of two whaleboat's crews, first toward a stake to the right, then toward one to the left, and then in the direction of one still further in the rear. These poles indicated the course of the channel, staked out at low water. It was very, very crooked. It turned and doubled on itself so often that the irreverent sailors intimated that the laying out of that channel was one of Nature's jobs performed in the dark. Some days we gained a position but a few hundred yards ahead of that left when the water was of sufficient depth to float the *Henry* and then once more we grounded, the schooner leaned over more and more, and in and out of his galley, inclined over forty-five degrees, the wretched cook carried on a series of nearly over-turned culinary operations, while the laboriously-inclined steward crept and slid and clambered along the steep and slippery deck, moving with two legs and one arm, bearing with the other to the cabin vessels of salt beef and coffee, which were deposited in convenient corners to leeward, and their contents partaken of by uncomfortably inclined men, sitting or lying at an angle of forty-five degrees.

Margarita Bay, about two hundred miles north of Cape St. Lucas, consists of a series of narrow lagoons, opening by narrow passages into each other, extending parallel with the coast for many miles. At intervals openings appear in the beach, connecting them with the ocean. Through these during the winter come the cow whales of that species known to whalers as "Californy Gray," "Graybacks," or "Muscle Diggers," to avail themselves of the warm and quiet lagoon waters for breeding purposes.

Our mission was to kill and boil the skins of these great mothers for oil. After three weeks of towing and kedging we anchored in a small round lagoon, bordered on all sides by thickets of low, dense, green bushes, limbless as to their trunks and umbrella-shaped tops, birds among them singing and flitting about, while at intervals of a few minutes the round, smooth, glossy back of a California Gray would emerge from the surface, with an attendant puff of spray and a blow sounding like the rush of steam through the escape pipes of a high pressure engine; or, suddenly, a cable's length off, the immense black bulk would shoot half its length out of water and half back with a tremendous splash.

Here we set to work immediately. The crews tumbled into the boats and were soon in chase. Near as the Gray-backs came to the schooner, they were shy of the boats. They had been chased before and knew something of our deadly intentions. Two hours elapsed before we managed to creep up near one of the great fish. The oars were handled without noise; the men spoke not a word; they came within a few yards of the black mass; the suspense and half dread was akin to that experienced by the soldier in the hush before the battle. That immense creature, whose ribs rivalled in size and strength the timbers of our vessels, whose vertebra was a linked series of blocks of bone, through whose arteries at each beat of the giant heart pulsated great jets of blood, had but to turn lazily round to move those flukes, as you would crook your little finger, and our boat would be a crushed mass of wood as when, with your spoon, you playfully tap an empty egg shell. There was an upright figure in the bow, braced firmly back, poising above his head with both arms a heavy harpoon. The iron shaft is set in a heavy oaken pole, and the inexperienced arm cannot throw it as many feet as "Jake," our black boat-steerer, can send it yards. On his great bared black arms the muscles stood out under the skin like ropes of twisted wire. Suddenly it shot in a curved line from his grasp; point downward it buried itself to the wood, impelled by its own weight through the thick coating of blubber, deep in flesh, muscle, and cartilage. The rowers, their oars braced for the critical moment, sent the boat backward: for a moment the water foamed with the thrasing of flukes and fins, the whale blindly and madly struck out in every direction to crush the creature which had stung her. She disappeared under water, with a final angry flirt of the powerful flukes. Coil after coil of neatly laid line sprung from the tub in the boat's bottom; it ran smoking about an upright round block in the bow; the boat buried to the gunwales, flew through the water, the long oars were high in the air apeak, and the men sat in their seats, being now idle but interested spectators.

All action was now confined to the two upright figures at the boat and stern. The whale being "fast," they changed places; Black Jake stepped aft and handled the long steering oar, the other came forward and made ready the keen round-edged lance. The whale commenced gradually to slacken her speed; the boys slowly hauled in the line and coiled it away. Soon just ahead the smooth waters were seen simmering and full of little whirlpools; it was the commotion caused by the passage of the mighty mass underneath. There! the great head burst through the surface — there came a snort, a jet of water, and foam from her "blow-holes" — a great gulp of air for the laboring lungs, the light lance darted from the boat-header's hands. It pierced her side, but she was down again in an instant. There was a tinge of blood passing by the flying boat; the lance was pulled back by the attached light hempen line; the boat-header, his eye on the boiling surface, signalled to the steersman, by a wave of either arm, the proper direction. The light craft obeyed the slightest motion of the long steering oar. Again she came up for a breath; again the lance was buried in her side, and the jet from her blow-holes was reddened with blood — a sign of victory to us, of death to her. The iron had entered her lungs.

There was another party concerned in this murder. Alongside of the whale swam another fish of similar proportions, ten or twelve feet in length. It was the calf. For it, the mother was sacrificing herself. The young one was weak. She retarded her speed that it might keep up with her. And this gave us double the number of chances for sending the lance to her vitals. There was then a slackening of speed; the men looked anxiously around. These Gray-backs have at times gleams of sense and cunning; sometimes they cease at once their flight and grope about beneath the surface. Suddenly under the water there is felt a rub and a jar, and up come the submerged tons of flesh, bone, blubber, and wrath, and up from the black back flies boat, men, tubs, lines, lances, harpoons, and scattered amid the floating ruins are seen heads and hands clinging to oars, paddling feebly from the enraged thrashing monster and waving their caps for assistance.

But our first whale was taken without such disaster. The jets grew redder and redder; we hauled off at a respectful distance, warned by the signs indicated the coming of the "flurry," her death throes. There is something awful in the giving-up of life by these great animals. They rush about in great circles and tear through the water like a swiftly speeding steamer. They cease suddenly and belabor the waves; then the blind rush again commences; there are death shudderings and tremblings sensible even to those watching from the boats. Life leaves the great animal with a harder struggle than when the beetle dies.

We towed the upturned carcass to our vessel. But the poor calf still followed the dead mother. It was playing about the body in the morning, as like a huge bladder it swelled, rising buoyantly foot after foot out of the water, quite to the bulwarks, while the quickly generating gases arising from internal decomposition hissed and blubbered through the gashes cut by the lance in yesterday's struggle; and still after we had stripped from the carcass the blubber and turned it adrift to float up and down the lagoon, a festering mountain of rottenness, its back crowded with gorged gulls and cormorants, the poor, helpless, starving creature still swam by the dead mother's side. It was foul murder. The whale has all the instincts and affections of a mammal. It deposits no spawn and then swims heartlessly away. We would often from our decks watch these same Graybacks give suck to their young, and in unwieldly sport roll over and over with them in these warm and sheltered lagoon nurseries.

The carcass alongside, a great iron hook was fastened to that part nearest the head; the strongest "tackle and falls" we had on board clapped on the old-fashioned windlass; and amid its clink, clank, and a rough sea chorus from the dingy-looking sailors, great strips of blubber were slowly hoisted on board; the whale rolled slowly over and over; and his oily wealth was taken from him, something as one rolls the ribbon from its block. The try-work fires were kindled, at first with wood, afterward with the "scraps" bailed with great cullenders from the seething cauldrons. Black smoke enveloped the vessel by day; greasy flakes of soot covered the men, the rigging and sails, and penetrated hold, cabin, and forecastle. The uncomfortable cook murmured as he broke his newly-baked loaves, and found them tinged with the sooty shower. The steward vainly endeavored to hide his towels, so that they might not on his plates leave more blackness than they wiped off. By night, the masts and cordage stood out in a glare of light. And in this, the "gang" moved about like maritime witches — some feeding the fierce flame, some stirring up the seething oil, bailing it out into the "coppers," ladling in fresh blubber, and ladling out the dripping scraps; some chopped the long strips of blubber into oblong blocks called "horsepieces," then minced them fine with long, sharp knives. Slender tree-trunks, covered with small oysters, were held in the blaze until the shell-fish gaped open, and eaten with great relish. The tree of umbrella-shaped foliage bears oysters. The tide covers the limbless trunk at high water. Those who have seen mussels growing in a similar manner will not think the story surprising. We cut them down by day, and roasted them by night. So also, doughnuts were fried in the "coppers," filled with hot oil to cool. They were not flavored with lamp-oil. Whale-oil, newly tried out, is quite as tasteless and limpid as water.

In thirty-six hours after the whale was "cut in," chasing was resumed. There is no intermission of labor when the school is by. It is the whalemen's harvest time. He pulls an oar all day and stands his watch at the flaming try-works at night. But the work seems light. It is like taking out "big pay" from a placer claim. Every additional gallon of oil puts a few more pence in his pocket. He is on a "lay." It may be one barrel out of ten, or one out of two hundred.

We filled up in five weeks. They were five weeks of blazing fires, chasing, cutting in, hurry, toil, soot, grease, and excitement, with an occasional stoven boat, or a visit from the crews of the vessels whaling in adjacent lagoons. Our success was mainly due to the skill of Black Jake, in fastening to and killing the Graybacks. He was a Jamaica negro, a giant as to breadth of chest and strength of arm. He could throw the harpoon twice as far as any ordinary man, and drink three times as much rum. We had a poorer whaling outfit, and numerically, a weaker crew than any other vessel lying in Margarita Bay. Yet, coming in there last, we beat them all in taking fish, and sailed away before the rest, with nearly everything full of oil that would hold it. Black Jake's skill and prowess became noised abroad among the rest of the fleet. Cunning skippers came on board, ostensibly to "have a gam" with our own captain, in reality to delegate to some shrewd boat-steerer the office of descending the forecastle; and after the whaling compliments of the day had passed, and the pipes had smoked everything blue, and the rum, strangely smuggled on board, had warmed all hearts and revived the old-time recollections of "that season on the Nor'west," or when we were refitting at "Rio," or gallanting the dusky maids at Honolulu, or essaying the Portuguese tongue with the ladies at Fayal or the Western Islands, blubber-hunting diplomacy would be essayed, and tempting offers in a low tone would be proposed to Jake that he should leave the *Henry* and join another vessel. But the negro proved loyal. Indeed, he could not leave. He exercised a great moral supremacy over the ten Sandwich Islanders, constituting, besides himself, the sole inmates of the forecastle. He seemed their king. He spoke their language, and had sailed with the entire number on other voyages. They had shipped in a body on the *Henry*. He was the arbiter in their childish disputes, their adviser and interpreter. They regarded him as a great power. He was in his present position. He could have influenced them as he chose, and led them in a body to another vessel. But there, they would have been obliged to live with a white crew. They could not then uninterruptedly have sung their sad, monotonous native chants; nor, lying at night in their bunks, have, like idle children for amusement, made all manner of uncouth noises. All our Caucasian element was aft; Africa and Polynesia, forward. Jake was not ignorant of the prejudice among the whites against the negro. He was something of a philosopher. He knew it was the unaccountable trick the "nigger" had of killing Graybacks that was coveted — not himself. He might on another vessel be king, when within ten yards of the lazy giant rolling in the still waters he stood with uplifted weapon in the bow, his great arms and chest bare, his eye fiery and protruding, his gray, kinky hair uncovered, the dingy Scotch cap flung to the boat's bottom, in the excitement of the moment, with the faces of the rowers half turned toward him, waiting for the moment when, with a swaying back of his whole frame, he concentrated the strength of chest, arms, and shoulder in the cast, and away sped the heavy weapon with its line attached, and at the next moment there thundered the cry "starn all!" and every soul bent obediently and sturdily to the oar, for they knew that their lives were dependent on the skill of the black man. But when all this was over, and the dead

-169-

whale lay alongside, an inert mass, Jake knew that if not openly expressed, yet in looks, in gestures, in the little actions which may not be remembered, yet as a whole day by day leave their unpleasant impress on the mind, he would be merely the "nigger." So he stayed—a black father, an ebony dispenser of justice among his Sandwich Islanders.

He was also a natural philosopher on the subject of "de Californy Gray." He often held forth to interested groups of whalemen from other vessels: "Dese yere whales," he would say, "dey aint like oder whales. You got to humor em like. You got to creep onto 'em softly 's if you warn't a goin' a'ter 'em 'tall. No wonder de *Ontario's* mate's boat got smashed wid de big hole in the bow yesterday. Puttin' an iron in de calf! Wha' for you strike de calf? Don't yer know the mudder smell de blood in minit, and den she turn an' fight de boat."

This was true. The cow whales when chased and after being fastened to would patiently take the harpoon and the repeated lance thrusts, seeking only with flight, retarded for the sake of its weak offspring, to find the narrow passage through the lagoon beaches into the breakers where no boat could follow them. But when some keen sense told the animal that her pursuers had hurt the young one, there came trouble. In the mother's rage, there was forgotten the pitiful fear of her insignificant persecutors. Ceasing her flight, she would head short around and with thrashing flukes and fins smash the frail craft in her rear. Jake by accident once transgressed one of his own precepts. The calf following close behind received the lance intended for the mother. The cow smelt blood. The line slackened. Jake knew what was coming, but before any time was given, bang! came a smashing shock under the bow; one end of the boat was tilted high out of the water; the swarthy crew leaped like so many frogs from the thwarts and swam for shore. Nor was this all. Another of our boats was close by: The raging mother charged after it; the crew knowing her evil intent pulled with all their might for the shore but a few hundred yards distant. Ere they could gain it the coming monster's head touched the steering oar! Whalemen can pull their boats at great speed, especially when they sit facing such a black mass foaming after them and see the little black eyes twinkling with wrath and destruction. They gained the race. The swimmers from the stoven and capsized boat soon joined them. Madame drew too much water to venture nearer shore. She would have come however and swallowed us all alive had it been possible. But her throat was not large enough and her jaws instead of being lined with rows of great white teeth looked as if a number of scrubbing brushes, with long, stiff, black hair, had been set in them. Rushing to and fro, she laid off that beach for half an hour, waiting for us to commit such an act of folly as to venture out in our uninjured cockle shell that she might smash that to pieces. The capsized and wet crew sat in the warm sand and laughed at the blockade. At last she swam away and then we timidly ventured forth, fearing a ruse might be intended. For California Grays, with their wits rousted by anger are keen, wicked and vindictive.

This was our first and last accident. We took the disabled boat in tow, picked up tubs, oars, and water beakers, mourned over a lost whale line which Madame had carried off, attached to the harpoon sticking in her back, and rowed to the Henry. Jake, looking rather sheepish, went immediately below, took to his berth, and spoke to no one until the next day. But many of the vessels about us suffered terribly. Some scarcely lowered a boat but that it came back a wreck. The *J.L. Frost*, a neat, new schooner, fitted out from the Sandwich Islands expressly for this sort of whaling, had her boats stoven twenty-six times while lying in the lagoon next us. A stoven boat does not imply its total destruction. They may be smashed like an egg shell and a few hours' work by the carpenter inserting a thin slice of deal here and a slender oaken rib there, sets them once more to rights. Their weakness is their strength. But damage more serious than boat-smashing was not uncommon. The ribs and legs of men were broken. A captain was, late one evening, steering his boat from another vessel which he had been visiting. Suddenly, in the darkness, they found themselves in the midst of a school of whales, blowing, rolling and "breaching" high out of water. The steering oar was violently wrested from the captain's hands, and making a long and powerful sweep its handle struck him on the head; he was swept over the boat's side and that was the last ever seen of him. A whale in its gambols must have ran against it or struck it with its flukes.

The carcasses, after being cast adrift, floated hither and thither with the tides up and down the lagoons. Day by day, as decomposition went on, they smelled, and it must be added, smelled more and more. And more than once the body we had cast adrift days before would, as if impelled by a sense of retributive justice, be seen, the wind and tide favoring, coming directly for us as we lay at anchor. All hands on board would be called to fend off the "stinker," the technical name among whalers for a whale long dead, and the appelation is most proper if it be not elegant. Down upon us would come the white and unsavory mass, and we would run forward with poles and capstan bars, and in most cases it would become jammed against the cables and there, despite all our efforts, the yielding, flabby mass would stick and smell until the turning tide carried it off to torment the nostrils of some other ship's crew. After a while, grounding at low water, they were left high and dry on shore. There, a few Mexicans made it their business to cut an entrance through the giant ribs and entering the cavity cut the fat about the heart and lungs, and try it out. From two to four barrels were obtained in this manner from each whale. The Grayback is comparatively a small animal, yielding on the average about forty barrels each. But even these seemed gigantic, when fully exposed. You are called to see a whale from a vessel's deck on the ocean. You behold only a small portion of a rounded black back, and perhaps a jet of spray like a puff of steam. You are disappointed. You can have no realization of the mass under water with a heart as large as a hogshead, sending at each pulsation torrents of blood through arteries like stovepipes. Such was the appearance of the internal machinery of the animals that we peeped into on the shores of Margarita. And the men working around and on them seemed, at a little distance, like mice playing over a dead ox.

The Mexicans who employed themselves in this business borrowed of us all the apparatus for trying out the dead whale's fat. They swept the vessel of every spare pot, pan, and kettle. Nor did they, when on board, ever fail to accept an invitation to dinner. For the Americans they had no great liking. But they endorsed our cookery. They smelt it from afar. And after sitting down to our board, they never arose until they had swept it clean. The steward carried naught away from their repasts save empty dishes. The sugar bowl was empty. The butter plate was bare. It is needless to speak of beef, bread, and potatoes. Sugar and butter they devoured unmixed. At length, we made provision for these gastronomical raids, and put them on allowance. And after thus clearing every platter, they came on deck and commenced their never-ending requests for a little flour, and a little more sugar and butter. When they brough on board a few sour oranges or stalks of sugar cane, they demanded for them exorbitant prices. Reciprocity in hospitality never troubled their consciences. Our liberality in this respect was not prompted however by the highest motives. We were in Mexican territory and taking therefrom the oily treasures of the sea. Had their ruling powers not been so much occupied in setting up and knocking down revolutions, they might rightfully have ordered off every foreign vessel fishing in these inland waters. So we deemed it best to keep on good terms with the natives. Once a party from an inland settlement smuggled forward a few gallons of mescal, a fiery liquor distilled, I think, from the sugar cane. It evidenced its properties on our crew in a very short time. It was necessary that afternoon to kedge the vessel a short distance. This was accomplished. We reached the desired spot. "Let go the anchor" was the order. The individual charged with this duty, who an hour before had with great secrecy informed me that "some rum was coming on board to warm the cockles of our hearts," let go the anchor. The cable had previously for some purpose been unbent, nor had the omission been repaired. So the anchor went to the bottom and the *Henry* calmly sailed over it. Rum alone was responsible. We found room that day for the divine skill of our Sandwich Islanders. With legs tightly pressed together, one hand pinching the nostrils, they would sink like plummets to the bottom, and after groping about for the lost anchor for many seconds in the tangled swamp of submarine vegetation, shoot like corks above the surface at some spot where you did not look for them, the drops running from their smooth, tawny skins as from the duck's oily plumage. The anchor was recovered. The rum was ferreted out and pitched overboard — all but a dozen bottles which Jake some weeks afterwards informed us he had secreted in his bunk, and during the long passage up the coast to San Francisco, when no one dreamed that the ghost of a drop of spirits was on board save that in the medicine chest, when the watch below in the early evening hours were singing and smoking, when the Cerros

Island castaways, who were at this hour disposed to stray into the forecastle to obtain relief from the comparative dignity of the cabin, sighed for a few drops of something to warm the cockles of their hearts, this secretive Ethiopian, lying in his bunk, would sympathizingly re-echo their desires, and then turning over draw from under his mattress one of the still unemptied twelve bottles, quietly and unseen pour a portion of its contents down his throat, and then renewing his former position remark in substance, that a bottle of rum would then and there be a great help to kill time with.

Shortly after this there came a great, white day in our calendar — a day in which we "filled up." Yet it opened inauspiciously. Both boats after being fastened all the morning to a Grayback, were obliged to cut loose from him. He gained one of the beach passages, and there was no following him through the breakers. The disappointed crews rowed moodily back, ate their dinners, and again put off. They were soon pursuing another doggerel chase, for the Graybacks, although plentiful, had become very shy. The mate's boat was sweeping along within a cable's length of the vessel and the object of its pursuit was occasionally breaching out a few hundred yards ahead, when suddenly, to our surprise, we saw the oars peaked and the boat with increased speed shooting through the water. It was fast! There had been no cast of the iron, none of the usual turmoil and thrashing of the enraged animal, yet the boat was gliding along and the crew were actually engaged in "hauling in" on a line, and from time to time, as the whale burst through the lagoon's calm surface, an iron was seen implanted in her back. This is the solution of the mystery. That morning, like ourselves, one of the Nimrod's boats had been compelled to sever their connection with another whale as it entered one of those stormy and vexatious passages. The Grayback swam off with their harpoon and several hundred feet of line. Having thus baffled her pursuers she had immediately returned to her nursery. We disturbed her repose in the afternoon, and the boat-header, as she sped away, looking into the water and seeing a few inches from the surface a long, light yellowish worm-like length of something rushing with great speed in the same direction as ourselves, fished it up with his boat-hook and found it to be a ready-made whale line with a whale attached. A turn was thrown around the loggerhead, and the rowers gladly delegated to the victim the labor of propulsion. Meantime, the boat in the rear was pulling for another black outline in the distance. They neared it softly, not a voice raised, the oars working noiselessly; still nearer, and the practiced eye of the whale hunter saw by the inert yielding of the mass to the swell that no life was there. It was the whale we had cut from in the morning. One lance thrust had touched its vitals; it had died in the breakers and drifted back. Barely were these two alongside, when a great thrash of foam was seen about two miles from our anchorage. One look by the captain through his glass at the mast-head, and he called out: "A whale aground, by jingo. Lower away there, the J.L. Frost's boats are after him now."

There was hurrying for a minute; men tumbled over the side into their seats; oars clattered into their places; oaths and orders crossed each other, and then the confusion all settled into place; the long dripping oars swayed and bent regularly back and forth as if worked by machinery. The stranded Grayback was equi-distant from the two vessels. Rivalry, as well as the common excitement of the chase, lent an increased nervousness to the arms of our men. For the *J.L. Frost's* boats had many, many times invaded our lagoon where, by the whaling law of those waters, they had no business unless taken there behind a harpooned whale. Here they were again after a prize which had fallen in our boundaries. Our men pulled in desperate silence. No breath was expended in useless shouts or orders. The boat-steerer upright, controlling with one arm the boat's direction, swayed in unison with the long strokes, and with the other lent his whole force in vigorous pushes of the oar worked nearest him. And between the rapidly advancing boats the unhappy animal, trapped by the ebbing tide, struck about wildly with flukes and fins, splashing sheets of spray for yards around with a noise which might faintly be heard from the *Henry's* deck. Vain the terrific strength he expended, digging his fins into the yielding sand and rolling from side to side. He was only settled more secure on the flat. Down came the two rival boats in advance; in each stood the boat-headers with uplifted weapon, their eyes centered on the prize with an occasional angry glance at the other, for to the vessel whose iron was first driven in to the writhing mass it must belong, so read Whaleman's Law; and that iron sped first from the arms of Black Jake before the opposing boat-header dared to hazard a cast. The whale was ours; the opposing crew sullenly suspended the race and gazed at us half gloomily, half listless, not raising their voices to assist our boys' hurrah of triumph.

He proved to be a large bull who, violating the bounds of Cetacean propriety, had strayed into this Grayback lying-in hospital. Being aground we could not take off the blubber in the usual manner, but were obliged, in whaling parlance, "to range" it — that is, cut it off in longitudinal strips from head to tail. For the next four days the *Henry* dripped and overflowed with grease; all the availble space on deck was filled with blubber; we tramped over or rather knee-deep in it; the hot sun officiously gave unsought aid in trying it out; the scuppers were stopped to prevent this oil, perspiring as it were from every "horsepiece," from running overboard; it oozed however from crack and crevice; in the intervals of other duties we scooped it up with dust-pans; we filled therewith every spare barrel, tub and even monopolized the grumbling cook's pots and kettles. At length the last scrap was tried out, and we were full and more. We had of whale oil five hundred barrels, of seal oil a hundred more, of aulones some ten tons, of their variegated shells a ton or two more, and of the little pearls extracted from these fish every man had his pill-box full for "shore presents." Then came a general and vigorous scrubbing of deck, cabin, and forecastle with sand, soap, and hot water, as we slowly drifted along and worked out of the tortuous channels toward the mouth of Margarita Bay. A season of lashing barrels, spare spars, and boats, in preparation for outside weather, next ensued. Firewood and fresh water were laid in, the decks were cumbered with turtle, and thus accoutred everybody for twenty-five days was joyful, while the *Henry* struggled and beat against the steadily persistent "Nor' East Trade" toward San Francisco.

____ The Last of the Leatherstockings ____
by the Right Reverend W.I. Kip
May 1869

Thirty years ago California offered a strange contrast to its present appearance. Here and there throughout the country were the massive buildings of the Franciscan Missions, surrounded by the huts of thousands of their Indian converts — the land in their vicinity tilled like a garden, rich in vineyards and olive-yards — and their neighboring plains covered with their innumerable cattle. Then, there were the *ranches* (or farms) of the old Mexicans and Spaniards, stretching over leagues of country, but used only as pasture-grounds for their countless herds. The remainder of the land was filled with tribes of savage Indians, who made inroads, when they could, upon the quiet Missions, or waged a guerilla warfare with the Spaniards who had seized upon their rich hunting-grounds.

Far back in the country, in the mountains, and at the head-waters of the streams that flow into the Pacific, were scattered another class — the sole representatives of the Anglo-Saxon race. These were the trappers and hunters — men whom a love of adventure had driven out from the settlements at the East, until they wandered across the desert and made their homes in the fastnesses of the last chain of mountains which borders the Pacific. There they breathed freely in the air of the wilderness. They hunted the deer and trapped the beaver, returning occasionally to the outposts at the East to sell the furs and lay in a new supply of ammunition. They disputed for their homes with the grizzly bear — that monarch of the wilderness — and at times they joined the Indians, remained with them perhaps for years, took their squaws for wives, and engaged in their wars and huntings. Then for seasons they would live along on the streams where they snared the beaver, supporting themselves by the rifle, seeing no white man for months — perfect Ishmaelites, at feud with every living thing in the mountains, whether Indians or wild beasts.

Of this class at the East — the pioneers of our country — Cooper has given some faithful pictures in his Leatherstocking Series. But "truth is stranger than fiction," and the wild adventures of Hawkeye have been more than equalled in the experience of many a trapper in the Sierra Nevada Mountains, and in those broad valleys which form so beautiful a feature of the country in California. Some of them have found a biographer in Irving, and in the delightful pages of "Astoria" and "Adventures of Captain Bonneville" we find the true histories of some of the boldest spirits that ever looked along a rifle.

The last of these Leatherstockings we happened to know. During the summer of 1854 we met in San Francisco an elderly man, who was introduced to us as Mr. Blount. Though between sixty and seventy, "his eye was not dim, nor his natural force abated." Florid, hale, and hearty, he was able to undergo fatigues from which most men of half his age would shrink. We recognized him at once as one of the old mountaineers whose name is as "familiar as household words" to all Californians, and looked upon him with very much the same curiosity with which we should have regarded Hawkeye, had we met him the week after we first read "Last of the Mohicans." More fortunate than most of his comrades, he had escaped the bullet of the Indian, the hug of the grizzly, and the still more fatal influence of strong drink, and having at an early day secured a large tract of country in the rich Napa Valley, had settled down upon it in a quietness which contrasted strongly with the stirring years which preceded it. We gladly accepted an invitation to visit him, as furnishing an opportunity of seeing some primitive California life before the progress of refinement should deprive it of all its freshness. But some months passed away without affording the desired opportunity, and it was not until the middle of the following winter—as we should call it at the East, though here the climate furnishes no evidence of that season—that we were able to carry our wishes into effect.

It was a bright December day that the little steamer conveyed us up the Napa River until we landed at evening at Napa and found Mr. Blount's covered wagon waiting to take us up the valley. So we sat in the darkness as our spirited horses dashed over the dozen miles before us, now and then rattling down the bank where the road led over the bed of a stream, at a rate which made us hold our breath, and, like Ajax in the old Greek tragedy, pray for light. The country seemed to be one unbroken plain, with only an occasional enclosure, until at last we saw by the lights that we were approaching a ranch. Numerous dogs opened on us with all sorts of cries, from deep bass to treble, as we drew up at the door of a long-extended house, one story only, built part of adobes (bricks dried in the sun) and part of wood, evidently erected and added to as occasion required. The lights gleamed cheerily from the windows, Indian boys rushed out to see the new arrival, the dogs were whipped away, and we were ushered in.

The front door opened into a large hall or sitting-room, and before the fire sat our host, smoking his pipe, and surrounded, like a patriarch, by half a dozen of the men employed on his ranch in various capacities. The fire was none of your modern contracted apologies, but a broad old-fashioned fire-place, which (as the air had become cold with the advancing night) was every little while replenished, so that it burned and blazed with such a flame of oak logs as we had never seen since our childhood. A hearty supper was soon provided, after discussing which, with the appetite furnished by our long drive, we went to bed in an apartment opening out of the hall.

And now a little about our host. He was trained from his earliest years on the frontiers of Missouri, where his first labors were in the forest, and his youthful adventures hunting parties or conflicts with the Indians. A fit preparation for his eventful future! About fifty years ago he left his early home and came down with a trading party to Upper Mexico, where he joined a band of trappers and for some years hunted the beaver on head-waters of the Gila and Colorado. The first season — he told us — he took about a thousand dollars' worth of skins. So he lived for several years, returning occasionally to Sante Fé to dispose of his spoils. On one occasion they were seized and confiscated, on some frivolous pretence, by the Spanish Governor, and Blount was obliged to work as a laborer till he gained enough money to purchase another outfit. These were years of stirring adventure. He became familiar with the whole range of country for a thousand miles, and met every tribe of Indians, either in amity or war. Most often it was the latter, and many were the times when his life was staked upon the accuracy of a single shot from his rifle. He was known, however, as one of those "dead shots" found on the frontiers, whose nerves seem never to fail, and with whom it was only necessary to "draw a bead upon an Indian" (to use border language), and the savage had ended his career.

After many vicissitudes, he wandered down into the Napa Valley, about 1835, and, attracted by the beauty of the country, obtained from the Mexican Government a grant of two leagues. "I might," said the old man to us, "just as well have had thirty miles as six! If I had asked for the whole valley they would have given it to me." And so they would, for it was of no use to them, and grants were often made, at this time, of twenty and thirty leagues of unoccupied country. General Sutter's grant in the Sacramento Valley extended for sixty miles. Here Blount determined to settle. It was, however, only a continuation of his adventures, for the next fifteen years were spent in fighting the Indians and the grizzlies. He built a block-house, and with one white man and occasionally a few friendly Indians, set the rest of the world at defiance. His enemies often besieged him for days, but he coolly fought his way through, and every savage who came within range met with a certain fate. When the Missions were threatened by the wild Indians, or General Vallejo called out the Spaniards to anticipate a threatened attack, Blount's rifle was always at their service.

In one of these battles — we were told by one who knew his history — he killed eighteen Indians in eighteen shots. He missed but twice during the whole engagement, and those were in this way. He and an Indian "treed" (took post behind trees) at the same instant. The Indian kept firing, while Blount but once caught sight of him, when his ball only inflicted a slight wound in the Indian's thigh. He then drew sight directly on the edge of the bark, intending to fire the instant the Indian exposed himself. He did so, but shooting a little too close, the ball glanced off. These were his two failures. A second time he tried the experiment with better success. As the Indian uncovered to fire, Blount's ball grazed the bark and entered his breast. The savage dropped his gun, bounded into the air and pitched head-foremost on the ground.

At last, after years of warfare, the Americans came, the Indians retired before the torrent of emigration, and Blount found himself lord of many broad acres, his once valueless leagues of land having grown into a noble estate. And there he lived with his employés and servants, and a couple of hundred Indians who still lingered around his ranch and shared his bounty. The profusion and abundance, indeed, were rather like that of the old Norman barons, whose beeves and sheep were slaughtered as the household required. Far removed from the influence of cities, all of the features of primitive California life were preserved. Everyone came and partook of his open-handed hospitality, used his horses as they pleased, and departed without ceremony. No change was made for anyone. Blount sat at the head of his long table, his guests next to him, whether of "high or low degree," and his dependents and workmen below, like the picture Scott has given in the "Monastery," of Julian Avenel at table with his retainers. His cattle and his horses roamed in herds by hundreds over the broad plains, untrammelled until needed, when the Indians went out and lassoed them. And yet, free and unshackled as this life seemed to be, the old man pined for the still freer air of the wilderness. "If I were a little younger," said he, "I should like to return once more to the mountains."

One of his family was a well-educated Englishwoman, who acted as governess to the young grandchildren living with him. It was amusing to us to hear the horror she expressed for the vocabulary of the people among whom she lived, and its perverting influence on her pupils. She had not yet become reconciled to the difference between the *Queen's English* and the *President's Yankee.*

"I cannot," said she, "make the children say 'very.' They will say 'mighty.' For instance, a thing is 'mighty good.' And then, the other day, I asked a woman down the valley, who was ill, how was she? and she answered she was 'powerful weak.' Did you ever hear anything so absurd?"

We shouted, for we considered the last expression exceedingly forcible and felicitous. In truth, the English have to come to America to discover what magnificent results can be produced by the use of their own language.

His household seemed to be a general gathering. Orphan boys, whose parents had died in crossing the Plains, found here a refuge; old mountaineers dropped in to see their former comrade and "fight their battles o'er again;" and horse and cattle dealers came to purchase the old man's stock. On one occasion, he told us, he entertained for three nights Joaquin, the celebrated bandit, who in 1853 was hunted down and killed, after a large reward had been offered for his head. He came to the ranch, and although Blount suspected who he was, yet, as he denied no one his hospitality, he received him, and, in the fearlessness of his nature, gave him a bedroom leading out of his own. For three days he sat at his table, "eat his salt," and departed unquestioned.

Long before we rose next morning we heard the steady tones of conversation in the hall, and on coming out found the old man talking to a mountaineer who had just dropped in on his return from the head-waters of the Colorado, where he had acted as guide to a party of engineers of the United States army, who were surveying the country. They were evidently deep in the narrative of their adventures, for as we entered we heard Blount say:

"When we travelled through that country we had our wagons in two parallel lines, so that at the least alarm we could close up, put the cattle in the center, and have a breastwork from which to fire. Well, on that occasion the Camanches charged down to within a hundred yards of us" —

And so they went on for hours, telling one story after another, and relating adventures, each one of which would make excitement enough for an ordinary man's life, as if they were the most commonplace occurrences. And they were so to them. But to one who had spent his days in cities there was a charm in meeting with these men of the wilderness. They gave entirely new phases of life, and these adventures seem very different when read in books and when heard from the lips of one who had been an actor in them. Blount had, in his youth, personally known Daniel Boone, the pioneer of Kentucky, when, more than eighty years of age, he had wandered into Missouri to avoid the advancing tide of population, and still carried his trusty rifle to the buffalo and bear hunts. And as the old trappers talked we heard them quote Sublette and Bijou and others with whose adventures we had been familiar on the pages of "Bonneville" and "Astoria," until it seemed as if we had been personally acquainted with them.

Running about the house was a black-eyed, straight-haired boy, every feature and action showing his Indian blood. He was the son of an old comrade of Blount, named Smith, who often passed years in different tribes in company with some Indian wife he had picked up, of one of whom this boy was the son. We once heard while there his pedigree discussed in the following question and answer, which would have perfectly astonished Burke — (he of the "Peerage"):

"Wasn't his mother a Crow?"

"No; she was a Snake."

Referring to the two tribes of Indians which rejoiced in those poetical names.

On one occasion the father of this boy, in a skirmish with the Indians, received a ball in his leg, between the knee and ankle, which entirely shattered the bone, He was borne off by his comrades, but that night there was no one to aid them, for the camp was in a state of drunken revelry to celebrate their victory. So, sharpening his hunting-knife, he deliberately cut off his leg above the wound!

"But," said one of us to Blount, as he related the occurrence, "how could he live through it? I should suppose, there being no one to tie up the arteries, that he would have bled to death."

"I don't know about that," replied the old man, "but I suppose it bled till it had done and then it stopped."

This may seem very improbable, but we have had the story several times verified from other witnesses. We have frequently, indeed, seen "Peg-leg Smith" (as he was called from his wooden leg like a broom-stick), when he was stumping about the country. At the time of this visit he was alive and hearty, and down on the Colorado, on the borders of Mexico, among the Yuma Indians.

Some years afterwards we met with another old comrade of Smith, who knew all the circumstances of the case, but gave a more accurate account. Blount's narrative was true, as far as it went. Smith did indeed cut off his own leg; but they seared the stump with red-hot iron, and then bound it up in a cloth covered with pitch. This explains why the man did not bleed to death, but shows what nerve these frontier men had. To think of the red-hot iron fizzing against the naked stump! Eugh!

A short distance from the house were the wigwams of some two hundred Indians who had encamped there for the rainy season. A few poles were put up, and these covered with rushes so as to make a rounding roof impervious to rain, while the low entrance was enclosed with a skin. When the spring comes and the rains are over, they burn down their houses, and move off to the sides of the streams to fish; or to the mountains, where they erect still slighter tenements, sleeping most of their time in the open air.

And those were the wretched remnants of the powerful tribes which once filled this valley, and made it no secure dwelling-place for the white man. Blount said, that as late as 1837, the tribes through Napa Valley alone numbered five thousand warriors. They had melted away like the snow-drift, and the miserable survivors exhibited no trace of their former spirit. In connection with this there was a strange circumstance related to us by Blount, with regard to the Indians in the Sacramento Valley. In the spring of 1836 he passed up through it, and found the whole valley perfectly swarming with savages. Their *rancherias*, or towns, filled the country, and along the narrow Sacramento River they seemed to line the banks. In the autumn he returned, and hardly a survivor was to be seen. In the intervening time a pestilence had swept through the tribes, and their unburied bodies were lying in heaps upon the ground. In one settlement of fifteen hundred a single squaw along remained. It was just before old General Sutter, the pioneer of California, entered the valley, and it seemed to be paving the way for his settlement in their deserted hunting-grounds.

In that mighty crusade after gold, which is peopling California, and in which, by sea and on the plains, more have perished than in the Crusades of the Middle Ages against the Infidel, there have been some chapters of history more startling than any the world has ever before seen. One of them we will relate, on account of its connection with our host; and the story — strange and almost supernatural as it may seem — which we had from his own lips.

Among the parties which crossed the continent in 1846 was one, numbering in men, women, and children, about eighty persons, which by unfortunate delays did not reach the Sierra Mountains until late in the autumn. There they encamped on a little meadow close by the Donner Lake. We passed it a couple of years since, when — seen in a bright afternoon — it looked too peaceful and beautiful to have ever been the scene of such a fearful tragedy. There a snowstorm arrested them and blocked up the passes. Their animals died and were covered by the deep drifts, until it became impossible to advance or return. They necessarily encamped for the season; but provisions were soon exhausted, the cattle were eaten till every hide was devoured, and starvation in its most horrible form came upon them. And thus the long and dreary winter passed away — many dying of hunger and exhaustion, and the survivors sustaining themselves by eating the bodies of their comrades. But one of the most horrible features of these scenes was, that their cannibalism seemed to produce a perfect insanity. They lost every trait distinctive of human beings, and seemed to acquire the nature of wild beasts. When found, they exhibited the most perfect apathy with regard to their situation, and had ceased to feel any horror for the revolting way in which they were sustaining life. The party which rescued the survivors from this Camp of Death, described them as surrounded by circumstances so foul and revolting, that probably human life has not witnessed its parallel. They were living in the midst of filth and the relics of their horrible feasts. Parents fed on their offspring, and young children devoured the hearts and livers of their starved relatives as if they were delicate morsels. Exchanges were going on from hut to hut, and limbs were bartered and their weight scrutinized, as they would any marketable articles of food. Lieutenant Wise of the United States Navy, who saw some of the survivors, says, that one man boiled and devoured a girl nine years old in a single night; a young woman actually made soup of her lover's head; and a young Spaniard told him, he "eat baby raw, stewed some of Jake, and roasted his head."

Yet there was still a darker and more awful scene in this tragedy. So fully had this mania possessed them, that it was difficult to withdraw some of them from their cannibalism. They had actually to be dragged away, and, like the lion which once it has tasted human flesh prefers it to all other, they turned with regret to the supply of food which their deliverers had brought. Among them was a German, still living in the interior of the State, who was found, after the necessity had ceased and food was abundant, smeared with blood and cooking a meal of human flesh. He was removed by main force from his horrid repast, while there was also a strong conviction that he had added murder to the other terrible accompaniments of his situation, to gratify his ghoul-like appetite.

And now for the supernatural part of the story. While these emigrants were thus suffering in the mountains. Blount — we are giving his own narrative — dreamed one night of their situation and the horrors by which they were surrounded. He says the scenery was plainly pictured before him, particularly a huge perpendicular front of white rock cliff, and he saw the men cutting off the tree-tops rising out of the deep gulfs of snow. He had never been in that part of the mountains — yet, the next morning, in relating his dream to two old hunters, who were staying with him and were familiar with that section of country, they said he described the route and the location as faithfully as if he had passed months there. Struck by the coincidence, and believing there was something providential in the warning — "for I felt," said he, "if I did not obey it, some misfortune might happen to me" — he went that day eighteen miles up the Napa River to find an old hunter, who was familiar with these mountains, and was foremost in organizing a party to search, through whose means many lives were saved. About thirty survived, though many of them frost-bitten and crippled.

This is a strange story; but we find in the Rev. Dr. Bushnell's work, published after his visit to California, the same narrative given as he received it from Blount. He adds: "A gentleman present said — 'You need have no doubt of this: for we Californians all know the facts and the names of the families brought in, who now look upon our venerable friend as a kind of Saviour.' These names he gave and the places where they reside; and I found, afterward, that the California people were ready, anywhere, to second his testimony. Let anyone attempt to account for the coincidences of that dream, by mere natural casualties, and he will be glad enough to ease his labor by the acknowledgement of a Supernatural Providence".

The hills which hem in the house were still, in their ravines, the resort of grizzlies, which come down at night and leave their footprints about the house. No old hunter willingly attacks the grizzly bar (as they call it), for he has a tenacity of life possessed by no other animal, and even a ball through the heart does not seem for a time to diminish his strength. When Blount first came to the valley, he said it swarmed with these disagreeable neighbors, who made sad havoc among the Indians. In the season of clover, of which they are very fond, they descended to the plain; and sometimes, at sunrise, from the door of his house he had counted from forty to sixty in view at once. Hundreds have died before his unerring rifle. But when caught on foot, it required some nerve for the encounter. Imagine him standing before a huge monster, who, as he rises on his hind legs, is more than seven feet high, and only his rifle on which to depend. Should his hand tremble in the least, or the ball vary half an inch from the glaring eyeball, so as to glance off on the skull instead of reaching the monster's brain (the only wound which is instantly fatal), all is over with the hunter! He never has a second chance.

Among other things, Blount told us of the massive remains of the old cities (similar to those described by Stephens), which he found in his wanderings in the center of the continent. There are wrecks of huge buildings which have already been ruins for centuries, and, in one instance, he traced the remains of a canal, fifteen miles in length, which had been dug to bring water to the city from the distant mountains. Who were the inhabitants of these vast and deserted cities?

But the strangest of all was his account of the Moquos—so strange that we might consider it exaggerated, had we not the testimony of other witnesss. It was in 1828, when about two days' journey from the Little Red River, the trappers were toiling on, the horses wearied and worn out, that they found themselves approaching the territory of this strange race of Indians. It is a lofty table-mountain land, to which there is but a single passage, scarcely large enough for two men abreast. Here their houses are built of a beautiful sandstone, easily quarried. They are generally entered from the top. Their land is not naturally very productive, nor is it irrigated, so that they have to depend on the annual rains to produce their crops. In many of their customs they differ widely from all the Indian tribes. They bury their dead with suitable services, and annually elect their rulers, instead of having hereditary chiefs.

Pacific in their character, men and women are industrious, laboring in large work-houses constructed underground. In one of these you find only men, and in another women alone, except one gray-headed father who acts as overseer. Here, they spin, weave, make blankets and garments. They have large granaries well-filled as security against a year of famine; and in each of them is placed a male and female image cut in stone. Their laws with regard to marriage are strict and rigidly enforced, and anyone detected in their infringement is banished at once and regarded forever as an outcast. The young females, before marriage, wear their hair on each side of the head like a half-moon, while after marriage it is combed loosely over the shoulders. Their dress is neat, without any of the ornaments or tawdriness which mark the American Indians, nor is paint upon the body allowed in either sex.

The appearance of the Moquos shows plainly that they are not of the blood of the tribes by which they are surrounded. Their complexion is much lighter; and Blount said that instances of red hair and blue eyes were not uncommon among them. They saw there some of the most splendid physical specimens of humanity they had ever met with—forms of the most perfect symmetry, showing in either sex the most beautiful development.

Their religious rites, too, are peculiar. Besides the stone images we have already mentioned in the granaries, they were to be seen also in various other places. The trappers saw one spacious apartment, destitute of all furniture except a massive stone altar. A venerable old man, whom they took to be a priest, would at intervals sprinkle the altar and the floor around, for a considerable distance, with the finest wheat flour. On the borders of their towns, too, in every direction, were large stone altars in the open air, on which were sacrificed, at intervals, sheep, goats, and other domestic animals. The remains, after sacrifice, were thrown as high as possible in the air, from the top of a precipice, so that they might fall far below the town upon the arid plains and wastes by which they were surrounded. These remnants were left to decay or to be devoured by the beasts and birds, but were never taken up by the inhabitants. On these altars, too, they offered every variety of their manufactures and mechanical productions.

During the preceding year (1827) a trapper named Williams wandered into that country, the first white man the Moquos had ever seen, and spent much time with them. He became familiar with their rules and acquainted with all their customs, mingling with them in their dances and religious rites. Struck with the simplicity and purity of character they exhibited, he told them of the Christian scheme as he himself remembered it in the teachings of his youth. He narrated to them the history of Jesus Christ, and assured them that he himself was a disciple of that great Saviour. They reverenced him greatly, asked his prayers when he departed, and as the following year was remarkable for prolific crops of grain, they attributed it to the efficacy of his petitions. This fact had given him such an influence with the people that, had he returned there, it would have been in his power not only to have acquired the supreme rule over them, but to have converted them all to Christianity.

As the little party of Blount, almost exhausted, drew nigh to their town, they at once experienced their hospitality. "The people," said he (for we will try to give this in his own words), "came out and flocked about us, unpacking our horses and giving them water with great caution, lest they should be injured, and then led them off to pasture. We ourselves were taken into their houses, where a great feast was spread and a fine, spacious apartment, spread with mats, allotted us. And in this way we were feasted daily, the different families vying with each other in bringing us food and luxuries."

They spent about a fortnight among this interesting people, in recruiting their strength, and when they departed, it was after a scene as strange as any which had preceded it. "When the time came for us to leave," — to adopt once more his own language—"there was a stir through the whole tribe. They all tried to bestow upon us the best possible demonstrations of respect and love, and every profession was evidently sincere and hearty. In their simple piety they brought their little ones for our parting blessing. We could not but reflect upon ourselves as we received these evidences of their veneration. We were rough trappers of the wilderness, too little accustomed to respect ourselves. In our hunting-dresses we had anything but a sacred appearance. We were young men, too, inconsiderate; but for once we were obliged to be serious. Whether you think it manly or not, we wept. Our horses were brought out, sleek and well recruited, having been daily groomed and fed. We were loaded down with gifts and our animals with provisions for the journey. Their women and children accompanied us to the border of their territory, the last clinging round us for our parting notice. And as we went, they begged our prayers and heaped blessings on our heads."

We listen to this account and it seems to us as if it could not be anything but a fiction. Yet others have since corroborated its more important features. But how strange that this people for so long a time — for they have lost the traditions of their own origin—have been preserved not only distinct, but with their pacific habits even, in existence in the midst of the warlike tribes surrounding them! And whence came this people, so different in appearance and customs from all the other tribes in this country? In many respects, in their habits and rites, we are forcibly reminded of the ancient Jews.

It is strange—to give the finale of their history—that sometime afterwards, in the interior, we met with a man who had just crossed the continent through New Mexico, and whose route had led him to the residence of the Moquos. He said there were but few of them left. The small-pox—that scourge of the Indians, which the whites had introduced—had swept through the tribe, almost entirely destroying it. As a distinct people the Moquos are among "the things that were."

Another curious circumstance related by Blount was, his discovery of gold in this country thirty years before. Somewhere at the head-waters of the Colorado the members of his party found large lumps of what must have been virgin gold. They collected and examined some of them, but never having before seen gold ore, were ignorant of its value, and decided that it was copper. In later years, since he had become acquainted with this precious metal, he remembered the appearance of those specimens he formerly saw, and was convinced that they were gold. It is evident, therefore, that in those parts of the country there must be countless undiscovered treasures, and only during the week which preceded our visit, Blount had been solicited by a company in San Francisco to be their guide in seeking the place. It is, however, a long and dangerous journey, and he felt that he was too old to encounter its fatigues.

There seems, indeed, to have been quite a series of these discoveries prior to the final one which proclaimed that this was the El Dorado. A few years before that time gold was found by a trapper, who, knowing the value of the fact he had discovered, returned to the East, acquainted his brother with the secret, though without describing to him the location, and after laying in a stock of mining implements, they set out on their journey across the Plains. One morning they were attacked by the Indians and the possessor of this valuable secret killed. But "he died and made no sign," and his brother therefore inherited no benefit from his discovery. He continued on to San Francisco, where he sold his implements and then returned to the East.

The next morning we accompanied our host down the valley. Our walk was protracted from one point to another, until we began to wish ourselves back at the ranch. But the old man, with nearly threescore and ten years on his head, tramped on hour after hour as if he knew not what weariness was. At last we crossed a deep ravine by a single round log, over which he walked as firmly as if it was two yards wide, while we went over with head twisting round, as if we might be found, in another minute, at the bottom of the ravine.

"Mr. Blount," said we, "were you ever ill?"

"Never, sir; never yet gave the first dollar to a doctor."

"But in all your living in the mountains were you never attacked by any of the dysenteric complaints which such exposures produce?"

"Yes; I once had some cholic cramps, but I took assafoetida."

"But where did you get assafoetida up in the mountains?"

"Why, I had it to mix with my beaver bait."

We suppose, indeed, it was the only nauseous thing the old hunter had in his possession, and therefore he thought it would do for medicine.

He took us to the site of his first block-house, some of the beams of which were still lying on the ground where it once stood. It was only about a dozen feet wide, with the second story projecting over the first, so that he could fire down upon anyone attempting to break in the door. In this little building he was often beleaguered, and around it many a hostile savage bit the dust. The old man, strange as it may seem, in all his various encounters through forty years, was never touched, so as to draw blood, by Indian or wild beast. After a time the Indians believed he bore a charmed life, called him a *Great Medicine*, and desisted from their attempts. "They might perhaps have killed me, if they had kept on," said Blount, "but they stopped trying."

This was an adventure, he told us, which happened to some of his comrades, in a block-house of this kind. There were three men (one of them a French trapper) and two women together, when they were unexpectedly startled by a wild yell of hundreds of savages who had surrounded them. At the first fire of the Indians an arrow glancing through a loop-hole killed one of the men. The Frenchman, perfectly paralyzed by fear, at once threw himself on the floor and was no further assistance. The remaining hunter, with the three rifles which the women kept loading for him, watched as well as he could at the loop-holes, and brought down many an Indian who ventured too near. After a while they changed their mode of attack, and rushing upon all sides at once, hurled burning brands upon the roof. Fortunately the roof was light, and with poles which were inside, the gallant defenders succeeded in pushing it off, leaving themselves entirely uncovered. The brands then descended among them, and the only fluid they had to extinguish them was a barrel of betheglin, which the women ladled out on each burning piece which descended. In this way the defense was continued through the entire day. At last, impatient of the protracted struggle and the loss of so many of his braves, the chief imprudently advanced too near the block-house and planting his spear in the ground, prepared to give his orders for a more vigorous assault. At this moment the sharp crack of the trusty rifle was heard from within, and the Camanche warrior fell. His followers at once set up a loud wail, and taking the remains of their leader, in a panic abandoned the assault and retreated.

Another long evening's talk and the next day our visit ended. There had been a freshness about it, and the associations into which it led us, highly delightful. And now that the tide of population has spread over those valleys and the last Indians have gone, our stay with the old hunter comes back to us as a memory of times which can never be repeated. New men have occupied the ground, the pioneers of '49 have displaced the old trappers of thirty years earlier, and the generation of frontier men has gone. We never saw our old host again, and when, a couple of years ago, we read the announcement of his death, we felt that with him passed away "The Last of the Leatherstockings."

Rt. Rev. William Ingraham Kip *(1811-1893) was the first bishop of the Episcopal Church in California. The New York native was elected missionary bishop of California in 1853 and reached San Francisco in January of 1854. The local Episcopalians had recently organized a diocese and, by church law, had the right to elect their own bishop. For three years he served by mutual consent until his first election by the diocese in 1857. His church work in California was pioneering in every way. It took three to four days to journey to Los Angeles by steamer, while the mining camps were reached on horseback. He traveled constantly, laying the foundations of the church.*

In 1862 he accepted the rectorship of Grace Church in San Francisco and established it as his cathedral, the first such for the Episcopal Church in America. Kip was a scholar and enjoyed studying the early history of California, especially that which concerned the Spanish missions of old California. He was an able writer and published many theological papers.

It is interesting to note that the editor was never able to find a mention of Mr. Blount in connection with the fur trade. Bancroft makes no mention of him and neither does Hittell. Was Reverend Kip hoodwinked by a tale-telling stranger or did Mr. Blount really exist?

Adventures
in
Other Lands

Saint Saviour of the Bay
by G.T. Shipley, M.D.
October 1868

I never saw any other city in my life that was half as beautiful by night and from the sea as San Salvador de Bahia de Todos los Santos. It is called Bahia, for short, by the world in general — all the world, that is, which knows anything about it — and "Bah-*hee*" by the men before the mast. Sailors have a queer way of twisting words out of shape.

One cloudless evening, in 1864, we rounded the northern side of the entrance to the bay. Less than ten minutes' steaming from the desolation of the open sea sufficed to bring us into full view of the city. It lies on a crescentic hill-side; a hill so steep that its streets are impassable for wheeled vehicles; and through its seven-mile sweep around the curving northern side of the bay these streets are as visible from the deck of a ship as are those of a city on a plain from the basket of a balloon floating in mid-air. Lamp-posts are planted in lavish profusion; and at night their gas-lights, abnormally brilliant in the tropical atmosphere, blaze out the lines of every avenue, from the beach to the crest of the slope, with the grand effect of a special illumination.

Bahia, you know, is a large city. It doesn't make half the noise or brag that any one of our five hundred American "centers-of-trade" glories and delights in; but it's big enough, and populous enough, and wealthy and magnificent enough, to buy and sell the entire half-thousand pretentious abortions aforesaid, despite their liberty and ugliness and filth. It is painful to a traveller to think of the astounding amount of ignorant cockneyism that our glorious institutions give rise to. I have never wondered at Dickens's *American Notes* — they told perhaps too many unpleasant truths. We are gradually growing civilized, of course, and when he made his second visit, we were on our best behavior, but there is immense room for improvement yet.

Well — we dropped anchor in Bahia harbor. Next morning we went through the usual exchange of courtesies with the fort — which is a funny little Martello tower lying off the city — and with two Brazilian men-of-war. After much flag hoisting and dipping, and firing of guns, and all that sort of international trifling, we stopped, and they stopped; and then Dunallan and I went ashore in the second cutter to buy fresh provisions and to look at the city. This second cutter was one of those boats in which you have to part you hair in the middle to keep her on an even keel. She was far more pleasant to go ashore in than she was to use for returning. Because, in coming back you see, some of the men at the oars are, almost to a certainty, verging towards inebriation; and if any one of them *should* catch a crab or foul his oar, the entire establishment is overboard in less than no time. I went through this experience once in that favorite resort for sharks, the harbor of Charlotte-Amalia, Saint Thomas, Virgin Islands, and once was enough. We effected a partial cure of this eccentricity of the cutter's after a while, by putting a few rifled shell along the keelson for ballast; but she never was exactly what she should be till a sea struck her at the davits, in a gale off Patagonia, and knocked her into kindling wood.

Years ago, when I was a little boy, and given to making clandestine visits to the afternoon performances of the theatre, it was a source of everlasting amazement to me to look at the wings and flats of street-scenes. Such incredible architecture. Doors opening into nowhere; columns carrying nothing; windows giving light to nobody; stairways ending in vacancy; red walls, green walls, blue walls, yellow walls, all jumbled up together. I came to the conclusion that they must be portraitures of unreal houses — houses having no existence more actual than that given them by the imagination of the scene-painter. Growing with my growth, and strengthening with my strength, this belief met absolute annihilation before Dunallan and I had been ten minutes in the spiritual capital of the Brazils. The originals of the wings and flats were before us, behind us, around us. As I haven't the faintest idea of how long Bahia has been built, I can't tell when the scene-painter first made his sketches in its streets; but that he did so, I am certain. I was very sorry to have this cherished belief of my boyhood's days so ruthlessly upset; but I could not close my eyes to obvious truth.

Our stay on shore that morning was very short. Beef, vegetables, fruit and soft-tack were more important needs than anything else just then. We secured an ample supply of all the delicacies of the season, and had our return half-mile of danger in the cutter. None of the men had had time to get drunk on the excellent liquors of the town, and the passage was consequently made in safety. How different it might have been in almost any one of the seaports of our own beloved land! I have seen a man-of-war's-man go to bed on the sidewalk in Brooklyn within two hundred yards of the Navy Yard gate, in less than fifteen minutes after he had come out of it, dead drunk and helpless from the comparatively limited number of drinks possible to be absorbed in that brief period of time. After travelling all over the world, I have found that there is no place like home — for the most abominably bad liquors on the face of the whole earth.

Day after day we swung idly at anchor in the beautiful bay. There was little or nothing to do, and we did it. Yellow Jack had left the city several weeks before we came, on his annual visit north. Sometimes we were on shore, enjoying hospitalities there; sometimes on shipboard, giving our own in return. Nobody cared how we looked. The airiest of costumes could create little sensation in a city where bathing-drawers for men, and chemises, and skirts reaching only to the knee, for women, were walking suits; and where children went naked. In a week or ten days we had lounged through the whole extent of the lower town, sometimes going on foot, sometimes in *caderas*; but none of us had found energy enough to mount the hill.

We had one sensation during this time. Several of us had started to go ashore one sultry morning after a late breakfast of tropical fruits and claret. We had gone about half-way from the ship to the shore, when there came after us, across the water, the sharp ringing report of one of the brass howitzers on the hurricane deck of our ship; and, turning at the sound, I saw a ball of bunting flying up to the fore-royal-masthead and dropping lazily in the breezeless air into the unpleasant shape of the cornet. Not the wind instrument, but a small flag so-called, which means "come on board;" and when hoisted in conjunction with the firing of a gun, "come on board as if the devil was after you."

Now, naval officers may wonder as much as they please at the sense or reason of an order, and may growl about it as much as they want to, if they only growl quietly and to themselves; but they must obey the order never-theless. We growled accordingly, but turned round and went back. Before reaching the ship, the coxswain whispered to me, bending over from his seat on the gunwale at the tiller, "It's something about that steamer outside, sir." I looked towards the entrance of the harbor, and saw a vessel heading in, some three miles away, burning English coal and flying an ensign in-distinguishable to the unaided eye, but which gleamed with traces of red in the sunlight. As I went over the side, our signal quarter-master was just hauling down our own flag.

I went up on the hurricane deck for a better look. My first glance through my marine glass explained everything. A light puff of the commencing sea breeze blew the colors of the incoming stranger straight out from the halliards at his mizen-peak, and showed me the Confederate "stars and bars" blazing in their brilliance of massed red and white. I have wondered since why he flew that flag, because the C.S.A. had changed the original for their would-be national ensign to the St. Andrew's cross studded with stars, in a crimson field on a white ground, some months before, I think. The rattle sounded to the quarters as I stood there, and I hurried below to my station at the ward-room table.

It was a flash in the pan. It was such a pity too. We had everything so beautifully arranged for the reception of the rebel steamer. We were in a neutral port, and of course had no right to attempt her capture; but all our plans were completed for sinking her as she lay at anchor that night or the next day; and that without firing a shot or violating a single rule of inter-national courtesy or neutrality.

Our engine was partially in pieces for cleaning and slight repair, but in ten or twelve hours it could have been put in order, steam raised and the ship got under way. A circuit of a mile, with a return to the neighborhood of our anchorage; a few orders given by the officer of the deck, which the quartermaster at the wheel would by direction misunderstand and reverse, and our iron stem, rising straight from the water, unencumbered by bowsprit or appurtenances, would have gone through the wooden sides of the rebel vessel like a knife through cheese.

Such a pity! Months afterward we learned that the rebel was the notorious *Florida*. Curiously enough, she was taken by the *Wachusett*, in defiance of neutral laws, in that same harbor of Bahia, long after we had sailed southward. But then the *Wachusett* had no means of playing the game we proposed, on account of being encumbered with head gear.

The rattle was sprung again. Quarters were over. The men and monkeys of the powder division closed the magazine, triced up the screens of woollen cloth which shut off its hatch from the rest of the ship, and restored the wardroom to its usual appearance. I suspected what had happened. I went on deck, passing the men who were hand-spiking the big pivot Parrott and the ten-inch side guns back into their normal positions, and hastily mounted the mid-ship ladder to the hurricane deck.

Our flag had been lowered too late, we imagined, or else the stranger had smelt mischief instinctively. Nothing about our appearance, save our ensign, would indicate our nationality. Indeed, in later days and other waters the governor at Castro insisted we were Spanish, from our "devil's mourning" — black and yellow paint. Our ship was the first of her type that had gone on foreign service. But at any rate and from whatever cause, when within a mile of us the rebel steamer had turned and put out to sea again as fast as her legs could carry her, while we lay helplessly looking after her. There wasn't the slightest use in trying to follow. Ten or twelve hours, as I said, would have been requisite to put us in condition to start, even had our fresh supply of coal been on board; and by that time the enemy would have been a hundred miles at sea, east, north or south of Bahia, practically lost to us.

Well — I wanted to tell about our getting lost in Bahia. Not the ship, but Dunallan and I.

After being in port awhile, we found that the evening and night were much pleasanter parts of the twenty-four hours to travel about in than were the days of sultry heat and torrid sunshine. We were unlearned in tropical rules, or we should have understood this from the first. Aside from the absence of the sun, night brings a breeze from the land to the sea in localities near the equator that border on the ocean — a wind stronger and cooler in Bahia than in almost any other port I have visited in the tropics.

The magnificent opera-house, rising from the hill-side on its Cyclopean foundation walls of solid masonry, was closed during our stay off the city. But one day news came to us that the imperial band was to give an open-air concert in the hanging gardens on the cliff that overlooks the ocean, two miles or more from the boat-landing in the harbor. We had heard a great deal about these gardens, and were naturally curious to see them. Our Brazilian friends had told us, very modestly, that in their opinion they were magnificent, and they were anxious to have our ideas about them. Bahians are mostly stay-at-home people, and know little of other countries except by hearsay. Our plain duty, as Americans of the North, was of course to pooh-pooh such an idea as the possibility of there being anything worth seeing outside of the United States — but we didn't; to have astonished these ignorant Brazilians with the fact, that the Central Park of New York beats anything else of the kind in the world; that the Mississippi is twenty-five thousand miles in its dirty length; that the falls of Niagara are seven hundred and seventy-seven feet high — but we refrained. Naval men and travellers in general, are apt to forget these minutiae of etiquette which are taught every American from his birth. It's unfortunate, I know, but they will do it. The public at large must console itself with the existence of some travelled Americans who are exceptions to the rule. Men who never let up on the Central Park, the Mississippi and Niagara, and who never fail to insult the people and the government of any foreign country where they may be, by predicting disaster and ruin to both, unless the stainless ward-politicians, the righteous congressmen, the unbiased elective judiciary, the filthy streets, the swindling taxation, the want of care for the lives and property of citizens, and all the other blessed fruits of popular rule, are at once introduced and adopted.

Sunset came, and Dunallan and I made ready for our evening excursion to the gardens.

Who first circulated that interesting lie about the suddenness with which the tropical night comes on? I have never yet seen an article or book regarding the equatorial regions that didn't reiterate this stereotyped nonsense about the sun sinking below the horizon at one minute, and the darkness of night coming on at the next. The twilight isn't as long, of course, as it is in high northern latitudes; but I have often read ordinary print with perfect ease a full half-hour after sunset, within two or three degrees of the line. I have often seen lingering light in the western sky for another half-hour later. The fact is, that most people who journey to foreign lands are told before they go of the things they ought to see, and instead of believing the evidence of their own senses, expend their time and energy in trying to find what other people say they have found.

Our friends were to meet us with *caderas* at the landing. A *cadera* is an arm-chair with a buggy-top covering, upholstered in dirty blue-and-white cotton cloth. It is almost as unclean as an ordinary American "hack." Two men carry the *cadera* by means of handles projecting fore-and-aft on either side. It looks like a bier condensed and canopied. The bearers keep grunting as they go, but never keep step. If the unlucky inmate has ever happened to ride camel-back, he finds the motion and noise reminding him forcibly at every step of his men of that excessively uncomfortable and dromedarian way of getting over the ground. Then the bearers are always unwashed and everlastingly perspiring; so that whether the wind is ahead or astern, it comes to him redolent of animal exhalations. On the whole, I used to prefer travelling on foot.

We reached the landing, but there was no one there. We waited a few minutes, but no one came. Half an hour, but our friends were still invisible. It began to grow late. It was very near the hour assigned for the commencement of the concert. Our boat had gone back to the ship and would return no more until midnight. Something had evidently occurred to detain our friends, perhaps to prevent their coming at all. Still, Dunallan and I had come ashore to see the gardens and to hear the music, and we had no idea of going back before both purposes were accomplished. Neither he nor I knew the way to our destination further than its general direction by compass, but waiting any longer at the landing was out of the question. We left word with the watchman at the gate, so that he could tell any one who might come for us where we had gone, and started up the hill to find our way unaided. Before getting under way, we had taken our bearings as accurately as we could. We knew that by heading E.N.E., and as far as possible "keeping her so," we should eventually reach the oceanside somewhere in the neighborhood of our destination, if we only went far enough. It was perfectly plain sailing at first. Not exactly under *easy* sail though. The grade of the principal street from the water, up which we went, is considerably steeper than that of Kearny, here in San Francisco, between Broadway and Vallejo, and about ten times as long as that particular block of our own amazing metropolis. Its trend was almost exactly that of our course as given above.

After many struggles and much puffing and blowing, especially on the part of Dunallan, who was fat and scant of breath, we reached the top of the street and sat down at once on the pavement to regain our wind. It was our first visit to the heights. Looking down across the city into the harbor was a view worth remembering. The sky was overcast and foreboded rain. The darkness of the night was intense. Above the magnificent sweep of the city around the crescent of the northern shore, there hung a misty splendor of light — low-lying clouds reflecting the rays sent up from ten thousand street-lamps beneath them. The bay — still, and black, and vast — was gemmed with glittering points, "the ship-lights on the sea." The night-wind blew gently and refreshingly over us as we rose and resumed our course.

They had told us that, beyond the crest of the hill, were the suburbs of the city, and we very naturally supposed it would be an easy matter to find our way through them. At the outset we encountered several serious obstacles to this. Instead of consisting as such districts usually do, of detached houses and open lots of ground, these suburbs were as compactly built as the town itself, but of houses of a meaner type, while the gas-lights ceased at the summit of the hill behind us. Before we had gone a quarter of a mile from our resting-place we were involved in an intricate maze of lanes and alleys—

were completely turned about, and had lost our course as thoroughly as if we had never held it. Not a star could be seen, and the breeze which we knew came from the north, was only palpable at the angles and intersections of the narrow streets, in eddying whirls from every point of the compass, giving no clue whatever to its actual direction. There was no use in trying to go ahead until we knew which way was ahead, of course. We came to anchor in front of a villanous-looking liquor shop, where a bright mulatto, half negro and half "Portergee," ("g" hard, as in "good-for-nothing") was dispensing rum behind an extemporized bar—a board on tressels. The door of the shop was open and we went in. Two or three small tables of rough wood were standing near the walls of the room, each one occupied by a couple of the lower order of the Portuguese population, seated on fragmentary chairs and stools. Dunallan asked the proprietor in English, if he could tell us the way to the gardens. The man stared stupidly at him, but said nothing. I repeated the question in French. The man stared again but made no reply.

"Ask him in Spanish, Dunallan," said I. He did so, but still the bar-keeper said nothing. By this time the other occupants of the room had gathered about us, each one talking rapidly and with many gestures in the Portuguese tongue, of which neither Dunallan nor I knew a single word. We repeated our questions in the only three languages at our command, but it was evident that no one could understand what we wanted. We declined a gesticulated invitation from the proprietor to drink something, and went out into the street. The place reminded me of a similar resort on the upper Potomac, where late one night, when I was employing a month's leave of absence from my ship in serving as a volunteer aid on Burnside's staff—it was on the eve of the battle of Antietam—two or three of us, travelling from Washington to join the army, had gone in after a long ride over wretched roads in wind and rain, to get something hot if possible. Just such a room as this one in Bahia, earth-floor and all except the tables—your Brazilian never takes a perpendicular drink, but must always have a table to sit down at—and just such a looking mulatto as bar-tender. Only in Maryland the mulatto spoke English, and asked us to "nominate our pison."

We walked on a little farther. If we couldn't find our way out by ourselves, and couldn't make anybody understand us, how were we ever to reach our destination? The question became more decidedly pertinent, and the labyrinth of lanes and alleys more bewildering than ever, as we advanced. After a few minutes' walking we came to another gin-mill. This one was a little dirtier and a trifle more disreputable in appearance that the first. Here, the proprietor as well as all his customers were Portuguese, and we repeated the same unsatisfactory questions with the same unsuccessful result. There was no use in going on, and none whatever in trying to retrace our steps. We should be traveling in a circle, in all probability, whichever way we went; and yet to stay where we were was an unpleasant impossibility. By daylight an observation from the roof of any one of the low houses around us, would have given some distinct bearings by which we might shape our course. This was impossible now. The darkness of the night, relieved only at intervals by a gleam of light from some unglazed window or open doorway, seemed to grow deeper and denser every minute, and the first heavy drops of a shower began to fall.

"We'll find a woman," said Dunallan. "She can understand us if the men can't. There must be one around here somewhere."

There was. She came towards us as he spoke. She was neither very pretty nor very young; and as she groped her way along the filthy road, it was very evident that she was three-parts drunk. Dunallan addressed her in a desperate compound of English and Spanish. She muttered something without looking up at him and kept on her way. He followed her and laid his hand on her shoulder.

"Look out! Dunallan," I said, "Don't touch her!"

My warning came just too late. She turned on him like a tigress, clawing at him with her skinny fingers, and yelling at the top of her unmusical voice.

"Make for the corner ahead there!" I shouted to Dunallan, starting for it at the same moment myself. A few yards from us, a dead wall at right angles to a house closed the lane in that direction. We rushed for the angle of junction and stood in it, side by side, with our back against its walls. In less than a minute the lane was filled by a crowd of half-drunken men and women, with flaming torches and glittering knives, hurrying towards the woman whom Dunallan had accosted, as she stood screaming and flourishing her arms, and pointing every now and then at us.

Dunallan had a loaded revolver in his belt. I had my brace of solid steel breech-loading Derringers with me, which were susceptible of almost as rapid handling as a revolver is, and which had, besides, the advantage in a street-fight of being useful as artificial knuckles, in event of one's ammunition giving out. We cocked our pistols and waited the onset of the Portuguese. "Don't fire till the last minute," said I, "and then *aim to kill.*" "Aye! aye!" replied Dunallan, and the infuriated crowd closed around us, yelling, hooting and brandishing their knives, but leaving a quarter-circle of some ten paces radius between us and them as we levelled our arms. They had caught sight of the pistols and hesitated. I have seen a good deal of all sorts of fighting in the course of my life, but I don't *like* to look into the open muzzle of a firearm in the hand of an enemy, and never saw anyone yet who did. One hears any quantity of brag about this sort of thing, of course; but when a man tells me he really loves a fight, I regard him as either a liar or a lunatic. I make these assertions by a right gained from close personal observation in more than twenty battles by sea and land; and I know that people who have ever smelt much of an enemy's powder will sustain me in them.

The Monitor came gaily up Hampton Roads one morning in March, and saved our sea-board cities from destruction. Our rescue from impending death came just as unexpectedly. At the instant our pistols gave temporary check to the enemy's advance, the tall and massive form of Long Mullen, our coxswain, hove in sight round the corner of a cross-lane, not a hundred feet from us, with the crew of a second cutter, twelve men good and true, at his back; each one armed with cutlass and revolver. Mullen was a New York Sixth-Ward Irish Hercules, and had picked out a crew after his own heart and build.

The lane was illuminated by the torches of the Portuguese. Instantly on turning the corner, Mullen's quick eye comprehended the whole situation, and instantly he and his men went in. How splendidly they came down towards us! Each man cutting and slashing right and left, Mullen leading with superb and sweeping blows, until such of the howling and cowardly mob as were neither killed nor wounded fled cursing into the darkness.

Our sailors gathered round us. Where had they come from? How did they happen to be on shore again so early in the evening? The explanation was simple enough. After returning to the ship, Mullen had asked and obtained permission for himself and his crew to go back and hear the concert. Just as they were shoving off, some gentlemen of the city came alongside in a shore-boat, to say that the gate-keeper at the landing had reported that two American officers had gone into a dangerous quarter of the town alone, and that aid ought to be sent them. Arms were quickly passed down into the cutter, and Mullen was ordered to follow us with all possible dispatch. Two of his men had been in Bahia before and knew the suburbs well; so that he had no difficulty in threading their mazes.

We gave our men substantial rewards for their energy and courage, treated them all round to brandy in a shop known to the two who had been there before, and soon found ourselves and our powerful escort at the entrance to the gardens. It was amusing to see the wholesome dread inspired by our visit to the last-named bar-room. The *habitues* skulked away in terror as we went in; and the proprietor, trembling and frightened half out of his wits, placed his entire stock of liquors at our disposal; utterly refusing to take any pay for what we drank. The story of the fight had spread; although if the gate-keeper hadn't been such an ass it need never have happened.

We weren't so very late for the concert after all. It began at nine, and it was only half-past that hour when we reached the gardens.

The precipitous cliff, on the verge of which this Bahian pleasure-ground is placed, is about three hundred feet in height above the level of the sea. Two terraces, excavated from its ocean front, lie in succession below the ten or twelve acres of plateau on the summit of the hill. At the outer edge of the plateau a parapet-wall of white marble, cut into a continuous bench or seat on its inner side, guards the visitor from a fall to the first terrace forty feet beneath him. A similar wall protects the ocean side of the first terrace, and still another that of the second. Stairways of stone go down from the highest ground to the level next below, and from that to the garden nearest the water. Tesselated pavements of marble, in various colors, make the floor of the footpaths on each of the levels. They had told us in the city that these gardens contained every variety of Brazilian vegetation, and I saw no reason to doubt it. Even on the plateau, before Dunallan and I had gone down the marble stairs, we found nearly every sort of tropical tree and flower that we had ever heard of: and the terraces below held many which were wholly unknown to us.

Hundreds of gaslights made the gardens visible and brilliant. Under the dense and heavy leafage of the tropics, and among the masses of low-growing shrubs that struggled for air and life beneath their self-begotten load of buds and blossoms, fragrant and rare and strange, the men and women of the city went up and down the winding walks, Dunallan and I following suit.

What was there in the air that night? Why should he and I have stayed so long, sitting on the parapet-bench of the plateau, listening dreamily to the music that came down to us on its way to the sea, smoking leisurely, talking or thinking as the hours went by, until over the ocean there came the first faint rays of dawn?

We hadn't taken anything to drink, and we hadn't gone to sleep. But it was sunrise when we reached the landing—broad daylight and breakfast time when we went over the side of the ship.

George T. Shipley, M.D. (-). *The only record of Dr. Shipley which we have uncovered is his naval service record. Born in Massachusetts, he was appointed to the Navy, September 16, 1861, and was commissioned an Assistant Surgeon in January of 1862. He first went to the receiving ship, Ohio, in Boston harbor. In 1863 he was aboard the gun steamboat, Wateree, which was on its way around the Horn to the Pacific in 1864. It was on this cruise in the famous part of Bohim, Brazil that he gathered the material for his story reprinted here. Dr. Shipley resigned from the Navy on September 6, 1865.*

Dos Reales

by G.T. Shipley, M.D.
July 1868

He had to have a name of course. So one day when he met us on the Mole and I had given him a quarter of a dollar by mistake for a copper "dump" or two-cent piece, and he had hurried off, throwing glances of trepidation behind him every now and then as he ran up the wharf lest I should overhaul him and demand return of change, I called him "Dos Reales." And always after that he seemed to know the name.

But that was a long while ago. Years before the Spanish fleet knocked the lower town to pieces. Dos Reales must be getting on in years by this time, even if he still lives.

He was a large brown dog, of no particular breed, and of the color of a ripe horse-chestnut. A dog of no vices. He scorned to run in debt, always paying cash down for what he ate, and lodging no one knew where. I haven't the slightest doubt, however, that he paid for bed as well as board. A very Beau Hickmann of a dog. Courteous, affable, self-possessed, never seeking an acquaintance but always glad to meet any friend of a friend of his, always opening his mouth for money when anyone whom he knew came near him. Bones and garbage he left to the plebeians of his race. I have often seen him turn up his nose with quiet contempt at ordinary pups squabbling for refuse edibles, as he, having dined well, lay at full length in the sun with an air of lazily smoking his after-dinner cigar.

No one knew where he came from. Dr. Reid, the wholesale druggist, whose shop is in Cochrane or Commercial street, I forget which, at any rate it isn't far from the Custom House which stands or did stand, before the Admiral Nuñez shelled it, right across the way from the gate of the Mole – and you turned to the right from the Custom House to go there – Dr. Reid, who knew more about the town than any other American in it, told me that he believed Dos Reales was left on shore by some merchant-ship's boat when quite a little puppy, and that when he found himself thrown upon his own resources, as you may say, he organized and adopted his own method of support in life.

It seemed to me that the dog deserved a good deal of credit for this. In fact, everyone gave it to him.

He would stand on the upper step of the long flight of landing stairs, watching our boat as it came from the ship. He knew the flag perfectly well, and would bark a hoarse and gruff "good morning!" as the officer in charge called out "way enough! trail oars!" and the coxswain steered her in towards the stairs, and the men let their oars swim loose in the beckets that hung alongside and threw over the little fenders of stuffed leather that looked like biscuits over-done, and the bow and stroke-oar, each armed with a boat hook, made desperate dives at piles and stairs to check her headway.

The gruffness was all put on, however. He would come up to us as we landed, laying his big, honest head in the hand of one and giving his paw to another, while he winked at a third and wagged his tail vociferously as the last one out of the boat came over the cap-sill. Then he would draw back from the group, sit down, open his mouth and look a request for money. Usually each of us gave him a "dump." He would close his teeth on the coin, wave a good-bye with his tail, and walk away to the town.

He patronized two butchers, a baker, and two cafes. At the butcher's he bought beef or mutton. He never ate pork. He always selected some choice cut, with plenty of juice and not too much bone in it. He liked a little bone for medico-chemical reasons probably. From the butcher's he would go to the baker's or one of the cafés, and purchase either plain bread or sweet cake, either or both as his taste or his means dictated, and then he would lie down in some quiet corner and eat his breakfast, or lunch, or dinner, like a Christian.

I wanted to tell you about his habits and peculiarities first, you know, so that you might feel acquainted with him.

We were all going to dine at Henry Caldwell's one night just after we arrived. Henry was a good-hearted, whole-souled fellow, who liked nothing better than to have his friends come to see him. He was a lumber merchant. His partner, Don Somebody-or-other, I forget his name, lived away down in the Patagonian woods, near the German city of Port Montt, where he cut lumber and sent it to Valparaiso, and Henry attended there to its sale.

Caldwell's home was a snug little house on Concepcion Hill, right up in the air three hundred feet above the lower town, and not half that distance back from where Cochrane street would have been had its location marked the summit instead of the base-line of the precipitous front of the hill. A zig-zag path, for mules and foot-travelers only, ran up the face of the bluff.

David Page and I were the only officers going from the ship that evening. Harry Finn, once on the stage in Boston, (you remember his father, the great comedian, dead long ago, a man of immense dramatic genius in his day and generation) was at that time in commercial business in Valparaiso, and three Chilean gentlemen were to complete the party. Henry Caldwell's cosy little dinners were perfection, and Page and I were anticipating a delightful evening.

"Don Ricardo isn't well enough to come to-night," said Henry.

He and David and I were walking slowly up the zig-zag path. "He's quite sick, in fact. Almost dangerously so, his clerk told me this afternoon."

I was very sorry. Don Ricardo was a civil engineer, at that time engaged in some way on the Valparaiso and Santiago railroad. He was most agreeable company, speaking English perfectly, and appreciating fully, which is one of the hardest things that a foreigner can do, all the points of a joke in our language. I was very sorry we shouldn't see him, and very sorry to hear of his illness.

Dinner went off very well. Mrs. Caldwell always handled her table and her guests in the most pleasantly efficient manner possible. Everyone was naturally a little subdued at first by the Don's absence and its cause, but as the wine went round we grew more like ourselves; and when our coffee had been poured and our cigars lighted, and Peta, the pretty table-girl, had made everything about the table snug and comfortable for a long sitting, we talked of people and things and felt certain Don Ricardo would be better by morning.

Perhaps he was.

There came a knock at the door, and one entered whose face was a face of sorrow and mourning.

Don Ricardo was dead.

Burials are such sad necessities! Why isn't the old classical incremation better? A retort to hold the body; a furnace to reduce it to ashes; an urn to hold the dust. I doubt if the daily, sickening thought that the hands which were ever devotedly ours for every need and tender care, the eyes that read love in return in our own, the lips that kissed us into life and light, are going back to their dust in slow and loathsome and crawling decay and corruption, is as pleasant as it might be. Still, tastes differ. Burials may be more Christian-like. It doesn't seem so to me—that's all.

Sincere mourners carried Don Ricardo's body to its grave.

And when we came back to Caldwell's and sat there at the open windows in his little parlor, and talked about the dead man, wondering what friends or relatives he had in his old home somewhere up near Santiago, wondering what they would say when they heard of his death, we grew melancholy. We were all away from home, too. Very far away. All with stout hearts. All with good courage. But what befell Don Ricardo might come to us, would in all certainty reach us somewhere. Perhaps while we were still strangers in a strange land.

Page and I said "Good-night" to Mrs. Caldwell, and started to go down town.

"I'll go with you," said Henry. "I can't sleep just yet. And Lizzie, why don't you go to bed, child? You're tired out, you know. I'll be back soon."

The night was perfect. Still and cool. The moon was nearly full.

At our feet, so far below us that the houses and ships were toys in size, lay the crescent of the lower town traced in triple lines of gas-light from the three business streets: lay the bay of silver undulating in slow magnificence as the ground-swell came in with the first of the flood.

At our left was the hill of the "Main-Top," looking by day like a gigantic leprous abscess ready for the knife; reeking both by night and day in its dens of misery and disease with more than the leper's foulness; a thing of beauty in the moonlight now.

Behind us, peak above peak, rising in snowy splendor till their king, Aconcagua, 23,000 feet above the sea, carried earth in unearthly grandeur to heaven, reigned the Andes of Chile.

And the Southern Cross shone out. Dimmed in glory by the moon, yet still radiant with the everlasting light that its stars gave forth ages before the world was, it hung in the midnight sky just over the churchyard where Don Ricardo slept, and point upward to God.

"Let's go round to his quarters a moment." said Henry. "The outer door was left unlocked this afternoon, and somebody may take a notion to steal something. You'll have plenty of time to reach the Mole."

Our boat had orders that night to wait till we came, and as the house where the Don had lived wasn't much out of our way, we went.

There's a sort of irregular, three-cornered plaza in the lower town. I don't remember its name. Perhaps it has none. Four or five streets make it in uniting and crossing each other. It's the only open space in the city of that especial shape, however, and it is near Cochrane street. There is a long two-story building on one side of it, that has a balcony or open veranda running the entire length of its front, on a level with the floor of the second story. Its projecting width is some seven feet, about that of the sidewalk below it. At each end a stairway, set against the wall, goes from the sidewalk to the balcony. These stairways are about four feet wide, and are set sloping towards each other. Nearer each other at the top, I mean, than they are at the bottom. Convergent. One word would have told what two sentences didn't. The ground floor is cut up into eight or ten retail shops, each one the width of an ordinary house-lot here in San Francisco, and forty or forty-five feet deep. The second story has as many suites of rooms as there are shops below. There are three rooms in each suite; the front one lighted from the balcony, the second and third by windows in the roof. These rooms communicate with the balcony only, each suite being isolated from its neighbor, and the only way to reach them from the street is by the outside stairways and the veranda. Just remember how this is, so that you can understand what I tell you.

We walked slowly along and stopped on our way at the English club house to get some brandy and cigars. We hadn't felt like either drinking or smoking before during the evening, but the mental and physical fatigue of the day began to tell. We talked with the manager, Whip, (I wonder whether he's still in existence, what he did in the bombardment, and whether he'll remember me if he sees this) lighted our cigars at one of the tiny braseros of burning charcoal that stood on the bar, came out into the moonlight and walked on towards the plaza.

We came into the plaza in such a direction that the house where Don Ricardo had lived was always directly before us. To reach either of the stairways leading to the balcony it was necessary to make a detour either to the right or left. The moonlight fell squarely on the face of the building, but just as we entered the open space a cloud dimmed and almost quenched it. The stairs on the left were a little nearer to us than the others, (we had come down on the left-hand side of the street from Cochrane) so turning that way, Caldwell leading, we traversed one side of the triangle and began to go up the stairway. Caldwell first, I next, and Page last.

Henry's head was just above the level of the floor of the balcony, when he stopped and looked intently forward. I was two or three stairs below him and stopped when he did. He looked ahead, put his left hand back with a gesture of warning, and then said, without turning round, speaking in a hoarse whisper, "for heaven's sake, doctor, look!"

I passed up by his side. Page followed. We three stood together on the same step of the stairway.

The moon shone out with renewed brilliancy, and there, leaning against a stanchion of the veranda rail not a dozen yards from us, and looking down into the plaza, dressed in his old-time wear, standing in his old familiar attitude, was Don Ricardo! Dead — buried fathom deep in red clay — and here!

As we stood the figure turned. The moonlight fell across its face, showing it white and ghastly and still. Then with slow and noiseless steps it entered the open door of Don Ricardo's quarters.

The little plaza was silent. From a distance came the sound of the foot-fall of some vigilante walking his beat, the bark of vagrant dogs, the deadened roar of the surf on the beach of the bay.

Regarding the right of a man, alive or dead, to enter his lodgings, there can be no doubt. The question is one of ability merely. To the best of our knowledge in the case of the Don, this ability had no existence.

Caldwell went along the sidewalk to the right hand stairway. Page took up a position in the road that enabled him to command a view of the veranda from end to end, and I began to re-ascend the stairs on the left. Henry and I reached the veranda at the same time and walked towards each other and the door where the figure had disappeared.

The front room was vacant of everything but its ordinary furniture. The chairs stood in their usual places. Books, instruments and papers lay undisturbed on the large table on the center of the floor. Caldwell lighted a match and with it the standing gas-light on the table. Every portion of the room was visible then, and no living beings were in it but ourselves. Walking out on the balcony I called Page and he came up.

The door of the middle room was closed but not locked. We opened it and went in.

Don Ricardo had used this second room for a work-place. Drawing boards, surveying implements, and two or three chairs were its only contents.

The back room door was shut. Lighting the gas in the working room we opened it cautiously.

A draft of air blew towards us and the gas-jet in the second room fluttered and flapped and nearly went out. Closing the door quickly, Caldwell scraped a match on the heel of his boot and ignited the gas at the bracket on the wall at the head of the bed.

The sky-light was open. Left so by the undertaker's attendants to ventilate the room, about which the odor of chlorine still lingered from the disinfecting agents used after the Don's death. The blank wall checked our further progress.

The bed was stripped. We looked below it. We looked in the movable closet or wardrobe standing on the right. We opened the doors of the bureau on the other side of the room. We made a variety of absurd investigations into every nook and corner—and found nothing.

Page sat down and lighted a fresh cigar, offering one to Caldwell at the same time and another to me. The smell of chlorine was unpleasant and we joined him in smoking. Thus far our search to understand the mystery ended in nothing more tangible. Ended in smoke.

Sailors are almost always superstitious. I have been one myself and I know of what I speak. Things come to men who go down to the sea in ships and do business in the great waters that landsmen never dream of. Old shell-backs believe in marvellous happenings because they must. Wouldn't the testimony of a dozen witnesses, men of truth and honor, combining to tell how each and every one of them had seen me kill you or you kill me, send me or you to the gallows? Very good. I can bring you the attested oaths of a thousand men who have seen that embodiment of the terrible, the Shrouded Demon of the Sea; who have found themselves working away up and out on a yard-arm in some night of storm and darkness, side-by-side with *something* that wore the form and features of a shipmate dead, sewed in his hammock and launched overboard days before, with a thirty-two pound shot at his heels; who have seen a ship with everything set, mannered by no mortal men, drive straight into the teeth of a gale and vanish, shadowy masts and spars going over the side of a ghostly hull, which rose and plunged and sunk while groans and shrieks of men and women came over the surging sea to the ears of the horrified witnesses, and have had this drama of death three times repeated in their sight in an hour. Superstition is hardly the term to apply to this sort of thing. It's simply a belief in facts as patent to the eyes of those who see them as are the ordinary scenes of a city to a lounger in its streets. What's the use of saying they can't be, when they *are?*

So two of us being of the sea, we sat, and smoked, and talked of this apparition. If one of us only had seen it, the others might have doubted its reality, and attributed the whole thing to the fumes of Mr. Whip's strong water acting on a system wearied with the toil of the day. But it had been seen by all three. And, as if to confirm its reality, the portrait of the Don, hanging on the wall directly beneath the skylight, parted its fastenings suddenly, as if unseen hands had cut the cord, and fell on the floor with a crash that shivered its heavy frame and tore the canvas from its stretcher. Fell at our feet—and the painted face, rent from forehead to chin, looked up mournfully at us from the ruin.

"Let's get out of this," said Page. "I'm going aboard ship."

He threw his half-smoked cigar away, and went through the other rooms to the balcony. I saw no reason for remaining, and went out after him. Caldwell turned off the gas in each room as he left it, and followed us.

We stopped at Whip's again on our way to the Mole. I have great doubt of either the need or benefit of brandy under ordinary circumstances. But there's probably no fact more firmly established than the one of there always being some especial reason why a drink should be taken. We had taken our first one that night to revive us. Page suggested the second to quiet our nerves; and Page being then and now a man using but little stimulant, a suggestion of this sort from him carrying weight, in consequence, and meaning something, we agreed to it.

Two or three men had come into the club-house since our first call, and we went up stairs the second time we heard them talking and laughing out in the moonlight, through the open door at the end of the central hall. There was a balcony there that overhung the water.

Caldwell recognized their voices, and asked Whip to send our brandy out there after us.

Page knew one of the party, an old Scotchman, named McLerie, and Henry was evidently well known to all of them. They made room for us at the table where they were sitting. Presently the servant in attendance at the bar brought out our decanter and glasses, and we all drank together.

"What's the matter with you three?" said McLerie. "Caldwell there looks as if he had seen a ghost. What has happened?"

Then Page told him about what we had seen on the balcony, and how we looked through the rooms and found nothing, and wanted to know what he thought of it.

"Well, said McLerie, after a pause of a few minutes, during which he emptied his glass and lighted a fresh cigar, "I think that whoever or whatever you saw, went out of the third room, through the open skylight. I don't believe there was anything unreal about the affair. You were all thinking of the Don; there was somebody standing at his door. The moonlight is uncertain at best. I haven't the slightest doubt about there being a man there, but I am perfectly sure that it *was* a man, and no ghost. That's my idea. Page and the doctor know very well how easily an active man might mount on the bureau, cling to projections here and there in the wall of the room, and be out on the roof in less time than it took you to get there from the front door. I don't believe in supernatural agency when I can account for a thing by ordinary rules."

We sat there and talked the matter over for a long time. As usual, each one of the party had his own theory to advance and his own illustrations to tell. Whip was a remarkably patient man with good customers, the summer night was short, and the bay below us began to reflect the first faint approach of sunrise before our conversation ended. We had forgotten all about our boat. Caldwell had unwittingly far overstayed his promised time for returning home. But we knew our men didn't care, and we trusted that the captain would find but little fault when he heard our reasons for delay, and Henry's wife had undoubtdly gone to bed to sleep quietly till he came. She was a very sensible woman.

So we all got under way for the Mole. Caldwell and our new friends insisted on going down to see us safely off for the ship. Our boat lay bumping gently every now and then against the lower stair of the landing. There was one man in her, fast asleep. Page woke him up, and started him off after the rest of the crew. We all sat down on the long bench that runs along inside the railing on the cap-sill of the pier, and waited for the crew to come.

Dos Reales had preferred camping out that night to retiring to his usual lodging-house, wherever that might be. So we judged, at least, for after the sound of several prolonged yawns, and a variety of scratchings and slippings of claws on the wooden floor of the wharf, had come to us from a little distance, he made his appearance, walking sleepily towards us, through the morning twilight. He rubbed a "good morning" against each one of us, and then sat down and opened his mouth for money for his breakfast.

"You're too early, old fellow," said I; "there are no shops open yet. Lie down, sir!"

After waiting a while and looking wonderingly at the absence of his usual remittances, he appeared to think so too, and curled himself up at my feet to resume his interrupted slumbers.

The coming daylight came nearer. The lanterns on the Mole began to grow dim, and the chilly land breeze from the mountains to lessen in strength.

There was a steady footstep coming down the pier from the entrance gate.

"There comes the coxswain," said Page. "The crew are close behind him. Let's get into the boat."

We were shaking hands with our shore friends, and saying "good bye," when Caldwell exclaimed: "McLerie! Look there!" We turned and looked up the Mole.

The steady footsteps had ceased, but a figure stood about a dozen yards from us, shadowy and vague in the dim light, wearing the features and dress of the dead Don Ricardo—stood in his old familiar attitude, looking far out seaward, unconscious, apparently, of us or anything else of this earth.

McLerie shrank back.

"What do you think *now*?" whispered Page.

McLerie braced himself as if against some physical shock, waited a moment, and then exclaiming, "Man or ghost, I'll make it speak!" he started with a firm step towards the figure.

But Dos Reales was too quick for him. With a bark of joyful greeting he sprang up and ran towards the apparition, satisfied that he had at last found someone who would give him what he wanted. After his usual manner, he sat down close to the figure, and opened his mouth for the expected coins.

The apparition burst into a loud laugh.

It was a twin-brother of Don Ricardo's. The affair of the night before had been impromptu on his part. He had seen our heads above the upper step of the balcony stairs, suspected what we thought, and resolved to carry out the delusion by doing exactly what McLerie surmised he had done—climbing rapidly out on the roof through the open sky-light, and dislodging, or rather loosening, the nail that sustained the picture, as it gave him a momentary stand-point in his ascent. This morning he had merely walked out for fresh air. At the gate of the Mole he had heard our voices, and supposed them to be those of boatmen. Coming nearer, he had recognized us, and resolved to maintain the illusion of the balcony of the night before; but Dos Reales interfered.

The affair didn't lessen either Page's belief or mine in ghosts, however.

———————————————

The Panama Fever

by Thomas M. Cash

December 1868

"My dear, the captain says that to-morrow morning, early, we shall arrive in Panama, and I think it would be well for us to take a few grains of quinine to-day, to be sure and prevent any possibility of an attack of fever on the other side. You know how you suffered the last trip, and a little precaution this time will probably prevent a recurrence." I heard the above remark made by a lady to her husband, and am assured that the same occurs frequently among passengers to and from California for a day or two prior to their arrival at Aspinwall or Panama, so great is the fear of contracting disease during the day that intervenes between the arrival at one, and departure from the other port. We will follow this lady from one ship to the other, and observe what she does to aid the three five-grain pieces in their good work of preventing an attack of *calentura,* as the natives term it.

The steamer is made fast to the buoy, and then the passengers are informed that on account of the tide not serving, the steam tender with the mails, baggage, etc., will not leave for two or three hours, and that they must pass the time as best they can. Waiting under such circumstances is not pleasant, and our lady friend, whom for convenience, I shall term Mrs. Prudence, exclaims: "How provoking!" Now Mr. P., who is a staid, sober, sensible personage, sees no particular hardship in having to seek a cool, shady spot on the commodious deck, and waiting until the time comes to be transported from the anchorage to the railroad wharf; but his better-half can't stand it; her small traps — even to the ice pitcher — have been consigned to the tender care of the obliging baggage master, who for a fee will see them safe on the other side, and she is unable to remain quiet; at last, turning to her husband — who has been watching the back fin of a shark moving about on glassy surface of the bay, waiting for something or somebody to tumble overboard — she remarks: "Mr. P., we have two hours before us; now, instead of staying here doing nothing, let us get into one of these boats and go on shore; we can see the city, and I can purchase some linen dresses and other matters *very cheap* — and you know that I will want them this summer at the East, and will have to pay much more for them in New York. Mrs. _____ has gone, and I am sure she will select the prettiest patterns if much before us. So come along; don't be stupid — it will do you good, and you will enjoy it, for it is not very warm." Poor P.! if there is one thing more than another that he dislikes, it is boating, even under the most favorable circumstances; but to be compelled to go three or four miles under a blazing tropical sun, with the thermometer nearly up to ninety degrees in the shade, is a little too much; but Mrs. P. continues her importunities, and it does not take him long to discover that refusal will only add to his discomfort, and hence he gives a most unwilling consent. For a few *pesos fuertes* a boat is secured, and Mrs. and Mr. P., with probably a few friends that she has persuaded to join the party, take their seats, and off they start with no other protection than a sunshade, or, at the most, an umbrella.

From the anchorage in the Bay of Panama to the *puerto del mar*, or seagate, is at least three miles—a long pull even in a man-of-war's gig; but in an ordinary boat, with only two oarsmen, especially on the ebb tide, it is of prodigious length, and so our friends found it. They had not gone a mile before Mrs. P. even would have turned back; but pride gained the day, and she would not have said the excursion was not delightful on any account — she would have died first! The sun first, and the reflection from the mirror-like surface of the bay, rendered the heat insufferable; and after an hour of such discomfort the boat is grounded on the reef, and the company are told that they will have to walk some hundreds of yards before they reach the entrance of the city, for the tide being out the boat can go no further. They start off over the slippery, slimy rocks, mentally saying very many hard words, but trying to look pleased. The gate is reached and the city entered, and then another walk follows over rough sidewalks or cobble stones to the Grand or Aspinwall Hotel; and a more uncomfortable looking or feeling party it would be hard to find. The woman portion, with muddy boots and skirts, from walking over the reef, and with faces red as so many poppies, are fanning themselves in the most frantic manner; the men, in scarcely better condition, are looking anything but pleased. All, however, seek a cool place, and throwing off all superfluous clothing, they seat themselves where there is a breeze, probably in a strong draft; and then sherry cobblers, or something of the like character, are sent for, to be disposed of while waiting for the breakfast that has been ordered: probably an orange or two may be devoured in the mean time as an appetizer.

A Panama breakfast is no ordinary meal; in fact, it is the meal of the place, especially with Americans, and ample justice is generally done to it, particularly by those who may have had the exercise that Mr. P. and party have been subjected to. There is a kind of novelty about it; and Mrs. P., in the variety set before her, forgot all about the little silver-coated balls that she had swallowed the day before to ward off the effects of a tropical climate. Mr. P. was in a better humor also, and though, now that the trip was over, and he had "cooled off," that it was not so bad after all; and like the others, forgot all else than his appetite, and thought that while in Panama he would do as the Panameños did, and accordingly stowed away a large portion of a bottle of St. Julien, while his wife did the same—it was "so very cool and refreshing." When breakfast was over, the time was found to be limited; the train would leave at a certain hour, and all the sight-seeing and shopping had to be done in a hurry. The latter being the first consideration, of course, the stores were sought — and in Panama their name is legion — and as a rule they contain the most obliging proprietors and clerks, willing to put themselves to any amount of trouble and inconvenience to gratify California passengers, who are all supposed to be heavy with *oro Americano*, worth generally about five per cent premium. A lady can purchase a large amount of dry goods in a very short space of time when the necessity arises for so doing, and Mrs. Prudence and her friends proved no exception to the rule. Half a dozen dress patterns were selected, an indefinite number of yards of plain linens, and many dozen of hem-stitched handkerchiefs were also purchased; and when all were tied up and delivered, Mr. P. found out that the bundle under his arm was far heavier than the amount of coin his pocket had been relieved of. Mrs. P. now discovered that the time was up; that if they did not "hurry up" they would be too late for the last omnibus for the station, and that they might be compelled to walk; her shopping was over, she had secured all that she came ashore for, and more, too; she cared nothing for ruined churches and mouldy, crumbling walls now; her only desire was to get to the train and into the cars, and give her female passengers a list of her purchases, knowing that thereby she would excite their envy, and make them wish that they also had come ashore, instead of waiting for the more comfortable passage afforded by the *Ancon*.

The omnibus was reached by our again overheated party, for the sun's rays were coming down in full power; fans were again moving; the perspiration was streaming down the faces of more than one, and it was with a sigh of great relief that Mr. P. deposited his bundle and seated himself in the "bus", at the moment of its starting for the station. On reaching the cars they found that the passengers had been ashore for sometime, and it was with great difficulty that seats could be obtained, for it is seldom that the "steamer trains" of the Panama Railroad take more cars than there is necessity for; but they were found at last, and when all were stowed away, bundles included, then it was that more than one of our party *thought* that they had eaten too much breakfast. The pills were beginning to have their proper effect.

At the wharf of the Panama Railroad, when the California passengers arrive, the native merchants in fruit, birds, shells, and other commodities, appear in swarms; they are nuisances of the first class — thought so by all who come in contact with them — and yet they are liberally patronized; they will cheat you in the most unblushing manner; poison you legitimately and take your coin for it; in fact, they will perform almost any little service for you; provided they can get three prices for it. You are no sooner off the gang plank than they beset you on every side; they are in the cars and out of the cars; they take hold of you, if they cannot attract your attention in any other way, and if you resent their continued and repeated insults, you will get more than you bargained for in the shape of abuse, and a mob could be raised in a moment were it not for the squad of ragged, dirty native soldiers that are always on hand to keep the peace. These natives are themselves quite sufficient to give one an attack of Panama fever, even if there was no malaria or other exciting cause in the place; and yet they remain the same all the time, and will, until some other power rules the country.

Mrs. Prudence dotes on several things; among these are silks, laces, the last new bonnet, the Italian opera, and tropical fruits; the latter she has a decided weakness for, and says that Californians get surfeited with apples, peaches, pears, grapes, etc., and that when the opportunity offers of getting some really good bananas, oranges and pine apples, it should be taken advantage of. She acted upon this argument, but first purchased a parrot and a pair of paroquets for some of her junior relations in the East, that she had not seen for years; for, as she said, "it will be so pleasant for them to think that they have been remembered." Mr. P. had, under her instructions, and to gratify his own tastes — for he was fond of tropical fruits — laid in a large bunch of bananas, some pine apples and oranges, and had also secured a couple of bottles of claret to last them to Aspinwall. A young and interesting monkey had tempted him; but he had no way to carry it, the animal appearing too vicious for a passenger car; his wife had also taken a fancy to it, saying: "What a dear little monkey, how cunning it looks;" (she had no children) but the purchase had to be given up, and the sable son of Jamaica was compelled to leave with his monkey remaining upon his hands.

It is scarcely necessary for me to say, that the majority of the passengers that waited for the steam-tender to bring them ashore comfortably were refreshing themselves after the fashion of Mr. P. and his friends. Fruit met with more ready sale than other articles, but occasionally a passenger could be found driving a bargain with a native for what he supposed to be pearls, but which were nothing more than imitations carved from pearl shell, very pretty and having a tendency to deceive any but a practiced eye; many passengers being taken by these worthless articles, only finding out their mistake when taking them to a jeweler to be set. This desire to purchase everything the natives on the Isthmus offer for sale, is another description of Panama fever that quinine will not reach. The foreigners who reside on the Isthmus, and who flock to the station when the steamer arrives, look on at the excesses of those in transit, and laugh quietly when they think of the almost certain result of them. They "have been through the mill," and are willing that others should partake of their experience as a penalty for their imprudence.

There is always more or less delay in leaving after all the passengers are seated, and Mrs. Prudence has even found time before the train started to give her experience, and tell what a delightful time she had among the old buildings and dry goods stores; and it was not without strong remonstrance on the part of the husband, that she refrained from opening the bundle to show the pretty things she had purchased. The climate had for a time ceased to be thought of; the imprudence she had thus far been guilty of never entered her brain, and it was not until the moving of the cars told her that the train was off, that she remembered her situation, and discovered that she was in that unhealthy locality — the Isthmus — then it was that a shudder passed over her, and she exclaimed that she didn't feel very well, that the atmosphere appeared heavy, and that she'd better take another pill — and she did.

We will leave our party to themselves for a little while, and go through the train to see what the rest are saying and doing. It is a singular fact that so few among the passengers who pass from the Pacific to the Atlantic Ocean, find anything to admire in the varied and beautiful scenery of the Isthmus of Panama; they can talk of its miserable inhabitants; their dirty hovels and naked children; its fevers and other diseases; its venomous reptiles; its deluge of rain, and everything that is unpleasant about it; but seldom have a pleasant word for the numerous beautiful views that are to be seen, especially between the Chagres River and the Bay of Panama. Nowhere can tropical scenery be found more diversified than between Aspinwall and Panama; you have the dense jungle, the impenetrable forest, the mountain range, covered with foliage to the summit, the tortuous river and smaller streams, with the mangrove bushes growing to their edge; birds of the most brilliant plumage, and such flowers as are only seen within the tropics; and yet with all this to please the eye, and to call forth the admiration of those who profess to be fond of the beautiful, how seldom it is that an exclamation of delight is heard at such a combination of all that is lovely in nature! In the dozens of times that I have crossed the Isthmus with passengers, and at all seasons of the year, I have not failed to notice what I have stated above; and really, when I did hear someone break out with an exclamation of pleasure, I have felt like rushing up and embracing him or her for being an exception to the rule — for evincing some appreciation of a picture such as nature only can paint.

The principal topic of conversation, especially with cabin passengers, appears to be about the passage just concluded. The ship, her captain and officers, the accommodations and the table, are all raked up and overhauled. Gossip with her mischievous tongue pulls to pieces this one or that one, that may, in the eyes of these models of purity, as gossips generally profess to be, have been guilty of some act of indiscretion, in their opinion unpardonable. Captain _____ is abused by some who did not have places at his table; they charge him with favoritism. The purser comes in for his share of faultfinding; he showed partiality, of course, and the Company should find another to put in his place who would be the same to all. The table was, if you believe what is said, miserable; fit only for the lower grade of passengers; and as for accommodations — why, each person should have had an entire state-room to himself. The steamer the other side, the one they are to embark upon, is everything she should be; and reaching her deck is looked forward to with great expectations by those who, though claiming to be slighted on one side, suppose they will have everything their own way on the other. There must be something in the air of the transit of the Isthmus that causes so much complaint, and it may be one phase of the disease, for I have seen more than one person worked almost into a fever by recounting the terrible hardships passed through on the voyage just ended.

Mrs. Prudence is one of the kind mentioned. Very little on the passage has pleased her; she has not received the attention from the officers her well known position in society entitle her to; being the wife of one so well known as Mr. P. is, she should have had more privileges, and her husband must speak of it on his return. Tropical scenery has no charms in her eyes. She can see only her wrongs, and the little affairs that have occurred on board ship, which are termed by her, "horrible conduct." She continues her observations in the cars, and although not feeling well, keeps a sharp look on what is going on around her. Turning to her friend, Mrs. Caution, she remarks: "Do you see how Miss Flyaway carries on with that Mr. Easy? really, it is abominable, and her family should put a stop it it; the night before we reached Acapulco, I found her sitting with him on the guard, after all her friends had gone to their rooms, and dear knows how long they stayed there; she should be ashamed of herself, and have more respect for her reputation; but you know that she was always called fast, and would have been cut long ago, only for her parents." Mrs. C. fully coincides with everything said, and adds her portion to the conversation by wondering aloud if the widow that Mr. Savage is and has been so attentive to all the time, has any idea that he is a married man with a family?

Mr. Prudence, tired of wading through the columns of a New York paper that he managed to obtain at Panama, has succeeded in mixing a claret punch, and interrupts his wife in her conversation, by suggesting that, as the weather is very warm, she should take some—to which no objection is offered. Thereupon Mrs. C. produces a lunch, prepared on board the ship, among which are several hard-boiled eggs; and these are devoured with much gusto, and are washed down with the above-mentioned beverage. By the time this is over, the train is at Matachin, the half-way house, where some minutes are allowed for refreshments. Here, as at Panama, all kinds of fruit are offered for sale; cocoa-nuts, prepared in various forms, also, and the latter are seized upon with avidity. Mrs. P. takes her share, and expresses great amusement at the original and tasty manner in which the junior members of the society of Matachin are clad, and wonders if they never suffer from the heat by reason of having so much clothing. She soon tires of this, however, and yawning thinks the trip across is very long and tedious, and that it occupies more time than there is any need of. She has a slight headache; she closes her eyes, and leans against the back of the seat; she is not feeling as well as in the morning, and longs to be on board the other ship and in her state-room. Something is the matter. Is it the debilitating effect of the climate; is it the malaria? Who can tell!

In the seven or eight cars that compose the train, you will find many that are in the same languid condition. Of course, there are exceptions: you may find couples that have formed acquaintance on board ship, from which serious flirtations have arisen, carrying them on with the same energy in the cars; you will see jolly parties, that manage to make merry and keep alive at all times; and you may tumble over a crowd in the baggage-car, keeping up the "spree" that commenced within an hour after the steamer had cast off from the wharf. The latter are case-hardened individuals, that fever won't touch; they drink Bourbon to keep it off, and take the same to cure it; they make friends with baggage-masters and conductors; they are always on the right side with captains, pursers, and superintendents; they have money, and they spend it freely; they are on their way East to have a good time, and they commence early; they appear to have their own way in everything, and to control matters as if the steamships and railroad were their exclusive property.

Willie Thompson — one of the two regular passenger conductors of the road — like his brother in the service, (Mr. Lee) — allows every license possible to steamer passengers, consistent with the regulations of the Company. He is part and parcel of the concern; his good-humored Scotch face has nearly always a pleasant smile upon it, and he knows the passenger characteristics; he can tell you those that are soon to be sick by reason of imprudence; he knows a gentleman from a snob, and the lady from an upstart; he can "spot" a stowaway, and can put him out of the train if compelled to; and if the time is given him, he can tell you more of the Panama railroad than almost any man belonging to it. He delights in laughing at those who are afraid of the climate and who, like Mrs. P., take medicine to prevent ill effects therefrom. Years and years he has lived at all points on the road; he has been through wet and dry seasons so often, that he could scarcely do without the regular change from one to the other — and yet he looks the picture of health. He has had the fever over and over again, and laughs at it now; and if you want to know how to get it, and how to get rid of it, ask him — he can tell you all about it, and can tell you why it is that so many foreigners have died in the vicinity of Panama, and after leaving it; and why it is that so many live there, year after year, and retain almost unbroken health. You can find out from him, also, the reason for passengers taking the Panama fever, after being only a few hours on the Isthmus. Indeed, he is a guide-book on all such matters; and if you can get a chance at him, when off duty, you will find out in an hour more than you ever knew before about the Isthmus. Mr. Lee could give you nearly as much; but he is not talkative. In that respect he is Thompson's opposite; in others, he is much the same. Both are clever fellows.

Our friend, Mr. Prudence, was a kind and considerate husband; he would do anything within the bounds of reason, to oblige his spouse; his means were ample to gratify every expensive want; and he would submit to personal inconvenience, at any time, to keep peace in the family. Now, when the train stopped at the summit, ten miles from Panama, to take water, his dearly beloved wife saw among the bushes, at some distance from the track, a quantity of beautiful and rare flowers, and thought that a few of them would serve to adorn her state-room and counteract, in a measure, the smell peculiar to all ships, even to a first-class steamer. A wish so easily gratified was equivalent to an order, and Mr. P., without further thought, plunged boldly into the bush with all the ardor of a young man desirous of serving his first love. Poor P. — he thought that he might run through the grass, on the Isthmus, with as much impunity as he used to at home, when a boy; he little dreamed of what was in store for him; and when the flowers were seized and brought back in the train, he imagined that his trouble was over — that his work was fully accomplished. If he had known of the *garapatos* (wood-ticks) that were on his person in that short space of time, and that were destined to cause him many sleepless hours, by reason of the intense itching they create, he would not have felt so joyous at having given his wife gratification, by complying with a wish so moderate as hers. There is a moral in this for all men who may be crossing the Isthmus: Never, under any circumstances, when passing from Panama to Aspinwall, rush away from the track into the grass, or bushes, to cull flowers for a lady — no matter how young or attractive she may be — unless willing to submit to the torture of those little insects that are there to be found in countless numbers. Many, through ignorance, have done what Mr. P. did, and have suffered for days before knowing the cause of their trouble, or where the "confounded things" came from.

The train has passed Gatun, the last station before reaching Aspinwall, and little change could be noticed in the situation of the Prudence party. True, the claret punch had disappeared; many of the bananas and oranges had gone the same way; but a cloud was there and hardly energy enough was left to express pleasure at so soon being at the end of one portion of the journey. When the prolonged sound of the whistle came which announced the approach to Aspinwall, and the waters of the Caribbean Sea and the masts of the vessels in the bay appeared to view, they did begin to brighten up; and as they gathered up the articles that had not been given to the baggage master — the precious bundle included — they did, with one voice, almost say, that if they had not felt so dull and languid, so oppressed with the heat, the journey would not have appeared so long after all. 'Twas over at last, however; the train had been brought to a stand-still; the cars were disgorging their loads of human freight; the Jamaica negroes in crowds were hanging on to the skirts of the passengers, seeking for a "job" as porters, and abusing those who did not see fit to patronize them. All Aspinwall had turned out to see who had arrived, as Mr. P., family, fruit, dry goods and parrots, descended from the car and sought the shelter of the Howard House, the hotel whereat first-class passengers most do congregate. The site of one of these Isthmus palaces is enough to give one the fever almost. And so Mrs. Prudence thought, for depositing her packages in a safe place, she insisted that Mr. P. should take her a walk up the track, to see what was to be seen of the town. It was about four P.M. when this little piece of exercise was taken, and still very warm, for the sun was nearly as powerful as at noon-day. Mr. P. didn't want to go, but his wife insisted; she wanted to walk off the dull feeling that had bothered her all day; it would do her headache good. These with other excuses were enough—and away they went. About the time they started, certain dark, heavy clouds were rolling up from the southwest, and the mutterings of distant thunder could be heard from time to time. This is nothing uncommon in the tropics; but as the sun was shining at the time, they gave it no attention. The north portion of the island was reached, the new church had been examined, the company's mess house had been peeped into, and they were on the return, when drops of rain began to fall; the sun was obscured, and it had become almost as dark as night. Soon the drops increased in size and number, and our devoted couple, with no other covering that the sun umbrella of Mrs. P., hurried forward in the direction of the hotel. Before they reached there they were wet to the skin, and in this condition they remained, for a change of clothing could not be had. True, the sun came out again,nd they tried to dry themselves a little thereby; but they had wet feet, and when the gun fired from the steamer, giving signal that the passengers could come on board, they were chilled through and felt anything but comfortable. They soon found their state-room, and after undressing, Mrs. P. concluded that it would not pay to go on deck again, even to see the steamer go out of the harbor. So she wisely "turned in" and thought to get warm: the chill and headache remained, but they gave her no uneasiness. She though they would pass off soon, and that the next morning she would be as bright and as merry as ever, and con-gratulated herself that she had got through the transit so well.

Mr. P. was better off; he had turned over a new leaf, *i.e.*, got on dry clothing, and had taken the deck for it, watching the last moments before the plank was hauled ashore. He made the acquaintance of the U.S. Consul at Aspinwall, who is always in Panama, and listened to his story of how he was obliged at one time to *visé* the passports of all California passengers; and how the rinderpest had broken out among the cattle; and how he had to have an order issued that no hides coming from the Isthmus could be landed in the States without his certificate that they had covered the bodies of healthy cattle—indeed, he was going on with a history of his trials and vicissitudes as Consul of the United States in Acapulco and on the Isthmus, when the "all ashore" cry came, and the conversation had to be broken off, much to the sorrow of Mr. P., who being a practical business man, had listened to the information given by our Consul with more than ordinary in-terest. He had hoped to learn something of the Panama fever, but was too late, and this information had to be postponed for another visit.

The following morning broke bright and clear; scarcely a cloud was to be seen, except the heavy bank that hung over the land to the southward. The mountains of the Isthmus had sunk below the horizon, and the Caribbean

Sea—that dread, as a rule, of California passengers—was as smooth as possible; the long, heavy swell rolled in from the northward, to which the noble steamer bowed and courtesied as politely as a French dancing master; but the surface of the water was not even broken by the gentle easterly breeze, that served only to fan the cheeks of those who had ventured on deck to enjoy early morning in the tropics. Although Mr. Prudence made his appearance at the breakfast table, Mrs. P. did not—her place was vacant; and to the questions asked him by everyone about her absence, he replied, that although not sea-sick, she was far from well. The truth is, that when Mrs. P. awoke, instead of feeling refreshed, and ready for a pleasant day on deck, she found that her headache remained and had become worse; that pains in her back and limbs had set in; that her skin felt dry and parched, and her mouth seemed unnatural. As all these symptoms remained, she thought it best to send for the doctor, and ask him what was the reason for them all. The medical officer came and had a talk with his patient—for Mrs. P. would talk even when a little under the weather. After hearing all she had to say about how she felt, his diagnosis was a mild case of fever—Panama fever. This he told her at once, and was about to prescribe the necessary remedies, when she broke out with great vehemence, and said it could not be so, it was impossible! The doctor asked her if she had not been guilty of any imprudence. "No," she replied, "I have not. I only went on shore from the steamer at Panama in an open boat; cooled off at the hotel with a sherry cobbler; refreshed myself with claret; ate a hearty breakfast with fruit; went shopping afterwards; ate lunch with fruit and claret on the cars, and got a little wet in the shower last evening at Aspinwall; besides all this both myself and Mr. Prudence took fifteen grains of quinine before reaching Panama. So you see that I have not been imprudent at all." This argument was, of course all-sufficient with the medico. He saw through the case at a glance—only another of the many he had treated of the same kind in traveling to and from Aspinwall. He dared not contradict the lady; but he told her that notwithstanding her *prudence* she still had the fever; not an alarming case, or one that would not yield in a few days to proper medical treatment; but still it was the fever. Her reply was: "Now, doctor, you don't say that with all my prudence and care I have the fever?" "Yes, madam, you have, as I have told you." "Well, then, doctor," she said, "it must be the climate alone that caused it; for with the precautions I have used, nothing but malaria could have brought on this attack." The doctor left his patient in no pleasant frame of mind. She vowed that she never would return to California until enabled to do so overland. She still lives, however, and in her daily habits and tastes is a remarkable example of the insidious character, which no precaution can avert, of the Panama fever.

Thomas M. Cash (-   ). *We were fairly convinced that nothing was* to be found on the life of Mr. Cash when we discovered a small book in the Library of Congress written by him and titled, A Plain Statement of Fact for the Perusal of Those Interested, published in 1872 in New York. Much to our surprise and delight the forty-three page book was a chronicle of his wife's infidelity during an illicit love affair.

According to the author, he and his wife, Ellen J. Lewis, were secretly married in Philadelphia in June of 1860, to the displeasure of her father. The young couple was estranged from her family for the next six years.

We do not know if marital problems contributed to his dismissal from his position at the time, but he lost his job and was compelled to accept an appointment for six months in the flotilla on the Potomac. Naval records show his service was as an Acting Master from January to August of 1861. He resigned in November and got a job as a War Correspondent for a prominent New York journal. They sent him to Key West, Florida, where his wife joined him early in 1862.

From October 1863 through 1866 the couple was in Panama, except for a voyage in 1865 to San Francisco and back aboard the Pacific Mail steamship, Colorado. To Thomas Cash's surprise, the commander of the ship was an old colleague from the days when Cash had been an officer in the opium trade off the coast of China. His friend invited Cash to become his Executive Officer on the voyage and he was kept quite busy with his duties. It seems that Mrs. Cash found a way to beat boredom, as she and an Irish born U.S. Infantry officer began an affair. Cash discovered them but forgave his wife. Later, when the couple returned to San Francisco and Cash resumed work for the New York journal, she resumed her illicit love affair with the officer.

In the Spring of 1869 Cash was sent overland by his newspaper to write a description of the Pacific Railroad, then nearing completion. His wife was with him but left in Chicago to go to her father's home in Philadelphia. Cash resigned his position with the newspaper since they wanted him to remain in New York and his wife wanted to return to San Francisco. Eventually he discovered that his wife had renewed her affair with her lover. Cash then told how he took his pistol and planned to kill his wife. Luckily, his neighbors were able to stop him. She fled to her father's home in Philadelphia where Cash later went to effect a brief reconciliation.

Cash eventually discovered his wife's secret letters from her lover. One of these told of her lover sending her a garter which he requested she wear for a few days and return to him. This so enraged Cash that he tried to have the Army court martial the officer, but to no avail.

One may now wonder if his small treatise could have served in any way to heal the wounds inflicted during the unfortunate marriage.

Tea Leaves

by W.M. Tileston

December 1869

We were tired of Hankow—the Judge and I. The trip from Shanghai—six hundred miles up the grand old Yang-tse-kiang, in a North River steamer, surrounded by all the appliances and comforts of modern traveling—had been most enjoyable. The *Poyang* was her name. Commanded by Captain George Briggs, of the old Collins Line, with a steward from the same fleet, and a cook from the Astor House, could one ask for more? We had seen Chin-kiang—where the British troops suffered so in '41, from the combined effects of Tartar pluck and a China sun—with its lovely Silver Island, where poor Captain Townsend, of our Navy, since met his death from the latter cause; Nankin, the old capital of the Empire, where lies buried the last of the Ming dynasty—now in possession of the Tae-ping Rebels, with the Imperialists encamped on the opposite side of the river, and who, by the way, amused themselves as we passed by firing a few shots *over* us at the rebel outposts; "The Orphans," those remarkable rocks, standing in solitary grandeur near the mouth of the lake from which our steamer took her name—their apparently inaccessible summits crowned with temples; and lastly, Kiu-kiang, a most uninteresting and dilapidated specimen of a Chinese city, where a few poor "exiles from Erin," and the sister isle, passed their time in smelling tea and shooting snipe.

We had "done" Hankow most thoroughly; been duly dined and tiffined; visited Wu-chang, the Viceroy's residence, opposite, and searched the *curio* shops for old bronzes and crackled China; been duly mobbed by "braves," as they call the native soldiers, and hailed as *Yung-qui-tsi* (foreign devils); had ascended the Han-yang hill, and from its summit viewed a lovely panorama, embracing three cities, with, according to the veracious Abbé Huc, a population of three million souls.

And yet we pined for a new sensation.

It came one morning, while we were lounging in the tea-room of our host. The *cha-sze*, (tea-master) a native of bonnie Scotland, "with an eye like a hawk, and a scent like a hound," was leaning over his dark-green table, where the clear north-light came through the broad window, poking his nose into a series of little porcelain cups, and going through the orthodox sipping and spitting—when entered Ah Lum, tea-broker, a fine specimen of the genus Chinaman. The "pidgin English" which followed, was too much for our untutored intellects to comprehend; but the result made itself both apparent and acceptable, in an invitation to accompany Mr. Ah Lum on a trip to the Tea Districts, some two hundred miles distant. The season being just about to open, here was an opportunity of witnessing the whole *modus operandi* of picking, firing, and packing, not to be lost; so, in spite of sundry misgivings as to the security of our heads should we chance to meet with hostile "braves," we decided to accept the invitation; and the following day found us again on broad bosom of the Yang-tse.

Both craft and *cuisine* suffered somewhat from comparison with the *Poyang*. Our conveyance was what is called a mandarin boat — a craft used by those gentry in transporting themselves and families about the country — Noah's Ark on a small scale, without the animals, but *with* the insects; flat-bottomed, housed all over, and divided into compartments from stem to stern; provided with light sails, but propelled mainly on the canalboat principle — coolies taking the place of horses — enabling passing travelers to work their passage by taking hold of the rope, as George Christy used to say he did once on the Erie Canal. The country through which we passed varied but little from what we had seen on the lower river: the same compact system of farming; the hills terraced to their very summits, and every available spot cultivated, apparently, to supply the wants of the immense population, which seemed to increase, rather than diminish, as we journeyed westward.

On the evening of the second day, we left the main river; and after going a short distance on a tributary stream, entered a broad canal, which, we were informed, led direct to the heart of the Tea Districts. The country, which was completely cut up by intersecting ditches and canals, looked "flat, stale, and unprofitable," and was entirely without the luxuriant tropical vegetation found in the southern districts. Immense *paddy* or ricefields stretched in every direction, with here and there the thatched roof and mud walls of a farmer's dwelling showing themselves above the horizon. The tedious tracking of the boat was frequently intercepted by huge nets planted on the banks, which the fisherman raised and lowered by means of levers and a windlass worked by the feet. Sometimes we passed a lonely temple, shaded by a grove of waving bamboos; but the general appearance of the landscape was so monotonous, that it was an immense relief when Ah Lum, pointing to a line of blue hills rapidly rising above the horizon, told us that beyond them lay our destination.

Turning out of our rattan beds on the morning of the fourth day we found the boat moored to the banks of the canal in the shadow of a large one-storied brick building, which proved to be the *hong* of the tea merchant to whom the neighboring plantations belonged, and casting our eyes around, we found that we were really in the tea country at last. On every side of us, as far as the eye could reach, the dark green tea-plants were growing in their beds of reddish, sandy soil. They looked thin, having lately been robbed of a portion of their covering of laurel-shaped leaves.

The cultivation of the plant which produces our common drink is by no means confined to any one district or spot, but is scattered about through the different provinces, each producing its peculiar description, known to the trade by its distinctive name. For instance, our visit was to the Hupeh, or Oopack country, as it is called respectively by the local inhabitants and Cantonese, through the latter of whom most business with foreigners is carried on; and the tea produced is the heavy-liquored, black-leafed Congou, which forms the staple of the mixture sold in England under the generic name of Black, and which sometimes finds its way to this country as English Breakfast Tea. Kiu-kiang shares with Hankow the exportation of this description of leaf, and is also the point of shipment for the fine Green teas manufactured in the Moyune District, the larger proportion of which find their way to this country. Next in importance — or possibly first, as a port of shipment — is Foo-chow-foo, on the coast, about half-way between Shanghai and Hongkong. From here are sent forth the red-leaf Congous, or old Boheas, to England, and the Oolongs to the United States. Still farther down the coast is Amoy, from whence is shipped an inferior description of Congous and some scented teas; but the bulk of the latter are exported from Canton and Macao, being, together with a peculiar description of Green, manufactured at these ports from leaf grown in the neighborhood.

Jumping ashore, regardless of the entreaties of the cook to wait until *chow-chow* was ready, we found ourselves in the midst of a noisy crowd of coolies, moving in every direction, each with his load slung at the ends of a bamboo, singing the monotonous *"Aho, Aho, Aho,"* in unison with the rapid dog-trot at which they move. Some were carrying chests to the canal-bank, and loading them in long, narrow boats. Others were bringing in baskets of freshly-picked leaves, and depositing them in the *hong.* Entering this building, we found the various processes of firing and curing in full operation, and, aided by our friend Ah Lum, were not only let into the secrets of the trade, but passed a pleasant day, wandering about from furnace to furnace, and among the thickly-growing plantations which covered hill-side and plain alike for miles on every side.

The plants themselves were from two to six feet high, according to age, and, from repeated cutting down, had grown into dense masses of small twigs. Many of them were covered with little white flowers, somewhat similar to the jasmine, and seeds enclosed in a casing not unlike that of the hazel-nut, but thinner and full of oil. The first picking, in April — the month of our visit — is when the leaves are very young and tender, which of course command a higher price than those subsequently plucked. The second is a month later, when they have attained maturity; and as unpropitious weather would be likely to ruin them, great expedition is used in gathering the crop, the entire population turning out *en masse.* A third, and even a fourth, follow; but the quality rapidly deteriorates, and but a small proportion of these last pickings is prepared for export.

The process of making tea for home consumption — that is, the great bulk of it used by the population generally — is very simple: a mere drying in the sun, subsequent to which it presents a dry, broken appearance, like autumn leaves. The plantations were filled with men, women, and children, all engaged in stripping the bushes as rapidly as possibly, throwing the leaves into bags slung over their shoulders for the purpose: a merry, laughing crowd, screaming at each other in their harsh, guttural tones, and pausing in their work only to cast glances of astonishment at the barbarians. As their bags were filled, the pickers trudged off to the curing-house, and deposited their loads on the heap. Here was the most interesting operation of all: at least thirty young girls were engaged in assorting the leaves, picking out all the dead and yellow ones, and preparing them for the hands of the rollers and firers. Our entrance caused quite a commotion among the damsels, and they were evidently preparing for a rapid exit — only waiting for a lead, like a bevy of quails — until a word from Ah Lum quieted them. No wonder the poor things were frightened. Foreigners have the reputation, in the interior, of living entirely upon fat babies, with no objection to children of larger growth, if they are plump.

On one side of the room was extended a long furnace, built of rough brick, with large iron pans placed at equal distances, and heated from charcoal fires below. Into these pans were pouring huge basketfuls of leaves, which were stirred rapidly for a few minutes, and then removed to large bamboo frames, where they were rolled and kneaded until all the green juice was extracted. They were then scattered loosely in large, flat baskets, and placed in the sun to dry. Subsequently, the leaves were again carried to the furnaces and exposed to a gentle heat, until they curled and twisted themselves into shapes so familiar to all lovers of the beverage which cheers without inebriating. Some of the finer kinds of tea, prepared for exportation, are rolled once before being fired. The great object appears to be to prevent the leaf from breaking; hence, in the commoner kinds and that intended for home consumption, which do not receive the same amount of care, the leaves are found to be very much broken.

Green tea, although grown in particular districts, is prepared in a similar manner, its peculiar color being imparted during the firing by dropping into the pans a small quantity of gypsum and Prussian blue. Chinamen wonder at the taste of "outside barbarians," in preferring tea so colored; but would furnish them with a leaf of bright yellow, if there was a market for it. Little do they know of the comfort it affords the ague-shaken dwellers of our Western river-bottoms, when varied with the regular doses of quinine.

The entire operation pertaining to the business appeared to be carried on under one roof, and afforded occupation to an immense number of persons. In one room men were engaged in making boxes; in another, lining them with thin sheets of lead. Farther on, the outsides of the boxes were being pasted over with thin sheets of paper, on which were stamped the *chop* of the tea and the maker's name. Finally, they were being filled, soldered up, and carried off to the boats, perhaps not to be opened again until reaching the shop of some London grocer. It is a common thing to hear English travelers say that they find it impossible to get as good a cup of tea in China as they can at home. With regard to the quality, they are probably in error; but it is quite likely they can not get tea to suit their taste as well, for this reason: in England, the art of mixing tea has been reduced to a science. The assimilating of different kinds—a little Congou, a little Oolong, a little Orange Pekoe—until a palatable mixture is produced, is so thoroughly understood, that but little pure tea of any one description is sold. This prejudice is even carried to China, where each *hong,* or mercantile house, has its own mixture prepared for its special use. It has been a recognized fact for many years, that the Russians have the best teas of any nation outside of China, and this can be accounted for in three ways. First: The Russians pay high prices, and buy the best. Second: A great deal of their tea is received overland, *via* Miamatchin and Kiachta, the Chinese and Siberian towns, standing one on each side of the boundary line between the empires; hence, not having made a sea-voyage, its properties are not impaired, nor is it compelled to undergo the strong curative process. Third: The Russians know how to *make* and *drink* tea better than any people in the world, the Chinese not excepted. Their implements are a small China tea-pot and a *samovar*—the latter a huge brass urn, with a cylinder running through the middle of it, in which is placed burning charcoal, heating the water to an extreme temperature, on the principle of a tubular boiler. The tea is made strong in the tea-pot, and the cup filled up from the urn. The use of the *samovar* is universal, and it is as much of a domestic institution in Russia as a waffle-iron in Yankee-land. The Chinese usually make their tea in the cup from which it is to be drank; and the leaves, after being subjected to several applications of water, are often redried and used again. To drink with comfort, it is necessary to invert the saucer over the cup, and sip from between the edges of the two. An immense quantity of what is known as Brick tea—tea pressed into cakes, not unlike bricks—is exported from the northern districts to Russia and the Siberias, for the use of the poorer classes of the population.

Our mandarin boat was to convoy a fleet of tea-junks back to Hankow; and their cargoes being on board, but little time was given us to remain among the plantations. The last evening of our stay was to be devoted to a *sing-song,* given in our honor—an entertainment comprising a great deal of eating and drinking with a surplus of native music. The latter was furnished by a company of professionals from a neighboring town, consisting entirely of gorgeously dressed young women, some of them quite handsome. The dinner was like all Chinese dinners: an immense number of little dishes, containing all of the delicacies known to Chinese culinary art, and the usual *piéce de resistance* of boiled rice. Visions of fattened puppies and plump rats would obtrude themselves, sadly to the detriment of our appetites. We had agreed to dispense with knives and forks, and essay to use the national

Chopstick; but it was like eating soup with a hairpin. While the Judge was laughing immoderately at my attempts to get a fair mouthful from my plate at once, an antiquated Celestial, who was sitting next me, with an evident compassion for the barbarian's ignorance, coolly lifted a piece of what appeared to be fat pork on his chopsticks, and, after biting off a portion, passed it over to me. This, I was informed, was an act of great courtesy; but it was the "last straw," and I left the table incontinently. After the repast, the music commenced—and such music! We asked Ah Lum to translate one of the songs for us; but the effort to put the words of one of his native poets into "pidgin English" was too much, and after a few moments of mental agony, he feelingly replied, "No can." How much more accomodating is our language! Witness the ease with which Longfellow's "Excelsior" is transformed into "Topside Galah," and "Norval's Address" becomes—"My name belong Norval, topside that Glampian hill-ee my father—you sabe my father?—makee pay chow-chow he sheep," etc., etc.

The women appeared to be in the charge of an ancient *duenna*, who watched them most jealously. For a "lark," we requested a Chinaman to ask the old lady the price of one of her *protégées*. Taking a scrutinizing glance to see if we really "meant business," she informed us that $1,000 was the lowest price for a choice. With the utmost gravity, our friend said: "More better you no buy. Suppose you want one piecee woman, Hankow can buy for five hundred dollar."

The custom-houses were probably the most interesting places we saw on our return trip—large whitewashed buildings, with the everlasting mandarin-poles and dilapidated banners. They are farmed out by the Government to local mandarins, who, for a certain annual sum, are allowed the privilege of "squeezing" all passing boats to the greatest extent they will bear. There appears to be no recognized tariff, but each gets what he can; or, if a man comes down liberally, he may be given a *chop*, which carries him past several stations. After getting into the Yang-tse again, the strong current carried us rapidly down the river—the fleet all beating down, tack for tack, together, making a very lively and animated picture. On the afternoon of the second day, the Han-yang hill loomed in the distance; and soon we could make out the four large Joss-poles which mark the Viceroy's residence in Wu-chang. An hour later, we landed on the jetty at Hankow, heads safe on our shoulders, and without even an adventure of consequence to relate.

We are at Vernon now—our travels, for the present, over; and, as we sit on the porch in front of our little house, the cool breeze comes from the sea through a gap in the hills, kissing the tops of the waving mulberries, and gently rustling the leaves of the orange trees—the Judge's terrier, Jack, and the setter, Rose, having a game of romps under and around our chairs, and the sleepy Muscovy ducks winking and blinking in the warm sunlight. The Judge says: "Colonel, do you remember our trip to the Hupeh country? Why could we not import some tea-plants, and try to produce the leaf here?

Those hills, now looking so bleak and dry, might be made to bloom and blossom like the rose; and what a change it would effect in the landscape, if they were covered with a rich, dark, verdue, instead of withered weeds."

"Labor, my dear Judge, labor is the rock on which we'd split. Why, if we were to import Chinamen enough to carry on a tea plantation, these fierce Democrats around us would never forgive us for robbing the Irishman of his birth-right. I notice, however, these same violent anti-Coolieists are glad enough to employ the Celestials in their vineyards. But the time will come, when, this troublesome labor question once settled, these hills, now so valueless, will be made to give their share of the blessings designed by Providence for the use of man."

William M. Tileston (-   ) *has not yielded to our efforts to uncover significant biographical information about him. We have learned that he edited a weekly journal entitled* The Country *which was devoted to the gun, the dog, yachting, fishing and other outdoor sports from October, 1877 to September, 1878, and also published a book called* Points For Judging the Different Varieties of Dogs *in 1878.*

In addition to Tea Leaves, *Tileston authored at least one other work on the subject of tea, a six-page illustrated article entitled* A Trip to the Tea Country, *which was published in* St. Nicholas *magazine, New York, 1878.*

A Cup of Rio Coffee

by Rev. J.D. Beugless

April 1869

Physicians have not entirely agreed whether or not tea and coffee are generally injurious to the health. One of eminence in his profession remarks: "The Turks, who drink great quantities of coffee, and the Chinese, who make equally as free use of tea, do not exhibit such peculiar effects as render it easy to decide whether they are in reality deleterious to the human system." The natives of the region of the river Platte in South America, and especially the women, sip or suck through the *bombelâ* their *maté* or Paraguayan tea from the time they rise in the morning until late at night, without any apparent marked effects; and this might almost be called the concentrated lye of tea.

Climate, however, has doubtless much to do with the effect of these beverages upon the health — coffee specially appearing perfectly harmless in the tropics, whereas in colder climates it often produces acidity of the stomach, with headaches and other nervous affections. All of which is, however, irrelevant to our main purpose, which is simply to give the reader a brief sketch of the history of his morning cup of coffee.

The plant belongs to the Madder tribe, the botanical family *Rubiaceae*, deriving its generic name from its red berry. The *Rubiaceae* are divided into three sub-families, known as *Stellateae*, *Cinchonae*, and *Loganiae*. The second of these is the particular family with which we have to do; and the species is known among botanists as the *Coffea Arabica*.

Not having been present at its birth, and finding no reliable record, I am unable to say whether coffee is a native of Arabia, Ethiopia (Meroë), or Abyssinia. All these countries claim its parentage; and intelligent writers, both of our own and other lands, have accredited it to them all. It is yet found growing wild, not only in the above-named countries, but in Liberia as well, thousands of miles away. In its wild state it abounds especially in a rocky district of Abyssinia, called *Kaffa*, whence the berry is said to have derived its name. The entire region of country bordering on the southern half of the Red Sea, both in Asia and Africa, may have been its home at the time of its discovery. Those who claim for it an exclusively African origin, say it was not taken to Arabia until the fifteenth century, where soon thereafter and from that time until this present it was cultivated with remarkable success, both as to quantity and quality, especially in the district or kingdom of Yemen.

Mocha, the seaport of this province, has given its name, with a world-renowned reputation, to the coffee shipped thence, amounting to many thousands of tons annually. But notwithstanding this large exportation, Mocha coffee is something like champagne in this: manifold more of it is used in the United States alone than is produced in all Arabia.

It is uncertain when coffee was introduced into Europe; but in 1538 the Mahometan priests issued edicts against its use — because, as they said, the faithful pay their devotions more generally at the coffee shops than at the mosque.

In 1643 the first coffee-house was established in Paris, by an adventurer from the Levant; but for want of patronage did not succeed. A few years later Solomon Aga, the Ambassador of the Sublime Porte at the Court of Louis XIV introduced it again in Paris, from which time coffee drinking became the *mode* among the aristocracy. Many influential Parisians stoutly resisted its introduction, among whom was the celebrated Madame de Sévigné, the special partisan of Corneille in opposition to Racine, who predicted: *"Le Racine passerait comme le café."* (Racine will be forgotten as soon as coffee.) She was right in her prophecy, but egregiously in error as to the time of its fulfillment.

An English merchant of Constantinople first introduced coffee to the people of London; and his wife, whom he had introduced with his berries, being a young and beautiful Greek, proved a most successful saleswoman. And here, by way of parenthesis, let us say to all the bachelor tribe, take warning from the difference in the success of the London merchant and the Levant adventurer, and get the right kind of a partner before you engage in business.

During the Protectorate coffee-houses multiplied so extensively and were patronized so generally that the taverns and beer-shops were in a fair way to close their wooden eyelids and sleep the sleep of death, when Cromwell, to avert this calamity, issued a decree closing the coffee-houses instead.

In 1699 President Van Horn, of the Dutch East Indies, had coffee plants introduced and cultivated in Batavia, with such success that Java soon became one of the foremost coffee-growing countries of the world — while the berries of that country have attained a reputation second only to those of Mocha. There is exported from the island of Java alone about seventy-five thousand tons of coffee every year.

In 1710 a coffee shrub was sent from the Dutch East Indies to Amsterdam, and planted in the botanical gardens of that city. From this a shoot was sent to Louis XIV and placed in the *Jardin des Plantes*. This succeeded beautifully; and from it slips were sent by M. Isambert for the garden at Martinique; but both the slips and Isambert died on the way. In 1720, however, three shrubs, which had been produced in Royal Botanical Gardens of Paris, were sent to the same destination by Captain Declieux. The voyage was long and tedious, and two of the plants died in transit. The ship's company was put on a small allowance of water, and the captain generally shared his *quarte* each day with his remaining *cafier*, and so succeeded in getting it to its destination. From this single plant, which made its transatlantic voyage amid such perils, have resulted all the myriads of coffee plantations of the West Indies and of Central and South America.

In 1754 a Franciscan friar, by the name of Villaso, placed a coffee plant in the garden of the San Antonio Convent at Rio de Janeiro. In 1809 the first cargo of coffee was sent from Rio to the United States. The present year, with the average rate of increase for the last quarter of a century, Rio alone will ship to the United States a million pounds per day, Sundays included. About three-fourths of all the coffee imported into this country comes from Rio.

The three great coffee-growing provinces of Brazil are, stated in the order of their production, Minas Geraes, San Paulo, and Rio de Janeiro. And it is our purpose to make a short trip into the interior of this greatest of all coffee-growing regions of the world.

We suppose ourselves already landed at the city of Rio de Janeiro. Being too late to start to-day we take rooms at the Exchange Hotel, kept by a most respectable English gentleman. We can, however, glance at some features of the coffee trade as it appears in Rio. Our hotel fronts to the southward on Rua Direita, the principal business thoroughfare of the city. As we descend to the street we find ourselves amid the bustle of the business center of this great metropolis of South America. Turning our faces eastward, a few steps bring us to the *Praca do Commercio* (the Merchant's Exchange), and adjoining this the *Alfandega* or Custom House. At both these establishments all business is transacted between nine A.M. and three P.M. No vessel is allowed to discharge or take in cargo outside of these hours. At the Custom House three or four cargoes of coffee are cleared almost every day, having paid a moderate export duty to the Government. Negro drays (each a cart with five stalwart Africans pulling, pushing and shouting at the top of their voices), mule carts, omnibuses, and hacks are all mixed up in apparently inextricable confusion. But above all the confusion of Rua Direita a stentorian chorus of voices is heard "responding in quick measure to the burden of a song." Casting our eyes in the direction whence comes this measured succession of musical grunts, we see above the heads of the multitude "a line of white sacks rushing around the corner of Rua de Alfandega" (Custom House Street). Elbowing our way through the crowd, we discover that each of these sacks is borne on the head of "a living ebony Hercules." This is a train of Brazilian coffee carriers. They go in companies of a dozen or twenty each, of whom one selected as captain takes the lead. Their only dress is a short pair of pants, reaching from the waist to the middle of the thigh — the limbs and body being left to the fullest and freest play of the muscles. Each has upon his head a bag of coffee weighing five *arrabas*, or one hundred and sixty pounds; and they move on a measured and rapid trot, keeping step with the double-quick time of some wild Ethiopian ditty. In perfect accord with this we have heard a strange, rattling music, which we now perceive proceeds from an instrument resembling exactly the mouth-piece of an ordinary watering-pot. This is partly filled with gravel, corked up, carried in one hand, and rattled in the time of the ditty, in a style resembling that in which a negro barber plays his wisk, or an auctioneer's boy rings his bell.

The strength of the spinal column and the amount of neck muscle that these coffee carriers develop are truly astonishing. I have seen one of them carry on his head a full-sized crate of crockery; and another carry from Rua Direita to the summit of Corcorado (a distance of three miles, and a height of two thousand eight hundred feet), over a rugged mule path, a box containing a ham, a turkey, a leg of mutton, a roast of beef, ten loaves of bread, two dozen of claret, two dozen of ale, two dozen dinner-plates, three large meat-dishes, a coffee-pot, coffee, cups and saucers, tumblers, knives and forks, napkins, etc., by way of breakfasting and dining a party that made the ascent by moonlight, one fine morning, in order to see the god of day come up from his morning bath in the old Atlantic.

From the time the coffee reaches Rio until it is stowed away in the hold of the American clipper, it is all handled and carried by these coffee carriers, and all in sacks of one hundred and sixty pounds each.

After dinner and a turn up Rua do Ouridor, which is at once the Rue Virienne, Regent Street, Broadway, Chestnut Street, and Montgomery Street of Rio de Janeiro, though neither very broad nor long, we give orders to be called at five, and retire. We are aroused at the appointed hour, and after our *almôço*, we walk through the city, passing on our way the City Hall, the Mint, the Assembly Building, the Penitentiary, and other prominent public buildings, reaching the depot of the famous Dom Pedro Legundo railway, at the southwest corner of the city, just as the numerous church and convent bells are ushering in the new-born day. After securing our tickets we have a moment to glance at the building, the rails, the engine, and the cars, and are a little disappointed to find them all to be of English manufacture and construction. We take our seats in an English boxcar, and are locked in, according to that detestable and dangerous English custom. The first forty miles of the road is in a northwesterly direction, over a level plain, mostly covered with marsh and a coarse, file-toothed grass — the road having little of interest along it after we leave the Palace San Christovao, which is the Emperor's principal residence. This is but three miles out of the city, bordering the railway on the north. The Emperor has a summer palace, at Petropolis, thirty-six miles distant, a little above the head of the most magnificent bay in the world.

We hurry along, with few stoppages, until we reach the foothills of the *Serra do Mar*, or coast range. Here our door is unlocked and we get out to stretch our limbs and look about us. Here is quite a depôt, and here are changes made. The track from this point onward is of American iron and American construction. An eight-driver American engine of the camel-back coal burner pattern, made by M.M. Baldwin and Company, of Philadelphia, takes the place of the little greasy John "Bull-gine" that has brought us over the Plains. We are again locked in; and fortunately have for a companion in our box Major Ellis, of Harrisburg, Pennsylvania, the constructing engineer of this part of the road. He tells us that in the next forty miles we are to make an ascent of four thousand feet, without a single switch-back, the grade being in places three hundred feet to the mile, while some of the curves on the heaviest part of the grade are made to a radius of two hundred and eighty feet. Slowly but steadily we are dragged up, up, up, the old camel-back seeming at times short of breath and just ready to give out. Within these forty miles we are plunged into and thundered through seventeen tunnels, one of which is a mile and a half in length, and cost a million and a half dollars. Between these we skirt along, and sometimes over, immense precipices, where we look down into the dizzy depths of the dark and dense Brazilian forests of the ravines and valleys below. As our iron horse stops for food and drink we hear the monkeys and the parrots chattering to each other in an unknown tongue, and the keel-bill and bell bird put in their ringing reply. The old trees are festooned with mosses and decked with the many-hued flowers of the *orchideae* (air plants), while the sons of these fathers of the forests are stayed on all sides with rope-like ipecacuanha, popularly known as *cipo* in Brazil. Away across the ravine on an opposite slope a sunlit cascade pours its silvery flood into the insatiable depths beneath. We reach the summit at last, where we find an extemporized village of the railroad's creating. The railroad stations are built of mahogany logs. A neighboring slope, newly reclaimed from the forests, is planted with coffee, and in one corner of it is a native's hut of satin-wood. The station-master's pig-pen is of solid rosewood, and every house, stable, and fence in the vicinity is built of the precious woods of commerce, because the owners cannot afford oak, or chestnut, or pine. But it must not be supposed that these have the polish and beauty of a mahogany "four-poster," or a rosewood piano. On the contrary, they are of a dark, dead, dirt color; and in their weather-beaten condition as unattractive to the eye as a black-oak fence built in our boyhood, upon which have beaten the storms of many winters.

We start down the western face of the *Serras*, with brakes down and engine reversed, and still making an almost frightful degree of speed. We are diverted from the immediate source of alarm by our friend Major Ellis who, in answer to our questions, informs us that this road was built by the Brazilian Government in conjunction with private enterprise, at a cost varying from two hundred thousand to one million dollars per mile. Meanwhile, down, down, down we rush, head foremost, to the banks of the Parahiba, a river which forms the boundary line between the provinces of Rio de Janeiro and Minas Geraes.

We have had the pleasure of seeing and riding over the greatest marvel of railroad-engineering skill that America has ever produced; and if at the outset of our journey we felt a little piqued at the thought of finding everything English, we are now compensated by the knowledge that when this marvelous work was to be done, American skill and American material superseded those of the mother country.

But what has all this to do with our cup of coffee? Just this: that this mighty work was constructed expressly to develop the resources of the interior coffee regions of Breazil, and to bring the fruits of those broad acres to market; and not more exclusively is the Pottsville and Reading, or the Broad Top and Huntingdon Railroad devoted to carrying coal than the Dom Pedro road is to carrying coffee.

Where this road intersects the Parahiba is a great *porto de embarque,* or shipping depot of this *caminhos de ferro,* or railroad.

The mountain air has been bracing, and we are a little tired and much more hungry; so the moment our box is opened we follow the lead of other ravenous ones to the *taverna.* Even here they have the fashionable hours of eating, and though well in the afternoon we are entirely too early for dinner, so we must order a *segunda almôço* (a second breakfast). We are set down to a grilled roach, some jerked beef, black beans, fariña, fried potatoes, and the inevitable but ever welcome cup of coffee. This beverage is almost a syrup, and yet as clear as brandy. Brazilians know how to make coffee as well as to produce it. But we have not yet become accustomed to the strong and almost bitter taste of this condensed extract of the berry whose mysteries we have come to explore, so we take our coffee *au lait.* One, two, three cups are swallowed, and we wish we dare drink more, but the ghost of a bilious temperament rises before us and in a churlish, snappish, bilious way puts in a prohibition.

We call for our bill, and it is presented thus:

CONTA.

Dous Peixes	80
" de Vacca	200
" des Bagens	80
" de Fariña	80
" des Batatas Fritas	320
Leis Chicaras de Café	240
	1$000

Great Zeus! what does this mean? We look first at the frightful *conta* and then at each other; seize our slim purses; turn out their entire contents and find ourselves jointly possessed of less than fifty dollars, for we have left our funds in the London and Brazil Bank, taking only what we supposed we might possibly need on our trip. The *moco* comprehends our ignorance, and picks up an American half dollar, bowing his satisfaction and withdraws. In our gratitude at being thus so easily relieved we throw another half dollar after him and puff away our mortification in the clouds that roll from our Bahias, and leave the *taverna* to reconnoitre the surroundings.

Outside we confront a thousand or more mules, which we are informed have come in laden with coffee from the neighboring province. We make our way to the *Estaço*, where we find piled in every direction thousands of sacks of coffee, somewhat as we see wheat on the California Steam Navigation Company's wharves and in Friedlander's warehouses.

We take a mule each and cross the Parahiba to see where all this comes from. Immediately upon reaching the western shore of the river we are plunged into immense forests of coffee. The trees resemble somewhat the *Rhamnus Catharticus*, or familiar buckthorn, the color, size, and character of the berries being different, and the coffee plant having far less spines. The trees are planted about six or eight feet apart each way, and grow naturally from twelve to thirty feet high, although for the sake of convenience in gathering the fruit they are seldom allowed to attain a height of more than ten or twelve feet. This region of country is very hilly, and the soil is light, dry, and silicious, the prevalent opinion being that coffee will not thrive in moist ground. If, however, you shall have time, on our return to Rio, to visit Bennett's, in the valley of the Tijuca, just go up to the bath in a spur of the valley and you will find growing close by the water side a *cafier* many times larger and more prolific than any we shall see in Minas Geraes.

The shrubs are transplanted with care from the nursery at one year of age, and in two or three years thereafter become fruitful, and will continue to produce two crops per annum for ten to twenty years. An occasional tree bears well for twenty-five or thirty years; and instead of two there are often three gatherings from the same trees during the year. The tree is an evergreen, while the blossoms are a most delicate white, emitting an exquisite fragrance. We find on the same tree, and indeed on the same twig, the blossom, the newly-formed berry, the green and the matured fruit. When ripe the berry very closely resembles the cranberry in external appearance, though somewhat larger. Each berry contains two seeds or grains of coffee in the centre of the pulp, with their flat sides or faces opposed to each other. Each grain is covered with a tough integument or membrane; and they are additionally separated from each other by a layer of the pulp interposing.

Each tree produces from one to eight pounds of berries, the average being about three pounds. It is now the gathering season, and we see hundreds of negroes in every direction; some shaking the berries upon gathering-sheets spread on the ground—others picking the fruit directly from the trees. A negro will pick about an arroba (thirty-two pounds) of berries per day. These are dried by being spread upon pavements or level tables of ground prepared for the purpose, which pavement or table is called a *terrene*. These should be sheltered from the sun. As the fruit dries the pulp forms a sort of shell or pod, as we perceive in examining some that have been longer gathered; and which being perfectly dry are now being passed through a coffee huller, a machine in which a fluted roller is closely opposed to a breast-board, between which roller and breast-board the berries are made to pass. The pulp is washed away, leaving the beans free. These are again dried as before, after which the tough membrane is removed by a somewhat similar process with heavy rollers. The chaff is next separated by winnowing; and the coffee is now ready to be bagged and stored, or taken to market.

Coffee, like some other articles of commerce, is greatly improved by age; and for this reason we find immense quantities of it stored for a time, although the difference in market value between the old and the new does not pay the interest on the money. Mocha coffee, it is said, will attain its seasoning in three years, while Rio, St. Domingo, Laquayra, Maricaybo Costa Rica, and all other American coffees require from twelve to fifteen years to perfect their flavor.

When we return to Rio I will take you to the Café Americana, where we can get a cup of Rio coffee quite equal to the best Old Government Java, and rendered so almost entirely by washing and age.

We have now traveled many miles through the very heart of the greatest coffee region of the world. We have met numberless trains of mules, each without harness or halter, carrying his two sacks of coffee and following the leader over many weary miles of unfenced and in many places almost unbroken road or mule track to the *Estaçio* or depot of shipment.

A man and a boy, with a train of thirty mules, entirely unharnessed, carry thus at a single trip nearly a thousand pounds of coffee to the depot; the man attending the leading mule of the train, while the boy simply sees that none of the animals straggle by the way.

Until within a few years, we are told, this great coffee-growing province produced only sufficient coffee for home consumption, the labor and expense attending the shipment consuming almost the entire proceeds of the crop. Now, through the agency of the Dom Pedro Railroad, it has become the rival of the best, and in turn outstripped all its rivals.

The name Minas Geraes signifies general or universal mines; but these newly-developed coffee plantations of the province are worth millions more every year than all its gold, copper, iron, and precious stones. Indeed, although Brazil is known to us as the land of diamonds, the coffee crop of this single province yields an annual return a hundred-fold greater than that of all the diamonds of the Empire.

Reverend John D. Beugless (-1887). *Although a record of Rev. Beugless' early life and schooling could not be located, we have learned through his naval service records that he was born in Pennsylvania and then relocated to Rhode Island where he entered the Navy in July of 1864. He was commissioned a chaplain with the rank of Lt. Commander and his first duty station was with the ship* Susquehannah, *then being repaired in N.Y. harbor.*

The records between 1864 and 1867 are missing, but we assume his time was spent aboard the Susquehannah *cruising the Atlantic sea lanes and* making ports of call. One of these trips must have been around the Horn, since he was assigned to the Mare Island, California, Navy yard in 1867. It is more than likely that he gathered the material for his story on Rio coffee during the 1867 voyage.

Rev. Beugless was a resident of California until 1870 when he was transferred to Philadelphia. In 1875 he began service on the Franklin, the flagship for the European station. The rest of his duty years were spent in New York City and aboard the ship Brooklyn, which was a member of the North Atlantic Squadron. Rev. Beugless died on active duty in Nagasaki, Japan, July 31, 1887.

An interesting sidelight to Rev. Beugless's career is that he was a recognized expert on cremation. The Princeton Review published his article, "Incineration", in September of 1883 and he presented a paper, "Cremation as a Safeguard Against Epidemics," to the twelfth annual meeting of the American Public Health Association in 1885.

The Cruise of the *Monadnock*

by Rev. James S. Bush
July - September 1869

No. I

At the close of the late civil war, the United States Government found itself in possession of a number of vessels belonging to a class popularly known as monitors. The efficiency of these vessels for operations in still water, and for harbor defense, had been thoroughly tested. The disabling of the *Merrimack* in Hampton Roads, and the capture of the *Atlanta* before Savannah, established at once their claim to be the right arm of the American navy; and it was soon conceded on all sides that in a close engagement no ships afloat could stand before them. With an impenetrable armor, and the smallest possible surface exposed to the enemy, with a weight of metal hitherto unknown to naval warfare, and equal to the piercing of the most formidable ironclads, they seem to have fairly solved the problem of their distinguished constructor, and to have met the demands of the nation for a navy, as well as an army, that should prove invincible.

Happily, the war was too short to determine what were the sea-going qualities of the monitors. An experimental trip by Commodore Rodgers in the *Weehawken*, had done little more than excite admiration for its boldness, and gain for himself a vote of thanks from Congress. The *Dictator*, to which he was transferred, ventured only upon one or two excursions along the coast. And the opinion was current, both in the navy and in the merchant service, that while the effectiveness of the monitors for attack and defense, was unapproached, they were lacking in the necessary conditions of speed and safety, and would therefore be found of little value on the open sea, where rough weather and an active enemy were to be encountered. Indeed it was seriously questioned by sea-faring men whether it would be prudent to risk a voyage across the Atlantic in one of them. Scores of the most daring officers in the navy pronounced it foolhardy, and made no disguise of their reluctance to be transferred to them.

The monitors, however did not want for a champion. Commodore Rodgers, who had so gallantly tested their fighting qualities, and by his brilliant exploits in command of one of them had added fresh laurels to an honored name, was eager now for a trial of their capabilities in the undertaking of a long sea voyage.

Accordingly it was determined by the Government to fit out the *Monadnock* for a cruise to the Pacific, making San Francisco the port of her destination. This vessel was the mate of the *Miantonomah*, afterwards placed under the command of Captain Fox, whilom Secretary of the Navy, and the first of her kind to cross the Atlantic and cruise in European waters. Both were inferior in size to the *Dictator* and the *Puritan*, but were fair representatives in respect of efficiency and completeness of the class to which they belonged. The United States steamer *Vanderbilt*, formerly of the merchant service, and the gift of her patriotic owner of the same name to the Government, was selected as the *Monadnock's* convoy. Two other vessels were ordered to the Pacific in their company, and the four, constituting what was known as "the special squadron to the Pacific," placed under the command of Commodore Rodgers. The *Vanderbilt*, Captain Sanford, and the *Monadnock*, Captain Bunce, proceeded from Philadelphia to Hampton Roads, the port of rendezvous. Awaiting there the arrival of the *Powhatan*, Captain Ridgely, and the *Tuscarora*, Captain Stanley, the squadron set sail for St. Thomas, West Indies, on the second day of November, 1866.

It is to some of the incidents of the cruise that followed, with the writer's impressions of "life on a man-of-war," that the reader's attention is invited in this and other papers hereafter. Favored by the commander with a temporary official relation to the squadron, and therefore furnished with every facility for observation, the writer had also the advantage of a *non-professional point de vue*. He must beg the indulgence of his naval readers, however, if he shall occasionally venture with something of the freedom of an outsider to speak of matters in which they are more especially concerned.

It has been well said that the personnel of the American navy, more than the construction of its vessels, has been the secret of its successes. A civilian comes to understand this in a few days' contact with the officers of a man-of-war at sea. Drawn for the most part from the best class of American citizens and carefully educated at the Naval Academy, they bring to the service a culture both of mind and body, and a spirit equal to the highest achievements in their profession. Physical courage, dashing and sustained; a romantic love of adventure; traditional and personal pride, springing from the knowledge of great deeds, and the consciousness of power to emulate them, are some of their most noticeable characteristics. Nor are the more noble qualities of honor and patriotism wanting.

Most of the officers of the squadron had seen service in the late war, and had shared in the glory of the victories at Fort Fisher, Mobile, and New Orleans. Some had won distinction by deeds of personal daring. In the blockade at Charleston, Lieutenant Commander Bunce (who afterward took command of the *Monadnock*) with a small boat's crew left his ship under cover of the night, ran by the fortifications in the harbor, reached the city, captured the sentry on the wharf and brought him off to the ship. Another instance of courage that well deserves recording is given of Lieutenant Commander Franklin, of the *Vanderbilt*. A fire had been discovered in or near the magazine of a ship, of which at the time he was in command. The danger of explosion appeared imminent, and the men rushed forward in great consternation. Not one was found daring enough to obey the order to go below and extinguish the fire. Seizing the hose in his own hands, Mr. Franklin leaped into the hold. The gunner instantly followed him, exclaiming: "Mr. Franklin, you are a brave man—you sha'n't go to h—ll alone." The fire was soon put out, and the ship, with its precious freight of life, was saved.

If the space allowed, the writer would gladly give in full the narrative of another gallant officer, Lieutenant Haswell, as received from his own lips. His ship was wrecked on the coast of a desert island, and the only mode of relief was to send one of her boats to another island, at a distance of several days' sail. The boat, with Mr. Haswell in command, encountered a squall the first day out, followed by weather so boisterous that the most serious apprehensions were felt for the safety of himself and crew. On his return, after the successful discharge of his duty, he was asked by the commanding officer why he did not put about and return to the ship when the storm struck him. "That was not in my orders, sir," was his reply.

Men like these—and there were others in the squadron none the less brave—were fitly placed under the command of the Commodore, who had won among the sailors the soubriquet of "Fighting Jack Rodgers," than whom a more accomplished officer, and a braver and more prudent commander, never trod the quarter-deck. As modest, too, as he is brave, he is not the man to sound his own trumpet in the ears of the public, nor to gain promotion through the favor of politicians.

Intercourse with officers such as I have described, as kind and courteous as they were brave, could hardly have failed in itself to make an eight months' cruise interesting. The hours at sea were beguiled of all tedium by the lively humor of the ward-room and the graver conversation of the senior officers. Deck and port afforded each its novelties, and a most agreeable alternation in the employment of one's time. For the coaling of the *Monadnock* instructions were given to put in at all the principal points, both on the Atlantic and Pacific coasts, and thus a rare opportunity was given to visit cities and countries quite out of the ordinary course of travel. At sea, the monitor was of course an object of unceasing interest, and speculation was rife for the first few days out as to her nautical powers. It was soon found that her average speed in good weather was not much beyond six knots, and that this was very considerably lessened when the sea ran high. The first day out from Fortress Monroe the sea was still rough from a late gale. Off Hatteras, as we entered the gulf-stream, the atmosphere was murky, with frequent showers. This was followed by a strong southwest wind, which increased to a gale. The night following was one of no little anxiety to the Commodore. The rain came down in torrents, making the air so thick that the lights of the other vessels were for a time quite lost. Presently the monitor was observed making signals that she was lying-to for repairs. It turned out that one of her tiller-ropes (of wire) had parted, an accident which occurred once or twice afterward. To repair it, however, was the work of only a few hours. It may be remarked here that provision had been made on the *Vanderbilt* for taking the *Monadnock* in tow in case of any accident disabling her. Happily the necessity for this did not arise in the entire cruise.

The order in which the vessels sailed was in a square, the *Vanderbilt* diagonally ahead, the *Monadnock* on the right quarter, the *Tuscaroro* on the left, and the *Powhatan* directly astern. Until the accident to the *Mondadnock* they kept well together and were sometimes within easy hailing distance. The next morning the *Tuscarora* was out of sight, having sailed on for St. Thomas. We learned there that she had suffered from the gale much more than the monitor. The Commodore's solicitude for the latter during the storm can be well imagined. He had staked his reputation as a sailor upon her success. Day and night he kept his place on the wheel-house of the *Vanderbilt*, glass in hand, with a sharp lookout toward "the chicken," as the officers had christened the monitor. Signals were constantly making to inquire the condition of things on board. The response was almost uniformly cheering and satisfactory. Her decks were swept fore and aft by the sea. Not a sailor was visible there, except for a moment on some special duty, and then with a life-rope round his waist. At times the waves dashed over her turrets, almost to the top of her smoke-pipe, and an occasional intervening wave would hide her entirely from the view of one standing on the deck of the *Vanderbilt*. But she rode the sea like a bottle well corked, all right and tight below. The Commodore's only apprehension was, not that the principle of her construction would prove at fault, but that some defect of detail in her making might appear, or that some accident might befall her machinery, rendering her unmanageable. Of the power of such a vessel to withstand the violence of the sea he was as confident in the outset as at the end of the cruise. The chief defect was discovered on reaching the tropics, in her ventilation. In bad weather, when the ports were closed, and officers and men were confined below, they were subjected to great discomfort. On arriving in port, however, the defect was partially remedied.

A passage of nine days brought us to anchor in the beautiful bay of St. Thomas. The monitor immediately became the central point of observation, and was soon surrounded by a fleet of boats filled with curious spectators from the shore. The sailors, too, from the foreign vessels, looked on wonderingly. "My eyes, what a bloody craft *that* is," exclaimed a jolly jack tar, belonging to a British man-of-war in port. Here, as elsewhere, she was more carefully inspected by naval officers, who to their knowledge of what the monitors had done against the confederate ironclads, could now add the fact of their success in fighting the sea. Their verdict could hardly be otherwise than favorable to the naval science of the United States, and the reluctant confession was more than once made of our advance in naval warfare beyond all other nations.

The harbor of St. Thomas is said to be the finest in the West Indies, being almost landlocked, and with an abundant depth of water for the largest vessels. In the event of a foreign war, the possession of it as a coaling station and general *entrepot* for our own ships would be of incalculable value to the United States. We are not now the owners of a foot of land in the West Indies. The islands belong to England, France, Spain, and Denmark. The convenience of Nassau to the English blockade-runners during the late war may have suggested to Mr. Seward the necessity of sharing the advantages enjoyed by other nations, and may have been the occasion of his visit to St. Thomas a few months after our squadron was there, and the rumored negotiations for its purchase. Whether the present be the most favorable time for the acquisition of foreign territory may well be doubted; but surely the sagacity of the Secretary of State in directing attention to the importance of a foothold in the West Indies cannot be questioned. This may be needed by and by for the protection of our commerce with South America and Asia, when the waters of the two great oceans shall commingle in the ship canal across the Isthmus of Panama. Cuba itself could be purchased by the savings of a single year under a more honest and economical administration of public affairs.

The appearance of St. Thomas from the harbor is highly picturesque. Rising in the midst of an amphitheatre of the mountains, the town is chiefly built upon the sloping sides of three separated hills — giving the effect of three triangles with their bases on the water, and each having for its apex a conspicuous structure of brick and stone. One of these is a grayish-looking tower, called "Blackbeard's Castle," the refuge of a famous, or rather infamous, buccaneer of former days. Many years ago, the pirates who infested the seas of this region made St. Thomas their rendezvous, affording as it did shelter and protection and sufficient commerce with the few inhabitants of the island. Another angle is made by the Governor's house, a fine dwelling of red brick. Directly beneath this is the residence of Santa Aña, who made this place his home for several years, and from which, a short time before our arrival, he had sent forth his manifesto to the Mexicans, urging resistance to the Empire of Maximillian. On another eminence near by, is the handsomest structure on the island, called by the sailors "Bluebeard's Castle," for no other reason probably than to match it with "Blackbeard's Castle." The town is built chiefly of a light yellow colored brick, and of stone stuccoed and washed with various colors. The roofs are painted a reddish purple, thus heightening the picturesque effect given by the location and shape of the town.

To one just entering the harbor all that meets the eye is inviting. The palm trees that line the shore, the background of hills clothed in richest tropical green of varying shades; the colors, here and there deepened by the shadows cast along their sides by the passing clouds, offer a feast of beauty to eyes that for days have been confined to the wilderness of waters. One has only to put his foot on shore, however, within the thickly-settled part of the city, to be disenchanted. The town itself is for the most part poorly built, and filled with a miserable degraded population of all colors, mostly black, using a lingo of negro-English. The blood of Europeans has been mixing here with African blood for near two hundred years, and it is doubtful whether the latter has been much improved. Here and there one meets with a good-looking mulatto, or a finely-shaped negro. But the prevailing type of humanity is sadly inferior, and affords not much encouragement to those who contemplate the possible admixture of the two races in our own country. No humanitarian abstractions should lead us to slight this testimony of fact. Doubtless there are moral as well as physical causes for the degradation of the mixed populations of the West Indies and South America. The marriage-tie is lightly regarded; the moral training of children is almost unknown; the lower classes multiply and live more like brutes than human beings. So it has been, and so it is likely to be for generations to come.

While in port the squadron was visited by Santa Aña. His coming had been announced; and although his well-known character made any demonstration of honor distasteful to most of the officers, etiquette required the usual salute of twenty-one guns due to an ex-President. In person the General is tall and of rather commanding presence. His physiognomy, however, does not belie his reputation for lust and craft and treachery. His house is called the harem, and his life outrages the moral sense even of St. Thomas.

After a week's anchorage the squadron set sail again for Cayenne, South America — our course taking us in sight of the islands of St. Dominic, St. Christopher, Barbadoes, and Martinique. The passage was a delightful one. Our eyes were feasted by the sight of the lofty mountain summits and rich green slopes of the western coast of Martinique, as we sailed along some two miles distant through a sea of glass and under a cloudless sky. This was the New World to Columbus, for the islands around us were among the first that he discovered, and we could well imagine the rapture with which he gazed upon their beauties. On the twenty-sixth of November we approached the Salut Islands off the port of Cayenne, in French Guiana, South America. The depth of water not being suffcient near the town, we anchored close under a little island, some twenty miles distant. One of the vessels, however, the *Tuscarora*, steamed up to Cayenne. This is a penal settlement of the French, containing some three or four thousand convicts. On the island near us were about a thousand more, guarded by a hundred soldiers. We learned that Orsini, who attempted the life of Napoleon, was confined there — but were not allowed to see him, his confinement being close and rigorous, and therefore, in this climate, little less than a lingering death. The convicts are variously employed: some in the building of roads, fortifications, and terraces; others, in the different mechanical trades. Houses sufficiently comfortable are erected for them, and their hours of labor are not unreasonable. When not at work they are allowed to go about the island, enjoying all the freedom that its narrow limits can give. They attend religious services in a neat little chapel, and when sick are kindly cared for in the hospital. On the whole, so far as one could observe, they are humanely treated while conforming to the discipline and regulations of the island. For misconduct they are imprisoned, or put in irons, in which also they are compelled to labor. The officers in charge were uniformly courteous; and our visit to the island would have left only the most favorable impression of French kindness and humanity, but for a single melancholy incident.

While standing on the quarter-deck of the *Vanderbilt* one evening, in conversation with the First Lieutenant, I was startled by the cry of a *"man overboard."* I listened for an instant, and could distinctly hear a voice as of one struggling in the water. The Lieutenant immediately gave the order to lower a boat, and in another minute one was in the water, making toward the man, whose head was now visible some thirty or forty feet from the ship. Before the boat reached him I distinguished the word "American" repeatedly uttered with a sound unlike the tone of one of our own men. My surmise that he was a convict trying to escape proved correct. The poor fellow was soon brought aboard, nearly exhausted, with no other clothing that a pair of thin pants rolled above the knees. The Commodore and Captain hearing the commotion, had come on deck, and the man was at once brought before them. His story was soon told. He had been a soldier in the French army and was sentenced to transportation for ten years for knocking down a corporal who had insulted him. His time was nearly out, but he had no hope of returning, for no one who came here ever found his way back. He supposed that under the American flag he would find liberty and protection, and had accordingly ventured, under cover of the night, to swim out to the ship. His desire for liberty must have been strong indeed! for if retaken, he was sure to be shot, and in swimming to the ship he had run great risk of being devoured by the sharks, with which the harbor abounds. When told that he could not remain on board, but must go back to the island, his face was the very picture of woe. He quietly answered that he should be shot if his attempt at escape were discovered; but the tones of his voice, no less than his look, indicated the agony of the poor fellow's mind. Every heart, both among officers and men, was moved with sympathy; but no alternative was possible. We were in a French port, partaking of its hospitalities. We could not interfere with its laws, nor harbor those whom we knew to be amenable to them as criminals. Of this the Commodore told the man, at the same time assuring him of his sympathy and willingness to do all in his power for him. The choice was then given him either to stay on board overnight and be sent back in the morning, or to return immediately. He chose to go at once, hoping to be in his place again before the roll was called for the night. Accordingly the boat was lowered, and he was taken ashore to a part of the island the farthest distant from the usual landing-place. The night, however, was not dark, and the guard on shore must have watched the movement; for the next day we heard that he had been taken and shot. Visiting the island that day with one of the officers, as we stood before the chapel witnessing the funeral service of three deceased convicts, whose remains were near the chapel door, I expressed to my companion the fear that the body of the poor fellow of the night before was in one of the coffins. So, alas! it proved. The laws of the island were inexorable. In the light of early morning he had been led out by a band of soldiers to his doom, and the heart that panted with the desire of liberty a few hours before, had ceased to beat forever. Let us hope his wish was found in death; that the prayers said over his dead body were heard by the Good Father above, and that in the divine justice and mercy his soul has found a refuge from the cruel severity of which he was the victim here. "So I returned and considered all the oppressions that are done under the sun, and beheld the tears of such as were oppressed, and they had no comforter; and on the side of the oppressors there was power, but they had no comforter." The event I have narrated gave rise to sundry very animated discussions among the officers of the squadron. Some insisted that the duty we owed to society, no less than comity to the French Government, required the immediate delivery of the convict to the authorities on the island. Others held that we ought not to have refused him the protection of our flag, and that we had no right to treat him as a criminal, except upon legal proof and a formal requisition. The majority, however, sustained the Commodore in refusing to harbor a confessed convict, and after treating him kindly on board, simply returning him to the place of his own choice on the island.

No. II

The course of our squadron lay from Cayenne to Bahia, in Brazil, in which port we came to anchor on the 17th of December. The weather was fine, and the soft land-breeze that came over the bay reminded one of a pleasant summer day in the North. The harbor is a beautiful one, the banks around rising gradually to the height of a hundred feet or more, covered with the richest foliage, and crowned, here and there, with the villas of the Brazilian gentry. Bahia is the port where, during the late war, the Confederate ship *Florida*, then lying at anchor, was cut out by the *Wachuset*. The act was in violation of the rights of a neutral nation; and the reader will remember that the Government of the United States was obliged, afterward, by the laws of nations, to disown it, and tender an apology to Brazil. The Commander of the *Wachuset* was not ignorant of the offense he was committing; but determined, nevertheless, to risk his commission for the benefit that might accrue to American commerce, already damaged very seriously by the depredations of the *Florida*. He escaped, however, with a reprimand. The Brazilians were satisfied; but the English residents of Bahia, who profited largely at our expense, were loud in their indignation.

The town of Bahia is well located, on a point of high table-land that runs out into the sea; and as the breezes, both from sea and land, sweep over it constantly, is not unhealthful, nor oppressively hot. It is one of the oldest cities on the continent, having been founded by the Portuguese, in 1539. The population, at present, has a considerable share of the same element, both immigrants, and the descendants of others in former days, of pure blood. Some of them are intelligent, enterprising men, largely engaged in commerce and manufacturing. I visited quite an extensive cotton factory, owned and run by one, in which the labor was performed chiefly by slaves. Nearby, was a fine plantation, belonging to the same person, with an orange grove, said to be the finest in South America, producing the variety known as the navel orange, so called from a little protuberance in the rind, containing the seeds. The pulp of the orange is solid throughout, and deliciously sweet. No variety so fine finds its way to the Northern markets. Most of the Portuguese, however, in Bahia and vicinity, have intermarried — or, rather, intermixed — with the aborigines and the negroes. It is in this class, chiefly, that the nobles and grandees of the realm are found, under the name of Creoles. They are often miserably inferior, in body and mind, but as haughty and exclusive as any princes of the blood in the old world. There seems to be, throughout Brazil, very little of race antipathy, and African descent carries no taint with it. Mulattoes, and even negroes of full blood, having gained their freedom, sometimes accumulate considerable property, and their wealth is generally the passport to social favor. A negro was pointed out to the writer as the owner of a large number of slaves, among whom was a woman whose color could not distinguish her from the fairest of the whites. She was purchased of her master by a subscription among the European residents, and her freedom given her. Three-fourths of the population are negroes, and many, perhaps most of them, of African birth; Bahia being the port from which the slave-trade is chiefly carried on. The streets are full of them, the men half-naked, and the women nearly so; their faces and breasts often tattooed in true savage style. Physically, they are by far, as a class, the finest-looking people there; for the most part, tall, erect, and well made, the men being often upward of six feet in height, with a magnificent development of muscle, and the women equally fine in shape and figure. Of course, they have the African type of feature; but their expression is sometimes pleasant, and even handsome. These Africans are the beasts of burden, horses and mules being little used. They carry you about the town in sedan-chairs. The lighter burdens are borne on the head; the heavier, on the shoulders of men, suspended from poles; half-a-dozen stout fellows carrying, in this way, a ton's weight, or more, of merchandise, stepping together to the tune of a rude chant, with different parts, in which they all join.

Many of the foreign residents of Bahia are English, who, by the way, are the most successful merchants in all the ports of South America. They have here a very pretty chapel, in which, every Sunday, they attend the service of the English Church, sustained in part by the English Government, and partly by voluntary subscription. By invitation of the Chaplain, some of the officers of the squadron attended the service of Christmas-day. The weather was very warm, in singular contrast with a Christmas at the North. But the chapel was tastefully decorated with green branches and flowers; and the service, in which an American clergyman joined, recalled the joyous solemnities of the day at home. As it continued, we could hardly help thinking how sadly incongruous would be the scenes of another war between England and America, and how Heaven would smile upon the mighty energies of these two Christian nations if united always in the peaceful triumphs of their religion. What blessings of civilization might they jointly share, and confer upon other nations and peoples besides, if their power and enterprise could be employed only in a spirit of honest and friendly competition, and never in the work of mutual destruction!

The English Chaplain we found to be a man of culture and refinement, very much interested in the topography and geology of the country, making them the studies of his leisure hours. It was refreshing enough to listen to the conversations of such a man; and we could hardly decline his kind invitation to share the hospitalities of his country house, some twenty miles from town. Meeting him at the station, we soon found ourselves drawn along on a Brazilian railway, at the rate of about fourteen miles an hour. Some English capitalists were persuaded to build a road of sixty miles in length; the Brazilian Government pledging seven per cent on the outlay, and agreeing ultimately to take possession by paying the cost of construction. It proved a poor investment, being built at great cost, and without judgement in the route chosen. The country through which it passes is uninteresting, and not very productive. Sugar-cane, cotton, and tobacco were seen in the adjacent fields, but for the most part of inferior quality, their culture evidently being careless and thriftless. The planters work their land, as they do their negroes: to get as much out of them as possible, and give as little back as possible—a process of exhaustion which the richest lands will not endure for many years.

While at Bahia, we were questioned as to the probability of immigration from our own Southern States. A number of gentlemen had already visited Brazil with a view to obtaining grants of land from the Government for the colonizing of several thousand families. Of course, the very limited observation allowed by our brief stay in the country, hardly afforded the means of judging fairly of its agricultural resources. The production of coffee in some districts is well known to be profitable, and all that travelers into the interior have reported of the surpassing wealth of soil may be true. But it seemed to the writer that no greater blunder could be made than for American citizens to migrate with their families to Brazil. Their own domain was broad enough and rich enough for generations to come; and even the reverses and sad privations attending the social revolution at home, would be less grievous than the evils they would encounter here. The event has justified this opinion. The few who left their homes in the United States for Brazil soon returned, disheartened and disgusted, and the thousands whose thoughts were turning for a time in that direction, are now attracted by the richer soil and more genial climate of California.

A passage of four days, with no incident worth recording, brought us to Rio de Janeiro, whose magnificent bay, so much "finer than the Bay of Naples," with its "Sugar Loaf" and "Cercovado" overlooking the town, and the loftier heights of the "Organ Mountains" in the distance—strangely unique and piercing the clouds with slender cone-like peaks, or standing against the sky like the battlements of heaven, along which Milton's fallen angels contended till hurled into the abyss beneath—has been so often described that I need not attempt the description here. The city of Rio, aside from its surroundings, which are delightful, is an ill-built, filthy town, with a population of about one hundred and fifty thousand, and every way inferior in interest to Bahia. Commercially it is, perhaps, the most important place in South America, and for this reason, as being also more central than any other large city in Brazil, has been made the residence of the Emperor. The city was all astir when we arrived with preparations for the war against Paraguay. Most of the soldiers appeared to be negroes, and those not of the best class. Recruiting, we were told, had not been very successful; but, as the allies were to furnish most of the men and do most of the fighting, while the Emperor was to foot the bills, this mattered very little. The revenue of the Brazilian Government being small, money was to be raised by negotiating its bonds in Europe. The investment there has probably not proved to be a good one. Notwithstanding the loss of Asuncion, his capital, Lopez still holds out, and Paraguay is not conquered, nor likely to be very soon. It would not be surprising if the Emperor found himself, at the end of the war, already having continued nearly four years, without having gained his object, cheated by his allies, and overwhelmingly in debt. The war seems to have been undertaken chiefly to secure to Brazil, the Argentine Confederacy—whose capital is Buenos Ayres—and Uruguay—whose capital is Montevideo—the free navigation of the rivers rising in Brazil, tributaries to the Plata. A secondary object, and really the first, with the Argentine States, is to compel Paraguay to come into their Confederacy. Should Lopez ultimately be overcome, this latter object might be gained. But, in this event, it is probable that the Confederate States, which will one day include Uruguay, no doubt will themselves control the navigations of the Plata and its tributaries, subjecting Brazil itself to their exactions.

An issue like this seems the more probably from the growing importance of Montevideo and Buenos Ayres, and the strength and rapidly increasing population of the countries which they represent. Montevideo, our next port, near the mouth of the river Plata, an interesting town in itself, was especially so to us, from the evidence it gave of the life and energy of its inhabitants. The buildings, for the most part, were good, and those in process of erection much finer than any in Rio. The streets, too, are broader and cleaner, giving the town more the appearance of a North American city. One could hardly fail to notice the superior *physique* of the inhabitants, in part the effect of blood, and partly of climate. There is no admixture of negro blood discernible, and very little of Indian. The original Spanish stock has been pretty well preserved, and this in a climate favorable to health and physical development. The women are fair, bright-eyed, and sprightly; the men active, robust, and often handsome. We saw a number of fine-looking fellows from the interior, and could readily understand the contempt in which they hold the Brazilian soldiers, who were just then arriving, on their way to the seat of war. The town has a population of fifty or sixty thousand, and rapidly increasing. Beside its natural trade as a seaport, it does an immense business in hides, tallow, and jerked beef. In the outskirts of the city, along the opposite shores of the harbor, are immense slaughter-houses, called *saladarios*, or salting places. Here thousands of cattle, driven in from the surrounding country, are slaughtered daily. An English gentleman, the proprietor of one of the largest, invited us to visit his establishment and witness the process of killing and curing. Our curiosity overcame the imagined repulsiveness of it, and as it proved to be a little beyond anything of the kind in the known world, and by no means disgusting, a description of it may not be without interest to the reader. Some fifty or a hundred cattle were separated from the herd, and driven into a small *corral*, in which a man stood with *lasso*. As he threw one end over the animal, it was immediately drawn from the other, by machinery, and the victim was quickly hauled down a slippery inclined plane to a barrier, over which the executioner stood, with a strong-pointed, double-edged knife. This he instantly thrust into the back of the creature's neck, where the spine joins the head, pushing it forcibly into the spinal marrow. Of course, the animal dropped at once, paralyzed. Its body was received upon a platform car, on which it had stood, and on this drawn immediately out some fifteen or twenty feet. There it was quickly removed; and a man with a long sharp knife stood by, first to cut the throat, and with another thrust, seemingly to penetrate the vitals. A large stream of blood immediately followed; and, in another minute, the body was drawn a few feet farther, where men stood with sharp knives, to remove the hide. This they did with incredible quickness, and passed the carcass along to others, who cut it in pieces; separating the lean from the fatty portions, and passing each along to their proper places. The former were wheeled away in barrows, and thrown upon tables, where men stood with sharp knives, to lay them open and reduce them to proper thickness for curing. This being done, they were dropped into vats, from which they were soon withdrawn and thrown upon each other, with layers of salt between. Immense piles were made of the flesh thus thrown together, to be measured only by the cord. After one of these is made up it is pressed under huge beams and weights, and after the water is expressed, the pieces are removed for drying. This is done by the sun, in the open air, the pieces being hung upon wooden frames. The hides are dried in a similar manner. The fatty portions are conveyed to huge caldrons, from which, after melting, the tallow is drawn off into casks, for shipment. The bones are boiled to remove the fat, and then burned to make bone-ash, for manure. The hoofs and a portion of the bones undergo a similar process, for neat's-foot oil. The shin-bones are carefully cleaned, dried, and shipped to England, where they are manufactured into knife-handles. Thus every part of the animal is disposed of, and with such celerity, that the whole process of killing and distributing it did not occupy more than ten minutes. In this one establishment the slaughtering of a thousand cattle was considered an ordinary day's work, and one man did all the killing, which for two hours would be nearly at the rate of two every minute. The whole bloody process was conducted with so little pain to the animals, and with so much order and neatness, that the most sensitive person could only look upon it with interest. Some conception may be formed of the magnitude of the business thus carried on from the fact, that twenty or more of these *saladarios* could be counted along the shore, in which an average of ten thousand cattle were slaughtered daily. Of course, the supply from the interior must be correspondingly great. To furnish this, the ranches are stocked more abundantly than any that were known here, in the early days of California. Ten, twenty, and fifty thousand were often the property of a single person; and one ranch, owned by a woman, was said to contain 240,000 cattle. In the interior, horses were also formerly raised in such numbers that they were killed, like the cattle, for their hides and tallow.

While in Montevideo, we had the pleasure of meeting, besides a number of agreeable American and English residents, several very intelligent gentlemen, who were natives of the country. From conversation with these, we concluded that it might be here, if anywhere, that Napoleon's dream of the dominancy of the Latin races on this continent, so absurdly sought to be realized in Mexico, might be, in part, fulfilled. The immigration from Italy, France, and Spain is very large, and rapidly increasing. There are few English and Germans, comparatively, and still fewer North Americans. In the city of Buenos Ayres, out of a population of 250,000, (the largest city in South America) there are said to be 80,000 Italians. The preference of all these foreigners here, however, is for republican institutions. All the more intelligent of them have a high admiration of our own government and laws. They are familiar with the writings of our ablest statesmen, having translated the "Federalist" into Italian and Spanish. There can be no doubt that, in time, a powerful and stable republic will be established in South America, making the present Argentine Confederacy its basis, and ultimately drawing to itself Uruguay, Paraguay, and Chile; that the Andes, ere many years have gone by, will be crossed by railroads, and, as at the North, the Atlantic and Pacific be united by bands of iron. The country in the interior is described as surpassingly rich and beautiful, with a variety of productions hardly known elsewhere, and with the finest climate in the world. North

America, including Mexico, is the Western home of the Anglo-Saxon. There, for centuries to come, he will find room for his energies, and the rewards of his industry. South America will continue to invite to her shores the overplus of the Latin races, offering all it delights in, in the old world, and tempting it by a wealth of production more abundant, and by a wiser and juster apportionment of earthly blessings.

No. III

While we were lying in the harbor of Montevideo, a boat came off to the *Vanderbilt*, one morning, bringing a well-dressed, good-looking young fellow, with an unmistakably German accent, announced himself to the officer of the deck as an American citizen, and inquired if there was a Chaplain on board. He was told that no Chaplain was officially connected with the squadron; but that a clergyman from the United States, at the request of the Commodore and other officers, frequently held religious services on board; while in port, however, he was generally ashore; and the man was directed to one of the hotels in town, where he could be found. Returning immediately, he sought the Dominie's address, and made known his wish to be married on one of the American ships. He said he was of German birth, but, on reaching manhood, had come to the United States, and there been naturalized — the evidence of which he presented in his certificate and passport; thence he had come to South America, and was now doing business in Montevideo. In religion, he was a Protestant. His *fiancée*, however, was a Roman Catholic, and by the laws of the country their marriage, to be valid, must be solemnized by a priest of that Church; and he must either renounce his religion, or obtain, at considerable cost, a dispensation from the Pope. In this dilemma, he had sought the American Consul, and learned from him that the Government was bound to recognize the validity of marriages legally solemnized in other countries; and that, as an American citizen, he could be married with the like effect on board of an American vessel in port, according to the usages of his adopted country. He had been waiting, he said for a year or more for such an opportunity, and was now most anxious to avail himself of the presence of our squadron, and of the services of its Chaplain. The latter were cheerfully promised; and it was soon known among the officers that we were to have a wedding on board the Vanderbilt. An occasion so novel was not to pass without a bit of a frolic. Some of the *Monadnock's* officers, thinking to give piquancy to the affair, urged upon the Chaplain the choice of their ship for the ceremony; and it was accordingly arranged that the couple should be made happy under the huge guns of the Monitor. The next morning, a sail-boat, containing the bridal party, with a proper escort of officers, was seen approaching the *Monadnock*. The wind was blowing a gale, very much to the discomfort the groom, whose "full dress" was not much improved by an occasional dash of salt water. The bride — a very pretty Italienne, carefully enveloped in an officer's cloak — was as smiling as a May morning; and though the boat came alongside the ship, at no little risk to her safety, and looks of alarm were exchanged by her companions, her own radiant face gave the assurance, once given in the like fear before: *You carry the bride.* The ceremony soon followed in the cabin; the substance of it being translated for the bride, who understood nothing of English. The groom, having won an heiress, and himself being well to do in the world, accompanied the service with suitable presents to the Captain, the First-Lieutenant, and the Chaplain. The entertainment that followed was worthy of the occasion. Bumpers of champagne were swallowed to the health of the bridegroom, the Stars and Stripes, etc.; the groom, in one of his responses, declaring that the first child, whether boy or girl, should be christened "Monadnock."

We sailed from Montevideo on the 25th of January, 1866; and after a pleasant passage of eight days, came to anchor on the Patagonian shore, off Cape Virgin. There we remained a day or two, waiting for a favorable wind and tide to enter the straits of Magellan. The weather in this region is generally rough and stormy, making the passage through the Straits very difficult to sailing vessels. The Commodore, however, had so timed the departure of the squadron that we should reach this part of the cruise at the least trying season in the year, and, by the aid of steam, make the Pacific side without delay. In this we were singularly fortunate. We encountered, neither on the coast of Patagonia nor in the Straits, those violent tempests in which the accounts of this region abound; and we could hardly recognize, for this reason, the various localities described by Captain (afterward Admiral) Fitzroy and Captain King, of the British Navy, who cruised in these waters many years ago — the latter of whom lost his reason and his life through excessive care and hardship. Thanks to their labors, the amended charts now in use have made the navigation of them comparatively safe. It was thought prudent, however, by the Commodore, to proceed through the Straits leisurely, coming to anchor each night in some sheltered place. The first anchorage was in Possession Bay, which we made on the 4th of February. The reader will bear in mind, by the way, that the winters in the north are the summers here. The next day we proceeded as far as Gregory Bay, meeting no bad weather, and witnessing nothing very remarkable. We had, as yet, been able to see no more of the land than we could distinguish from the ship. It had very much the appearance of prairie land in the West, late in the fall. No mountains were in sight, and no trees; but everywhere, long stretches of undulating plain, covered with coarse, withered grass. The sky was generally veiled with clouds, driven rapidly along by cold winds-- the temperature being about that of November in the Middle States, and Nature, on all sides, wearing a cheerless and forbidding aspect. At Gregory Bay, however, we anchored under the lee of some bluffs, and the next morning were gladdened by a clear sky, and a tolerably warm sun. Here we gladly improved the opportunity to go ashore, and examine the country; not forgetting the Commodore's injunction to go armed, partly in the hope of finding something to shoot, and partly that the natives, who were represented as cannibals, might not make game of us. We had no occasion, however, to use them for either purpose. We found the land very much as it had appeared from the ship. Ascending the bluff, except a range of hills, a few miles distant, we saw nothing but a slightly rolling tract of prairie. Glad to escape the confinement of the ship, we ran over this like boys out of school, separating at length into little parties in pursuit of the *guanacos*—a species of llama, of which we had seen, here and there, a few along the shore. The day seemed likely to pass without incident, save the simple fact of our first landing, in the Straits, on the shores of Patagonia. Toward night, however, while strolling about the beach, I learned from one of the men that some of the natives had been seen, and that a number of the officers had gone out to meet them. I ran immediately up the hill, and saw, a little way off, three or four on horseback, galloping toward me like mad, with a crowd of officers and men in pursuit. They soon reached the beach, and there halting, we had our first sight of a Patagonian. In this we were very pleasantly disappointed. The gigantic stature and forbidding visage, which many travelers have recorded, and which make up the description of our older school-books, are a fable. Their average height is not greater than that of the North American Indians, to whom, also, in form and feature, they bear a very close resemblance. The tallest of the party measured about six feet. He was handsomely and powerfully made, with rather a pleasant expression of countenance. He could say a few words of English, picked up from a chance interview, now and then, with sailors—the most noticeable of which were "rum" and "bread." Pointing to the ships and one of the boats nearby, he expressed a desire to go on board—in the hope, no doubt, of regaling himself with those delicacies. The Commodore gratified his wish, by taking the party off to the *Vanderbilt*, when they soon returned, with a bushel or two of hard-tack, and, happily, none the worse for the entertainment on board. The spokesman, who seemed to receive from his companions the respect due a chief, was amusingly jealous of his dignity. Observing that the officers were borne on the backs of the sailors, through a little shoal, to the boats, he, too, insisted on keeping his own feet dry, and would not stir until the Commodore directed one of the men to carry him.

Their only clothing was a *guanaco* robe, which was wrapped about the body, and strapped or tied around the waist; leaving their bare arms free, with leggings and rude moccasins of the same material. Their hair hung long behind, with a tuft on the crown, and shortened near the forehead. Each one carried a long, sharp knife, and what in South America is called a *bolas*, made of two round stones about the size of a hen's egg, covered with leather, and united by a thong of hide some eight or ten feet in length. This they cast toward the legs of their prey, entangling and throwing the animal, and then riding up immediately and dispatching him with their knives. We observed the carcasses of an ostrich and a fox, just killed, tied upon the backs of their horses. They had, also, a number of *guanaco* skins, which they had brought down to barter for the commodities above-named. The fur of these is soft and fine, making very beautiful sleigh-robes, which, in New York, command a very high price.

Toward nightfall they left us, evidently pleased with the attention and kind treatment they had met, and promising to come again the next morning, with a large number of their people, who were then encamped a short distance away. They were as good as their word; for soon after sunrise the beach was swarming with men, women, and children — all eager to see the wonders, and share the bounty, described by their companions. We were compelled, however, to disappoint them — the order being given to weigh anchor, and none going ashore to meet them but the Commodore, with a small escort of officers. Unhappily, our next sight of them was only to repeat the old story of what rum does for the "poor Indian" everywhere. This was at Sandy Point, our next anchorage in the Straits, where a number were still lingering from a large encampment of several hundred, broken up a short time before our arrival. They were all beastly drunk, except one of them — a woman, with a child some two or three years of age — and she was half wild with drink and trouble. I feared for the lives of both, from the violence of a drunken brute who appeared to be the husband. But somehow the mother succeeded in mounting a horse, and rode away, with the little fellow in her arms. He was a handsome child, with chubby cheeks and bright black eyes, and seemed quite undisturbed by the wild scene about him. The reader must not infer that the rum which produced this scene had been furnished by our own squadron. The natives had procured it from some of the Chileno traders at Sandy Point, in exchange for their furs.

The identity of the Patagonians in race with the Indians of North America, as indeed with all the aborigines of the continent, can hardly be doubted. One observes among them all the same high cheek-bones, the same breadth of jaw, and the same general cast of features. Climate, food, and occupation will account for all the variations among them. These are nowhere greater than between the "horse Indians," as they are called on the main-land of Patagonia, and the "canoe Indians," on the island of Tierra del Fuego. The latter, of whom we saw a few, are of the lowest type of humanity — inferior, if possible, to the Diggers of California. Stunted in growth, their necks sunk into their chests, and their legs shriveled and spindling, they present the most decided contrast to the natives on the opposite shores of the Straits. Yet the differing habits of life will explain the unlikeness. The latter live on horseback, subsist by the chase, and are comfortably clad in furs. The former live in their canoes, with mussels and other inferior kind of fish for their only food, and often with neither rags nor skins to cover their nakedness. The islanders, too, are isolated — each family building its hut, and lighting its fire, on the lonely shore, by itself and for itself. Their neighbors opposite, in larger numbers, find something of a community of interest, and therefore the need and the advantage of social order and discipline. A few generations only would need to come and go, to produce all the diversity now witnessed; and yet one can easily trace in the features of these islanders their descent from the people on the mainland. (The reader will be interested in some of the "speculations" of the Duke of Argyle upon the primitive condition of the human race, illustrated by facts narrated of the Fuegians by Darwin, the English naturalist. *Vide* No. IV: "His Primitive Condition.")

A painful incident added very much to the sympathy with these poor creatures, which their forlorn condition naturally awakened. A chance-shot from the gun of one of the sailors, who was shooting ducks, struck a little child in the canoe of a native, as he was paddling from the shore to one of the ships. The wound was a dangerous one, though not mortal under proper treatment, and caused the little one great suffering. The man paddled up to the sides of the *Vanderbilt*, and the distressed mother held her poor child up to show the officers the injury it had received. Of course they were taken on board, and the wound dressed by the surgeon. But beyond this, nothing could be done. Of the probable pain and sickness of the child that followed, in their miserable and destitute condition, we could only indulge in sympathetic conjecture.

We remained at Sandy Point several days. It was formerly a penal settlement of Chile; but, a few years since, the convicts overpowered their keepers, and escaped. Since then it has been maintained as a military post, with a garrison of about a hundred men. These, with the officers and their families, form a population of something less than two hundred. No attempt at fortification is made — a fact that speaks well for the disposition of the natives, who could easily, with their superior numbers, assault and destroy the garrison. They are well treated, however; and they have the wit to see that so long as this continues, it is their interest to be on good terms with their neighbors. The Chileno settlement is a neat little hamlet, with small, but tolerably comfortable houses of wood; that of the *Commandante* being quite a respectable mansion, with some pretensions to ornamental shrubbery around it — all the prettier and more interesting to us because of its incongruity with our former thoughts of Patagonia. There is also a neat little chapel, alongside of which lives the *Padre*, whom we found a pleasant-looking person, very polite and kindly disposed. After a little conversation with our own Dominie — introduced to him as a Protestant *Padre* — he embraced him very cordially, seeming not at all reluctant to acknowledge him as a brother. From what we heard afterward, however, of the little man, the relationship was not one to boast of. An English-speaking Russian, who lived in the settlement, told one of our officers that the cock-fight which often followed the Sunday service was not unfrequently attended by the *Padre*, himself acting as umpire, and sometimes betting with the rest. He added that it was generally safe to stake money on his side, as it was very apt to be the winning side. The story — no doubt for the most part a slander, for there could have been no better way of breaking up the amusement – did not efface the impression which the *Padre's* good countenance and kind manners left upon me. Doubtless his religious teachings, without raising very much the standard of morality about him, were adapted to the customs and usages of the community. And, on the whole, his people were probably not worse, but better, through his influence.

Attached to each house was a little garden, containing about an eighth of an acre. The vegetation in these was strong and luxuriant. Green peas, potatoes, cabbages, lettuce, etc., were produced, they told us, in abundance. Patches of wheat and barley promised, in appearance, an excellent crop. The summer was too short, however, to bring them to maturity, and they were cut for the horses soon after heading. Cherry-trees and pear-trees grew thriftily, but yielded no fruit. The cattle and horses were in good condition, finding excellent pasturage in summer, and in winter good browsing in the forests. In these the trees grew to great size. We saw live-oaks from six to eight feet in diameter, some of them a hundred feet or more in height. The woods were filled with wild flowers, the fuchsia – in the Eastern States a delicate and carefully nurtured plant – here growing wild in the greatest luxuriance: plainly showing – what we learned otherwise – that the winters here, though more protracted, are much less severe than there. The summers, too, in this region are short, and the heat never intense. Though February corresponds to the northern August, snow was visible on all of the mountains about, at a height of not more than fifteen hundred feet. It should be remarked that around Sandy Point the face of the country was diversified with mountain, plain, and forest, presenting an aspect much more agreeable than any we had yet beheld in the Straits. In a clear morning, the solitary peak of Mount Sarmiento was seen glittering in the sunlight, near a hundred miles away to the south-west – the first snow-clad mountain of any great height that we had seen, and interesting, besides, from the name it has received of the great Portuguese navigator, who was among the first to explore these regions.

While at Sandy Point, we were told of a coal mine, some eight or ten miles from the coast, which the Commodore and several other officers expressing a desire to visit, the *Commandante* furnished them with guides and horses for the purpose. Making an early start, we reached the place before noon, our course lying through a dense forest, and along the bed of a mountain stream. The weather was fine, very like a Northern May-day; and as the party was well made up, the horses of the best, and ample provisions made in the way of creature comforts, the excursion was altogether one to be enjoyed. Let the reader imagine a picnic – for such we made it – in Patagonia! the cavalcade winding through the forest, or fording the stream; the Chilenos, with their bright, scarlet riding cloaks, and the officers in the neat, close-fitting uniform of American blue; and then the feast and merrymaking that followed, until very little time was left for *prospecting*. Business, however, was not forgotten. All along the bed of the stream we had observed small fragments of bituminous coal, and more than once had noticed signs of it in the banks by its side. At our stopping-place a stratum of it, several feet in thickness, was visible, and the guides told us of other beds still finer a few miles beyond. Not having brought the tools, however, for a very thorough examination, we contented ourselves with a survey, as we could best make it, at this point. From this, the evidence of good coal was decided enough to determine the Commodore in arranging another more effective expedition the following day. In this the Chief Engineer of the *Vanderbilt*, with several picked men, and the necessary tools and bags, were included. An excavation of several feet was made into the bed, and a considerable quantity of the coal brought away for trial. The Engineer pronounced it good, and believed it would be found still better, the farther the bed was penetrated. It was amusing to observe how the characteristic spirit of Yankee enterprise and speculation was set to work by the report of what was found. The report was at once conceived and seriously discussed throughout the squadron, of forming a company with sufficent capital to procure a grant of the mines from the Chilean Government — which lays claim to Patagonia — and work them on such a scale as to monopolize the trade in all the ports of South America. Besides this, a fleet of steam launches should be built, procuring cheap supplies of coal here, to take in tow through the Straits all the sailing ships that now double Cape Horn. Of course, the profits of such an enterprise would be enormous; and the New York and San Francisco capitalists would be glad enough to take the stock, while naval officers of ability would not be wanting to exchange their commissions for an active interest in the concern. I need hardly say that the bubble burst before anybody was hurt by the glitter of it. But many a fortune has been lost in speculations more foolish. No doubt the time will soon come when some similar project will become a reality, and the mines we visited be worked with profit.

From Sandy Point onward, the grand scenery of the Straits opened before us. The hills were covered with rich masses of verdure. On all sides the mountains — now fronted with plains, and then rising abruptly from the water's edge — lifted their white crests to the sky. The wild grandeur of the scene seemed to culminate as we rounded Cape Forward, the southernmost point of the main-land, where "the backbone of the continent" has been broken in one of Nature's convulsions, and the two oceans have embraced each other over the ruin. Traces of this ancient war of the elements may be found the world over; but in few places are its ravages, and the signs of its continued violence, more interesting than here. Immense glaciers, numbers of which we saw, are still rasping the mountain-sides, and adding breadth to the valleys beneath. Some of them, in the distance, under the heightening power of the imagination, were like mighty cataracts, as if Niagara were pouring down its blue waters from the clouds.

On the western coast of Patagonia, coming to anchor in the Bay of San Estevan, we were fortunate enough to have a sight of the three glaciers briefly described by Darwin, the English Naturalist, who accompanied Captain Fitzroy thither, some years ago, in H.B.M. ship, the *Beagle*. He speaks of them as the largest in the world, except one in Greenland; though, from the very meagre account he gives, it is probable that the fogs and tempests, which he describes as incessant, rendered any more than a partial and interrupted view of them possible. It happened to us in the *Vanderbilt* to approach them on one of the exceptional days of the year, under an almost cloudless sky. To paint the beauty and magnificence of the scene that gradually opened before us, would baffle the art of one much more skilled than the writer. I was called on deck by the officer in charge, about midday, to see the mountains that had just come in sight. Two cloud-like peaks were faintly visible to the northward, which one could hardly believe were mountains, so great was their height above the horizon and the darker cloud-masses beneath. The glass, however, left no doubt of what they were. As we drew near them, hour by hour, their outlines and surface came out more distinctly. Gradually the clouds rolled away, revealing other summits still loftier, until, at length, a magnificent range of mountains, covered with snow, and fronted with thickly-wooded hills, was before us. Presently, in an opening of these hills, we noticed a small, triangular-shaped space, perfectly white, with a point touching the water. As we drew near, this slowly enlarged, changing at the same time its shape, until we could distinguish it as a river of snow and ice, pouring down from the mountains beyond. Very soon another similar space appeared, some distance to the left; and then a third, of greater dimensions, in the center—both of which opened gradually to view, like the first. Here, then, as we came to anchor, toward the close of a beautifully clear day, were these three immense glaciers directly before us, each several miles in width—the mountains towering loftily above and beyond, and the still waters of the bay edged all around with foliage, whose rich dark-green faded into purple in the distance. Let the reader picture to himself the scene, as the sun was calmly sinking into its water bed behind, its light being reflected by the snow as by burnished silver, and its last rays tinging the mountain-tops with gold.

But Nature is chary of her most beauteous gifts in these regions. It was by extraordinary favor that we were allowed to approach, in a day so clear and still, a spot but rarely visited, and to gaze upon a scene closely veiled, through most of the year, by mist and storm. The next day the sky was overcast, and the clouds gathered around the mountains. Nor was the view upon which our eyes had feasted the day before, restored during the week that we lay at anchor in the bay. Thank God, the memory of what we saw remains. The sight of all outward things must soon pass away; but the images of beauty and of glory which the mind has once received it may retain, if it will, forever.

The Reverend James Smith Bush *(1825-1889) was rector of Grace Episcopal Church in Orange, New Jersey in 1865, and there is little else we have learned about him. Although his voyage on the* Monadnock *might indicate that he had served as a ship's chaplain in the navy, we have discovered no proof of that fact.*

Bush did author at least one religious work entitled More Words on a Bible *in New York in 1883, but despite the implications of that title we do not know what other works may have preceded its publication.*

Adventures in the South Seas

Trade With the Cannibals

by E.A. Rockwell

March 1869

But little has been told of those whose enterprise and daring first opened Commerce in the Pacific, and prepared the way for the occupation of California by a commercial people. The efforts of the early traders were confined to hide-droghing, whaling, and *bêche de mer* gathering. Although the latter occupation became one of the lost arts with the discovery of gold, and the consequent opening of larger and more profitable fields for commercial enterprise, some reminiscences in connection therewith may not prove uninteresting, as faintly outlining the nature of the hazards taken by the pioneers of commerce in the Pacific.

It was several years ago. No matter how many. I was just entering upon the world, and revolving in my mind what should be my future course, and where I should next direct my footsteps. One day, while cogitating upon these matters, I met Captain Hawser, an old family friend, who had been "down to the sea in ships." His vessel, the clipper brig *Addie*, was then being fitted out for a voyage of trade and adventure, in the South Seas—for in those days, which were working out the destinies and shaping the future greatness of the Pacific Coast, trade was oftentimes adventurous in more than one sense.

"The *Addie* will be ready for sea in ten days, and then I am off for a year or two. How would you like to make the voyage with me? Come, go along. You are doing nothing; I have a spare berth in my cabin at your service; the voyage will do you good, and teach you more than you will learn here in five years. Come, go with me, and learn how some of our merchants make their fortunes. If you will go I will give you a chance for a small venture on your own account, and you, perhaps, may lay the foundation for a fortune of your own."

The idea was a novel one to me, and the inducement for gain was tempting. I hurriedly revolved the proposition in my mind. Since then I have discovered that it is usual for persons just entering upon life to "hurriedly" revolve every proposition affecting their future welfare. Early days are not days of reflection.

The captain went on to inform me that he was to proceed on a trading voyage to the Southern Pacific Ocean, from the islands of which the materials for large profits and great fortunes were obtainable. But what he did not inform me was, that those materials were obtained under circumstances the most exciting — so exciting, in fact, that had I been informed of them in advance I should not now be in a position to pen these pages as a result of actual observation. During the geographical studies incident to adolescence, my imagination had been intensely excited by the brief descriptions given of those far-off regions — descriptions, allow me to remark, parenthetically, that I afterwards discovered to be as far from the truth, metaphorically speaking, as the sun is from the earth. Suffice it to say that the proposition of Captain Hawser was accepted; all necessary arrangements were perfected; and, in due course of wind and weather, the good brig *Addie* was speeding on her way.

I do not propose to weary the reader by describing the voyage. At the best sea voyages are monotonous and sickening; and my experience is, that descriptions thereof can properly be placed in the same category. One from me certainly would be — for, at the best, I could only faintly describe my feelings and impressions, and they assuredly were of the most unpleasant character. A succession of gales and calms; of high seas, and flat, glassy ocean; of "salt junk" and "hard tack", sandwiched with nautical oaths and general *ennui* — is anything but pleasant to think, write or read about.

We were bound for a trading cruise among the Fiji and other islands of Polynesia. Our object was to purchase *bêche de mer* from the natives. *Bêche de mer* (literally a "sea spade") is a sea-slug (*Holothuria*) found in great quantities on the rocks and coasts of some of the Polynesian Islands, the Fijis being the most abundant source of supply. Up to the time of the gold discovery in California, and the consequent revolution of commerce, the *bêche de mer* trade was one of those branches of general traffic which attracted adventurous spirits to the Pacific, and from it enterprising merchants of Salem realized handsome profits. But to what use was the article put? asks the uninitiated reader. It was carried to China, and exchanged for silk and teas — the Chinese esteeming it a great luxury as an article of food. For, your Chinese epicure ransacks earth, air, and sea, for delicacies wherewith to tickle his palate. *Bêche de mer* is the rarest delicacy obtained from the dominions of Neptune. The *Addie* was laden with second-hand flint-lock muskets, ball and powder to match; calicoes of "loud" pattern and glaring colors; tobacco; cheap sheath-knives, etc. The Fijians would have little or nothing but muskets and ammunition; other islanders would sell all they had — wives and daughters included — for tobacco; all would trade for knives; and "loud" calicoes found a ready market. Thus much I learned during the voyage, and pending our trading experience among the savages of Polynesia. In addition to *bêche de mer*, rare and beautiful shells were often obtained from the natives, and they commanded a ready market and good prices in civilized portions of the world.

Before we arrive at the islands, it would be well to enlighten the reader as to the manner in which the *bêche de mer* trade was conducted. Whenever a vessel appeared, for barter or otherwise, at one of the islands, the natives would surround it in their canoes in large numbers; the commander, however, would take good care not to allow any of them to board his vessel—for, should they once get a foothold, the voyage would be summarily ended, the cargo confiscated, the crew made food for cannibals, and the vessel destroyed. Hence, great caution, shrewdness, and courage, were necessary on the part of the captain. His object would be to get on board his vessel some high chief, to be kept as a hostage for the good behavior of his allies and retainers during trading operations. The object of the real chiefs would be to palm off upon the captain someone of the "lower orders," whose carcass was worth no more than the low price of meat in that market. After much maneuvering and "backing and filling," the Captain would, if he "knew the ropes," get what he wanted—a real, live chief. With him on board, the necessary arrangements for commercial intercourse would be made. It would be stipulated that, while the chief remained on board, a party from the ship should proceed on shore with a supply of muskets, ammunition, and calico, and there purchase the articles they desired. The prices of everything were arranged beforehand. So much *bêche de mer* for a musket, so much for a fathom of calico, and so on. The preliminaries being thus arranged, the trading party, with its stores, would take leave of the vessel, and proceed shoreward, escorted by an immense fleet of native canoes, all filled with armed and savage cannibals; at the same time, the brig would be put out to sea, keeping close watch over the hostage chief—since, should he escape (and he always used his utmost endeavors to elude the hospitality of his entertainers), the lives of the shore party would be sacrificed. And as the fellows could swim several miles, it was necessary for a vessel to sail out of sight of land, and stay there long enough for the trading party to collect all the *bêche de mer* within reach of its post. Though closely watched, the hostage was always treated with "most distinguished consideration," and nothing was omitted that could contribute to his creature comforts. As a matter of fact, the supplies necessary for this purpose were few—plenty of rum, tobacco, and food. While the vessel was thus at sea, the natives on shore would be busily engaged in collecting and drying the *bêche de mer*, and bringing it to the trading post, where, under the supervision of a chief, inferior in rank to the one on shipboard, it would be exchanged for the goods of the traders. The utmost good faith was scrupulously maintained in these transactions by all parties; the natives were bound to it by the life of their chief, and the traders by motives of policy, looking to future trading operations, and to the safety of other parties who might come after them.

In due course of time the *Addie* reached one of the Fiji Islands, and as she approached the roadstead, was met by a flotilla of the Fijian navy, armed with spears and muskets. The sight was strange and exciting to the new voyager. In the background were high, cone-shaped mountains, draped from base to summit in rich tropical foliage; and in the foreground was a smooth, pellucid sea, dotted with grotesque vessels filled with the most terrific beings in human shape that had ever met a civilized eye. Far beneath the vessel, through the depths of translucent waters, vast coral forests displayed their magnificent beauties and filled the mind with wonder and delight. The varied sensations of the moment amply remunerated for the vexatious trials of the long voyage, and nearly obliterated all memories of its tedious monotony. But not much time was allowed for simple admiration. Polynesian tactics soon began to display themselves, and the work of Polynesian and Yankee diplomacy commenced in good earnest. First, an attempt was made to board the *Addie,* but that was promptly and firmly, but quietly, vetoed by the chief magistrate of the brig and his cabinet. Then efforts were made to pass off a "low down" native as a chieftain of note and power. But Captain Hawser was conversant with all the tricks of Polynesian strategy. In due time matters were arranged satisfactorily to all parties. A live, unmistakably real chief was on board. I soon learned that no one of experience could possibly mistake a "low down" for a chief, so marked was the difference in their looks, actions, and general bearing. The pride of rank and power, and the habit of command, were as visible in the one, as the habit of subjection and servile obedience were manifest in the other. When the proper magnate came on board a trading party (of which I was one) was detailed for operations on land.

The vessel turned her prow seaward, and we proceeded to the landing, my mind filled with a variety of emotions, which may be defined as delight, wonder, fear, admiration, gladness that I was there, and a wish that I was somewhere else — even in Boston. The trading party was inducted into a commodious building, constructed according to the most approved style of native architecture, and the work of trading commenced. Of the bartering, dickering, and haggling, it behooves not to speak. Trading there, except in kind, was pretty much as it is everywhere else. Each party strove to get the most for what it had to part with, and each endeavored to make it appear that its poorest commodity was of superior order.

The Fijians are a superior class, among the Polynesians. Superior in physical manhood, superior in pride, superior in the art of war, superior in ferocity, and superior in treachery and bloodshed. They were quick to learn the value of the musket as an implement of war, and being almost constantly engaged in fighting, the musket and its accompaniments they demanded in trade. Their buildings are superior to those of the natives of other groups; their cooking apparatus is far superior, even approaching barbaric excellence. The latter consist principally of earthen pots and ovens, and are usually devoted to the stewing and roasting of human flesh, an article of food much in demand in Fiji. I am sorry to be compelled to give it as my opinion that most if not all their wars were occasioned by the desire to procure this delectable article of diet. They would go on a hunt for human beings wherewith to appease their appetites pretty much as our Indians hunt for game, and would kill, roast, and eat a Fijian of another tribe with as little compunction and as much gusto as a white man would kill, roast, and eat a turkey on Christmas day. Every day, if possible, was, in this respect, made Christmas in Fiji. The time of the Fijians appeared to be mostly divided between two pursuits — raising people and slaughtering and eating them.

For relaxation they diversified their occupations by dancing, carousing, and priestly exercises in their imbous, or temples, where they worship their gods, and glorified themselves exceedingly. There is a substratum of human nature which is just the same whether it occur in civilized or savage life, and in this substratum is to be found religious egoism and the propensity for self-laudation.

A happy condition of society was that in Fiji for an unsophisticated youth just entering upon life to find himself placed in! It was not comfortable to reflect that some day I might grace the table of the man from whom I was purchasing *bêche de mer* for the purpose of tickling the palate of some epicurean Chinaman!

A week or two previous to our advent the tribe with which we were holding harmonious and profitable commercial relations had been engaged in one of its periodical hunts. As a result of the *battue* some fifteen head of game were captured. All but three of these had been devoured before our appearance. The three had been fattening for several days, and were in tolerable condition. The Fijian epicure delights in having his human flesh fat and juicy. The labors of *bêche de mer* gathering and trade trickery made our mercantile friends hungry for a "meat dinner;" and, as a relaxation from their arduous toils, as well as to invigorate themselves for further efforts in the industrial way, they resolve upon having a feast.

The day was appointed, and we were honored with an invitation to dinner — this, by the way, as a token of appreciation of the excellent quality of our goods and our commercial integrity. On the morning fixed upon fires were lighted, the cooking pots brought out, and the fatted prisoners led forth. There were two girls and a boy, ranging in age apparently from thirteen to sixteen years. The old and tough game captured in Fijian hunts is condemned to slavery — a fate somewhat worse than being killed and eaten. They manifested no signs of fear; but a look of stolid resignation pervaded their countenances. They had been educated in such matters, and education forms the common mind in Polynesia as well as in countries where civilization predominates. The victims of Fijian cruelty and appetite were taken to the slaughter block, and their hands and feet tied, amid shouts and songs of joy on the part of the assembled cannibals. The butcher, with a sharp-edged, heavy club of wood, soon despatched the poor creatures by a well-directed blow against the base of the skull. Each died without a struggle. They were then, amid hideous incantations and outcries, cut up, pretty much as one of our butchers would cut up a hog, placed in the pots, and cooked. We did not stay to see the feast. Already we were sick near unto death with the horrible sight we had witnessed. It was a scene, once viewed, never to be effaced from the memory. Nothing but an earnest desire to gain knowledge, even under the most repugnant circumstances, could have induced us to withstand even so much of the terrible operation. Though we saw no more, deep into the hours of the night we could hear the howlings of the feasting revellers — for so long as there was a mouthful of the food or a drop of their exhilarating drink left the cannibals kept up their brutal revellings — their hideous howlings. While discussing the horrible affair in our quarters, a philosophical member of our party, who had been blessed — or cursed, as the case may be — with more experience of Polynesian manners than his fellows, endeavored to console and tranquilize the remainder with the following comforting remark: "Boys, mayhaps it's just as well. If them ere black devils hadn't been eat up now they'd most likely have eat up somebody else! And who knows," he reflectively queried, "how many they helped to eat already!" And saying this, he coolly knocked the ashes out of his pipe and went to bed.

An incident occurred during our stay which, in a manner, serves to exhibit some of the peculiar characteristics of manners not only in Fiji, but throughout all Polynesia, except in those rare localities — rare as relative to the whole — where missionary influence has prevailed. The *locum tenens* chief experienced a sort of savage friendship for one of our party, and, in consequence, heaped upon him every attention known in the code of Polynesian hospitality. Among other marks of his esteem he presented him with a girl of some fourteen summers — a comely specimen of cannibalistic beauty. The girl, however, was not attracted to her new lord and master. She was absolutely afraid of the white skin of the chief's donee, and sought every means of escape. The chief tied her to a tree, as one would a horse, to prevent her from running away. Then, his proprietary interest in the article having terminated, he ceased all further control over her. On being informed by the donee, while the two were smoking a sociable pipe together — that is, passing it back and forth from mouth to mouth, taking alternative whiffs — that the girl was too wild for him, the chief gruffly blurted out, in his broken English: "Kill um! Kill um! Gaw dammum!" Very naturally his knowledge of English was limited to only a few of the strongest and most ferocious expressions to be found in the language.

In addition to their ferocity and blood-thirstiness, a notable characteristic of the Fijian aristocracy was their indomitable pride. The pride of Lucifer, though different in character, was, as to intensity, humility, in comparison. No thing of lower degree was allowed to come between the wind and their nobility. The life of one of their retainers was worth no more than that of a dog. They would strut and fume with as much pomposity and arrogance as if they were lords of all creation — as they were, of all of which they had any knowledge or conception, for in their mind those who came to trade with them appeared as beings of another world. Of unequalled physique and imposing appearance, the chiefs delighted to add to the majesty of their bearing by all the appliances of art. For this purpose each one retained a corps of barbers whose duty it was to make, dress, and keep in order various wigs of different styles, some of them in circumference as large as a half-bushel measure, and others of enormous height. George the fourth was never more precise in the matter of apparel than were these scions of Fijian royalty and aristocracy.

Everything must have an end, even the business of trading with cannibals for sea-slugs. It was a bright morning with the brig *Addie* hove in view, and welcome was the sight to the trading party. A little time sufficed to embark with our collection of food for aristocratic Chinamen; the noble hostage was dismissed, none the worse for his rum and tobacco, and we left the roadstead (amid the wailings of a flotilla-load of natives, who were sorrowing because they could not despoil our vessel and cargo) for other portions of the group, to undergo similar experiences.

Six weeks' enjoyment of the hospitalities, dangers, and horrors of cannibal society sufficed to give the *Addie* her fill of *bêche de mer*, and to relieve her of the warlike though not very dangerous material with which she set sail from Salem.

Our commercial enterprise then diverted us to a group of islands some distance from the Fijis, where it was thought some rare and beautiful shells might be procured.

These islands, so far as geographical appearance is concerned, do not differ materially from the Fijis, but there is some difference in the character of the inhabitants. The natives are as treacherous, and more thievish in a small way than those of the Fijis, but they are not as bold and bloodthirsty; for the reason, perhaps, they neither eat each other nor their enemies. Hence, by taking care not to allow too many on board at once, and keeping watch that those who did come on board did not steal all that was in sight, we made our commercial transactions less complicated than when we were engaged in the *bêche de mer* purchase. Forty or fifty would come on board with their shells, and after bartering them for tobacco and calico, they would be forced to make way for another detachment. In this manner a very profitable trade was driven; so profitable in fact, that what was done in two days resulted in the end in a clear gain of over ten thousand dollars.

On the second day we were astonished by the appearance on deck of a fair-haired and light-skinned native. We were more surprised to hear him deliver himself in tolerably plain English. In short, the man was a naturalized citizen, so to speak, of the islands. He was a human "flotsam," that had drifted away from civilization and been picked up by the primitive people of that out-of-the-way portion of the globe. How came he there? was the query. Here was a new sensation. The man has a history, thought I, and in view of finding it out I induced him to visit the little "cubby-hole" which was called my state-room. By dint of the use of the socializing influences of rum-toddy, tobacco, pipes, and a little "soft tack," he opened his mouth and spake. He was a native of an interior town of Massachusetts. At that age when male humanity vibrates between boyhood and manhood he had a *liason* with the daughter of a neighbor of his father, much to the scandal of his friends and family. The selectmen of the town took the matter up with virtuous indignation. The youngster became alarmed and fled to New Haven, where he shipped on a whaler for the South Seas. After two years' hard service and harder usage the ship put in at the islands where we found him. He watched his chance and made his escape. He preferred the uncertainties of life among savages to the certainty of harsh treatment on board a Christian ship. Luckily the savages were not cannibals, and in their way treated him kindly. They did not, as did the savages we read of in storybooks, make a king of him, but they allowed him to become one of them and gave him as many wives as he wanted. (Wives were cheap and plentiful in Polynesia in those days.) No ship having passed that way for years, he had vegetated among the savages until he had become in reality a naturalized savage. Though he had not forgotten his language, as storybooks say men do under such circumstances, he had nearly outlived all desire for a return to civilized life. He had dropped out of the world, as it were, and floated far beyond all care for its concerns.

Having secured the complement of our voyage, which was to result in a plethoric cargo of silks and teas for the Boston market, the *Addie* was steered for the Celestial kingdom. Passing through King's Mill group, we stopped at one of the islands, not to trade, but to make observations. The people here have nothing of use to sell, and appear to be about as near to first principles as can be. They make swords and spears of sharks' teeth, which are curious and useless enough. They feed principally on sharks and other fish, with cocoanuts and a small variety of other fruits. In this group the mode of dress which was in fashion during the first days of Paradise prevails in all its glory, and every man and woman is an Adam and Eve so far as costume is concerned. The natives are notable for three weaknesses, to wit: a weakness for tobacco, a weakness for iron implements, and last, though by no means the least, a weakness for stealing. With great dexterity they will steal any movable article of iron to be found on deck and drop it overboard into the translucent water; a watching confederate in a canoe will instantly dive after and obtain it before it reaches the bottom.

It was at this island that an unfortunate occurrence, some three years later, befell Captain Spencer, commander of a whale ship. With a boat's crew of five men he went on shore to make observations, leaving the ship in charge of his mate. While he was visiting the shore his ship was visited by swarms of natives. When he attempted to return to his vessel his embarkation was forcibly prevented. At nightfall the natives on shipboard made a rush upon the crew and drove them beneath the hatches. Finally the crew gathered arms and made a sally on deck, driving the piratical rascals overboard. Not hearing anything of the captain, and fearing for the safety of his ship if he remained longer in such a neighborhood, the mate made sail for the whaling grounds of the Northwest. In about five months after this occurance an English vessel touching at the islands found the captain and his men all safe and well. The English captain ransomed Captain Spencer and his men with a box of tobacco, and conveyed them to the haunts of civilization. In time Captain Spencer found his way to Honolulu, where he now resides, a prosperous merchant and sugar-planter, none the worse for his captivity among the Adams and Eves of King's Mill group. He is a well-preserved type of the class of pioneer adventurers who in early times risked their lives to develop the wealth lying hid throughout the coasts and islands of the great Pacific.

Who was **E.A. Rockwell** *and what did he really see? We have no straightforward answers to either of these questions.*

Shortly after we finished reading Trading With the Cannibals, *our attention was caught by Gina Kolata's article in the March, 1987* Smithsonian *which she entitled* Cannibalism, Fact or Fiction? *In it the author wrote that some anthropologists claim the practice as a tribal custom has never been reliably documented, while others accept it as fact. We immediately put ourselves in the camp of the believers, since we had just read E.A. Rockwell's "eye witness account."*

The Smithsonian article went on to state that of the thousands of reports of cannibalism by early explorers and adventurers, virtually all were based on hearsay, with one tribe claiming that a neighboring tribe — their enemies — were true cannibals. The article included several other persuasive arguments rejecting cannibalism as anything other than an occasional religious or survival practice. We now had a foot in each camp — there remained the Rockwell account.

The next few weeks were spent in libraries discovering details of the lives of the authors contributing to this book. Not once did we find any mention of the name of E.A. Rockwell. We re-read Trading With Cannibals *for dates, but only found vague references like "Several years ago, never mind how many." We also took note of the fact that Rockwell, in describing his face to face encounter with cannibals, did not stick around for the actual meal — he only presumed they ate. We were now suspicious enough to conclude that Rockwell might not have understood what he witnessed, and indeed may have been privy to a portion of some other strange tribal custom or bizarre ritual not readily interpreted correctly by more "civilized" persons.*

In the reading of stories like Rockwell's, we have decided to beware of preconceived notions concerning such practices as cannibalism on the part of the author, as well as the distortions of fact which may occur when the writing of the account takes place long after the event. Such tales may even be artistically enhanced to add color or importance to the narrative.

Whoever did write this story — and it may very well have been E.A. Rockwell rather than another author using a pen name — the fact remains that he presents a reasonably accurate account of the practices of the South Sea traders, whether or not the reader concludes that the portion dealing with cannibalism remains above suspicion.

A Consulate Among the Fijis

by W.T. Pritchard

April 1869

In September, 1858, I arrived in the Fiji Islands, to assume my duties as Her Britannic Majesty's Consul. At this period there were living in the group not more than forty or fifty Europeans and Americans, and but few trading vessels went there. The unenviable character of the natives, their insatiable cannibalism, their frequent outrages upon the few whites already settled amongst them, and their constant intertribal wars, deterred the neighboring Australian traders, and the enterprising New England whalers, from visiting them, though they frequented the contiguous Samoan and Tongan groups, where missionaries of various sects had induced the natives to abandon heathenism for Christianity. The reported intricate navigation of the group also led ship-masters to give it a wide berth; and the character attributed to the whites themselves, represented them as little better than the carnivorous Fijians. Much to my disgust, when I landed at Levuka, the chief trading port and settlement of the whites, I found no house suitable for a consulate. The Wesleyan missionary alone had a weather-boarded house, half finished. From him I managed to rent, temporarily, two rooms. But before I had made my arrangements for opening the consulate — indeed, within a week of my arrival, not less than twenty complaints were preferred by British subjects, some against their own countrymen, and some against the natives. Being the first British Consul appointed to this extensive and savage group, my countrymen, many of whom had spent thirty years and more amongst the cannibals, entertained very indefinite ideas as to the duties of my office. Most of the complainants stated their cases verbally, though some few ventured to put them upon paper, and then simply *demanded* my interference on their behalf. The following is an average specimen of these complaints, and illustrates the manner in which they were preferred:

"Levuka, 13 September, 1858.

"Sir — I beg to inform you that last night I was on board the Sydney brig *Vulture*. I went on board to spend the evening with the mate. We had something to drink together, and then we went to bed. In the morning my watch was gone; the mate stole it, sir. I wish you to detain the vessel until the mate gives up my watch, and you have punished him. I request you to attend to this matter at once.

"I am, sir, a British subject, and your obedient servant,

Charles P — g."

The writer of this epistle delivered it in person, and was so drunk after his bout with his friend the mate, that he could hardly stand. He was a Fiji pioneer, having been there over twenty years. As he handed me the letter, he said:

'I shall wait here for the answer, sir. I have been robbed, and I'm an Englishman, sir. My cousin, Dan E — , is a member of Parliament in Sydney, sir."

I read the letter, and then quietly told the colonial M.P.'s cousin that I could not interfere, as I had not yet assumed the duties of the consulate.

"Then you won't see an Englishman righted, sir? What are you come here for then, sir?"

I told him to be off.

"Very good, sir. I'll go down and write to my cousin Dan, in Sydney, and show you up in all the papers, sir. You won't see an injured Englishman righted, eh, sir?"

"Decidedly not, under existing circumstances. You may hereafter be punished for your insolence."

"All right, sir. We shall teach you your duty yet. My cousin Dan will fix you up in the Sydney papers; yes, sir, we shall show you up in the papers."

"That is just what I want, my good fellow," I remarked; "and if you will oblige me by sitting down here and writing an account of me *now*, here are five dollars towards the cost of putting it in the papers."

I put five dollars on the table, and placed pen, paper, and ink ready for his use.

"Blow me, sir, if it's just what you want, I'll be d — d before I do it. You *want* me to write to my cousin Dan to show you up in the papers, eh? And yet you tell me to my face you won't see an outraged Englishman righted. Damn me if I'll do it to please you."

And away he sullenly trudged, rollicking from side to side of the road, assuming all the dignity of an inebriated, outraged Britisher.

Another of the cases thus early brought before me was against the natives of Waea, a small island on the western limits of the group. Mr. B., a Wesleyan missionary at Levuka, had several boats, manned by mixed crews of whites and natives, trading amongst the islands. A few weeks before my arrival, one of his boats had gone to Waea, in charge of two white men and some natives; one of the former was an Englishman, and the other an American. The natives of Waea had captured the boat, killed and eaten the crew, and appropriated the merchandise. Mr. B., as a "British subject," and owner of the boat and cargo, now pressed his "claim for redress and indemnity." While I was listening to the sophistry by which he sought to convince me that there was no possible connection between John B., Wesleyan missionary teacher, and John B., oil trader, and that the cannibals duly appreciated the distinction, the United States corvette *Vandalia* arrived at Levuka, and at the request of the American Consul, her commander, Captain Sinclair, took up the case on behalf of the *devoured* American, and whom the good Mr. B. now admitted into part ownership in the boat and cargo — a fact which did not appear in his earlier statement of the affair. And Mr. B. had suddenly become convinced that it would be better for the savages, and less prejudicial to the Wesleyan Mission, that Captain Sinclair should inflict "retributive justice," than that I should adopt the tardy measure of demanding from the savages "redress and indemnity" for his calicos and hatchets. And so, much to my satisfaction, the case passed out of my hands into those of Captain Sinclair. A party of fifty men was quickly despatched to Waea, to demand the murderers, and to punish them. The Waea people, mustering some five hundred fighting men, for the most part armed with muskets, defied the party, and declined all communications. The handful of Americans gallantly attacked them in their fort, on the summit of a hill, eight hundred feet above the level of the sea. Some twenty of the natives were killed, as many more wounded, and the town and fort reduced to ashes; of the Americans five were slightly wounded.

Another case was more legitimately within the province of my duties. When the Sydney brig *Vulture*, already referred to, was ready for sea, the mates refused duty, and the master appealed to the consulate. Knowing from past experience in another consulate which I had held, that vessels of this class often carried the very roughest of crews, I arranged with Captain Sinclair that if I made a certain signal from the quarter-deck, he would send an armed boat to my assistance, in charge of a lieutenant. Going on board to investigate the case, I found the whole crew drunk, and some four hundred hogs on deck. The vessel was a colonial sandal-wood trader. From Sydney she ran to Fiji, where pigs were bought and taken to the New Hebrides, and other contiguous groups, and exchanged for sandal-wood. A peculiarity of this trade was that the natives would exchange their sandal-wood only for *male* pigs; they held *sows* in abomination, as too feminine, and unfit for food. The mates stated their objections to proceed to sea, and in a fit of virtuous indignation alleged that the captain paid more attention to a *lady* he had on board, and who had joined the brig in Sydney without the knowledge of the owners, than to his duties as master. After carefully hearing the case, I decided to take the mates out of the vessel, as it was quite evident they would cause a mutiny on board, if compelled to proceed to sea. But, though when first stating their complaints against the master they declared their intention to leave the ship, they now refused to go ashore. They quietly set me at defiance, threatening to put the master and his "woman" ashore, and to throw me overboard, if I ventured to interfere. At once I showed the preconcerted signal, which the quick eye of the quartermaster speedily saw, and in a moment the *Vandalia's* boat was alongside. Seeing they were now powerless, the two bullying mates quietly got into her, and went ashore, as the vessel proceeded to sea, amidst the music of her four hundred hungry hogs. It was customary among the islands for English and American vessels of war to assist the Consuls of both or either nation when they could do so without compromising their own nationality.

A few days after my arrival, my worthy countrymen, accompanied by several "prominent" Americans of long residence in the group, called upon me to say that they welcomed me amongst them, and hoped that I would duly protect them from the aggressions of the natives; but they wished me clearly to understand that they "wanted no Consul to interfere in their *family arrangements.*" I was politely given to understand that the purchase of women from the Fijians was one of the ordinary trading operations of the white men. The price of a smart-looking girl from fifteen to twenty years old, with a good figure and well rounded limbs, was from one to five muskets (of the old English tower, or the American Springfield patterns). The girls thus purchased were attached to the white men's households as servants, or "housekeepers," but were in reality so many wives. And *these* were the "family arrangements" with which these worthy pioneers intimated they "wanted no Consul to interfere." In fact, these runaway sailors, escaped convicts from Sydney, and half-savage white men, had brought themselves to the level of the man-eating Fijians, and like them revelled in all the luxuries of the Fijian polygamy — and now gave me formal notice that their "peculiar institutions" should not come within range of the consular supervision.

The idea that I would interfere with this "peculiar institution" had arisen from the fact that the commanders of the British vessels of war who had occasionally visited Fiji, had denounced this traffic. The same worthy Englishman, whose note to me is inserted in an earlier column, with cool impudence, declared to Admiral Erskin, who was remonstrating with him upon the impropriety of his mode of life, that with reference to his "housekeepers" his conduct was perhaps open to some slight objections, though on all other points his conscience was clear, and at ease; he had, in fact, been gradually reducing the number of his women, as he found himself growing old, and the relief he had felt since he had got rid of a *dozen or two* would, even without a higher motive, be sufficient to induce him to perservere in his good intentions. Every white man in Fiji, indeed, lived with his harem of from ten women to the highest number he could manage to purchase; and it was the one thing with which he would not brook interference.

But these pioneers of civilization had another little amusement of their own. I have known a party of three or four buy a hogshead of rum or brandy from a vessel, and deliberately set themselves to drink it out, before even quitting the neighborhood of the cask. Some of these men have been drunk for three months, without an interval of sobriety. As they drew off the spirit, water was put into the cask; and by the time the contents became pure water they became sober. This is what they technically termed "tapering off," and they alleged that it prevented *delirium tremens* resulting from these prolonged "sprees." While in the state of helpless intoxication to which they came in the second or third day, their "housekeepers" provided for the maintenance of their families, and otherwise looked after them personally. And sometimes it was the duty of these "housekeepers" to pour the spirits down the throats of their "noble lords," as they lay stretched out on their mats! A woman who felt herself aggrieved also sometimes made these drinking bouts the opportunity to run away; but when the white man became sober, at the end of three months, the present of a musket to the chief of her tribe invariably brought her back.

Amongst the old white settlers in Fiji were men whose nationality it would have been hard to identify. But, to suit their own purposes, and to be able to threaten the natives with the broadside of a man-of-war, these nondescript whites generally hailed for American citizens, or British subjects — a more appropriate term, perhaps, would be British *objects*. Amongst this class of white men was one who had assumed the name of Clarke, and claimed to be a British subject. This man had taken offense at something Mr. Williams, the then American Consul, had said, or was reported to have said; and he deliberately walked into the American consulate, struck the table on which the Consul was writing, called him a "d — d liar," and threatened all kinds of vengeance, whenever he might find Mr. Williams in his power. He was one of the most reckless, desperate fellows in Fiji, and would as soon have taken a man's life as look at him; in those days life was somewhat precarious in Fiji, as well amongst the Fijians themselves. Mr. Williams could do nothing to the man, and came to me with his complaint. I was at a loss how to punish the fellow. To pass the case over quietly would be simply to submit myself to similar treatment — a prospect I did not much relish. Fortunately, an English man-of-war was in port — the *Cordelia*, Captain Vernon. I consulted the captain, together with the American Consul, and we decided to summon Clarke to the consulate. So far from attempting to deny the charge, he simply sought to justify his conduct. In the absence of any semblance of local authority to take cognizance of the case, we condemned him to five days on board the *Cordelia*, on bread and water, in charge of a sentry. This gave him a quiet time to ponder over his erratic ways, and when he came ashore, he went straight to the American consulate, and apologized to Mr. Williams. From that day he became a "reformed man," and has since been one of the quietest, well behaved men in Fiji. In former years he had lived just as a Fijian — half-naked, and painted. He had been thirty years in the group, and had attached himself to a late chief, Tui Kilakila, noted as one of the most ruthless, insatiable cannibals in Fiji, and in whose wars he had always taken part. In due course Clarke became the chief's right-hand man, and even went so far, it was said, as to join his chief in cannibal feasts, even to partaking of human flesh — the bodies of the enemies he slew in battle!

The white men in Fiji all produced large families. One of them used to boast that he had at least *eighty* sons and daughters; up to that number he had been able to keep an account of them – but there he had "lost his reckoning." And many others there were who counted their forties and fifties. These offspring of the white men and native women were called *half-castes*, and generally possessed all the energy of their father's, with all the cunning of their mother's race; indeed, the vices of their parents seemed united in them without inheriting any of their virtues (if any they had to transmit). Many of these half-castes had grown up to be able-bodied, smart young fellows; and following in the footsteps of the progenitors, purchased all the "housekeepers" they could find muskets for, and had their periodical drinking "jollifications." For some time there had been a rivalry between them and a "select party" of whites as to their prowess with the *club*. There happened to be a good muster of both parties in Levuka about this time; all drank together, and then took to quarrelling, then came to blows, and ultimately to the much-vaunted *club*. One was damaged on his head, another on his leg, another on his arms, and every one was more or less mauled in the face. Both parties came to the consulate for protection against the other. The whites charged their half-caste offspring with being "niggers," and the half-castes retorted that the whites were "outcasts without home or country;" and only with much difficulty I prevented a renewal of the battle in the consulate.

To give variety to life in Fiji, occasionally there were little family scenes. In consequence of the war in New Zealand, many settlers deserted their homesteads and came to Fiji, in the hope that some day it might become a British colony, and in the belief that under the aegis of the British consulate the islands were suddenly becoming habitable. Amongst other new-comers were one Spiers and his lady-love – a Scotchman accompanied by an Englishwoman. One fine evening, at the hour for retiring to rest, the fair spouse was nowhere to be found – she had eloped and gone to Rewa with another Scot of the name of Murray. Vowing vengeance on the destroyer of his connubial bliss, and with a pair of loaded revolvers hanging from his belt, Spiers came to the consulate full of rage. "If I find the villain I'll shoot him, sir, I'll shoot him, sir, as dead as a rat," was all he could say. From Rewa, the fair syren sent him word: "I can never live with you again. I have given my heart to Murray. You have beaten me so cruelly that if we meet again it will only be to die together, for I am determined to shoot you if you cross my path. Leave me with the man I have chosen, and I will leave you in peace. Take another bride as soon as you please; but as for me, I never can, and never shall, be yours again." Fortunately for the consulate, the chicken-hearted spouse, after a fortnight's intoxication, took the same romantic view of the case, and they both agreed to separate without any shooting. The one sailed on his solitary voyage for Sydney, there to forget his lost love; the other remained in the embraces of Murray — a unique example for the savages of the boasted virtue of civilization.

The trading operations of the white men not unfrequently were sources of dispute. A Mr. Israel Russell owned a schooner called the *Kate*, in which he sometimes made a trading cruise after cocoa-nut oil and tortoise shell. Having heard that two white men at Lakemba, a small island on the eastern limits of the group, had a ton or two of oil, he set sail from Levuka in search of the prize. Aware of their taste for brandy, several cases were put on board the *Kate* with the other articles of trade. In due course Russell arrived at Lakemba, and proceeded at once to the house of the two white men. Very seriously and with a very long face and many expressions of condolence, he pulled out of his pocket a great official envelope with an immense seal on it: "Now, boys, here is an order from the consulate to take you both to Levuka. What the deuce have you been up to? You are in for it when the Consul has you at Levuka." But before he would deliver the terrible document, the wily trader proposed they should sell him their oil and have a "grand spree" together before they fell into official hands. Completely upset by the alleged contents of the monster envelope with the big seal, the two men were willing enough and ready to seek relief from any source. Quickly the price of the oil was agreed upon, and the bargain closed. Then, as quickly, the brandy bottle was opened—and then another and another, until the men were on the mats. The oil was rolled down to the beach and put on board the *Kate*, while the "housekeepers" cared for their inebriated lords. A case or two of axes, a piece or two of calico, a few knives, and a few bottles of gin, were sent ashore, and the *Kate* sailed for Levuka. When the brandy and gin bottles were all emptied, and the men at the end of a week arose from their mats, they found, as they alleged, nothing near the proper payment for the oil—and the big envelope was in the careful custody of the chief "housekeeper." With trembling hands they opened the dreaded missive, and found it contained only a blank sheet of paper! In the course of a month or two the *Kate* again appeared off Lakemba, and the two men again had oil for sale. Proceeding on shore, Russell met his two friends who, without referring to the former transaction, readily sold him five hogsheads as containing each fifty-two gallons of oil. As usual, the bung of each cask was carefully knocked out to see that it was full, and one head of each was "spiled," or bored with a gimblet, to show that there was no water with the oil. Payment was promptly made, but this time without gin and brandy: the bargain was "half cash, half trade, no grog, and no reclamations." On arrival at Levuka Russell had the hogsheads rolled into his shed to be emptied as usual into other casks, but out of each there came *only one gallon of oil*, and yet they all appeared to be full. Russell was puzzled, and sent for the cooper to solve the mystery. The heads were taken out; the casks were full—of water! The men at Lakemba had put into each cask two pieces of bamboo filled with oil, so placed that when the bung was knocked out oil only was seen, and when the head was "spiled" oil only ran out, and then they filled the casks with water. This was their "liquidation" of the former transaction. Both parties came to the consulate, and both maintained they had right on their side.

Fiji had neither government nor laws in those early days, if we except the well-known code of *club law*, in which "might is right." Every foreigner went to one of the two consulates — the English or the American — in every trouble, in every fancied grievance, and we found we had more to do than we could get through. Agreeing to work harmoniously together, always to consult each other, and in every case to support each other, as necessary measures of self-defense, the two consulates gradually brought this horrible state of chaos into some little order. But the more we did for our countrymen the more they required from us; and as settlers now began to flock to Fiji we found ourselves every day more unable to entertain the cases that were referred to us. A meeting of the whites was therefore convened, when we proposed to them to establish a "mercantile court" for the adjustment of all white men's disputes, the Consuls sitting *ex officio,* and certain of the more respectable residents, not interested in the cases on hand, sitting as assessors. The proposition was unanimously accepted and the court forthwith organized, with the formal sanction of the chiefs. In the proceedings of this court some amusing scenes occasionally occurred. I remember a man by the name of Taylor brought a suit against a certain Mr. Wyer to recover the amount of a debt — some forty dollars. After a careful hearing the case was decided against Wyer, who was ordered to pay the amount within a specified time. Soliciting the permission of the court to make a proposition to the plaintiff, Wyer approached the table and said: "Now, Taylor, what will you take if I pay you at once, here in the court?" Taylor's eyes glistened at the thought of seeing the money and offered to accept two-thirds. "Will you take it here, *now,* in the presence of the court?" "Yes," said Tyalor walking up to the table, smiling all over his face. "Well, come, let me pay you then. You say you will take two-thirds now, in presence of the court, paid down to you here, on this table?" "Yes, I will, Mr. Wyer." "Then don't you wish you may get it?" and with a bow the rogue backed out of the court, leaving Taylor chagrined beyond description. Within the specified time, however, the amount was paid.

A very fruitful source of trouble we found in the early land transactions of the whites. They bought any fine tract of land from any petty chief for a mere song, without caring whether the seller had the right to alienate or not. Their object was to get a claim upon the land, and then trust to Providence to have their title confirmed hereafter. Often the real owners disputed the sales, and then bloodshed resulted. An amusing instance of this class came before us, in which English and Americans were equally concerned. Nearly in the center of the group is an island called Makongai, with a very fine harbor. Many years since the inhabitants rebelled against their chief, Tui Levuka, who resided on Ovalau, some seven miles distant. Failing in various attempts to reduce the rebels to subjection, Tui Levuka offered to give a portion of the island, including the harbor, to any whites who would assist him. Some ten or twelve Americans and English accepted the offer and accompanied the chief to the fight. The assault upon the fort at the back of the harbor was successful under the leadership of the whites. Two-thirds of the rebels were killed; the survivors were removed to Ovalau as slaves of the chief Tui Levuka; and the captured women were distributed amongst the victors of both colors, the whites, however, getting the lion's share, as they had led the assault that gained the victory. The chief, in a speech overflowing with gratitude to his brave and faithful whites, formally made over to them the portion of the island agreed upon, and ordered the bodies of the slain rebels to be cooked for a grand feast in celebration of the victory. After some time had elapsed, the chief allowed the survivors to return to the island to plant yams and catch turtle for him. About a year previous to my arrival a Mr. Binner had induced the chief to sell him the island, and now the white men who had conquered the rebels claimed the harbor and contiguous lands as theirs. Mr. Binner not being a very popular member of the community, not one of the claimants would make any compromise with him, and the question was referred to the consulates. In our efforts to bring about a quiet settlement of the dispute, one old man, from Salem, who had grown gray during thirty years of frollicking in Fiji, and who had been *clubbed* by the natives soon after his arrival amongst them to within an ace of his life, became considerably excited and declared: "I will never let Binner have my interest. The land is fairly ours. We fought and bled and *died* for it, sir; by heavens we did, sir." Not all the reasoning in the world could convince the old man that he had *not died* for the land, though he had "fought and bled for it." Ultimately, however, money bought the old man off, and Binner remained in possession of his island.

In the cases where natives were mixed up with the whites, there was often the mingling of the heroic and the ludicrous. Women have always been a source of war, and regardless of color they were so in Fiji. An Englishman by the name of Taylor had purchased a blooming young "housekeeper" for two muskets. But growing weary of her liege, and falling under the influences of the tender passion, she gave her heart to John Audette, a Canadian, who promised to marry her. Unable to check the course of her love, and to defeat the projects of her lover, Taylor gave the woman to the chief Tui Levuka, who, a week afterwards, gave her to the chief of a mountain tribe. To escape being carried to the mountains she fled to Mrs. Binner, the wife of the missionary, who secreted the fugitive under her bed. The mountaineers traced the runaway, and demanded that she should be delivered to them. But with true woman's pluck Mrs. Binner boldly refused. Tui Levuka appeared at the consulate, and gave notice that if the mountaineers could not get their own woman they would take Mrs. B. to the mountains as her substitute; and he hinted that already a large party, fully armed and painted, were in the bushes around the missionary's house watching their opportunity to seize his wife. The missionaries would not listen to my advice to give up the woman, for they imagined that by *marrying* her to the Canadian they would save another from the evil ways of those very loose followers of the Devil who kept so many "housekeepers." The superintendent missionary wrote to me, saying: "I judge one word from you would be sufficent to keep the chief from meddling with the man or his wife. I thought of marrying them at three o'clock this afternoon, if you see no objection." On receipt of this note I sent off at once for the chief, who still maintained that the mountaineers must have the one or the other—Rakil, or Mrs. Binner. If the missionary would defend his wife to the last, and the white lover fight for his sable bride, unquestionably there would be bloodshed somewhere. I used all my persuasion to get the runaway given up, but to no purpose; the missionary, with an eye to morality, was bound to marry the fugitive to his countryman; and the mountaineers, regardless of consequences, were bound to have *some* woman. There was but one resource left—to offer to *buy* the heroine, and then I could set her free. Tui Levuka dispatched a secret messenger to the chief of the war-party, hidden in the bushes around the mission house, and soon he returned with the acceptance of my offer. The mountaineer chief was summoned to the consulate; the bargain was struck; the axes, knives, cloth, powder, etc., were paid; the black-skinned Rakilu was at that moment my property; and by Fijian custom no one could ever again claim her. Going with the chiefs to the mission house to inform the missionaries of the contract just completed, Tui Levuka stepped out on to the verandah, and gave a peculiar shrill whistle. Suddenly there appeared from the bushes, in all directions, a host of painted, fierce-looking mountaineers, with clubs on their shoulders and spears in their hands. Mrs. Binner was safe; Rakilu was rescued; Audette claimed his bride; and the missionary was ready to perform the ceremony. At three o'clock that same afternoon the sublime climax was reached—John Audette, the white man, married Rakilu, the black woman! and the good missionary's blessing was duly bestowed on the wedded pair. But, sad to say, even in Fiji as elsewhere, love sometimes wanes with the honeymoon. Within three months the luckless Rakilu, *alias* Mrs. John Audette, again appeared in the consulate. This time *she* was in search of the fugitive. Her wedded husband, white man as he was, had joined a Sydney trading-vessel, and she was ruthlessly abandoned—again adrift in the wicked world of Fiji. Alas for the morality the good missionary had hoped to purchase by marrying them. Throughout the islands of the Pacific instances of this species of morality happen every day. A sailor, captivated by the comely forms of the island maidens, and seduced by the prospect of an idle life, as he roves amongst the towering cocoa-nut groves that line the coral beaches, leaves his vessel; to-morrow he marries a girl of fourteen, to have a lawful claim upon her. Soon he grows weary of his bride, and, disgusted with the listless *ennui* of the island life, he ships in another vessel, and leaves the girl trained to the white man's habits, and taught the love of handling a few dollars, and of wearing a showy dress. Inevitably she takes to the readiest means of obtaining money in a seaport; and another victim of the white man's civilization is added to the already long list.

When Captain Sinclair had disposed of the Waea business before referred to, he turned his attention to the matter which had brought him to Fiji—the

American claim for forty-five thousand dollars. Many years ago the houses and property of various Americans were wantonly destroyed by the natives, and in some instances the persons of these Americans were maltreated. After various careful examinations by successive naval officers sent for that purpose—chief amongst whom was Captain Boutwell, of the U.S. ship *John Adams*—the above amount was finally agreed upon as the compensation to be paid by Fiji. The King, Thakombau, promised to pay in cocoa-nut oil to the claimants, or their agents in the islands; but from time to time he shuffled off the payment, and it is more than probable that his conduct was influenced by the ill-advice given to him by certain missionaries who maintained that the claim was unjust — or if there were any claim, that the sum awarded was iniquitously high. Captain Sinclair now summoned the King to pay the amount of forty-five thousand dollars, as agreed with Captain Boutwell in 1855. The King appeared on board the *Vandalia*, and by urgent excuses and fair promises induced the gallant captain to give him twelve months more to meet the demand. Thakombau, well knowing his inability under the existing circumstances of his country (not from lack of resources) to pay the amount within the stipulated period, came to me for advice. Though taught to dispute the justice of the claim in its origin, he could not now evade his responsibiity for the amount named, since he had in 1855 agreed upon the sum with Captain Boutwell; and he now suggested a cession of Fiji to the British Crown, on condition that the British Government would pay the American demands. The King hoped to escape falling into the hands of the French by this move, and was most anxious that the question should be promptly settled. The result of our interviews was the formal cession of Fiji to the Queen, on the twelfth of October, 1858, on condition that the American claim be paid by the British Government, for which payment, as a direct equivalent, certain lands were to be transferred in fee-simple, besides the cession of the sovereignty of the whole group. Subsequently, on the fourteenth of December, 1859, the chiefs of the entire group, together with King Thakombau, "acknowledged, ratified, and renewed the cession of Fiji to Great Britain, made on the twelfth of October, 1858, by Thakombau." And the documents were "fully, wholly, and explicitly translated" by Wesleyan missionaries—the chiefs "affirming and admitting to us personally (the missionaries), that they wholly, perfectly, and explicitly understand and comprehend the meaning, the extent, and the purpose" of their act. I am thus explicit in this matter, because, when the question of the cession was first mooted, the missionaries as a body heartily and cordially coöperated, and most effectually facilitated the movement by every means in their power. They were already the greatest power in Fiji, and they hoped under the new régime to become the supreme and sole religious leaders of the group. But when I unwittingly stated that in an interview with the late Duke of Newcastle, then Colonial Minister, his Grace had asked me "what will the missionaries do when they see a bishop accompanying a governor—for the Church always goes where the State goes?"—there was a sudden change in the clerical tactics. The cession was looked upon with suspicion, personal motives were imputed, and ultimately from cordial coöperation they passed to sullen opposition. One reverend gentleman said to me: "Colonizing, colonizing—I don't understand the meaning of all this colonizing with bishops and governors. I only understand that if the British flag is hoisted over Fiji, the natives will not be allowed to fight, nor the traders to sell muskets and rum; and the natives will all become our converts.

Under the strong and well-organized opposition of the Wesleyans, the cession was finally declined by the British Government, after having had it some two years under consideration—and King Thakombau was left to his own resources to meet the American claim. The Australians were much chagrined at this result, for they had already learned to look upon Fiji as a natural dependency, and feared its falling into other hands—lying as the group does just at their very doors. After I left, and being still unable to pay the forty-five thousand dollars, the King mortgaged three of the islands for the amount. And now to save the islands from falling into the hands of Uncle Sam, a company has been formed in Melbourne to pay the debt and take over the islands, with the intention of growing cotton and sugar for the Colonial markets—a speculation which cannot fail to be most profitable, if the islands are under the control of a government that will avoid the mismanagement of the natives—such as has induced the New Zealand troubles.

It is not generally known that forty years ago there was quite a large and regular trade between Salem and cannibal Fiji. The Salem merchants used to fit out their vessels for Fiji with assorted cargoes, and there barter their goods for *bêche de mer* (commonly called sea-slug), which was taken to Manila or China, where in its turn this was again exchanged for sugar or tea for the homeward cargo. And on this bartering system, these voyages paid handsomely on the round trip. Several of the Salem merchants, or their heirs, are amongst the claimants to the forty-five thousand dollars due by Fiji, for goods and trading-posts destroyed by the natives. This trade has now, however, entirely died out; and to-day the chief trade of the group is in cocoa-nut oil, which the Melbourne and Sydney merchants purchase for shipment to England. In Fiji this oil is worth from eighteen to twenty pounds sterling per ton, without casks; and in London the average price is from forty-five to fifty pounds per ton. On the goods which are bartered for the oil, there is a further handsome profit.

The Fiji group numbers two hundred and eleven islands, of which eighty only are inhabited. Two only are really large—Viti Levu and Vanua Levu. The former is nearly round, with a circumference of about three hundred miles—while the latter is about sixty miles long by twenty-five in average width. The skin of the pure Fijian is dark, rough, harsh. His hair, naturally black and copious, is bushy, frizzled, almost wiry; indeed, it seems something between hair and wool. His beard, of the same texture, is equally profuse and bushy, and is his greatest pride. His stature is large; his muscular development is perfect; his limbs, well-rounded; his figure indicates activity and hardihood. His eye is restless; his manner, suspicious; his temper, quick; his movements, light and graceful. The soil of Fiji is so very rich that I have with my own hands planted kidney-seed cotton, at seven o'clock one morning, and at seven o'clock the following morning the plant was up with two full-blown leaves; and, incredible as this may appear, it happens every day in Fiji. In three months from the planting, the cotton crop is ready for picking; and, by a little management and care, three crops a year may easily be gathered from the same plants. The cotton is fine, and has a long staple. Sugar-cane grows in the same luxuriant manner. I have seen cane from twelve to sixteen feet long, and from eight to ten inches in circumference — and this is no uncommon growth. Coffee also grows well, and gives a good aroma. In fact, every tropical production can be produced in quantity and quality per given area equal to, if not surpassing, the same area in any other country. But the great drawback is — the Fijians are still cannibals.

Although we know that **William Pritchard** *was a regular contributor to the early issues of the* Overland, *our research has revealed precious little about him.*

An Englishman, he was appointed as the first British Consul to the Fiji Islands. We have also learned that he published a book entitled Polynesian Reminiscences; or Life in the South Pacific Islands *in 1866, two years prior to the first appearance of the* Overland Monthly.

Nevertheless, neither the body of his literary work nor his achievements as Her Majesty's Representative to the islands has led to our discovery of his enshrinement in any of the libraries or historical societies to which we have turned in pursuit of our authors.

____The Last of the Great Navigator____

by C.W. Stoddard

November 1868

Think of a sea and sky of such even and utter blueness that any visible horizon is out of the question. In the midst of this pellucid sphere in the smallest of propellors trailing two plumes of foam, like the tail-feathers of a bird of paradise, and over it all a league of floating crape — for so seem the heavy folds of smoke that hang above us.

So we pass out of our long hours of idleness in that grove of eight thousand cocoa-palms by the sea shore — the artist from Italy and the youth from the academy — seeking to renew our *dolce far niente* in some new forest of palms by any shore whatever. Enough that it is sea-washed, and hath a voice and an eternal song.

Now turn to the stone-quarry darkened with the groups of the few faithful friends and many islanders. They are so ready to kill time in the simplest manner; why not in staring our awkward little steamer out of sight?

One glimpse of the white handkerchiefs, fluttering like a low flight of doves, and then with all the sublime resignation of the confessed lounger, we await the approach of twilight and the later hours that shall presently pass silver-footed over this tropic sea.

Four, P.M., and the roar of the reef lost to us voyagers. The sun an hour high. The steams of dinner appealing to us through the yawning hatches — everything yawning in this latitude, animate and inanimate — and the world as hot as Tophet. We lie upon our mattresses, brought out of the foul cabin into the sweet air, and pass the night half intoxicated with romance and cigarettes. The natives cover the deck of our little craft in lazy and laughing flocks. Some of them regard us tenderly; they are apt to love at sight, though heaven knows there is little in our untrimmed exteriors to attract anyone under the stars.

We hear, now and then, the sharp click of flint and steel, and after it see the flame, and close to the flame a dark face, grotesque it may be, like an anitque water-spout with dust in its jaws. But some are beautiful, with glorious eyes that shine wonderfully in the excitement of lighting the pipe anew.

Voices arise at intervals from among the groups of younger voyagers.

We hear the songs of our own land worded in oddly and rather prettily broken English. "Annie Laurie," "When the Cruel War is over," and other equally, ambitious and proportionally popular ballads ring in good time and tune from the lips of the young bloods, but the girls seldom join to any advantage. How strange it all seems, and how we listen!

With the first and deepest purple of the dawn, the dim outlines of Moloki arise before us. It is an island of cliffs and cañons, much haunted of the king, but usually out of the tourist's guide-book.

It is hinted one may turn back this modern page of island civilization, and with it the half-Christianized and wholly bewildered natures of the uncomprehending natives, and here find all of the old superstitions in their significance. The temples, and the shark-god, and the *hule-hule* girls, beside whose weird and maddening undulations your *can-can* dancers are mere jumping-jacks.

Listen for faint music of the wandering minstrels! No, we are too far out from shore; then it is the wrong end of the day for such festivals.

A brief siesta under the opening eyelids of the morn, and at sunrise we dip our colors abreast charming little Lahaina, drowsy and indolent, with its two or three long, long avenues overhung with a green roof of leaves, and its odd summer-houses and hammocks pitched close upon the white edge of the shore.

We wander up and down these shady paths an hour or two, eat of the fruits, luscious and plentiful, and drink of its liquors, vile and fortunately scarce, and get us hats plaited of the coarsest straw and of unbounded rim, making ourselves still more hideous, if indeed we have not already reached the acme of the unpicturesque.

Now for hours and hours we hug the shore, slowly progressing under the insufficient shadow of the palms, getting now and then glimpses of valleys folded inland, said to be lovely and mystical. Then there are mites of villages always half-grown and half-starved looking, and always close to the sea. These islanders are amphibious. Their little bronze babies float like corks before they can walk half the length of a bamboo-mat.

Another night at sea in the rough channel this time, and less enjoyable for the rather stiff breeze on our quarter, and some very sour-looking clouds overhead. All well by six, however, when we hear the angelus rung from the low tower of a long coral church in another sea-wedded hamlet. Think of the great barn-like churches, once too small for the throngs that gathered about them, now full of echoes, and whose doors, if they still hang to their hinges, will soon swing only to the curious winds!

But if I remember, there was little moralizing then. We were getting tired of our lazy little propeller, and we watched the hills closely, and looked out for some opening which might be the harbor we were making for.

In and out by this strange land, marking all its curvatures with the fidelity of those shadow lines in the atlas, and so lingering on till the evening of the second day, when, just at sunset, we turn suddenly into the bay that saw the last of Capt. Cook, and here swing at anchor in eight fathoms of liquid crystal over a floor of shiny, white coral, and clouds of waving sea-moss. From the deck we behold the amphitheatre wherein was enacted the tragedy of "The Great Navigator, or the Vulnerable God." The story is brief and has its moral.

The approach of Capt. Cook was mystical. For generations the islanders had been looking with calm eyes of faith for the promised return of a certain god. Where should they look but to the sea, whence came all mysteries and whither retreated the being they called divine?

So the white wings of the *Resolution* swept down upon the life-long quietude of Hawaii like a messenger from heaven. The signal gun sent the first echoes to the startled mountains of the little kingdom.

They received this Jupiter, who carried his thunders with him and kindled fires in his mouth. He was the first smoker they had seen, though they are now his most devout apostles. Showing him all due reverence, he failed to regard their customs and traditions, which was surely ungodlike, and it rather weakened the faith of their sages.

A plot was devised to test the divinity of the presuming captain.

While engaged in conversation, one of the chiefs was to rush at Cook with a weapon; should he cry out or attempt to run, he was no god, for the gods are fearless; and if he was no god, he deserved death for his deception. But being a god, no harm could come of it, for the gods are immortal.

So they argued and completed their plans. It came to pass in the consummation of them that Cook did run, and thereupon received a stab in the back. Being close by the shore he fell face downward in the water and died a half bloody, half watery, and wholly inglorious death. His companions escaped to the ship and peppered the villages by the harbor, till the inhabitants, half frantic, were driven into the hills.

Then they put to sea, leaving the body of their commander in the hands of the enemy, and with a flag at half-mast were blown sullenly back to England, there to inaugurate the seasons of poems, dirges, and pageants in honor of the Great Navigator.

His bones were stripped of flesh, afterwards bound with *kapa*, the native cloth, and laid in one of the hundred natural cells that perforate the cliff in front of us, and under whose shadow we now float. Which of the hundred is the one so honored is quite uncertain. What does it matter, so long as the whole mountain is a catacomb of kings? No commoners are buried there. It was a kind and worthy impulse that could still venerate so far the mummy of an idol of such palpable clay as his.

Many of these singular caverns are almost impossible of access. One must climb down by ropes from the cliff above. Rude bars of wood are laid across the mouths of some of them. It is the old *tabu* never yet broken. But a few years back it was braving death to remove them.

Cook's flesh was most likely burned. It was then a custom. But his heart was left untouched of the flames of this sacrifice. What a salamander the heart is that can withstand the fires of a judgment!

This heart is the one shocking page in this history: some children discovered it afterward, and thinking it the offal of an animal, devoured it. Whoever affirms that the "Sandwich Islanders eat each other," has at least this ground for his affirmation. Natives of the South Sea Islands have been driven as far north as this in their frail canoes. They were cannibals, and no doubt were hungry, and may have eaten in their fashion. But it is said to have been an acquired taste and was not at all popular in this region. Dramatic justice required some tragic sort of revenge, and this was surely equal to the emergency.

Our advance guard, in the shape of a month-earlier tourist, gave us the notes for doing this historical nook in the Pacific. A turned-down page, it is perhaps a little too dog-eared to be read over again, but we all like to compare notes. So we took down the items of the advance guard, and they read in this fashion:

OBJECTS OF INTEREST RELATING TO CAPT. COOK.

Item I. The rock where Cook fell.
Item II. The tree where Cook was struck.
Item III. The altar on the hill-top.
Item IV. The river palms
Item V. The sole survivor—the boy that ran.
Item VI. A specimen sepulchre in the cliff.

Until dark the native children have been playing about us in the sea, diving for very smooth "rials," and looking much as frogs must look to wandering lilliputians. The artist cares less for these wild and graceful creaures than one would suppose, for he confesses them equal in physical beauty to the Italian models. All sentiment seemed to have been dragged out of him by much travel. At night we sit together on the threshold of our grass-house and not twenty feet from the rock—under water only at high tide—where Cook died. We sit talking far into the night, with the impressive silence broken only by the plash of the sea at our very door.

By and by the moon looks down upon us from the sepulchre of the kings. We are half-clad, having adopted the native costume as the twilight deepened and our modesty permitted. The heat is still excessive. All this low land was made to God's order some few centuries ago. We wonder if He ever changes his mind; this came down red-hot from the hills yonder, and cooled at high water-mark. It holds the heat like an oven brick, and we find it almost impossible to walk upon it at noon-time, even our sole-leather barely preserving our feet from its blistering surface. The natives manage to hop over it now and then; they are about half leather, anyhow, and the other half appetite.

Let us pass down to the rock and cool ourselves in the damp moss that drapes it. It is almost as large as a dinner table, and as level. You can wade all around it, count a hundred little crabs running up and down over the top of it. So much for the first object of interest, and the artist draws his pencil through it. At ten, P.M., we are still chatting, and have added a hissing pot of coffee over some live coals to our house-keeping. Now down a little pathway at our right comes a native woman, with a plump and tough sort of pillow under each arm. These she implores us to receive and be comfortable. We refuse to be comforted in this fashion, we despise luxuries, and in true cosmopolitan independence hang our heads over our new saddle-trees, and sleep heavily in an atmosphere rank with the odor of fresh leather. But not till we have seen our humane visitor part of the way home. Back by the steep and winding path we three pass in silence. She pauses a moment in the moonlight at what seems a hitching-post cased in copper. It is as high as our hip, and has some rude lettering apparently scratched with a nail upon it. We decipher with some difficulty this legend:

†
Near this spot
fell
CAPT. JAMES COOK, R.M.,
the Renowned Circumnavigator,
who
discovered these islands,
A.D., 1778.
—

His Majesty's Ship
Imogene,
Oct. 17, 1837
—

So, No. II of our list is checked off, and no lives lost.

"*Aloha*," cries a soft voice in the distance. Our native woman has left us in our pursuit of knowledge under difficulties, and now no trace of her and her pillows is visible — only that voice out of the darkness crying "love to you." She lives in memory — this warm-hearted *Waihena* — so do her pillows.

Returning to our lodgings, we discover a square heap of broken lava rocks. It seems to be the foundation for some building — and such it is, for here the palace of Kamehameha I stood. A palace of grass like this one we are sleeping in. Nothing but the foundation remains now. Half-a-dozen rude stairs invite the ghosts of the departed courtiers to this desolate ruin.

They are all Samaritans in this kingdom. By sunrise a boy with fresh coffee and a pail of muffins rides swiftly to our door. He came from over the hill. Our arrival had been reported, and we are summoned to a late breakfast in the manner of the Christians. We are glad of it. Our fruit diet of yesterday, the horrors of a night in the saddle and a safe and certain mode of dislocating the neck, make us yearn for a good old-fashioned meal. Horses are at our service. We mount after taking our muffins and coffee in the center of a large and enthusiastic gathering of villagers. They came to see us eat, and to fumble the artist's sketches, and wonder at his amazing skill.

Up the high hill with the jolliest sun shining full in our eyes, brushing the heavy and dew filled foliage on both sides of the trail, and under the thick webs spun in the upper branches, looking like silver laces this glorious morning—on, till we reach the hill-top.

Here the guide pauses and points his horse's nose toward a rude corral. The horses seem to regard it from habit—we scarcely with curiosity. A wall half in ruins in the center, rising from a heap of stones tumbled together, a black, weather-stained cross, higher than our heads as we sit in the saddle. It is the altar of sacrifice. It is here that the heart of the great navigator survived the flames.

No. III scored off. At this rate we shall finish by noon easily. The sequel of an adventurous life is soon told.

After breakfast, to horse again, and back to the little village by the sea. We ride into a cluster of palms, our guide leading the way, and find two together, each with a smooth and perfectly round hole through its body, about three feet from the roots, made by the shot of Cook's avengers. A lady could barely thrust her hand through them; they indicate rather light calibre for defence now-a-days, but enough to terrify these little villages, when Cook's men sent the balls hissing over the water to bite through the grit and sap of these slender shafts. They still live to tell the tale in their way. So much for No. IV.

We pause again in the queer little straggling alleys of the village, planned, I should think, after some spider's web. They are about as regular in their irregularity. It is No. V this time. A bit of withered humanity doubled up in the sun, as though someone had set him up on that wall to bake. He is drawn all together; his chin sunk in between his knees, his knees hooped together with his dreadfully slim arms, a round head, sleek and shining as an oiled gourd; *sans* teeth; eyes like the last drops in desert wells; the skeleton sharply protruding; no motion; apparently no life beyond the quick and incessant blinking of the eyelids—the curtains fluttering in the half-shut windows of the soul. *Is* it a man and a brother? Yes, verily! When the uncaptained crew of the *Resolution* poured their iron shot into the tents of the adversary, this flickering life was young and vigorous. And he ran like a good fellow. Better to have died thus in his fiery youth than to have slowly withered away in this fashion. For here it is the philosophy of mammon left to itself. When you get to be an old native, it is your business to die. If you don't know your business, you are left to find it out. What are you good for but to bury?

Let us slip over the smooth bay, for we must look into one of these caverns. Cross in this canoe, so narrow that we cannot get into it at all, but balance ourself on its rim and hold our breath for fear of upsetting. These odd-looking out-riggers are honest enough in theory, but treacherous in practice; and a shark has his eye on us back yonder. Sharks are mesmeric in their motions through the water, and corpse-colored.

A new guide helps us to the most easily reached cave, and with the lad and his smoking torch we climb into the dusky mouth.

There is dust everywhere and cobwebs as thick as cloth, hanging in tatters. An almost interminable series of small cells, just high enough to straighten one's back in, lead us further and further into the mountain of bones. This cave has been pillaged too often to be very ghostly now. We find a little parcel of bones here. It might have been a hand and an arm once, cunning and dexterous. It is nothing now but a litter. Here is an infant's skull, but broken, thin and delicate as a sea-shell, and full of dust. Here is a tougher one, whole and solid; the teeth well set and very white; no sign of decay in any one of these molars. Perhaps it is because so little of their food is even warm when they eat it. This rattles as we lift it. The brain and the crumbs of earth are inseparably wedded. Come with us, skull. You look scholarly, and shall lie upon our desk — a solemn epistle to the living. But the cave is filled with the vile smoke of our torch, and we are choked with the heat and dust. Let us out as soon as possible. The Great Navigator's skeleton cannot be hidden in this tomb. Down we scramble into the sand and show by the water, and talk of departing out of this place of relics.

We are to cross the lava southward where it is frescoed with a wilderness of palm-trees: for when the mountain came down to the sea, flowing red-hot, but cooling almost instantly, it mowed down the forest of palms, and the trunks were not consumed, but lay half-buried in the cooling lava, and now you can mark every delicate fibre of the bark in the lava, as firm as granite.

Still farther south lies the green slope that was so soon to be shaken to its foundations. I wonder if we could discover any of the peculiar loveliness that bewitched us the evening we crossed it in silence. There was something in the air that said "Peace, peace;" and we passed over the fatal spot without speaking. But the sea spoke under the cliffs below us, and the mountain has since replied.

This place is named prettily — *Kealakakua*. You see that mountain? There are paths leading to it. Thither the gods journeyed in the days of old. So the land is called "the path of the gods."

It is a cool, green spot up yonder; the rain descends upon it in continual baptism. The natives love these mountains and the sea. They are the cardinal points of their compass. Every direction given you is either toward the mountain or toward the sea.

There is much truth in the Arabian tale, and it is time to acknowledge it. Mountains are magnetic. The secret of their magnetism may lie in the immobility of their countenances. Praise them to their face, and they are not flattered; forget them for a moment: but turn again, and see their steadfast gaze! You feel their earnestness. It is imposing, and you cannot think light of it. Who forgets the mountains he has once seen? It is quite probable the mountain cares little for your individuality: but it has given part of itself to the modeling of your character. It has touched you with the wand of its enchantment. You are under the spell. Somewhere in the recesses of this mountain are locked the bones of the Great Navigator, but these mountains have kept the secret.

Charles Warren Stoddard *(1843-1909) was a regular contributor to the* Golden Era, *writing his poems under the pseudonym "Pip Pepperpod". Influenced by Thomas Starr King, he attended prep school until 1864, when his poor mental and physical health took him to the Hawaiian Islands. For the next twenty years he traveled widely. Trips to Hawaii and Tahiti furnished material for his* South-Sea Idyls *(1873). In 1873 he went to Europe as traveling correspondent for the* San Francisco Chronicle, *and for a short time served as Mark Twain's secretary. Stoddard wrote many books about his adventures in foreign lands including* Mashallah *(1881), and* A Cruise Under the Crescent *(1898).*

During Bret Harte's time in San Francisco, Stoddard became his companion. Stoddard, Ida Coolbrith and Harte spent many hours socializing and exchanging thoughts. Together they were known as the Golden Gate Trinity, and contributed much of the poetry for the initial issues of the Overland Monthly.

Stoddard's mental health was partially restored by his conversion to Catholicism in 1864. He lived in Hawaii from 1881 to 1884 and while there wrote A Troubled Heart *(1885), the story of his conversion. His* The Lepers of Molokai *(1885), is thought to have interested Robert Lewis Stevenson in the work of Father Damien. Following this last Hawaiian visit, Stoddard taught English at Notre Dame and Catholic University in Washington, D.C. for a number of years.*

When Stoddard died in 1909 the flag of the Bohemian Club in San Francisco flew at half mast. He had been one of the earliest members of the group and was responsible for giving the club its patron saint. "It was at the Christmas jinks of 1881", an old member recalled, "when Stoddard brought to the Club's notice 'the saint who wouldn't tell'. John of Nepomuk was the confessor of a thirteenth century Queen of Bohemia, whose husband suspected her of infidelity, and tried to force secrets of the confessional from the lips of the priest. Taking him to the Moldau bridge, the king told the saint to furnish the desired information or be cast into the stream. The holy man refused and in he went. Then came a miracle, for five brilliant stars suddenly shone around his head as he went floating down the stream unharmed.

"This saint who wouldn't tell so appealed to the Bohemians that he was then and there elected its patron. At that dinner was Count Thun, one of the wealthiest noblemen in Bohemia. He praised Mr. Stoddard's recital of the

virtues of this patron Saint of Bohemia, and several months later the club received a statue, graven by the most celebrated woodcarver in Bohemia of St. John of Nepomuk from Count Thun." It remains one of the most valued possessions of the Bohemian Club as a remembrance of Charles Warren Stoddard.

A Lady's Trip to Hawaii

by Agnes M. Manning

July 1869

Far out on the wide Pacific; the steady trades and pleasant days vying with each other in their rapid flight; the demon Nausea fairly buried, and being safely on what sailors call your "sea-legs," you begin to realize the singular charm of the measureless sea.

The grand orchestra of ocean winds is far beyond anything to which you listen when the curtain rises at the opera, and, half heedless of the familiar airs, your eye wanders over the audience, with its shimmer of opera cloak, silk, and lace, its touch of bright flower or ribbon nestled in ladies' hair, its gleam of small, white-gloved hands relieved against the orthodox black of the modern masculine figure.

But the "weird music of the sea" admits of no such divided attentions. Only the silent sky, the large, lonely albatross, and the boundless distances are its auditors; unless, indeed, some wandering waif of civilization like our ship, sailing alone, and tossed like a child's toy at the will of this mighty deep.

And then, the long, delicious days in mid-ocean calms! Days when the vast expanse lies stilled in one magic dream of Peace. What marine painter ever found the wonderful blue of these waves, bent over by the answering blue of Heaven? What sky drapery was ever so soft as the white cumulus clouds of these latitudes? The warm tropic sun casts the idle sails, tall masts, and great awnings into long shadows across the sea. There is not even a ripple to gurgle against the ship. Occasionally, some straying breeze, forgotten by the wind-god when he withdrew from this region, passes over your face and stirs your hair with the lightest touch of a fair coquette.

The morning passes; the drowsy afternoon steals on; the glorious colors of sunset bathe the lofty dome with marvellous floods of amethyst, gold, and crimson. From horizon to horizon, the masses are wrapped in folds of royal purple, and the atmosphere is aglow with a million brilliant tints.

It is worth much to one to rest through days like these; to lie back in your light wicker chair with the unopened book on your lap, and a dreamy consciousness of rest and calm enjoyment pervading your senses.

The dust of the world's thronged highways is lost across this trackless deep. The roar of its noisy life comes not so far. Its fevers, its pettiness, its bickerings, its wild unrest, its tragic moments of bitterness and pain, its hours of dull, inert endurance, its sea of human sorrow for every small bright drop of human happiness, have all passed like a far-off troubled dream, and you have wakened in the domains of silence, where, about, above, below, and around you is a blessed calm, giving the soul a foretaste of that after-rest we mortals must ever more or less hunger for on earth.

You will do well to let yourself float idly with the "silver-stealing hours"; to steep yourself in the dreamy luxuriance of a quiet like that of the lotus-eaters on the shadowy Nile. It will bring to your brain the recuperation you need; it will gather into your purposes fresh earnestness and strength for your future life.

I know the glories of the summer on the land; I know of its sweet, aimless saunterings through leafy wood, or by breezy upland — the pure scent of hay-meadow and wheat field, and the hallowed stillness of lonely roads. I know the charm of the brown birds' whirr, the lazy hum of bees, the long grasses in the sedgy water, the music of trembling leaves, the glints of light athwart massy tree boles, the slant of our soft south wind, the pale blue of northern skies; and I know that all are as "water unto wine" in comparison to the glistening splendor of this tropic ocean calm.

There comes a morning when we are roused from our slumbers by loud cries of "land!" through the cabin. In a trice we are all on deck, rubbing our eyes, peering into the blue horizon, declaring "there is no such thing," and denouncing the hoax played upon us. Those who have "been before" enjoy our discomfiture and point to the sky nearly above. There, crowned with its eternal snows, on which the pale beauties of the dawn cluster, belted by masses of cloud that lose themselves in the dark ocean, rises in its isolated might of more than fourteen thousand feet the vast volcanic Mountain.

As the morning advances, it looks still more beautiful — the clouds catch the rosy light and play with it, in and out through thin, airy columns; the snows reflect a thousand tints, while overhead the ultra-marine of the sky is only equalled by that of the tropic waves below.

You realize a little the meaning of Guido's "Aurora" now, and you can easily fancy the clouds taking the place of his aërial chargers and long-robed maidens.

The listless enjoyment of our sea days is now over; stray volumes are gathered up, trunks and valises brought forth, invitations are exchanged of visiting in the future, and in the midst of all the usual hurried preparations for landing, we do not lose the regret that our pleasant sea days and genial sea friends will soon be "things of the past."

All day we skirt the land, and it is not until the late afternoon when we round Cocoanut Point, and find ourselves in the long low swells of Hilo Bay.

An enthusiastic admirer of these islands calls this the most beautiful bay in the world. Those of our passengers who have seen Rio and Naples dispute it at once. I can myself imagine nothing more lovely than the semicircular stretch of dark water, backed by the greenest of uplands, that reach far off to the purple distance of foot-hills, from which rise the snowy peaks of Mauna Loa and Mauna Kea. In the foreground is a dense mass of foliage, through which peep quaint churches and the white houses of the foreign residents. Tall cocoanuts skirt the beach, under which cluster rows of grass huts, and long lines of surf break in a silver fringe across the coral reefs.

We land in a motley crowd—the inhabitants of the village, both native and foreign, are on the beach. They crowd about us and are evidently as delighted with the advent of so many strangers as we are with their queer costumes and beautiful landscape.

Dark-eyed, swarthy girls, with yellow and scarlet blossoms tied in their hair, *ohilo* flowers for necklaces, shell bracelets, and bare brown feet, are matched by stylish youths in all the pride of cast-off man-of-war's-men's clothing, with gay flowers also decking their heads and ornamenting their button-holes, their black hair shining with rancid cocoanut oil.

Little children, in mother Nature's gear only, peer at us from behind obese matrons, who smile and say "*Aloha!*" with that frank kindliness for which the Kanakas are justly celebrated.

One rakish-looking young man, in all the pride of white canvas and blue jacket, from the pocket of which streams a yellow bandana, is introduced to us bearing the euphonious title of "Sam Weller," and our party advising him to "spell it with a We," proceed to our quarters.

The natives accompany us *sans ceremonie*. They have not the least idea of being deprived of their sight-seeing. In the van a lad starts a melody, and when the chorus comes they all join. The voices are very musical and the song is a welcome to us.

We walk on through an avenue of strange trees, shrubs, flowers, and perfumes, and strangest of all, these groups of fantastic savages singing about us. The women and girls all wear the *holokoa*, a long, loose garment, made with the skirt gathered on a yoke and falling straight to the ankles. Of hats they have a strange conglomeration, from the high-peaked fright of the Italian to the modern "turban," all trimmed with a profusion of flowers, feathers, and faded old ribbons. They are not pretty, these women, any of them, but they have soft, kindly, dark eyes and exquisitely formed little brown hands and feet.

At last we come to a garden and enter its wide open gates. A heavy odor weighs on the air. Great bell-shaped blossoms line the walks and bend as if they, too, would bid us welcome. We are here greeted with true Hawaiian hospitality, and this is the signal for our motley escort to leave, though not before they have favored us with another melody.

Three gentlemen who have just crossed the island are staying here. Of course we are very anxious to know if the feat is possible for ladies. They are of the opinion, on the whole, that it is not. They tell doleful stories of their horses dying under them, and one who is an old traveller, says it is the very worst road he has ever known.

We sat on the verandah until it was very late, enjoying the rare beauty of the night. Light arm-chairs and Mexican hammocks furnish the balconies of this climate, where one can sit or lie at leisure, musing on the beautiful surroundings.

When the house, with its inmates, native and foreign, was hushed in repose, I went softly out from my room into the garden on which it opened. For I could not sleep; I could not bear to close my eyes and shut out this strange enchantment — this vision of Eastern story.

The high, blue sky was unflecked by a single cloud. The broad moonlight was such as we never see in our latitudes. Its clear radiance threw into full power the flowers, shrubs, and trees. A soft sea-breeze stirred the plumey palm-tops and rustled through the dark *ohias*.

A thousand voices from the insect-world seemed calling to me to note their marvels. Gleaming fire-flies glowed under the heavy shadowing of breadfruit and mango as if beckoning me to follow and see the wonderful nooks into which they could penetrate. The beautiful pandanus seems to ask me if in all my life I have seen anything like her. My eyes wander afar, only to rest on groves of bananas, coffee-trees, limes, and guavas. The golden balls of the orange gleam amidst its dark foliage; and the feathery tamarind sweeps its light leaves down on my hair, wondering how I, a lover of trees, can have never known her before. The very flowers, I think, press out a heavier odor as if to imbue my senses with the wonders of this tropic world.

Far beyond the village, like a sea of silver sleeps the great ocean we have crossed. I can see our ship like a white bird against the dark horizon. I went down among the flowers and looked at their great, sleepy petals; lifted the broad leaves that choked my path, and examined their wondrous beauty. The breeze freshened in the palms, and the low sough of the waves on the coral reef stole like a sigh of satisfaction on my ears. Alone with Nature and the Night, they were determined to send me back to my colder clime, with a vision of their glories printed on my brain.

I thought on the time, not far distant, where from out of the sea rose these islands like a mirage of splendor on the gaze of civilization; of the early voyagers who first told the tales of their magic charms; of the time, in the far-off home, when I had devoured every meagre account of them with that hunger for travel that seems born with some of us.

What a glorious thing is such a night in such a tropic wealth of subtle odor, flower, and foliage! Why should you not linger on such scenes? Steeped in the glamour of novelty, they are rare events in life.

The world, heaven knows! will soon enough drive its juggernaut car of Care over you. Ten to one but your daily fare has a salad that you have learned to swallow without either oil or vinegar. Here is a cup of shining sweets that glitters like the foam on champagne, held to your lips by the dainty fingers of the fairest of dryads. Why should you not drink deep the draught that thrills you with a new sensation?

There is plenty of time, believe me, to be your commonplace self again; to fit smoothly into the grooves of the humdrum society and very respectable mediocrity you have left.

We are thoroughly roused from the dreamy luxuriance of Hilo, and facing a most practicable Tuesday morning, with the weather paying up for past civility, and the rain coming down as it can only come down on the windward side of Hawaii. We are mounted on a train of meek-eyed steeds, who according to their owner's asseverations were possessed of every virtue in a horse's calendar. They were fleet of foot as English racers, sound of limb as Arabian chargers; they could go through a crater blindfold, extract sustenance from a sulphur bank, and rival a camel when we should come to the rainless regions of Kona. Alas! that such a paradise as Hilo is not yet clear of the trail of the serpent; and that the Pickwickian trustfulness of our army should be rewarded by a small army of brutes, any one of which might be fearlessly ridden by Mr. Winkle himself, with little danger of "shying" or getting excited into anything beyond the lamest of walks.

Gray is the sky and wet the trail; dripping wet the uplands of sugar-cane, and behind spreads the ocean a mass of driving mist. We have lain on the lilies of tropic calms, and slept on the blossoms of tropic shores; wandered on shining sands of coral-reefed bays, through ferny nooks of the silvery Wialuka; and, now armed with umbrellas and clad in water-proof—both useless in a land of small deluges—we are on the far-famed, rugged road to Kilawea.

At last, after some hours' *walking* we catch our first sight of lava. It is an inky sea, washed wild and wide over the landscape. A stormy sea, too, whose black metallic waves glitter in the rain, and tell as no language can tell the terrible story of destruction. Great slabs are standing loose, piled upon, or leaning against each other. Here you discover the only accomplishment of the sorry Rosinante you ride. When you come to some lava precipice that seems to bar all further progress, he will gather his feet together and slide down with the most perfect *sang froid.*

We pick our slow way across this broken waste; at intervals ferns and small shrubs struggle through the crevices; but after some time even these disappear, and nothing but desolation spreads about us.

Wet and weary we alighted at the Half-Way House, and lunched on the floor—being favored through the process with the serious attention of a score of natives who stood in rows watching us. This grass hut is precisely like the rest of the interior of Hawaiian hotels, consisting of one apartment covered by a mat, on any part of which you are privileged to select your resting-place.

It is queer at first to sleep without a pillow—or with the substitute of a carpet-bag—and open your eyes in the gray morning upon the outstretched figures of a horde of savages, but you soon learn to rest your tired head on the hard mat without a murmur, and find thereon the deep, sound sleep of the traveler. You soon learn that every Kanaka household has at least a score of "friends," and is, besides, thickly inhabited by dogs, pigs, goats, chickens; roaches that run about like young rats; ants that march and countermarch in battalions; and fleas whose audacity, size, agility, and peculiar *penchant* for "white ladies" ought to entitle them to the dignity of a new class in natural history.

We were foolish enough to allow our fastidiousness to start us on our journey at two P.M., in a wild storm, and with seventeen miles of a country whose miles are like nothing outside of Sweden, and whose natives have the most facetious ideas of distance.

All the afternoon we ride through endless scenes of lava. Nothing but lava: broken lava, old lava, new lava, streams of lava, hills of lava, smooth satiny lava, (called by the natives *pahoihoi)* diversified by occasional patches of pulu fern, and *ti* plant, break the dreary landscape.

From horizon to horizon stretches this vast field of horror that once swept its fiery floods to the distant sea, whose waves hissed and boiled for miles along the coast. One realizes to the full the terrible force of volcanoes only when one gazes upon scenes like this.

Our pack animals are endowed with a singular propensity for wading in lava ponds, to the imminent ruin of our baggage; running off into lava beds, browsing on stray specimens of pulu, and going any way and every way except in the trail, where the gentlemen of the party vainly endeavor, by yelling at, whipping up, and poking with umbrellas, to conduct them.

Our imperturbable guide never interferes with this interesting employment. He rides calmly ahead and never breaks into speech for the sufficient reason — his master's word to the contrary — he neither speaks nor understands a word of English.

Night brings us to higher altitudes; to roads whose pitfalls are a unique corduroy of lava slabs and mammoth fern roots; to a cold wind rushing down from Mauna Loa, penetrating one's wet garments and making one shiver.

At last the vagaries of our pack animals cease to elicit mirth. We are so wet, so cold, so very miserable, that we can only think of the possible luxuries of shelter and a fire — only speculate mentally whether these animals will go down before the feat is accomplished.

A young lady friend coaxes her brute once near enough mine to tell me she must "die" if this lasts two hours longer. I am so utterly chilled, so wholly weary, so thoroughly wretched myself, that I think "dying" would be a decided advantage.

The rain comes thicker; the night blacker; the storm grows louder.

By the beating of branches to and fro, and the shrieking of the winds, we know we are in a belt of trees. How the unearthly shrieks go madly through the forest, a fitting prelude for the Inferno beyond.

And now, as we emerge from this wood, we suddenly come upon a magnificent spectacle. A spectacle that calls the chilled blood back quietly to the veins and once seen will never be forgotten. It is the great Kilawea itself, making the night aglow, and shooting its giant tongues of flame against the black background of mountain and sky.

I remember sinking down, aching in every fibre, from my wet, weary ride. The wind was in my ears, the dash of the rain on my face, the roar of the crater mingling with its fierce flames. What does this woman want who will not let me sleep now, when the long-looked for shelter is ready—who snatches the rest that my very soul craves, and who tortures me by grasping, wrenching, and manipulating my shoulders, neck, arms, head, and limbs?

I open my eyes wide and find myself in the hands of a dusky savage. Very kindly this savage smiles, however, as she holds a cup of warm tea to my lips. I swallow the draught and beg her to go away, but she forthwith commences a kneading of the muscles that makes me scream. She does not desist for an instant when I scream, but smiles still more kindly and shakes her head. A dim idea that this must be the native practice of *lomi loming* goes in a rayless fashion up and down through my tired brain. In a little while I come to have faith in her; to understand the sympathy in her face; to let her wring out my wet hair and press my head as she lists. I remember something, indistinctly, of what Mungo Park said about the unfailing kindliness of savage women. A blessed assurance of rest and peace wraps every faculty. A soft drowsiness steals over my sense. What are sharp rains, chilling winds, or wild volcanic flames, or grass huts, mats, or *wahinas*, to me? I am luxuriantly wrapped up on a couch that is softer than eider down. I am in a wide, airy room, where the summer breeze enters, and beyond whose open windows lie pale blue skies; below the garden flowers. Bees are there and summer birds. The mignonette beds and heliotropes are heavy after the light showers. I was reading to-day of strange hardships endured by travelers in the Pacific Islands. Ah! how often I have longed to see them and counted light the perils of land and sea! And, so, through a sweet dream like this, I sink into a long, deep sleep, from which I do not awaken until very late the next morning, and then as refreshed as if I had just stepped out of the "marble baths of Stamboul!"

Look from this wide plain down across that vast pit of smouldering fires, some three and a half miles long by two and a half wide, and over a thousand feet in depth; and see how unlike it is to all stereotyped ideas of a crater. Here is no burning mountain, from whose lofty cone rises fire and smoke, to reach which you must climb upwards for long hours on "scoria treaders," through toilsome beds of ashes, loose lava, and under a broiling sun. Yet the historic Vesuvius and far-famed Aetna are toy cups in comparison, and on all this wide earth of ours there is no such escape valve for its internal fires.

The bed of this crater is a far-spreading, black, jagged mass, filled with thick smoke, clouds of sulphurous steam, and poisonous gases. Very horrible it all looks from above, and timid travelers go no farther. You smile, perhaps, a little contemptuously at this information, and are impatient at the deliberation of the guides who, with true Kanaka dignity, slowly proceed in packing bundles of shawls, an odd conglomeration for lunch, and a debris of utensils for picking up hot lava for specimens.

Long staffs are provided for travelers, and when the party is ready you grasp yours, and prove your belief in the easy descent by springing gleefully down the first grassy steps of the cliff. This glee is short-lived, however, for you soon find yourself obliged to cling to the jutting wet rocks and woefully scratched by the twisted, rough, branches of a terribly rustic staircase, whose steps are often narrow, slippery boughs, from three to five feet between, and down the black face of a volcano precipice nearly six hundred feet in height.

With a heightened respect for cliffs and less contempt for the cautious tourists who prefer taking observations at a distance, you thankfully find yourself at the bottom, in a shrubbery of dense growth, fostered by the condensed steams and almost endless rains.

A small red berry, rather insipid to the taste and something like our cranberry in size and color, attracts your notice. If you have read Ellis you know at once that it is the *Ohelo*, the bright little friend of many a hungry traveler in the mountain wilds of Hawaii. The guide tells you its legend, and how in the days of heathendom the presiding goddess of this Hades was propitiated by handfuls of this her favorite fruit being thrown towards her with the loud words: *E Tele eia ha ohelo!* which, being rendered into plain Saxon, reads: "Tele, here are your *ohelos!*" Numerous earthquakes, terrific eruptions, and lava flows, were believed to follow any infringement of this rite.

After this strip of flower and foliage — which was once the edge of the crater and must have been hurled down by some mighty convulsion — there is another easier descent, of more than four hundred feet, and then you are fairly in the old crater bed, with three miles of the hardest clambering through a very Valley of Desolation, before you reach the active South Lake.

Here, most of our party turned back, too fatigued to venture farther in the driving rain; and here we found that the fields of loose slabs and broken lava, over which we had yesterday ridden, were a smooth, safe, and easy path to the storm-tossed billows of horror that stretched far and wide about us.

It was as if some supernatural power had suddenly arrested a tempest-lashed ocean, sweeping over it a pall black as Erebus, that yet plainly shows all its sublime strength and wild motion.

You climb to the top of a petrified crest and watch the fierce waves just congealed as they reared against each other in their blind fury. Dotting this scene are great pillars of cones, from twenty to seventy feet in height, with thick columns of smoke rushing from their funnel-like tops, and a roar like a modern steamboat. We tie handkerchiefs over our mouths to pass vast sulphur banks, whose noxious gases make one half sick, and we descend into long hollows of smooth, shining lava, as if streams of ink once flowed through them. High walls of lava blocks are piled upon each other in a demoniac strata of architecture; over these you must climb as you best may, springing from block to block, balancing yourself on treacherous projection, and always with the inimitable prospect of mangled limbs as the price of a single misstep. The guide, Anthony, is splendid; vigilant, brave, active; exactly the guide you want when you hold your life on such precarious terms. If you are bruised or maimed it will be through no lack of care on his part, and you soon see that he will risk his safety for yours at any moment. He is thoroughly at home in these dangers, has plenty of coolness and courage, and what is far rarer in a Hawaiian than one supposes, he understands and speaks English.

Through clouds of steam, that are at times so thick you must needs pause for a gust of wind to clear your dangerous path, through stifling smoke, whose odor is nauseous, through a dazzling glitter of heat, that looks like that you have seen rise from some furnace, you slowly pursue your perilous way.

Wide-yawning chasms gape about everywhere. Many of them over a hundred feet in depth and from two to four in width, out of which ooze blue smoke and sulphur steams. Peering down into some of them you can see the cherry-red fiend himself, in his very lair, looking up at you with red, vengeful, eyes, and a shudder steals into your heart as you think that a one false step may send you into his clutches.

Sometimes the lava is spread in a thin crust over this chasm, and your only safety is in keeping closely in the guide's footsteps, who, from long experience, knows where they are.

Two long hours we toiled through these dangers; and, then, as suddenly as from the plain above, we came on the culminating chapter of horrors, the Kilawea proper, or great, active crater.

Wet with the incessant rain, weary with the toilsome way, half dizzy with the glare of heat and countless terrors, you sink on the lava cliff and every sensation is lost in that of awe.

Just below you lies a lake, over a mile in width, across whose steely-gray surface long, fiery ripples of molten lava twist hither and thither, and shoot in forks of flame against the black cones scattered on its bosom and the frowning precipices surrounding it.

These precipices, on one of which you sit, are beyond all things horrible. In all your life you have seen nothing like them. What is the broken granite in the wildest fastnesses of the Sierras to the grinning caves and horrid crags that surmount this entrance of an Inferno far more frightful than ever entered Dante's dream? Into the raging element that forever seethes here tumble at intervals great stones from the hollow cliffs, making hideous noises in their fall, and warning you that at any moment your precarious resting-place may follow them into the fiery depths. So great is the heat near the surface that you can thrust your staff into any of the fissures and bring it out charred.

Very fortunate is the cold wind and rain, else—though you suffer from the noxious steams—you could not obtain so eligible a position.

Suddenly the dull roar grows louder—that peculiar sound that accompanies earthquakes and sends a thrill of horror along the pulses of the bravest. A wild motion stirs the lake; it surges, heaves, rises. A long wave gathers force, rears a fiery crest and breaks in a sheet of crimson foam all over the surface. You spring to your feet in momentary terror, and see another and another follow in swift succession; you hear the guide cry: "That's a grand sight," and then it has all faded out into the silver tint—so rapidly does surface lava cool. But the black cones now come into action—belching forth showers of red-hot stones, and hissing long tongues of flame into the smoky atmosphere. The lightning lava winds like scarlet serpents about their inky sides and leaps over into the lake. High carnival is indeed held here by myriad demons, and the dread echoes wake to their unearthly orgies.

Nothing can surpass the terrible sublimity of this scene. Far and wide stretches the black and desolate wilderness of ruin you have crossed; awful precipices below and above, leading down to fearful depths and away up to the smoky level that shuts out your view of the upper world; and in the foreground this ever restless, foaming mass—with the rain beating down in torrents, and the wind sweeping past in wild gusts—keeping a weird minor to the roar below.

Hour after hour we sat there—heedless of wind or rain, heedless of personal dangers that at such times soon come to take a certain insignificance—fascinated by the awful grandeur of the changeful element beneath, until the gathering night warned us that the perilous way must be retraced.

The Volcano House is so far an improvement on grass huts in general, that it contains four or five divisions; but this effort in favor of the prejudices of civilization results in bare plank partitions that run up just high enough to allow an ordinary-sized person to see over into the neighboring apartment. A small library, consisting of a strange medley of old books and magazines, occupies the corner of a shelf. They were doubtless left here by travelers, and are as diverse as must have been the mental tastes of the donors. "Baxter's Saint's Rest" lies beside a Sue novel; a "Call to Sinners" jostles Voltaire; the passionate, brilliant, reckless Madam Dudevant reposes quietly near the staid, wise, and kindly Hannah More.

Not the least interesting is the visitor's book; where divers embryo poets have essayed to mount the volcanic Pegasus, who has certainly exhibited much more spirit than the Hawaiian steeds of our acquaintance, and refused point blank to let one of them succeed. "Ho! ye volcano fires!" "O, thou that *was* and *is!*" are only to be surpassed by the hero that discovered that "*that*" rhymed to "but."

The prices at this establishment are four dollars per day, exclusive of extras; said extras consisting of guide, fare, and the privilege of your

Rosinante luxuriating on the pasturage that may be expected from sulphur beds.

A nondescript Chinaman is the cook, chambermaid, waiter, and resident landlord. In a land where *"poi"* is the staple article of food, one ought, perhaps, to consider the fare excellent; though how it could be worse passes all civilized comprehension.

You will do well to remember that the brave, early missionaries lay here without shelter — often without food — in the bleak, pitiless nights, and let themselves down with ropes over the precipices. This may reconcile you to the hard bundle of dirty wet cloth, that turns out to be the remains of an intelligent patriarch of the fowl family; brought over, no doubt, with the rest of the live stock by Vancouver; to the soup in which his venerable body was stewed, flavored in addition with sulphur; to the bread — which is best of all — but was doubtless raised by volcanic gases, it is so bitter; to the utter abominations called tea and coffee, milkless, because the cows brought here have an inquiring turn of mind and tumble into craters in their exploring expeditions. The voice of birds has been silenced in the dread ruin of these regions, but ants, fleas, dogs, rats, and roaches bid defiance to flames and gases.

The cups, plates, and spoons are redolent of brimstone; the walls, floor, and furniture, including your garments, are all steamy, sulphury, and damp. All night the volcano is one mass of lurid flame, beating upwards at times in long columns against the mountain background. Its deep roar in the silence of midnight is terrible; and the occasional slight local earthquake shocks, swaying the grass house, make you feel the utter insecurity of your resting-place.

Rude is the couch and rough the fare; and yet, if you bring to them the true spirit of the traveler, your sleep will be deep and calm, while a strange pleasure will come and dwell softly with you in the consciousness that yours is the high privilege of standing face to face with the great works of Nature's God.

In reading the contributions of **Agnes Manning** *to the* Overland, *one senses the author's ability to take care of herself in "a man's world". The fact that she became one of the best known and most effective of San Francisco's suffragettes in later years is not hard to understand.*

A teacher at San Francisco's Lincoln Primary School, Manning became one of the city's first female principals and enjoyed a long and successful career.

A champion for several causes, she was well known in the 1890's for a number of papers read before local associations, including Because It Was A Woman's, *a paper on women's rights read before the Women's Press*

Association in 1891, and another read before that same group on the plight of homeless boys.

She held a variety of positions in the Women's Congress Association as an advocate of women's rights, and was a long time member of the Public School Teacher's Mutual Aid Society. The latter group, in eulogizing her shortly after her death, indicated that "Few, if any, have left a stronger or more lasting impress on the educational system of our city and our state... Miss Manning was a woman of extraordinary mind, great literary ability; broad, generous, unselfish. She devoted her life and powers to the betterment of all humanity."

Although we have been unable to ascertain the exact dates of her birth and death, we know that she died in October of 1901, since the above eulogy appeared in the October 19 issue of The San Francisco Call that year.

A Hawaiian Feast

by J.T. Meagher

May 1869

Of the many Hawaiian customs still in vogue a *"luau"* (feast) is not the least interesting to a traveler in search of knowledge concerning the ancient manners and customs of the semi-civilized natives of the Pacific islands. During a stay at Honolulu last summer, it was my fortune to be a guest at a native entertainment tendered to the officers of an American and an English man-of-war, then lying in the harbor, and to his friends in general, by David Kalakua, a member of the Hawaiian royal family, who completed extensive preparations for the carrying out of the project. The scene of the gala was at a grass hut a few miles from town, of sufficient dimensions to allow of ample accommodation for the amusements in contemplation. A large number of persons congregated in and around the structure, showing by their lively demonstrations that they were bent upon the full enjoyment of the occasion. Our horses were taken charge of by a dozen or more barefooted attendants, who vied with each other in attentions to us, no doubt under instructions from their chief, coupled with the expectation of a small reward on the departure of the *"houries"* (foreigners); for although the islanders have but little regard for money, they certainly evince a weakness for its accumulation with the least possible exertion, and are firm believers in the doctrine of doing nothing for nothing. Our dusky host received us with the politeness of his cultivated manners, and we were ushered into the presence of the assembled company who in turn contributed their share to our comfort, greeting us heartily with the salutation *"Aloha"* (Love to you), the most expressive word in their language. The internal scene was at once novel and picturesque. The walls were hung with the national colors, and strips of bright-colored calicoes, intertwined with green boughs and native gewgaws. Laughing, chattering Kanakas and Wahinces, dressed in their native simpleness, were squatting on the grass-matting which covered the floor. The women were enveloped in a single garment reaching from the neck to the ground, wreaths of red and yellow flowers encircling the head and neck. Some of the men wore nothing but pantaloons, whilst others were provided with more extensive toilets—all, except the chiefs and head men, were barefooted. We were invited to be seated on the mats, each receiving a supply of pillows on which to rest the arms, elbows, or head, as we might feel inclined. We were then crowned with wreaths of the sweet-smelling jasmine, by a rather pretty maid in waiting, and passively submitted for politness sake, to the trying ordeal of receiving from her a kiss administered in the native fashion—an operation so oddly peculiar, that a passing notice of it will not be out of place. Hawaiians kiss by touching, or rather violently bruising, noses—the flatness and fatness of that organ preventing the bone from interfering unpleasantly with the *delightful* sensation; a circular motion is observed, until full satisfaction seems to have been imparted on both sides. In order to please her visitors, the dusky maiden offered to kiss us in the good old way. "Not," as she expressed it, "that it gives me any idea of love or affection, but it gratifies the stranger." We were unanimous in our thanks for her intended *kindness,* and declined any further embraces. Nor do I wish to convey the idea that we submitted, in the first instance, to the bruising operation, admitting only that we touched noses with the Hawaiian beauty, who informed us, with pouting lips, that we knew not how to appreciate the tender salutation; nor did we, when received in the manner which she implied—for we agreed mutually that Hawaiian kissing was no exception to the general rule of native customs, which are all outlandish alike in foreign estimation.

Three dancing girls, dressed in short, gaudy garments manufactured from the tapa leaf—their heads, necks, wrists, and ankles, being decorated with flowers, wriggled and twisted through the motions of the *"huli huli"* (native dance, consisting of a series of indecent contortions of the body, accompanied by a graceful movement of the hands), to the dull and inharmonious sound of a half-dozen calabashes, which were thumped and pounded on the floor in the most energetic manner by native musicians, who added a low, grunting hum of their voices to the unseemly noise. Frequently one of them would spring to his feet, throw out his arms, slap his chest and sides violently with his open hands, tear his hair, make the most frightful grimaces, roll up his eyes, foam at the mouth—seeming in every respect as one possessed of an evil spirit—and suddenly drop on his knees, and calmly resume humming and thumping on his calabash.

The viands were spread on a cloth extending the full length of the floor; and it required no little scrutiny to observe and remember the contents of the dishes displayed. The array was imposing. I will enumerate the different joints, within my recollection.

The head of the table was graced by a smoking conglomeration of heterogeneous chunks of meat, of which dog and pig formed concomitant parts—for although the existence of cannibalism cannot, in truth, be traced with any definite certainty in the group, dog-eating flourishes in all its pristine glory. In this regard the natives exhibit a superior advancement in the matter of taste, evincing a decided preference in favor of dog meat. A large trout flapped his tail and expanded his gills, in the throes of death at the foot of the table; the sides were lined with raw and cooked fish of all kinds. One dish contained a quantity of minnows, which were hopping about in the liveliest manner, and were eaten by the natives in pairs. A delicious fish and a young porker cooked in taro leaves underground, possessing all the requisites to tickle the palate of an epicure, took a foremost place amongst the dishes. A calabash of poi was placed in front of each person, and quantities of the modern inventions of drink were introduced. Dishes and glasses were the only articles of civilization in use. Knives and forks had not yet become fashionable. As poi is a standing dish amongst the natives, the reader may like to know how it is manufactured. Boiled or baked taro is pounded into a dough with a smooth stone; water is added until it becomes of the consistency of thick starch, which it resembles in appearance; it is then allowed to ferment in stone pots until it turns sour, when it is fit for use. It is the staple article of food amongst the islanders, who are extremely fond of it. It possesses fattening properties, and, as flesh is the standard by which Hawaiians judge beauty, their vanity and love of corpulence may account for its universal use, as its peculiar flavor and mode of consumption is, to foreigners, simply disgusting. It is eaten by sucking it off one and two fingers, which members become white from the practice. But aside from a discussion of the demerits of poi, and to return to the subject — the company sat cross-legged on the mat, and dealt very summarily with the esculents, evidently in blissful ignorance of the teachings of Chesterfield. The natives helped themselves, and invited their guests to do likewise. Hands were thrust wrist-deep into the contents of the dishes, which disappeared marvellously fast. The foreign guests drew heavily on the baked fish and pork; but our entertainers importuned us to try to the dog, uncooked fish, and poi, as being the most toothsome dishes. A dusky maiden sitting near, displaying an evident anxiety to be extra-attentive, offered me some of the latter composition on the end of her finger, and assumed an air of offended dignity when I declined to partake of it. The King, America, England, etc., were duly toasted amid the deafening clatter of the calabashes, the noise of Hawaiian loquacity, and the general disposition of every Kanaka to elevate his voice above that of his neighbor. It is questionable whether the united din of a dozen boiler foundries in full operation could exceed the noise of a crowd of excited Kanakas. It was all well-meant, however, and conformed in every respect to the *native* ideas of how an entertainment should be conducted.

After the repast a bowl of water was handed round, in which we washed our hands, using our handkerchiefs for towels.

This revelry usually terminates in scenes of unbridled debauchery and drunkenness, wherein all restraint is laid aside; but, happily for the natives, this relic of their barbarism is fast dying out, under the salutary influence of the Missionaries.

J.T. Meagher *shall remain for us another of our most enigmatic authors.*

Despite research efforts the only traces of Meagher we have found are the above contribution to the Overland *as well as a second one entitled* Quicksilver, and Its Home.

Adventures of the True Bohemian

———— Duelling in the West Indies ————

by J.C. Cremony

December 1868

Who has not read Barrington's famous sketches of Ireland? Who has not laughed heartily at the lively episodes in duelling which he so graphically describes? Let it be fairly understood that we have no *penchant* for that fine art, which teaches us to "snuff a candle at twelve paces," as the school of practice for snuffing out the lamp of life at the same distance. But Barrington, with great good taste, rarely kills his men. There is always something ludicrous and amusing rather than shocking, in his anecdotes of personal *recontres* which portray the character of the people and the time. Ireland, however, was not the only theatre of personal warfare. In America it was very common; but in the majority of cases attended with fatal results. Our duels were fights to kill. The mere exchange of shots followed by an amicable arrangement, and a general invitation to dinner, at which, perhaps, another affair of the kind found its way on the *tapis*, was considered "mere child's play," and unworthy of men who went out with the avowed and determined purpose to kill or be killed. But in the West Indies — English, French, Spanish, Danish, Dutch and Swedish — the Irish principle, the real Barringtonian conception, reigned supreme. It is astonishing what climate and association will do for men. The phlegmatic Dutchman of St. Eustatius, the cold-blooded Swede of St. Bart, or the imperturbable Dane of St. Thomas, were quite as ready to enter the field as the fiery Frenchman of Martinique or St. Martin. It is also strange, that although Guadaloupe is the largest and most important isle of the French West Indies, its inhabitants were less frequently embroiled in duels than those of any other island in the Caribbean Sea pretending to anything like wealth or population. It was probably owing to the fact that its two great cities, Bassaterre and Point a Pintre, were mainly inhabited by commercial men, who were the factors for the planters of the smaller isles, and eschewed the "code of honor." Nevertheless, among the planters or "estated gentlemen," as they liked to term themselves, were many who had reduced duelling to a profound science, and whose sanguinary exploits were regarded by many neophytes with all the awe and veneration we may suppose a young aspirant for honors in the P.R. would recall the prowess of Tom Crib, Ben Caunt, Tom Sayers, John Heenan, *et id genus omne*. Foremost among the shining lights of the personal-satisfaction gentlemen stood Beauvallon, father to the young gentleman of that name who afterward distinguished himself in the same arena in Paris. Mons. Beauvallon was a "crack shot," and during the course of his life — some forty-five years at that time — had very satisfactorily to himself disposed of no less than thirteen opponents. Insensibly to himself, the man who sheds so much blood and murders so many of his fellow beings, becomes a sort of sanguinary bully. He may attempt to plaster his conscience with the sophistry that he had done nothing in violation of the law — for there was no law interdicting such meetings — and that he had only done as other men of his acquaintance and every-day intercourse would have done under like circumstances; the fact remains, that with every duel he gains a corresponding accession of ferocity and indifference to human life, which can only terminate in rendering him a monster to be avoided, or killed for the benefit of mankind. This was the pitch arrived at by Beauvallon; and unknown to himself he assumed an overbearing and intolerant air, which kept him employed in his favorite work of shooting people *selon le régle*.

In Basseterre, the capital of Guadaloupe, there is a beautiful promenade known as the *Course*. It is lined on both sides with wide-spreading, umbrageous trees, and is supplied with benches for saunterers, who crowd it on fine moonlight nights in that tropical region. On one side of the *Course* is a large and spacious stone building denominated the *Cirque;* a club house for opulent planters, merchants, and some of the more distinguished French officers of the army and navy. A young and accomplished captain of the *Infanterie de Ligne* was one evening playing billiards at the *Cirque* when Beauvallon entered. He had dined and felt his wine. His countenance wore a forbidding aspect, and his appearance soon caused the visitors to thin out. Chafed at this evident distaste to his society, Beauvallon fixed his eyes on Captain Duchampy, and passing behind him struck his cue just as he was about to make a shot. Duchampy believing that his own awkwardness had struck the butt of his cue against Beauvallon, immediately turned and asked his pardon. No recognition of the politeness was vouchsafed, but when the officer again attempted to make his stroke, his cue was once more struck by Beauvallon. "Is it you or I, sir, who is in fault?" inquired Duchampy. "Just as you please, sir; suit yourself," was the rejoinder, accompanied with a *farouche* look. Duchampy made no reply, but called for a glass of wine, and having received it, pitched the contents into Beauvallon's face. The consternation was general at this act of audacity, for the officer was a general favorite, and all present looked upon him as another sacrifice to Beauvallon's insatiable thirst for blood according to the acknowledged code. A verbal challenge was soon given and as soon accepted. Seconds were appointed, the time and place fixed, and the weapons, pistols, nominated. They were to fight at eight o'clock the next morning. The terms being arranged, Duchampy retired, but Beauvallon was at once surrounded by his jackalls, who seemed solicitous to offer their services. "Gentlemen," said he, "do me the honor to breakfast with me at ten to-morrow. I will go out at eight, kill this mushroom young fool, and then we shall return to a *déjeuner à la fourchette.*"

At eight the next morning, a large number of persons were congregated to see Beauvallon "plant" his fourteenth man. The principals, accompanied by their seconds, appeared upon the ground almost simultaneously. Duchampy was a recent arrival in Guadaloupe, and up to the time of his quarrel was totally ignorant of his adversary's powers in dueling; but there were not wanting friends who sought to convince him that he had rendered himself little better than a foolish sacrifice to a noted homicide, who had never suffered an antagonist to leave the field alive. The appearance and demeanor of the contestants were notable. Duchampy was pale, preoccupied, and silent, but the beholder could perceive a settled determination in the young officer's eyes; while his bearing was modest and unobtrusive. Beauvallon talked freely and in a loud voice while the preparations were being made. His carriage was defiant and haughty, while his whole demeanor evinced a desire to intimidate, coupled with undoubted confidence in his own skill. The principals were stationed; each received his weapon, and the party who was to give the word, said, "Gentlemen, you must fire between the words 'fire' and 'three'; there must be no reserve of fire. The man who reserves his fire after 'three,' falls by my hand." Then came the warning—"Are you ready?" "Ready!" responded the principals. "Fire!" "One"—but before the word "two" could be given, both pistols cracked upon the morning air. Neither had fallen. Beauvallon could scarcely credit the evidence of his own eyesight. He stood a moment, and then flinging his arms above his head, fell prone upon the earth. His ball had just grazed Duchampy's right ear, carrying away a small piece of the upper end; but Beauvallon was shot through the breast, the ball passing out below the right shoulder-blade. He recovered from this wound, but never after fought a duel. In describing his sensation, he said that when the air rushed into his wound, it seemed as if a ton of ice had suddenly been thrown into his stomach.

Rifle or brass-barrelled pistols were strictly forbidden. It was held that a duel was an affair of honor between gentlemen, and that nothing could be adopted which might tend to aggravage a wound or inflict extra pain or danger. "Ragged balls" were prohibited in all cases. Rifles, double-barrelled shot guns and bowie knives have been the creatures of American refinement, and their use was not known in the duelling codes of other countries. We have never adopted a custom without carrying it to excess. But perhaps there was no spot on the globe where the system was so neatly and thoroughly regulated as in the little island of St. Martin. For a small community, the planters were the proudest and most princely in the West Indies. Their houses were the abodes of luxury and elegant refinement. They were almost exclusive, none but "estated gentlemen" being admitted to their tables, although their every-day business demeanor was courteous and polite almost to the extreme. For the sake of society, dinner parties were of every-day occurrence, several uniting first at one house and then at another. All their wines were imported, fined and bottled by themselves. La Rose, Lafitte, Margeaux, were the clarets; Leacock, Cockroach, and other choice brands of Maderia, from ten to thirty years old, accompanied the dessert. Old homemade rum, selected Cognacs, and the best of Hollands, succeeded the repast after the cloth was withdrawn and the ladies had retired. Dinner commenced at seven o-clock P.M. and lasted until one A.M. The crops, the rains, foreign and domestic politics, were freely discussed after dinner, when every guest could boast his two bottles of claret and one of Maderia under his vest, beside several generous potations of "strong waters." They were "fighting cocks" to a man. No person could live among them who was not. Each planter had been "out" and proved his game breeding. An ambiguous expression, too much emphasis or violent gesture, were pretty sure to be followed by an invitation to pistols and coffee. Ten paces, and balls thirty-two to the pound, were the St. Martin terms.

This little island was owned by the Dutch and the French, each nationality boasting about one-half. It was a queer state of affairs; but never did two people agree better, and simply because the planters on both sides were almost all English, or of English descent.

A planter from Martinique had just arrived, and was invited to dine with Mr. George Dormoy, where six or eight other St. Martin planters were congregated to meet him, with the view of "passing him round," and showing him a bit of hospitality. After dinner the Martiniquen boasted of some splendid "tools" he possessed, made by Le Page of Paris. His pistols cost three hundred dollars, and his breech-loading double-barreled shot gun as much more, while his carbine was something extraordinary. Manning Rey was his *vis-a-vis*, and Manning was a "fire-eater" of the most approved pattern. He really loved a fight, but in that bellicose society he was careful "whom he kicked." Manning's eyes scintillated as he listened to the Martiniquen while extolling the quality of his "tools," and the wonderful feats he had accomplished with them. Leaning quietly forward he said, almost in a whisper, "Mons. Villefort, I am charmed at having made your acquaintance. We poor fellows of St. Martin boast only the weapons bequeathed us by our fathers. My pistols are two generations old already, and have done some service; but I long to test them against yours. Do me the honor to dine with me to-morrow, and remain all night. At ten the next morning I shall be pleased to meet you on the field. There is a snug spot not far from the house, and we can arrange matters admirably." "I will reply in the morning, Mons. Rey," answered Villefort, "because I must first take account of my engagements." "That will do," said Rey, and the repast continued until two A.M. without the slightest ruffle. That night Villefort chartered a small sloop in the harbor of Marigot, and returned to Martinique. He never afterwards honored St. Martin with his presence.

On another occasion, Manning was to fight with Gaspar Mauras. The men and their friends were punctual; the positions selected, distance paced, principals stationed, and the word was just about to be given, when Manning observed a straight little bush directly between him and his antagonist, and observed further, that Mauras had seen it, and had "lined" him over its top. Slapping his left hand to his side he made a *pirouette*, exclaiming that a sudden cramp had seized him, and asking pardon for the interruption; but he had changed his ground some three or four feet and no longer had the bush between him and his opponent. The word was at length given; both fired, and Mauras escaped with a bullet through his cravat. It was enough to satisfy the little "unpleasantness" between them. They were marched up to each other, shook hands, and dined in company with as much cordiality as two brothers.

A large dinner party was given by Philip O'Reilly, one of the richest and most aristocratic planters on the island. Among the guests were a French *chef de bataillon*, naming Beauperthuy, and a huge, bluff Englishman, named John Hodge, but more familiarly known as "Probin." The Frenchman was a most handsome fellow, full of life, and brimming over with wit and *repartee*. "Probin" was a heavy, good-natured, red-faced, orthodox Briton, abounding with common sense, and entertaining a perfect contempt for anything but the solids of conversation. It may be easily conceived that two such characters could not dovetail; but by some oversight they were placed opposite each other at dinner. After the cloth had been removed, and the ladies had retired, conversation became general and took a political turn, during which, "Probin" let fall some blunt animadversions against the government of Louis Phillipe, which were replied to by Beauperthuy in a brilliant series of pithy rejoinders which set the whole table in a roar. "Probin's" dignity was deeply wounded, and he sought a plaster by inviting Beauperthuy to a *partie à deux*, where the *Diable à Quatre* was to be performed. The invitation was cordially accepted, terms to be fixed next day. This little episode by no means interfered with the post prandial festivities. On the contrary, it lent them zest and piquancy, especially as everybody felt some fun would grow out of the meeting. The Frenchman, being the challenged party, selected swords, as the proper weapon for an officer. "Probin" knew as much about a sword as he did about the man in the moon; but being a tolerable shot he insisted upon pistols, which were, of course, ruled out, and he was compelled either to apologize or accept swords, which in this case happened to be sabres. The parties met; a second, holding two sabres by the middle, with a hilt directed toward each principal, bade each one take his weapon. "Probin," wholly unused to this style of thing, no sooner got hold of his sabre than he made a desperate lunge a Beauperthuy, who avoided the thrust by quickly jumping backwards. "Ah, ah! Zat is ze way you fight, Mons. Hodge; vary well, Monsieur, I will show to you how ze gentelman revange himself," exclaimed the irate officer. "Now, sar, I will take from you the left whiskare." A pass or two, and the keen blade whizzed past "Probin's" ear, carrying away his left whisker, and a small slice of skin. Wildly and furiously did "Probin" rain his blows; but he might as well have saved his strength. A wall of steel met him at every turn, and his cuts fell harmless on his adversary's ready weapon. It had become clear to all present, that Beauperthuy had no intention of seriously hurting his antagonist, for he had declined to avail himself of many opportunities to give him a mortal thrust. It was just as apparent that "Probin" could not hurt the Frenchman were he ever so anxious. Again their weapons crossed. "Now," said Beauperthuy, "I will cut you the pin from your shirt breast." No sooner said than done, a magnificent diamond being sent flying with a part of "Probin's" ruffled shirt-bosom, which served for the recovery of the gem. In the meantime, "Probin" had redoubled his efforts, his face as red as that of an amorous turkey-cock, and evidently laboring under the impression that there must be something terribly wrong in the laws of Nature, when the great physical force and power of a gigantic Briton were no match for the skill and coolness of a delicate, "frog-eating Frenchman." Once more the combatants met and crossed blades. "Now, Mons. Hodge," said Beauperthuy, fixing his glittering eyes upon "Probin," "I will take you off ze head, sar." "Probin" jumped backward, dropped his sabre, and picking up a huge piece of rock, roared out: "No, I'll be damned if you shall," and was about to throw it at his antagonist, when he was seized and held by the seconds and spectators, who were half-suffocated with laughter at the comedy. Matters were soon explained and arranged. The principals were induced to shake hands, and the whole affair ended with a most appetizing dinner at "Probin's," who did the honors with a huge patch of court-plaster on his left cheek, and shorn of the hirsute appendage he boasted on the morning of that day.

Another affair soon after occurred between a well-known and popular planter, and a diminutive little person, named Robinet. The planter was a crack shot, while Robinet was notoriously deficient as a marksman. The meeting took place on the open beach at Friar's Bay, at sunrise; and to equalize matters, the planter was placed directly facing the rising and glowing luminary. In vain did the planter try to shade his eyes with his hat and left hand; he missed his man every shot, while Robinet's bullets flew wide of the mark, and caused the seconds to fall back far from the line of fire. At last, the fourth shot — an unusual number — passed through Robinet's hat, which he immediately took off and with a polite bow, at the same time putting his finger in the hole, said: "*Mons. C., vous me devez un chapeau.*" The cool gallantry of the man entirely disarmed his antagonist, who advanced and offered his hand, which was as frankly accepted.

A very ludicrous affair occurred between a man named Richardson and one Robbins. Both were Anguilla men, and had crossed the narrow channel which divides that island from St. Martin, to sell a number of slaves. It had leaked out that the British Government was about to emancipate the slaves in its West Indian colonies, as it was understood that the appraisement allowed by the home government would not be so great as the negroes could be sold for in the French and Spanish colonies, English planters were anxious to dispose of their slave properties in the best markets. Richardson was the guest of Philip O'Reilly, and Robbins was a resident with Louis Durat. It was soon understood that both of these men were perfectly innocent of the "code," and measures were concocted to have a little fun at their expense. Being rivals, there was no difficulty in making each believe that the other was endeavoring to injure his property in the market. They met at dinner in the hospitable mansion of Dr. Alloway, and being unused to such rich cheer, they were not long getting "fuddled" on the Doctor's choice Madeira. Richardson gave Robbins "the lie." Everybody was shocked, as such an insult was unknown in St. Martin. Robbins had to be urged to send a challenge. Richardson was as earnestly besought to accept. O'Reilly was to act as second for the former, and Durat for Robbins; weapons, pistols; time, next day at ten o'clock A.M. When the hour arrived, both principals felt their courage going like that of Bob Acres; but being stimulated with liquor they came to the scratch, although with painful reluctance. The pistols were loaded with powder only. O'Reilly had armed himself with a huge, red prickly-pear, dead-ripe, and stood conveniently near his principal, who was in his shirt-sleeves, as well as his opponent, as they had been made to believe that this was *en régle*. At the word "fire," both men half turned their heads, shut their eyes, and banged away. At the same moment O'Reilly hurled his ripe prickly-pear full against the right side of Richardson, who instantly fell like a bullock, crying out most lustily: "I am killed; I am killed; for mercy's sake, call the doctor." Clapping his right hand upon his supposed wound, and seeing it covered with the red juice of the fruit, he exclaimed: "It is no use; I am dead — dead! What did I ever come to this devilish island for? I might have known how it would end." In the mean time Robbins' knees were knocking together with fright. He felt sure that Richardson was mortally wounded by his hand, and the poor fellow would have run off the ground had he not been prevented. Dr. Alloway soon assured Richardson that there was nothing desperate the matter with him; and in a few minutes the whole affair was explained, to the inexpressible delight of the principals, who reëmbarked for Anguilla that afternoon.

Mr. Benjamin Hodge, a brother to "Probin," but a man of diminutive stature, was a celebrated character. In his day he was the greatest and most fortunate cock fighter in the West Indies. Possessed of two large sugar plantations and some seven hundred slaves, he turned both properties out into "cock walks," hired out a number of his negroes, and kept the remainder to tend game chickens. "Uncle Benny," as he was familiarly called, was as game as his birds, but was as ignorant of the "code" as he was expert in "heeling" a cock, an art in which he was unequalled. Propositions to contend in "mains" were received and accepted by him from nearly all the neighboring West Indian Islands. A "main" consisted of twenty-one fights each between two cocks, the party winning the greatest number of battles to take the money. From fifty thousand dollars to two hundred thousand was "Uncle Benny's" "go," as he would never listen to inferior challenges.

"Uncle Benny" had been challenged to meet an old and oft-conquered antagonist in Antigua, the fortune of the dice having declared in favor of his opponent's battle ground. His finest of birds were selected and shipped two months before the "main" came off; but their arrival in Antigua was kept a profound secret. Three weeks before the contest, about thirty were picked out, trimmed, fed and trained after the most approved rules. Two days before the fight the rival cocks were duly weighed and matched against each other. "Uncle Benny" was the most intensely nervous of men, especially during a cock fight. Those who sat within his reach in the pit were certain to receive manifold spasmodic grips, pinches and nudges, until victory crowned one or the other birds. Whenever his cock killed that of his opponent, he would draw a long breath, and exclaim: "Absolutely, the child is christened!" The day came; the birds were pitted; the place was crowded with planters, merchants, and all sorts of people. "Uncle Benny" took his place on the front bench, but appeared as if he had no interest in the affair, although he was interested to the amount of seventy-five thousand dollars on the "main," and five hundred dollars on the result of each individual encounter. Next to him sat a planter who did not know "Uncle Benny." The first pair were put down and went at each other with the greatest animosity. "Uncle Benny" stood it for a few moments, and then reaching out his hand grasped his neighbor's thigh with vice-like grip, working and digging his fingers into the gentleman's flesh as if it were putty. "What the devil do you mean, sir!" cried out the injured individual. Completely absorbed in the fight, "Uncle Benny" paid no attention to this inquiry, but kept on digging away as the battle progressed and became more exciting; when, just at the moment his bird made a fortunate stroke and perforated the brain of his enemy, "Absolutely, the child is christened," said "Uncle Benny," giving his neighbor a farewell grip of reinforced pressure. The response was a slap in the face, administered with a heavy riding glove. Of course, there was nothing to be done but to assume the same attitude toward each other as the poor dumb cocks had so lately filled. They met next day at eleven A.M. Several prominent St. Martin's planters stood by "Uncle Benny," to see that no undue advantage was taken of his ignorance in such matters. The principals were stationed and the word about to be given, when "Uncle Benny" grasped his pistol in both hands, as he would a rifle, and took deliberate aim; his adversary at the same time raising his weapon and doing the same thing. The word being given, both parties fired, "Uncle Benny's" opponent falling, shot through the fleshy part of the thigh. "Absolutely, the child is christened!" shouted the victor, and having been informed that the affair was at an end, he walked over to his discomfitted antagonist, explained the whole matter, begged his pardon, and offered him the hospitality of his mansion and the unrestricted use of his purse.

Nicholas Heiliger was one of the most accomplished gentlemen of that time in the West Indies. He was over fifty years old, but straight as a reed, and a devoted gallant to the fair sex, by whom he was much esteemed.

Among his most prized possessions was a pair of old fashioned but excellent duelling pistols, which had descended to him as inestimable heir-looms through four generations. Locks, stocks and ramrods had undergone various changes and improvements, but the Damascus barrels were regarded with unaffected reverence. To dine in company with Nick was a treat; but to sit alone with him as his guest, with your legs stretched under his well burnished mahogany, and after a couple of bottles of the finest "Cockroach" had been comfortably disposed of, was the rarest of festive enjoyments. About eleven o'clock P.M. he would call "Harry!" "Sar!" "Bring my 'persuaders,'" and Harry would soon appear with an elegantly ornamented box containing the venerated family heir-looms. Then followed a series of historical and family anecdotes, describing past conditions of society, old family feuds, political and social changes, and above all, the part that the 'persuaders' had played in enforcing conviction when other arguments failed. Nick had consigned a quantity of sugar to a merchant named Capé, in St. Thomas, and for some cause or other, believed that he had been "chiselled;" but to be sure, repaired thither in person, taking his 'persuaders' with him, as no gentleman travelled, at that time, without his well appointed case of duelling pistols. Arrived at St. Thomas, he notified Mr. Capé of the fact, and requested his company that evening. Capé replied, "that if Mr. Nicholas Heiliger had any business with him, he would be happy to receive him either at his country house or at his residence, according to Mr. Heiliger's inclination." Next day Nick waited upon Capé at his country home, and had an interview which was not at all of an amicable character, and terminated in an invitation to look into the muzzle of a 'persuader,' which was quietly accepted. At the appointed time shots were exchanged, resulting in Nick receiving a flesh wound on the inside of his right arm, between the shoulder and elbow, narrowly grazing important blood vessels, and passing very close to the chest. Handing the empty weapon to his second, Nick advanced and said: "Mr. Capé, I am under the impression, sir, that I have done you a personal injury, for which I am truly sorry. You are a brave man, and therefore I believe you to be honorable. I beg, sir, to apologize for my rude and irascible remarks yesterday." It is needless to add that Capé instantly clutched the proffered hand, just in time to save Heiliger from falling, as he had become faint from loss of blood.

One evening several gentlemen were passing the *caserne*, or barracks, in Pointe a Pitre, Guadaloupe, when a dispute occurred between two French soldiers, one of whom challenged the other to meet him next day, the commandant permitting, at ten A.M. in the field back of the barracks. "*Je conviens*," was the response. Having never witnessed a duel of this kind, the conflict being peremptorily confined to the short sabres of the *Infanterie de la Ligne*, and the point being absolutely prohibited, considerable interest was felt by those present to see how this species of combat was to be performed. Permission to fight, in accordance with regulations, was immediately granted by the Colonel commanding, and at the appointed hour and place the men, attended by their seconds, met to hack at each other. It was well understood that the first blood drawn ended the quarrel so far as the men were concerned; for the fact was never lost sight of, that French soldiers were the property of the French Government, and had no right to sacrifice life except in the battles of their country. The same rule is rigidly enforced in regard to their officers when opposed to each other, but is ignored when an officer meets a civilian or an officer of some foreign service. The combatants were admirably matched, being two of the best *sabreurs* in the French service, each being an instructor or *Maitre d'Armes*. They were Parisians, *gamins* of the first water, and the insult consisted in one having called the other a *philosophie*, than which no greater term of opprobrium can be applied to a "rough" of the gay capital. *"Tiens, je te rougerais le nez, cette fois-ci,"* exclaimed one, as their weapons crossed. *"Blagueur!"* responded the other. The combat was carried on with great rapidity and violence, but yet with marked caution. Each felt that his reputation was at stake. Blows were returned and stopped in all directions; carte, tierce, prime, second, were resorted to without effect. Such splendid fencing had never before been witnessed by the admiring spectators. Faster and more furious became the contest as the parties warmed to their work, until both stepped backwards, pointing their weapons down, until they could recover from exhaustion and renew the conflict. An officer of rank, however, stepped forward and succeeded in obtaining an apology from the offending party, upon which the principals immediately embraced and started for the *cantine*, where their recent animosity was soon drowned in *petits verres d'absynthe*.

The Spanish islands formed the exceptions to the otherwise universal practice of duelling then in vogue throughout the West Indies. But it has since nearly died out with the decay and emigration of old families, which gradually subsided when slavery was blotted from the social system.

Colonel John Carey Cremony *(1815-1879) was an extraordinary man. He was a soldier, sailor and editor, a man of iron nerve, an accomplished swordsman and a graceful rider. His appearance suggested he was of Spanish extraction and, with his cloak slung over his shoulder, there was no mistaking him as an Iberian gentleman.*

Little is known of Cremony's early life. One source claims that his parents were planters from Santo Domingo, driven out by the black liberator Toussaint L' Ouverture. Another places Cremony's birth on the Island of St. Martin. Nevertheless, the family did leave the West Indies, settling in Portland, Maine.

As a mere boy he left his father's house and shipped out before the mast. He followed the sea for a number of years and it was his boast in more convivial times that he returned as Captain of the boat in which he had left as a cabin boy. Much of what we know about Cremony was gathered by his associates from his own lips. He told of his exploits as an officer in the French Foreign Service in Algiers and many other exciting adventures. He once told a story about an Indian who had him pinned down on the ground with a knife to his neck. Before Cremony could finish the story, one of his eager listeners interrupted, asking "Then what happened?" Cremony brought the house down with his reply: 'Why, sir, I died like a man."

Although Cremony was not college educated he was an accomplished scholar, fluent in French, Spanish, and Italian. He was a man who had looked upon every side of life and seen humanity in every form. He had visited most of Europe, traveled extensively in India, and had lived in South America and Mexico.

A veteran of the Mexican-American war, he came to California in 1853 as an interpreter for the government party which laid out the boundaries of the Gadsden purchase. Soon after, he became identified with pioneer journalism in San Francisco, as Editor of the Sun, and assisted John Nugent at the Herald during the vigilante times of 1856. Indeed, to his pen are attributed many of the stirring editorials which appeared in the Herald at that time. At the outbreak of the Civil War he joined the California Volunteers, riding with Major Carleton on his march into Arizona, New Mexico, and Texas to quell Confederate advances. Cremony served as Captain and eventually succeeded Salvador Vallejo as Major in charge of the First Battalion. He rose to the position of Lieutenant Colonel.

During his service, Cremony became interested in the study of Indian history and customs. He wrote the definitive book on the Apache tribe, "Life Among the Apaches", published by A. Roman and Co. in 1868. He also prepared an alphabet for the Apache Tongue. Cremony used to claim that the Apache book was written with a feather plucked from an American eagle.

After the Civil War, Colonel Cremony was Associate Editor of the Commercial Herald and was a daily contributor. He wrote with ease and clarity on any subject. Personally, he was a congenial gentleman. His military bearing attracted attention everywhere, and those who knew him would tell of his physical strength. Once he tried the stage in the role of Don Caesar de Bozan and although his appearance and style seemed to be perfect for the part, he was not a success. During his idle hours, Colonel Cremony taught fencing and other manly arts.

In 1872, when James F. Bowman and a group of friends were casting about for the name of a new club, Colonel Cremony saved the day with the name "Bohemian Club." Benjamin P. Avery proposed that a more sedate name be chosen so that none would go astray. With fire in his eyes and invective on his tongue, Cremony pictured his ideal club—a sanded floor, a deal table, a keg of beer, plenty of chairs and plenty of good fellows to sit in them. Single-handedly he won the day for Bohemians.

A Cruise On a Slaver

by J.C. Cremony
November 1868

It was in the Bonny River, on the African coast, that the writer who had been shipwrecked was offered a passage to Puerto Rico by the captain of a slaver called the *Saranac*. This offer was gratefully accepted, and from that moment Captain Scudder put away all restraint on his words and acts.

The *Saranac* had run into the river that afternoon. So soon as she came to an anchor, her royal and topgallant masts were sent down, and her top-masts housed, to prevent their appearance above the low lands of the coast. In all other respects the vessel was kept ready for immediate service. Twenty miles above and about the same distance below were elevated bluffs, from which a sail could be observed; and should such an one prove to be a British man-of-war, immediate notice would be given in time to assure the escape of the slaving craft, or in default of wind, to permit a complete change of rig.

"John Buckraw," said Captain Scudder, "how many niggers have you got on hand?"

"I got tree hundered at the bay barracoon, sar, and Jim Shiner has gone up to de upper barracoon for tree hundred mo'. I spect him héa' to-night at twelve o'clock."

"Very good; let there be no mistake, for I can't wait. If he don't come, I will trade down the coast with someone else."

This threat acted with effect on John Buckraw, a huge mulatto, and he hastened off to get on board the three hundred in the bay barracoon.

Down they came, and were about to be embarked, when Scudder appeared. "Avast, there," said he, "none of that, you old thief! You cheated me the last time, and I will inspect these darkies to suit myself."

"I nebber cheat you Massa Scudder; I always gib you good nigger, sar; but look for yourself, sar."

Scudder examined the men as they came down, boat-load after boat-load, and with some haggling accepted the main lot, with few exceptions on the score of old age or physical infirmity.

In a short time two hundred and eighty were placed on board the *Saranac*, and before day-light next morning she had completed a cargo of five hundred slaves.

"Time's up," said Captain Scudder to me, as he roughly shook me from a sound slumber; "send your dunnage aboard now, and go with me."

"I have no dunnage, Captain Scudder; I lost all when I was shipwrecked, except what I have on."

"Good," was the reply, "you can share with me; I have plenty, and you can occupy the port berth in my state room."

We went aboard and I was presented to a tall, dark man with coal-black eyes, and full beard of the same hue.

"This is the Spanish captain of the *Saranac*," said Scudder, "for you must know that she always sails with two sets of papers and two captains."

Don Ribero Guzman received me with politeness and something like attention.

"It is not often that we have a passenger," he remarked, "and I am pleased to welcome you, because I know that Scudder would not have made you the offer unless he felt convinced that you would do us no harm."

"Make yourself easy, Don Ribero, I am no English officer in disguise, but simply a shipwrecked American sailor, anxious to get home; and this being the only chance likely to offer for some time, I have accepted Captain Scudder's invitation."

"And you did well; I will see to it that your name is properly entered on the log book with all the circumstances; so that should we be unfortunate enough to fall into the hands of a British cruiser, you will be all right."

This man's gentlemanly address, and Scudder's frank and jovial manner, tended greatly to set me at ease, and reconcile me to the novel and somewhat extraordinary voyage I was about to make.

Two o'clock A.M., there being no wind, the boats, four in number, were got ahead with ten oarsmen in each, and by means of a tow line the *Saranac* moved gracefully and not sluggishly from the Bonny River. The rowlocks were all muffled; no conversation was allowed, and no noise made. Topgallant and royal masts and yards were speedily sent aloft, and every sail set that could catch a cap-full of wind. By six o'clock A.M., we were several miles clear of the river, and out on the broad Atlantic in one of those terribly dense fogs, never encountered except upon the African coast. The boats were called and snugly stowed, and as the wind began to freshen from the eastward, all studding sails were set. "Keep her west by north half north," said the captain, and the course was laid as directed.

The *Saranac* was a brigantine of four hundred and thirty tons measurement, and had been built for a privateer. Her lines were as fine as those of a dolphin. She had great length and breadth of beam, with a corresponding breadth of hold; but her floor was long and smooth as a plane. Her entrance was as sharp as a knife, and her run long, keen and elegantly modeled. Aloft, her rig was of the true Baltimore clipper style, with short, strong masts and enormous yards, long and tapering, but stout in the slings. She was provided with false bulwarks made of painted canvas, and so arranged that they could be turned up at a moment's notice to the height of three feet, giving her the appearance of being a heavy, wall-sided merchantman. The *Saranac* had made four successful voyages and was on her fifth, having enriched her owners after many almost miraculous escapes. Captains Scudder and Guzman had been in charge from the first, and were both possessors of large properties in the Spanish West Indies; but they had contracted such a love for reckless adventure, that they persisted in their nefarious career.

"Mr. Jerome, send a man aloft to see if he can overlook this fog. If there is anything in sight let him sing out at once."

In obedience to this order, two men immediately mounted the rigging. "All clear above, sir," shouted the men.

"Very well; keep a sharp look out," was the answer. In a few minutes the man on the fore royal yard hailed the deck—"Sail, ho!" "Where, away?" "Just forward of the weather beam, sir." "What does she look like?" "Only her royals and the head of her main topgallant sail, sir." "How far off does she appear to be?" "I should judge about two miles, sir." "Very good," said Scudder, "she has not seen us yet." Just then came the announcement of three other sails in sight, all apparently large ships and standing to the northward. Scudder immediately threw his telescope over his shoulder, mounted the rigging and took a quick, but comprehensive glance at the strangers, whose royals were alone visible. Quickly descending to the deck, he said: "They are British men-of-war, and we are right in the midst of them. There is a heavy frigate just forward of our starboard beam, another directly to leeward; a smart sloop ahead, and a first-class line-of-battle ship straight in our wake; but they have not yet seen the *Saranac*."

"Mr. Jerome, call all hands; but make no noise. In all stun' sails; clap on the lee braces; down helm; brace up sharp; board the fore tack; haul aft the sheets; keep her full and by, but let her go through the water; be sure and don't shake the sails." The *Saranac's* crew consisted of eighty able seamen, and these orders were obeyed almost as soon as given. Turning to me, Scudder remarked: "I am going to pass that fellow to windward; but must graze him very closely. If he sees us we may almost as well give up the ship; but if the fog holds until ten o'clock, and I think it will, we can get by him, and once to windward I will show him the cleanest pair of heels he ever saw." The breeze had been steadily increasing, and the *Saranac* was making nine knots on a taut bow-line. Scudder took his position on the fore royal yard and conned the brig. "Luff a little, but don't shake her." "Luff it is, sir," responded the helmsman. "Steady as you go." "Steady it is, sir." Becoming excited, I mounted to a place beside Capt. Scudder, in order to observe the whole affair. We were rapidly nearing a large ship, of which only the royals and a portion of the main topgallant sail were above the fog. She was heading nor'-nor'-west, with the wind two points free, and her consorts were on the same tack. "If she holds her course, and the wind remains steady, we shall pass within four hundred yards of her stern," remarked Scudder. The strictest silence was enjoined on board the slaver. Everything was hauled taut; not a rope nor a block swung in the wind; not a sound was heard but the rushing of the brig through the waves. In twenty minutes we were directly astern of the stranger, and in ten more nearly half a mile to windward, and more than a mile distant. We had descended to the deck, and Scudder was giving a description of the matter to Guzman, when the fog suddenly lifted and revealed the strangers in their full proportions. They were exactly as Scudder thought, two frigates, one sloop and a line-of-battle ship. The moment the *Saranac* was perceived all hauled sharp on the wind and gave chase, while the frigate we had just before passed fell off the wind two or three points, and tried the reach of her bow guns. The shot passed by without inflicting damage, and after three or four attempts, finding that she was losing ground too rapidly, the frigate filled away in pursuit. In two hours all the others were hull down to leeward; but the frigate held her own. "That is the *Thetis*," said Scudder; "I know her well; no other vessel in the British navy can keep pace on the wind with the *Saranac*. She has chased me before, and if I mistake not, will follow us across the Atlantic. Take another pull at those lee braces; sway up the halyards, and haul the sheets well home. Give her the main topmast and main topgallant staysails, and make everything snug fore and aft. Keep her full and by, and let her go through the water!"

The *Saranac* was then running ten and a half knots off the reel.

"I want no more wind," said Scudder; "the sea is smooth, and we are at our best sailing point. If the breeze should freshen much, the frigate's greater weight would tell against us in a heavy head sea." Night fell; there was no moon; the *Thetis* was four miles astern and two points to leeward. Guzman took the deck at eight bells. "Keep her away." The helm was put up until the *Saranac* was fairly before the wind, and once more on her direct course. "Take in all stay-sails, set all weather stun' sails; keep her west by north." Away she went, careering over the waves like a thing of life, rollicking and leaving a wake like liquid fire as she cleft the waters. Toward morning the wind increased almost to a gale.

At six bells, A.M., Scudder resumed the deck, took his spy-glass and went aloft, "Shake out all reefs. Man the lee braces and brace sharp up. Down helm; set jibs and stay-sails; keep her close to the wind." These orders were given with rapidity and as quickly obeyed. "By all that's devilish," said Scudder, as he returned to the deck, "there was that infernal frigate about three miles to the southward, on our port beam. We shall get the start of her this time; but it is blowing rather too heavily for the *Saranac*. Never mind, we shall see."

The brig was staggering under a cloud of canvas, considering she was close hauled. Her royals and outer jib were stowed; but beyond these she was carrying nearly all her standing sails. The only dry part about her was the forecastle deck, all abaft the fore rigging being drenched with blinding spray as she drove madly onward through the fast increasing head sea.

In the meanwhile the *Thetis* had hauled up in pursuit, and was cracking on at a fearful rate. Whenever a squall of unusual violence occurred, her royal and topgallant halyards were let go, the sails clewed up in a twinkling, and the ship luffed so as to shake the main force of the wind from the balance of the sails; but no sooner had the occasion passed than the light canvas was once more sheeted home and hoisted up to its utmost tension, while the frigate again fell off to a good "rap" full. After two or three hours of careful watching, it became evident that the *Thetis* was gradually gaining on the *Saranac*. Wind and sea had increased, and we had been compelled to hand topgallant sails, stow the flying jib, and single reef the huge fore and aft mainsail; the frigate still cracking on, with all sail set. The *Saranac* was jumping from sea to sea like a porpoise, and deluging her decks with water.

"Mr. Jerome." "Sir." "Come up with the mast wedges; slack off about three inches of all the weather lanyards; and rig up forty or fifty boatswain's chairs; put a nigger in each and run them up the fore and main stays, so that they may be about four feet apart. Be sure and have the darkies well fastened in the chairs, for we can't afford to lose them. Heave the log." We were going nearly ten knots through that sea way. The wedges had been slackened, and the lanyards eased off as directed. A string of negroes fastened in boatswain's chairs dangled and swung from the fore and main stays; the masts bent like whips, and with every plunge she went forward with greatly increased impetus. The log now announced ten knots and a half.

"Send the carpenters aft." Two men answered the summons. "Attend well to my orders," said Scudder. "Saw the plank-sheer down to the depth of two inches at the distance of every ten feet, and saw the main rail one-third through every eight feet." In half an hour these orders were obeyed. The log now indicated eleven knots large. The brig rose no more to the sea, but went straight through it like a dolphin. Night was again approaching; the *Thetis* had lost ground for the last two hours of daylight, and the weather had begun to moderate slightly. The negroes were taken down·and placed back in the hold; additional canvas set, and the brig kept at her highest rate of sailing, which increased as the sea fell, until at four bells, P.M., she was forging ahead with the speed of twelve knots and a half.

During all those exciting hours Guzman had kept the deck with Scudder; but gave no orders, limiting himself to assist Mr. Jerome in seeing the duty well and quickly done. All night we stood to the northward on a taut bowline, carrying every inch of canvas that the brig would bear. Day-light dawned with a fresh breeze still from east-north-east, but a smoother sea. The frigate was not to be seen. At day-break the look-out reported "nothing in sight."

The excitement created by the chase had almost obliterated other sensations, but with its termination came an ardent desire to comprehend the *manége* of the slaver. Eighty able-bodied and smart looking men, all picked seamen, composed the *Saranac's* crew. They were made up of Americans, Englishmen, Frenchmen, and Portuguese, with a slight sprinkling of other nationalities. There were two captains, two physicians, four mates, a boatswain and his mate, two carpenters, two blacksmiths, one pump and block-maker, two sail-makers and eight cooks; but all hands, except the cooks, were compelled to assist in working ship when required. The brig's armament consisted of eight twelve pounder brass guns, four on a side, a long thirty-two amidships, and a long twenty-four on the quarter deck, abaft the mainmast, and forward of the cabin companion way which opened toward the stern. Boarding pikes, pistols, and cutlasses existed in abundance and were properly stowed. She was flush fore and aft, and was of unusual beam and length, with low bulwarks, and the ends of all lanyards to her standing rigging belayed to iron pins strongly secured to her stanchions by a heavy iron cleet.

Although many of the crew wore the appearance of having no objection to a little profitable piracy, yet they were kept in perfect submission. Discipline was rigidly maintained. Scudder was the master spirit, but he had admirable backers in Captain Guzman and the first mate, Jerome, while the inferior officers manifested much zeal and ability. Each knew his station, and fulfilled its duties with promptitude and energy.

At four bells of the morning after we had got rid of the *Thetis*, Mr. Jerome gave an order to send a hundred of the negroes on deck to get up wind-sails in all the hatchways, and to place a strong guard over them. A hundred negroes were brought up and subjected to a regular purification; being thoroughly doused with salt water and roughly wiped with bits of old top-gallant duck. Their heads were then shorn entirely bare, and they were allowed to remain in the sun until noon, when they were sent below again. At one o'clock P.M. another batch of a hundred were sent up and put through a like process. Each relief, as it appeared on deck, was rigidly examined by the doctors, and should there be any indication of severe contagious or infectious disorder, the sufferers were immediately segregated and placed in a reserved room called the "Sick Bay."

At the period when these events occurred, slaving was carried on only with unusual risks, and every attention was paid to preserve those who had been secured. The average price paid for able-bodied men of from eighteen to thirty-five years, in the African barracoons, was about seventy dollars; but much of the payment was made in rum, cotton cloths, red blankets, beads, knives, condemned muskets, lead and powder, on which articles a profit of four hundred per cent was realized. Those negroes would bring from five to seven and eight hundred dollars apiece in Brazil, Cuba, or Puerto Rico. Young and likely girls, not over twenty nor less than thirteen, were worth about the same prices in the places named; but were bought for an average of thirty dollars each at the barracoons. Rum was the principal commodity in those transactions with negro traders on the African Coast. By a plentiful and shrewd use of this article, small tribes were led to make war upon each other, the main object being to take prisoners rather than to shed blood. Sometimes four or five villages would unite to capture the inhabitants of another. The promise of a few barrels of rum, with a proportionate allowance of useless muskets and almost useless ammunition, together with a few small looking-glasses and beads, would prove sufficient inducement for such a raid. It was not indispensable that the assailants should be of a different clan or tribe from the assailed; it was only necessary to stimulate them with a little liquor made palatable with sugar, to effect a raid at any time, and against any village not powerful enough to resist. The conquerors of one year would frequently be captured the next, and bought and sold with quite as little remorse by the very parties with whom they had formerly trafficked for the flesh and blood of their neighbors, and even of their kinsmen.

In such a condition of affairs no one felt safe at any time, and each seemed to resign himself, or herself, to whatever fate might be in store, with a degree of supineness altogether incomprehensible to us, but quite in accordance with their ideas of Fetish worship, and belief in unavoidable fatality.

A barracoon is the place where these wretched captives are kept until opportunity serves to dispose of them. Nearly all are some miles interior; but not so far off that their inmates cannot be placed on board ship in a few hours notice. No delays are permissible among slavers. No "niggers," — no rum, no muskets. When a slaver was sighted, bound in, the contents of interior barracoons were precipitated toward the port, a bargain soon made, and the captives immediately placed on board, where they were as soon hand-cuffed by twos and sent down to the berth deck prepared for their reception. Rarely were two days suffered to elapse before completing the "cargo," for delays were dangerous, and in the interval every means was adopted to insure immunity from surprise; or, if escape were impossible, to so change the vessel's appearance as to create the impression that she was a legitimate trader. To this end nothing was omitted. Two captains; two registers; two sets of papers; two styles of rig were employed, and all semblance of slave commerce put out of sight. With no tangible evidence on which to act, cruisers were compelled to be cautious. A mistake might provoke serious consequences. It were better to let three guilty ones slide, for the time being, than to do irreparable injury to one honest trader. Naval officers had to content themselves with maintaining a strict watch over the suspected craft, and then it became a matter of dexterity and chance, with pretty even results.

After the two batches of slaves had been shaved and scrubbed, as before related, orders were given to leave the hatches off during the night; but to keep strict watch fore and aft. Scudder had the deck. The night was magnificent beyond expression. A fine and refreshing breeze was wafted over the weather quarter, and bellied out the canvas in graceful curves. In that glorious tropical clime the stars scintillated with resplendent lustre. The vast ocean heaved and swelled, giving forth innumerable lines of living light, clearly defining even minute objects. It was a time for contemplation, and the remarkable expression of Israel's great king recurred to me with wondrous power, as I gazed into the mystical depths of that inscrutable firmament: "When I consider the heavens, the work of thy fingers, the moon and the stars which thou hast ordained; what is man, that thou art mindful of him, and the son of man that thou visitest him?"

In the boundlessness of that incomprehensible space; in the presence of its Creator; in the sight of the universal Alpha, what was I, or the wretched pigmy at my side, whose every attribute had been trained to traffic in the flesh and blood of his fellow man? While absorbed in these unprofitable lucubrations, I was aroused by Scudder's remark: "What do you think of the slave trade?" Astonished at such an interrogatory, I involuntarily replied: "I consider it the lowest point of moral degradation, with one exception." "What is that?" "The depth arrived at by the men who make your traffic lucrative."

Scudder was a man of superior mental ability and considerable culture. He felt that my remarks were not personal, but applicable in a general sense, although he was involved in their pertinency. I was not prepared for the philosophical manner with which they were received, and was agreeably disappointed when he said: "But do you not believe that we are doing a real benefit to the African by taking him from his savage life and haunts, and at least, giving him the advantage of coming in direct contact with civilized and christianized beings? Do you not believe that such affiliation must improve the moral and social condition of the negro, and elevate him to a higher and more useful sphere than he could possibly have occupied in his native state?"

"Before answering your questions, Capt. Scudder, permit me ask one or two. Do you believe that the performance of a wrong and outrageous act justifies him who does it, because the Almighty in his wisdom permits nothing without evolving some good from the operation? What amount of civilization and Christianizing do you think the five hundred men and women on board the *Saranac* will arrive at before they are called from this sphere of existence? What efforts are made to instruct them into the higher moral standing you speak of? Will they not adhere to their Fetish worship, their belief in Obeah, their faith in spells and incantations; and will they not die the heathen they have lived, so far as they themselves are concerned? The only change you effect is from freedom to life-long bondage; from one continent to another, or the isles of the Caribbean sea; from one description of savage and pagan life to its counterpart; from the manhood and courage of native independence to the craven terror of enforced serfdom. It is true, that after two or three generations have been swept away, some of the more likely ones may be admitted as house servants, and in that capacity brought into daily communion with more enlightened beings; but has that distinction been beneficial either to their moral standing or that of their owners, or has it proved only a small amount of intellectual sharpening, with a corresponding *quantum* of social iniquity on the part of their masters? Is an African in worse circumstances in his native wilds — free, untrammeled, and pagan though he may be — than he is under the lash of the slave driver — bond serf, slave, and no less pagan? Have those who fitted up this splendid brig, and employed you and others to trade in human flesh, built school houses, and furnished an improved condition for these people whom you hold manacled on board the *Saranac*? Were they not engaged in enterprises of this nature for the sole purpose of making money, and coining it from the blood of our fellow beings, although inferior, and at the compulsory sacrifice to them of all the sentiments which are natural to the human heart — the inalienable gifts of the Creator, and cherished by us as His chiefest blessings?"

Scudder listened with attention. Just then the forecastle bell struck twelve for midnight, and the deck was relieved by Guzman. "I am going to turn in," said the American captain, "so come below and 'splice the main brace,' " was his only comment upon my exordium.

The next dawn broke upon a sea like glass. The sails hung lifeless from the yards, flapping now and then as the *Saranac* rose and fell to the sea. Our main boom was guyed out and held taut between the boom tackle and the main sheet; every stitch of light canvas was set; dolphins and bonetas were lazily ranging from one side to the other and fore and aft, occasionally thrusting their noses into bunches of gulf weed, as we sluggishly passed them, in quest of small crabs and diminutive fishes which take refuge under their shelter in hot and calm weather. A thick, oily substance seemed to rest upon the bosom of the deep and impede its usual activity. About a hundred negroes were on deck reposing in the sun, apparently with intense relish. The pitch was boiling from the deck seams, and the rigging was sweating tar from every strand. "This would be a bad time to meet the *Thetis*," said Scudder, "for she would send her boats after us; but I think we could beat them off easily enough." "Would you add bloodshed to slaving?" I asked. The question was simply but emphatically answered by pointing to the guns and small arms. "They are for use, and not for show," said Scudder. At two, P.M., or four bells, the look-out hailed the deck. "Sail, ho!" "Where, away?" "Nearly in our wake, sir." "Mr. Jerome, send all the niggers below, and get all the boats ahead." In a few minutes forty strong arms were towing the brig through the water at the rate of two and a half knots. In the meantime, Scudder kept his glass fixed upon the eastern horizon. At three, P.M., he exclaimed: "I see her; it is the *Thetis*; I know her by the cut of her sails; she has got a light breeze, and is running along with all sail set. Probably we will get the breeze before she comes up; if not, she will run into this calm, stick, and down boats in chase. Clew up royals and topgallant sails; they only impede our progress. Brace the yards sharp on the port tack; slack away the boom tackle, and haul aft the main sheet; haul up the foresail." As there was no wind, and the yards had been squared, the impetus given by the boats had created a contrary current of air which impeded progress. In about an hour the topsails of our pursuer were visible from the deck, Scudder keeping his glass fixed on her movements. "So," he exclaimed, "she has run out of the breeze into the calm; her canvas hangs idly in the brails; she is at least seven miles off; we are going two and a half knots through the water, and it will be night before her boats can reach us, let them do their best. Mr. Jerome, put on the hatches, and send twenty more men to the boats, and let them double bank the oars." In ten minutes afterward we were going at the rate of three knots. Night fell; there was no moon, but the stars lighted up the ocean, and one could see clearly to some considerable distance. About eight o'clock, P.M., we could faintly hear the sharp click of oars in the rowlocks, proving that the *Thetis* had sent her boats.

"All aboard!" said Scudder. The brig's boats fell alongside, were taken in and stowed without noise. "Load the guns with grape and langrage! Distribute small arms, and prepare to repel boarders! Up with the false bulwarks!" Nearer and nearer came the sound of the approaching foemen. Presently a quick sensation of cold was experienced by those on deck. "All right," said Scudder, joyously, "the wind has chopped to the northward, and will be on us in less than half an hour." Twenty minutes elapsed. Intense curiosity and excitement kept me on deck. The advancing boats could not have been more than six hundred yards away, and would soon be upon us, when the mortal strife would commence.

Scudder appeared to take no interest in what was passing, but gazed intently over the taffrail, apparently absorbed with rudder fish. Guzman was commanding; the crew were properly stationed, and, everything got ready for a bloody resistance. Suddenly and sharply the order came from Scudder—"Round in the starboard braces, and trim sails to the wind!" No sooner had these mandates been obeyed, than a full puff of wind came from the northward, and filled the sails handsomely. The keen *Saranac* bowed in graceful acquiescence, and cut the liquid element at the rate of five knots, and the breeze was rapidly strengthening. As the boats had not been supplied with guns, we went away from them hand over hand, much to the chagrin of their occupants.

No more was seen of the *Thetis*, but to make matters sure, the *Saranac* was run to the northward of Virgin Gorda, St. Thomas, and the other isles of that group.

We had but passed Sail Rock Passage when the weather began to look threatening. It was in the hurricane months, the fourteenth of September; the barometer was falling fast, but there was not a breath of air stirring. The sky was of a deep lead color, and the ocean murky almost to blackness. The brig was placed under close reefed topsails, fore topmast stay-sail and balance reefed mainsail. All hands were kept on deck, and the braces manned to starboard and to port, while topmen were properly stationed. "The glass has stopped falling, and it is not likely that we shall have a hurricane; but there will be just as much as we can well stand up to," said Scudder to me, as he anxiously gazed around. "I thought you were bound to the south side of Puerto Rico," I remarked. "So I am." "Why, then, did you pass Sail Rock Passage?" "Because there is another further to the westward, called Serpent Island Passage, known to but few. It is short and contains no invisible dangers, and is safe for a line-of-battle ship. We can make the north side in less than three hours by this passage, and mislead any pursuer. If the gale bursts upon us from the southward, we can hug the northern shore and make a lee; and if it should come from the northward, we can soon avail ourselves of the southern shelter of Puerto Rico." We were heading due west, but without a breath of air. Directly, a sound like that of breakers, and a sharp, moaning noise were heard from the eastward and southward. Soon after came the first rush of the storm.

"Settle away the mainsail; up helm; keep her before it;" but before these orders were duly executed, our main topsail was blown clear of the boltropes. The *Saranac* fairly buried her forecastle in the now raging sea, as she acknowledged the power of the blast; but she soon gathered way and swiftly flew before the gale.

"Bend another topsail, Mr. Jerome. How do you head?" "West by north, Sir." "Keep her west-south-west. We must hug the land, and run for the passage." "The main topsail is bent and close reefed," said the mate. "Very well, have it set immediately." The wind was from east-south-east, blowing almost a hurricane. In an hour or two we sighted the northern entrance of the passage, which was dead under the lee of Serpent Island, and the water comparatively smooth, while the force of the gale was somewhat broken. "Keep her south-west; set the foresail and mainsail." The *Saranac*, was now going large and was rushing along at terrific speed. It was necessary to get through before night-fall, and she was staggering under all the canvas she could carry. The passage, in the narrowest part, was only two hundred yards wide. On either hand huge black rocks raised their foam-crested heads high above the water, while the lashing and surging of the waves denoted the existence of others just beneath the surface. The channel, though intricate, contained no hidden dangers, and by five o'clock, P.M., the *Saranac* was again on the open ocean to the southward and eastward of Puerto Rico. No abatement had taken place in the storm, so sail was shortened to the same canvas the brig was carrying before entering the passage.

Soon after four bells, the look-out aloft sung out, "Sail ho!" "Where away?" "Right in our wake, sir." Scudder soon satisfied himself that it was his old enemy, the *Thetis*. The frigate had evidently made out the *Saranac*, and was cracking on all the sail she could bear. She was probably six or seven miles off, and as a stern chase is a long one, there still remained time for new tactics; besides, it would be pitch dark in a few minutes. The *Thetis* was steering a half point more to the southward, clearly with the intention of crowding us between herself and the land. Once more the foresail was hauled down and set. The *Saranac* flew before the wind like a greyhound, but her pursuer was gradually gaining. At mid-night, all hands being properly stationed, Scudder roared out, "Port your helm; round in the port braces; haul up the foresail; keep her north by east," and we were heading directly for the land, which was not more than two miles off. The coast was low, and covered with a dense growth of mangroves, into which there was every appearance that the brig would be soon plunged headlong. Scudder was on the forecastle intently scanning the fast rising land. "Luff half a point; steady so." We were within two hundred yards of the mangroves, and madly rushing forward upon what seemed inevitable destruction. The brig's head spars disappeared behind the trees, and in a second more her trembling hull glided into smooth water, having shot into the mouth of the little, and then generally unknown, port called Jobos.

The entrance to this place is very narrow and intricate, being beset with several mud banks, to avoid which requires the aid of a skillful pilot. It is called the *Boca de los Infiernos*, or the "mouth of the Infernal Regions," on account of the serious difficulties which attend its navigation for four miles, when it opens into a handsome and perfectly safe harbor, entirely land-locked, and containing about three fathoms of water, with the best of holding ground. Jobos was a great resort for slavers at that period, and its existence seems to have been unknown to the officers of the British navy until several years later. Scudder was fully equal to the task, for in half an hour the *Saranac* was quietly lying at her moorings. Three large lighters were immediately got alongside; the negroes sent on shore, and run up into the interior without delay. All the water casks had been shooked up as soon as emptied during the voyage, and were now sent ashore. The calaboose was torn down and replaced by one of ordinary make and size. Royal and topgallant masts were sent down and replaced by stump topgallant masts. Topsail and lower yards were shifted for short, thick, and clumsy looking ones, painted white. The head spars underwent a similar change. Our false bulwarks were unshipped and landed. The seams made by the saw in her plank-sheer and mainrails were carefully puttied up and painted over, and by day-light the *Saranac* had undergone such a wonderful transformation that her oldest friends would scarcely recognize the keen and audacious slaver. A couple of boats were manned, and under the charge of Guzman, pulled out to discover what had become of the frigate. She had run past, evidently under the impression of being in full chase of the brig.

I had been most generously and kindly entertained by Scudder, Guzman, and the officers, and however much I might revolt at their wretched traffic, I could not help feeling some interest in the men. During the whole voyage I had witnessed no act of outrage or cruelty, and was assured that such instances were of rare occurrence, the officers receiving a *per capita* premium on all slaves delivered in good condition. Having made arrangements to set out for Ponce, where I could find an American trader, I took leave of my recent associates, and as I crossed the rail, Scudder remarked, as he squeezed my hand: "I have a nice place close to Puerto Principe, and should you ever cruise in that latitude, by sure to come and see me; but believe me, this is the last time I shall ever sail on a slaver."

An Ex-Pirate

by J.C. Cremony
April 1869

Surrounded by rugged granite hills, which rise loftily on all sides, and partly embowered by a superb forest, which is perforated by many a charming glade, lies a small, cozy town, celebrated for its lovely, land-locked, and tranquil harbor, its pure, invigorating air, and almost perfect seclusion from the outside world. Two miles east from this rustic burgh is a neat, well-kept hotel, located on the western declivity of a bold promontory, against which the angry Atlantic dashes its brine and spends its mighty fury. This hotel is the favorite summer resort of some who are esteemed our wisest and best men. Although unknown to the butterflies of fashion, its hospitable doors open regularly every season to receive the leading ornaments of our pulpits; the nation's sages; men of literary culture and refinement; artists of fame, and women who honor their sex by the exercise of manifold virtues. Riding through the stately woods, hunting amidst its leafy coverts, fishing from the granite wharf or graceful cutter, or engaged in some of the many pleasant entertainments always to be found, time passed delightfully and all too swiftly at that little nook, sheltered by the iron-bound front of Massachusetts.

I had just returned from the Mexican war, debilitated, worn down, and almost shattered by that harassing campaign to which so many fell victims long after hostilities had ceased. Being almost a stranger in Boston, and feeling the necessity of recuperating my weakened forces, I determined to pass the summer of 1848 at some retired and quiet watering-place, where I might be free from the conventional restraints and requirements of what is called "society." Balston, Saratoga, the White Sulphur Springs, Newport, Nahant, and a score of other places, suggested themselves, but were rejected in turn. While pondering on the subject I accidentally met two ex-officers, whose names are historical, and was delighted to learn that they entertained the same desire to rusticate for two or three months. In less than an hour our determination was made upon the recommendation of one who had already passed a season at the hotel already described. The next day, at 10 A.M., we occupied seats in an old-fashioned, jolting equipage, not much easier than an army wagon, but decidedly faster, and by 4 P.M. we were hospitably received by old Norwood, the landlord. Being rather early comers, the best rooms were secured, and we found ourselves ensconced in the loveliest spot on Cape Ann. As it was a strictly temperance establishment, we obtained vinous refreshments from the neighboring town, and then cast about to see how we might improve our comforts, especially as the regular annual visitors began to arrive in considerable squads. Foremost among our devices was the erection of a large and commodious brush house, or bower, to shield us from the sultry sun, while it afforded free passage on all sides for the balmy air, at that time filled with perfume from myriads of wild flowers. Close by — about three hundred yards — was the residence of a remarkable old man named Knowlton. He was about five feet nine inches high, straight as an arrow, with the vigorous, elastic gait of youth. His eyes were clear, glittering, gray; his nose thin, prominent, and curved; his mouth was large, with thin lips, and garnished with strong but well-ground teeth; his chin was square, firm, and rather massive, in comparison with other features; his forehead was of ordinary height and breadth, but his brows were thick, shaggy, and overhanging, making his eyes appear, especially when under any excitement, like live coals in a dark chamber. A thick, wiry, but silver-hued growth of hair covered his well-set head, and there was an air of such absolute indifference of other people's opinions in his manner, that it would have seemed to border on recklessness had he been a young man. A stranger would have placed his age at fifty-five or sixty years, but there was nothing in his demeanor or appearance to warrant such a verdict, except the innumerable wrinkles on his face and forehead, and the blanched whiteness of his hair. Knowlton was a well-to-do farmer, unmarried, and would no more suffer a woman to reside in his house than contract a mortal disease. When questioned on the subject he replied that he had no more objection to women than they had toward each other; but his experience went to show that perfect discipline could not be maintained where a woman had control of the house.

"It ain't in nature," said the old man, "for one woman to live in a house with five men, unless she kin get another woman to keep her company, and when that ere other comes, good-by to all discipline. No, gentlemen, I don't want none of them round my cabin."

In order to build our bower it was necesary to hire Knowlton, with his men and teams, which was done, *nem. con.*, for the trivial sum of ten dollars, the work to be finished in one day, according to specifications ready drawn, and upon a superb grassy spot, about forty yards from the hotel. The bower was to be ready for occupation in forty-eight hours, and to be fitted with ten rustic seats and centre-table, well covered with leafy branches, over which was to be thrown a large but well-worn sail, to prevent the sun from drying up the verdure too soon, and assisting in warding off the heat of his rays. On the morning of the second day we were surprised to see our long-coveted bower in full glory, admirably appointed, and filling all stipulations, on the plat designated. Everyone rushed thither impetuously, and was delighted to find two exquisitely-wrought grass hammocks, hung in true nautical style, and tempting one to enjoy the repose of an afternoon *siesta* in the tropical fashion. From that moment the bower became the chosen retreat of men and women whose names figure prominently in the history of our time. The sun had lost his burning heat for that day, and his radiant beams were falling askant with abated splendor, when old Knowlton made his appearance in the bower. Being well known to all present, he was cordially invited to make one of the party. A pair of "dungaree" trousers, with wide-cut legs and wider terminations, a white shirt, just from his bureau, white socks, neat seal-skin pumps, a dandy Panama hat, flowing black silk cravat, and immense Pongee silk-handkerchief, of many colors, completed his costume. He disdained to wear a coat or jacket in such weather, and the sleeves of his shirt were turned back half way up the forearm, revealing a strong, muscular, and well-strung limb. He evidently believed himself to be in irreproachable costume.

"Mr. Knowlton, we are delighted to see you. Walk in, take a seat, and help yourself to some refreshment. We are much indebted to you for this delicious retreat."

"Thank you, gentle*men*; thank you, kindly! I come to see if the thing suited. You don't owe me nothin'; all was paid fair and square. Ef I ever takes refreshment it's about this time, arter my day's work's done. 'Tis kind of comfortable, ain't it?"

"We find it exceedingly so; but, pray, help yourself; the decanter, glass, and water, stand before you."

"Gentle*men and* ladies, I looks towards you. May you all pass over the ocean of life with fair winds, and never be pooped by the sea of adversity!"

"Have you been long settled here, Mr. Knowlton?"

"I hev lived here forty year, and was fifty-six year old when I settled upon that ere farm," exclaimed the old man, pointing in the direciton of his house.

"What! Do you really mean to say that you are ninety-six years of age?"

"Every day on it. I went to sea forty year afore I come here, and was sixteen year old when I run away from my boss, who was a ship-builder in New York."

"Your life must have been very regular and exemplary; probably you were abstemious in your food, and especially your drink."

"Sartain! I never eat more'n I want, and ginerally limit myself to a quart of New England a day; but I hev seen the time when that much warn't counted worth talking about."

Here was a revelation which nonplussed the sages, shocked the disciples of total abstinence, and filled the ladies with surprise, while the military men present twisted their mustaches and slyly winked at each other.

"You say that you were a sailor for forty years; you must have seen much of the world, Mr. Knowlton."

"Reckon I hev. Many's the ups and downs old Knowlton hes hed, and none the worser for it neither."

"May I ask if you followed any particular line of trade, or did you ramble about indiscriminately?"

"Ramble! I didn't do anything else. I sailed the ocean in every kind of craft, from a first-rate line-of-battle ship to a sloop drogher, and follered all kinds of business, from a regular trader to a 'blackbird catcher,' and from that to a pirate."

"Good heavens! You really do not mean that, Mr. Knowlton. You would not make such assertion if it were true."

"'Vast heavin' and b'lay all for a while, till I tell you more'n you seem to know jes now. There ain't nobody alive nowadays as can prove anything again old Knowlton. No, sir*ree;* whatever I says here might or might not be true, and I reckon it would puzzle you to ketch old Knowlton a-doin' a fool thing at his time of life; but ef you hev a mind to hear a yarn, and the ladies ain't objectionable, I'll spin one for you, and tell you how I come to be a pirate."

"You certainly have no enemies here, Mr. Knowlton, and your life for forty years has been without signal reproach. You are called a good, generous neighbor, and you are not among those who would mislead you under any circumstances. We shall be only too well pleased to hear your narrative."

Knowlton arose, bowed his acknowledgments, gave his trousers a fresh pull, refilled his glass, squared himself in his seat, by "lifts and braces," as he termed it, and gave us the following episode in his eventful career:

"King George of England was King of Ameriky when I run away from old Mark Bolton, ship-builder, New York, and a devil of a life I led with him for two years. His wife was a goodish woman, who used to help out my 'lowance of grub, and parcel over my devilishness to keep old Bolton from boxin' the compass 'bout my ears every time he came home half drunk. Many's the time I'd a gone to bed without a shot in my bread-locker but for the old woman, who, arter Bolton had come to an anchor in his big arm-cheer, would bring me a bait of good meat and bread. But the good old woman was nigh wornout with trouble, and one night she slipped her cable and put to sea upon what parsons call the 'ocean of eternity.' I seed the old woman stowed away all right, and then shipped as cabin-boy aboard a West Injy trader. The skipper took a likin' to me, and showed me all the navigation he knowed, which warn't much, but would answer for the trade he was in. I sailed with Captain Jones three voyages, when he made me second mate. I was then nearly nineteen, and a smart, active lad, able to navigate the brig, and could stow a cargo of sugar or molasses, bilge and bilge, or bilge and cuntlin', 'gainst any man in the trade. Our next trip was to St. Jago de Cuba, where Capt Jones took the yaller fever and slipped his wind. All the crew follered except me, and there was a dozen or more craft lyin' there, without a soul aboard, and their yards playin' Isaac and Josh, whilst their riggin' was full of Irish pennants. Everything was goin' to the devil generally when I said to myself, says I, Knowlton, you ain't easy skeered, not as you knows on; for I knowed that ef I let down a peg I was a goner too; so I kep a stiff upper lip, clapped preventer guys on all my fears, and sailed in as bold as a shark. I hired a nigger crew, loaded the brig with molasses at high freight, and twenty-two days arterward made fast alongside the pier in East River, New York. The cargo sold high, and the owners of the brig talked about the voyage a good deal. I expected to go captain arter that; but they got what we call a 'ship's cousin,' which means a feller what is some near relative to the owner, but don't know nothin' 'bout navigation, nor handlin' a ship, and he was to be my skipper, while I was to be his sailin' master and first mate. Them as likes that ere sort of place kin take it — I didn't; but went and shipped as mate board the brig *Huntress*, Captain Breed, bound for the river Plate. We hed fair grounds and pleasant weather until we sighted the Cape de Verdes, when it commenced squally and rough, with heavy rain storms, contrary gales, and shifting breezes, from all p'ints of the compass, until we got six degrees south of the equator.

"Off Cape St. Roque we got the trades and went bowling along into the mouth of the Plate; but when we got off Maldonado P'int it fell dead calm, and as the ebb was runnin' strong we down killock and let her mull until we got a breeze. We hadn't been to an anchor more'n four hours when we seed a white cloud comin' off the northern shore, and it come so fast that we furled the light sails and clewed the others close, Perhaps you won't believe me when I tell you it was only a great army of big white butterflies, as long as my little finger and covered all over with down. Heaps of 'em come aboard us, and covered the decks fore and aft, and they was so thick that we swept up and hove overboard more'n three bushel of 'em. About half an hour arterward the butterflies was follered by the darndest lot of devil's darnin'-needles you can think of. There wasn't a piece of runnin' riggin', nor a reef nettle in the brig that was't fringed with them as thick as they could stow. By and by we heard a dreadful roaring from the north shore and seed the water a clear feather white; then we knowed that the devil was to pay. Afore we could git things snug the gale struck us, and capsized the *Huntress* as clean as a whistle. The tide was about half ebb and runnin' strong, and only five on us got back to the brig. Afore we could cut away her masts to right her, we had taken in so much water that she was a-sinkin' fast. We cut adrift a spare topmast and took to that, takin' care to git away from the brig as soon as possible. Soon arterwards she went down head first, and we was spicked up by a guardy costa which carried us into Monte Video.

"Talk about thunder and lightnin'! you never seed any and never will until you catch a pampero in the river Plate. I hev seed as many as four different streaks of lightnin' at the same time, and you couldn't hear yourself speak for the thunder. I hev been in typhoons, levanters, harricanes, and all sorts of gales, but fur spitefulness there ain't nothin' like a pampero. Captain Breed, the second mate, and four of the crew was lost along with the *Huntress*. I hed fifty dollars in gold in a belt 'round my waist, and when we got to Monte Video three on us shipped by the run aboard an English bark bound to Rio, where we arrived forty days arterward. One night I was a-settin' in a little out the way place I hed diskivered, a-drinkin' a glass of grog and smokin' my pipe, when a strange sailor chap comes in, and arter lookin' around a bit, comes to an anchor alongside of me, and says quite offhand: 'Shipmate your grog is out; fill up again at my expense and let us take a fresh observation.' 'Aye, aye,' says I, 'with all my heart.' So we took several snifters together, and in course of time got to understand one another's bearin's. Arter I hed spun him my yarn, he says to me:

"'How would you like to go a blackbird ketchin'?'

"'What's that?' says I.

"'Why, goin' to the Guinea coast for niggers,' he answers right plump and plain, for you see that sort of thing was all the go them days.

"'There is heavy merchants in Boston now whose fathers got their fust start that way. Ain't it strange that whot is right one time is wrong another?'

"'What the terms?' I axed him.

"'One hundred dollars a month wages, and five dollars a head bounty for every nigger that comes in alive,' says he.

"'I'm your man,' I answered straight, 'and you kin meet me here to-morrow night at eight o'clock.'

"'Wall,' says he, 'you told me you hed two messmates in Rio, and if you kin git them to ship I will give you twenty-five dolars apiece bounty.'

"I hed no trouble in gettin' 'em, and we all went to Pernambuco, where we found the brig *Cruiser*, Captain Leonard, bound for the Guinea coast on a tradin' voyage. She was a large and handsome-lookin' craft, built in Spain, and a fast sailer. She carried a crew of sixty men and hed six twelve-pounder carronades — three on a side — and a long twenty-four on a pivot amidships. Forty days arter we left Pernambuco we hed on board about five hundred likely niggers, and was a-layin' our course for the Brazils with all sail set. Things went along first rate until the ninth day out, when the lookout aloft sung out: 'Sail, ho!'

"'Where away?' says the captain.

"'Three p'ints off the weather bow, sir,' answers the man.

"'What does he look like?' axed the skipper.

"'She is a large, full-rigged brig, standin' this way, sir,' answers the lookout.

"We was a-runnin' nearly due west, and hed the breeze from the southeast on our port quarter, while the stranger was comin' along with the wind nearly abeam and forgin' through the water hand over hand. In half an hour he wa'n't more'n two mile from us. I noticed he kept fallin' off all the time, like he wanted to cut us off. I hed the wheel, and so I makes bold to say to Captain Leonard:

"'Ef you please sir, there is somethin' about that ere feller that I don't like the looks on.'

"'What is it?' says he.

"'When we fust seed him,' says I, 'he was headin' abot northest, and now he lies off to north by west, and the wind ain't changed a bit.'

"With that the skipper snatches up his glass, and after takin' a good look, he sings out:

"'Port the helm; keep her dead afore it, Mr. Black! Crowd every inch of canvas.'

"But 'twas no use; the stranger follered suit and come up with us hand over hand. When he got within range of eight hundred yards, he yawed three p'ints to port and let go a couple of feelers which made kindlin' wood of our main topgallant mast, and brought all above down by the run. At the same time he h'isted the black flag with the death's head and cross bones. He hed twelve long twelve-pounder guns and a pivot thirty-two pounder amidship. His decks was crowded with men; but we agreed to fight it out to the bitter end. The hatches was on, and the niggers all fastened down; the guns cast loose and manned, ammunition served and the ball set rollin' in earnest. 'Twas the fust fight I ever was in, but not the last, by a darned sight. We fought all we could, but the pirate picked his distance and let into us fearful. More'n half the crew was killed, besides a good many wounded. Two of our guns hed been knocked kitin', and Captain Leonard was bad hurt. There was nothin' else to do but to haul down the flag and surrender. You must remember that all this ere took place seventy-five years ago when slavin' was almost considered good, lawful business, and when the Spanish main swarmed with pirates. You oughter to hev seen them fellers board us arter our flag was hauled down. The fust thing they did was to iron every man of us, then they took off the hatches and commenced sendin' the niggers aboard their vessel. Our between decks was a sight — more'n a hundred niggers hed been killed by the pirate's shot, and a heap more hurt; but over three hundred were found alive, although half dead with fear and confinement, for the poor devils didn't know what *was* up. All the niggers as was bad hurt was left aboard; but everybody else alive, and everything worth havin', was carried aboard the pirate brig, which was named the *Shark*. The *Cruiser* was a-sinkin' fast, and went down starn fust in less than twenty minutes afterwards. I expected every minute they would make short work with us; but they didn't seem to hurry about it, just then. When Captain Leonard stepped aboard the pirate her captain stood on the weather quarter and says:

"'Welcome aboard the *Shark*. I reckon on your niggers is worth nigh a quarter of a million to us.'

"Captain Leonard spoke up, and said: 'I'm bad hurt; hev you got a doctor aboard?'

"'Yes,' says the pirate; 'I'll cure you. Doctor, come here!'

"The hail was answered by the cook — a great big nigger, who came up laughin', and says: 'What's to be done, sar?'

"'The captain of the cruiser requires your professional services; see what you kin do for him.'

"The darkey went up to our skipper, and axed him 'ef there was any one among us who knowed how to navigate.' Captain Leonard pointed to

-340-

me—for Mr. Black had been killed—and told the pirate cook I was a good navigator; and he no sooner got the words out of his mouth, than the cook lifted him up like a child and flung him over the weather quarter. We all had irons upon us, and Captain Leonard soon sunk from sight in the clear blue water. Then the pirate captain said to me: 'Kin you navigate?'

"'Yes, sir,' says I.

"'Will you navigate the *Shark*, and take a chance with us, or will you foller your skipper?' says he.

"'I ain't ready to take more salt water 'n my stomach will bear just now,' says I, 'and might as well make the best of this bargain.'

"'Spoke like a man,' he said; and then turning to the rest of our crew as was left alife and sound—the wounded ones being hove overboard—he axed them 'ef they would jine, because,' said he, 'you killed and wounded a lot of my fellows, and I want to keep a full crew.' There was no refusal on the part of the men; and the captain, who was named Simpson—a big, double-fisted chap, give the order to cast 'em loose, and take 'em into the forecastle, while he ordered me to take the forward port state-room in the cabin. You see, his mate had been killed in the action; and as he was the on-ly man aboard as knowed anything about navigation, my life was spared to fill his place for the time bein'. 'Lay her course for St. Jago de Cuba,' he said to me next day, and I did so. In course of time we got in all safe and sound. Simpson took the cruiser's papers ashore; passed the custom house all right, and sold the niggers for a average of about four hundred dollars apiece. We then up anchor, and stood for Samana, in San Dominger, where we had a great spree which lasted ten days. By this time I managed to get the weather side of Simpson, and he told me how he had murdered the first captain of the *Shark*, and took his place; but as he couldn't navigate the vessel, he pitched upon me for that sarvice. I ventured to ax him what he did with his wounded men, as I never seed any of 'em aboard. 'Pitched 'em all over-board,' he said. 'I can't afford to have a hospital on the *Shark.*' We cruised for more'n ten months, taking eight prizes in that time; a-burnin' and scut-tlin' the vessels, and makin' all aboard them 'walk the plank.' I was afeared to raise any conspiracy, because Simpson had a lot of spies amongst the crew, and they told him all that was goin' on, and he blowed out the brains of four or five men for almost nothin' at all; and told the rest that there would be just so much more prize-money to divide amongst them. One arternoon, about four o'clock, we was in the Caribbean Sea, watchin' out for traders, when we sighted a large ship, dead to windward, and under easy sail. 'That kind of looks suspicious,' says Simpson.

"'How so?' I asked.

"'Because,' says he, 'ef that feller was a merchantman he would be makin' the most of this ere fresh trade; but he don't seem to be any ways in a hurry.'

"Soon arter we seed that she was a ship-of-war, and Simpson crowded all sail to git away; but the ship amediately follered suit, sending out all his fly-ing kites and stunsails, and we knowed by the way he rose from the water tha he was gaining gradually.

"'Ef he don't come too close afore dark,' says Simpson, 'I think we can get clear of him. A starn chase is a long one, and in three hours night will shet down.'

"'But there will be nearly full moon to-night.'

"'Blast you,' says he, 'you're the navigator, and ef you don't git me out of this ere scrape I'll blow your brains out.'

"'Captain Simpson, says I, 'there ain't but one way as I knows on, and that is, to cripple his spars with our long thirty-two so soon as he gets within range.'

"About sundown we could see the bone he was fetchin' in his teeth, and then I knowed it was all up with the pirate. Half an hour arterwards Simpson trained the thirty-two and fired; but the shot didn't seem to hit. Just then the sloop yawed two or three p'ints and sent three messengers, one arter the other, at us, the third one takin' our main royal mast clean off; but as we was runnin' dead afore the wind it did not make much difference, as the fore one drawed all the better. We found out, howsomever, that the sloop had heavier metal and more of it, which wasn't a pleasant reflection to Captain Simpson. About half-past nine o'clock the sloop was within a quarter of mile, and roundin' to give us a broadside, which sent the splinters flyin' in all directions and made our scuppers red. I looked 'round for Captain Simpson, and found him flat on deck with a bad hurt in his head. He had been knocked senseless by a splinter, but wasn't serious damaged. That was my chance; so I called three or four men to come aft and help take the captain below. We laid him on the transom lockers, and I sent the men away to the guns, and soon as they was gone I clapped a pair of handcuffs on Simpson, and lashed his legs together, and then made him fast to a couple of ringbolts on the cabin floor so he couldn't help himself. All this time the sloop was a-pourin' it into us, and the pirate crew was answerin' the best they could. Among the men was one of my old shipmates I got to go blackbird catchin' in the *Cruiser,* and when I went on deck again I sung out for Tom Jackson and another man named Dick Brown. They came aft, and I says to them:

"Lads, you see how things is goin'; ef we get catched here we are bound to swing, but ef you hev a mind to save yourselves just put a breaker or two of water and a bag of biscuit in that starboard quarter boat, then get into her, cast off the falls, and lower away easy. No one will see or hear you in this rumpus and we kin git away in the dark.'

"In the meantime I kept encouragin' the crew to fight on and never give up the ship, a-tellin' 'em that ef they could only cripple the sloop we might yet git off with flyin' colors; and they did fight like wild tigers, for every man knowed there was a halter about his neck. The two men did as I told 'em, and steadily lowered away the boat, which was then under shelter, as I had put the help to starboard and we was then goin' with our port broadside to the sloop. Seein' everything all right, I got hold of the fall and was lowerin' myself away roundly, when I heard Captain Simpson roarin' and cursin' like thunder. 'Cast off,' says I, 'and let her fall astern.' In a few minutes we was a hundred yards clear of the *Shark*, and then we took to our oars, but we heard the roar of guns for several minutes arterwards. Next day we made Virgin Gorda, where we went ashore, and told the people that we had abandoned the brig *Cruiser*, which sprung a leak and foundered, and that the rest had gone on to St. Thomas in the long-boat, which was fitted out with a sail and plenty of grub. Two days arterward we shipped in a drogher for Kingston, Jamaica, and got there just in time to see Captain Simpson and twenty-two of his men hanged for piracy. The British sloop-of-war *Brisk* hed captured the *Shark*. I took care, howsomever, to keep a good lot of doubloons when I left the pirate, and with that ere money I bought my farm below there, and never went to sea arterwards."

The Story of a Survivor

by J.C. Cremony

January 1869

In the winter of 1849, the northeastern coast of America was visited by one of the most destructive gales recorded in the history of that section. From Prince Edward's Island to Montauk Point, the whole coast was strewn with wrecks. More than one hundred sail, large and small, went to pieces on the eastern and northern shores of Price Edward's Island alone; and the schooner of − − −, to which I then belonged, was of the number. I was among those who were saved; and six weeks subsequently, I shipped on board the bark *Jeanette,* of Westport, Captain Hosmer, for a whaling voyage in the South Pacific and Indian Oceans. The vessel was ready to sail when I joined; and on the twenty-second of January, we put to sea with a full crew. The voyage out was pleasant; and as we coasted down past the Atlantic shores of South America, we succeeded in getting three sperm whales, which put us in practice, and raised our spirits to a hopeful pitch. We had reached the Indian Ocean, somewhere in the latitude of New Holland; but as I did not keep the ship's reckoning, I cannot tell the exact location. The bark was under easy sail on a wind — the look-outs in the "crows' nests," and the crew employed in the normal avocations of a whaler — when on the twenty-second of July, just six months from the date of leaving Westport, the man on the main topmast cross-trees, sung out: "There she blows!" A fine school of sperm whale was observed on our port quarter, about three miles off. The sea was as smooth as glass; scarcely a ripple stirred its grand and solemn surface. The huge monsters were disporting themselves with the frolic of children just let out of school; but with the majesty of power and intensified vitality. Here and there the white, straight columns of water, curling gracefully forward, were ejected from their massive fronts; and every now and then one, more playful than the rest, leaped his whole enormous bulk from the foaming brine, to which it returned with a splash that sounded like the violent submerging of a promontory. The still greater animal — man — was watching these demonstrations with unfeigned delight: not with the relish of a naturalist, but with the intense gaze of the hunter — the glee of a miser who sees money within his grasp. In a moment the captain, mate, and second mate had their boats lowered, manned, equipped, and racing for the coveted prize. I belonged to Captain

Hosmer's boat; had the midship oar; and we were well in the lead: but the second mate's boat overtook and passed us, and was the first among the mammoth school. The officer stood forward—the harpoon ready in his practised hands; he raised it, and, with one powerful effort, fixed the barbed iron deep into the quivering side of a huge "bull." For a few seconds the warp flew around the "loggerhead" like lightning, and then stopped. "He has turned," cried the second mate," and will soon be upon us; so, look out!" Scarcely had the words been uttered, when the monster, with the widely-extended jaws, rushed upon the devoted boat, and seizing it between his massive teeth, reduced it to fragments—the men leaping far and wide each with his oar, to escape the dreadful gulf. Our boat pulled up rapidly, as did the mate's, and each took half of the second mate's crew—that officer going in the mate's boat. Again the chase was prosecuted with even more zeal than before. It was an object to get the "bull" which had been struck, as our iron and all the warp were still fast to his bleeding body. Presently he was seen not far off, and we immediately pulled for him. Again did the deadly iron find its way to his vitals, when hurled by the captain's hand; but the fellow's courage had been signally cooled, and after a sharp run, he gave in, when we administered the lance, and killed him.

"Good for ninety barrels, sure," exclaimed Captain Hosmer, as he took a leisurely survey of this behemoth. We turned him, took him in tow and made for the bark, expecting that the mate would pursue another whale; but instead of so doing, he laid his boat for the *Jeanette*, which was about a mile to leeward. Captain Hosmer could not understand this style of tactics, and expressed some surprise that Mr. Bennett had not followed and got another whale, several of which were not far distant. We had got within a mile of the bark, when to our intense astonishment she squared away before the wind, which was now blowing a six-knot breeze, spread all canvas and rapidly disappeared from view. What could be the meaning of this astounding conduct? Why had Mr. Bennett left his captain and nine of his crew upon the friendless ocean? Captain Hosmer tried vainly to repress the fears and anguish which at that moment agitated his mind. He endeavored to account for Mr. Bennett's course in a variety of ways, but that very variety was demoralizing. At length it became too evident that the mate had deserted us and gone off with the bark, leaving us to perish upon the broad bosom of the deep.

Three hours afterward the sun set and night fell, and with it the breeze, leaving a dead calm. "Men," said the captain, the *Jeanette* cannot be more than fourteen or fifteen miles away; she was steering east-southeast an hour before sunset, and cannot have altered her course in this calm; let us cut away the whale and pull for the bark, for I think we can catch her by midnight, unless the wind blows up; so cut away the whale, double bank the oars as much as possible, and give way with a will." The monstrous carcass we had been towing was immediately sent adrift, and each one bent to his oar with firm resolve. It was a pull for life. The night was cloudless, but no moon "o'er the dark her silver mantle threw." Bright and lustrous stars were reflected from the passive ocean; our boat rushed through the water impelled by the strong arms of nine stalwart men, endeavoring to save themselves from agonizing death. Her bows were crested with silver foam, and in her wake glowed lurid sparks, while the rapidly dipping oars, with their long, steady sweep, turned up myriads of scintillations, as if a host of fire-flies had been suddenly disturbed. On, on we pulled in the direction taken by the *Jeanette* until daylight broke upon us, when we stopped, laid upon our oars, and scanned the fast-coming horizon. In vain did we turn our anxious gaze in every direction. There was nothing framed by man in sight. Not a breath of air rippled over the boundless waste of waters; not a bird nor a fish broke the awful solitude. Up rose the sun, flaming, angry, merciless. A small beaker of water was in the boat, but it had been half emptied during the preceding night of trial and anxiety. Captain Hosmer immediately charged himself with the care of this desperately coveted beverage, to be doled out in regular rations to each man, no one receiving more than enough to moisten his parching lips and burning tongue. Then commenced that long sequence of unutterable horrors, compared to which all other human ills seem trivial. There were ten men in the boat, and the third day had come with the same lurid sun glaring upon us with relentless fury. At the captain's suggestion each man soaked himself in sea water, which seemed to afford some very slight relief; but our garments soon dried in that furnace-like heat, leaving a crust of salt all over our bodies, so that the experiment had to be constantly repeated. It is needless to describe the increasing anguish and torment suffered by that wretched crew as day after day came and went, leaving us still upon the glassy deep, which had begun to look more like molten lead than water. We were then so exhausted that all further effort to make way was out of the question. The pangs of hunger had become demoniacal, and men glared at each other with cannibal gaze and intent. Each felt what the others thought. We began to realize that one must die that the rest might live. Strange it was, that in the midst of this indescribable agony of mind and body, no one thought of committing suicide; no one contemplated self-sacrifice, but with insane despair seemed to prefer being killed and eaten. Psychologists may explain this extraordinary fact; I cannot. The love of life was still the ruling principle, and we clung to it with desperation.

"Oh, my God!" exclaimed the captain, "if we had not cut away that whale we might have been content." These were terrible words. They at once imparted a renewed sense of hunger which could not be appeased without food — food of some kind, no matter what. Among the crew was a Malay; a wonderfully active and vigorous man, with the agility of the tiger-cat and the muscular power of an anaconda. His savage eyes glittered like those of a basilisk as he proposed that we should draw lots to determine who should be immolated. Everyone at first recoiled with unfeigned horror; but in a few minutes the proposition familiarized itself to our minds, and in one hour it was adopted. An express stipulation was made to except the captain, who resisted the motion, but finally consented, as he was the only navigator among us, and the greatest sufferer. Our commander cut small slivers of different lengths from a harpoon-staff, and presented their ends while concealing their length in his hand, bade each one draw, the one pulling the shortest sliver to die. We were paralyzed. Had it really come to this? Perhaps in ten minutes after the victim had been sacrificed a vessel might heave in sight, and rescue us from so horrible a condition. Perhaps a storm might arise and destroy all hands. Perhaps some stray porpoise or other fish might come within the reach of our harpoons or grains. We hesitated, and agreed to defer the ordeal until after nightfall, for the double reason of waiting until the last hope was gone, and of securing the sacrifice as cool as possible when no other resource was left. Eight o'clock P.M. came full soon. The moon was riding in the heavens, and reflected from the vast mirror of the ocean. Slowly, and with suffocating trepidation, we approached the captain to draw our lots. His hands and frame shook as with an ague. One by one, with lank jaws, cavernous eyes and gaunt frames, we stretched forth our palsying fingers and selected our bits of wood. Not a word was spoken, but the commander, with the index of doom, pointed out the victim. Ten short minutes were given him to prepare for the awful change from life to death; from this world, with its attendant horrors, to the "undiscovered bourne." While engaged in commending himself to the throne of grace, and preparing to go where "the weary are at rest," he was knocked on the head from behind, and quickly dispatched with repeated blows — care being taken to shed no drop of blood. That was our first sacrifice to selfishness; but we were not in possession of rational faculty. The capacity to judge clearly and dispassionately had been lost. Our manhood had been taken from us, and we were but beasts of prey — the mere animal man. After two or three days, the same horrible ceremony was repeated, and again and again, until four of our number had succumbed.

Our fifth drawing was postponed longer than usual, for there seemed to be a reäwakened hope of rescue. It came not. Once more the captain held forth the fatal slivers, and the Malay drew the shortest. This was at five o'clock in the afternoon, and the time of sacrifice would not arrive until eight o'clock P.M. My feeble powers of description can give you no adequate idea of how the Malay's eyes glittered; of the foam which covered his lips; of the writhings his frame underwent; of the manner in which he gnashed his teeth, and howled like a wolf. These extreme expressions of unmitigated agony were beginning to operate in his favor, and elicit some tokens of compassion; but they were soon turned to hate and loathing. The after, or stroke oar, was propelled by a lad not over seventeen years of age. He had been the most heroic and uncomplaining of the crew. He was a meek, active, intelligent boy, who had won the favor of all, and we had unanimously determined that his life should be saved, if within our power. Seven o'clock arrived, The Malay was at the forward oar. One or two "heavers," short, heavy, thick, were lying under his thwart, and the captain saw him quietly reach down and arm himself with one. Suspecting some villainy, the commander quietly unshipped a lance and placed it by his side, ready for use. Half an hour passed, when the Malay, with the bound of a tiger, leaped over the intervening thwarts and made a desperate blow at the boy's head. As he sprang aft, Captain Hosmer raised his foot and kicked the boy off his thwart, causing the Malay's aim to miss its mark, and at the same instant drove the lance deep into his chest. The would-be murderer fell, and was instantly killed and shared out among the survivors. Hunger had been somewhat appeased, and we killed each other not so much for flesh as to moisten our mouths with the blood, which, although hot at first, soon cooled upon the lips and tongue, especially as a refreshing breeze had sprung up two days before the Malay's death. The sky had become overcast and threatened a storm. Water! water! Anything for water. The dreadful, the indescribable gnawings of hunger are feeble in comparison to the want of water. Oh! that the Majesty above would vouchsafe a rain storm, that we might drink, and not perish of thirst.

It was not so ordained. The clouds passed away and left us once more under the glowing firmanent. It was more than human nature could bear, and one of our number died under the infliction. His body was made fast to a rope and trolled for two days, in the hope of calling up a shark; but no such good fortune awaited us. Those who still cling to the belief that sharks will instinctively follow a vessel, on board of which some member is soon to die, may rest assured of its fallacy. We would have given worlds to have seen any of those voracious monsters at any time during our horrible sufferings. On the morning of the third day we cut our dead shipmate adrift, and again resigned ourselves to whatever fate might be in store. Only four of the original ten remained alive, viz.: the captain, the lad, one messmate and myself. It had been my fortune to escape so far, and only two of us were left to draw lots. Six days had passed since we shared the Malay, and we had been two days without food. There we lay, rocking silently upon great deep. The moon had come and gone, and was beginning to come again. Thirty-four days had been passed in this awful struggle for life. Not a drop of water had refreshed our systems after the second day; not a fish nor bird had been seen in all that terrible period. We had ceased to be human, and more resembled beasts of prey. Deep-sunk, bloodless eyes; gaunt, shrivelled and emaciated frames; lolling, swollen tongues, and trembling limbs; faces covered with thin, scraggy beards; nails like claws, and stained with human blood, may give a faint idea of how we looked, except that there was a fiendish, inexpressible glare about the eyes which spoke volumes. Our voices had been reduced to hoarse whispers; the power of utterance was nearly exhausted; men no longer spoke to each other, but conversed reluctantly by sluggish signs. Yet the desire to prolong life rose above all other considerations. It was for that we had killed and eaten our fellow men. It was for that we had undergone indescribable tortures of mind and body. It was for that we still hoped and struggled against an almost positive fate. As the next day dawned upon the cloudless ocean, although a gentle breeze fanned the waters, Captain Hosmer signalled us to come aft. In a hardly audible whisper he said: "Let us agree to die together like men. Let us have no more of this dreadful cannibalism. If we are to perish, it is God's holy will, and we should submit without rebelliousness. All proper measures should be adopted to secure life, if possible; but we have been sinful and selfish beyond ordinary parallel. Should we escape, our lives will become one harrowing grief for the deeds we have done in this boat; and if we do not survive, to what end will have been all the evil we have done?"

Freely each person reached out his hand, and grapsing that of our noble commander, acquiesced in his views, and solemnly pledged ourselves to their fulfillment. The thirty-fifth day came, and we had resigned ourselves to die, either by the slow and ineffable torture of famine, or by a hasty plunge into the deep. At ten o'clock A.M. a sail was descried to the westward, standing directly toward us with a fair wind. With all the haste our captain could command, he tore the ragged remnant of his shirt from his shoulders, and made it fast to a lance-staff. This was stepped in the mast-hole, and required the united strength of two men to keep it steady and upright. On came the ship, until within a mile of us; she hoisted her ensign in token of having seen us. We tried to shout, but could not; we tried to dance, and fell down exhausted; we tried to laugh, and wept from fountains long seared; we attempted to clutch each other's hands, and only succeeded in making convulsed motions. Presently the ship rounded to, just to windward, lowered and manned her boat and sent it to our succor. Then the long-sustained tension gave way and we all fell lifeless. When next I awoke to consciousness, I found myself on board the English ship *Malabar*, bound from Liverpool to Sydney. Every kindness and attention were shown us, and three days afterward we landed in Sydney, the shadowy wrecks of our former selves.

Buried Alive in the Sea

by Percival

January 1869

In the year 1840, I was serving as a midshipman on board the United States frigate *St. Lawrence*, then cruising in the Pacific. The *St. Lawrence* carried a crew of six hundred men—Americans, Irishmen, and men belonging to every nationality under the sun. The majority of them had passed the best days of their lives in the service, and were imbued with all the superstitions so common to their calling, thirty years ago. It was often my fortune to hear weird yarns of the sea told by men who believed every word of them, to comrades who scarcely dared to move while they listened. Some of the older sailors could, in dark, stormy nights, make the hair of a whole watch, including their own, stand on end—with their tales of seas that gave up their dead, and of ships that were haunted. On one of these occasions Larry McBlather, captain of the forecastle, spoke as follows:

"When I sailed on the *Sabine*, she was haunted, an' this is the way it happened. Ye see, it was a dark, stormy night just like this, an' the men were sent out to furl the flying jib. The captain of the forecastle was stowin' the head of the sail, an' all of a sudden he said to the man next to him: 'It blows hard, Jack;' an' then cut his throat, an' fell overboard an' was lost. Ever after that, of a dark, stormy night, when the men went out to furl the flying jib they would see a man sittin' on the end of the boom, an' he would say: 'It blows hard, Jack'; an' cut his throat, an' fall overboard."

Just as Larry finished, a voice which seemed to proceed out of the air overhead, remarked: "It blows hard, Jack." In an instant those who were not frightened too much to move were on their feet, and holding on to the rigging to keep their tottering legs from letting them down.

"Did ye hear that, Harry Blower?" asked McBlather, as soon as he had recovered himself enough to speak.

"Yes, I heerd it," replied Harry; "and like all yer other bloody ghosts, it wasn't a ghost, but the parrot, that said it."

"Man the flying-jib downhaul, clear away the halliards—haul down!—Layout, and curl the flying jib!" These orders were issued by the officer of the deck; but there was hesitation displayed by all whose duty it was to obey them. In the mean time McBlather turned to Blower, and said: "Now, Harry, I believe in ghosts—you don't. I hasn't the pluck to lead the men out on the flying jib-boom; I would be sure to see a man on the end of it. You have the pluck, an' you wouldn't see a man: therefore, Harry, will yez do me the favor to lead the men out?"

Harry Blower replied: "Larry, you're an idiot, a fool, and an ass. And ghost or no ghost, I don't lay out on the flying jib-boom, to-night."

"Come! Lay out there, you lubbers, and furl the flying jib. What are you about?" came from the quarter-deck, in a voice that smacked of a cat-o'-nine-tails and a dozen on the bare back.

In an instant the lubbers were scrambling out, led by McBlather.

"Do you hear anything, Larry?" inquired Terence Malone, who was the next man on the inside.

"No, blast ye," replied Larry; "and if you hear anything, don't let on ye hear it. Don't tell me ye hear it; and I warn ye not to show me anything ye see."

The sail was furled in short order; and the men "laid in," each one trying to get ahead of the other.

In a little while the watch was scattered about the decks — some to sleep, some to discuss the events of the evening, or any other subject which happened to interest them.

"I say, Jack," remarked Terence Malone, "they ought to git Simon Gobble out of the ship. He's been a pirate an' a murderer, an' the divil knows what. He swings close to me, you know; an' the other night jist as I was fallen into a doze, I felt something catch me by the arm. I sprung up in me hammock, an' there was Simon Gobble a sittin' up in his, and he was a sayin': 'Leave me; why do ye haunt me? Leave me, I say.' And his eyes were closed; and his ugly ould face looked so white, I thought it was dead. I tell ye, Jack, I niver was frightened so bad in all me life as I was thin; an' it didn't take me long to turn out uv me hammock. You may be sure I slept on a soft plank the rest uv the night, an' I've been a doin' uv it ever since. I wouldn't sleep along side uv that man agin for all the gold uv Peru. Did ever you see such a awful cold, sharky eye as he's got? And then his face is jist like the face uv one of the divils I used to see when I had the horrors. Mark me, Jack, if iver this ship comes to grief, it will be through Simon Gobble."

"Poor fellow," replied Jack, "I pity him. Sometimes he never speaks to anyone, and no one ever speaks to him. In all the ship there is not one man he can call his friend — and yet no one does his duty better. But then he has such strange ways about him; and there is hardly a man in the ship that he hasn't frightened out of his wits. We ought to try to be more friendly."

"Friendly? Is it friendly you mane. Bad luck to him; he'd better niver try to be friendly with me."

"That's what the men all say, and it's not fair; they should give the man a chance."

"He don't deserve a chance; an' I tell ye, Jack, he has done something awful. If the dead could spake, they would tell us terrible stories about Simon Gobble. Jist before you joined the ship, we were caught in a hurricane. All hands were called to reef top-sails. I was on the maintop-sail yard, and Gobble was at the weather earing. Well, all at once there was a long flash of red lightning, an Gobble gave a yell that made ev'ry body turn pale. The men on deck an' the men on the yard looked, an' there on the yard-arm, right behind Gobble, was a man with his throat cut from ear to ear, an' the blood streaming down his breast."

"Terence Malone, I never saw such a bloody set of Irishmen as there is on board this ship. When I joined her, I was not afraid of the 'Old Harry' himself; but now I don't dare to go about in the dark, unless someone is with me. Every time I go aloft in the night, I don't dare to look around me for fear of seeing a ghost. For all that though, Terence, I never believed in ghosts, and I don't believe in them now. But I've got the panics, and so I'm just as much afraid as anybody."

About this time the other watch was called. Terence turned in on his soft plank, and his friend Jack turned into his hammock — both to pleasant dreams, it is to be hoped. In a few days the *St. Lawrence* arrived at Tahiti, where she was visited by a large number of ladies and gentlemen, principally missionaries and their families. One day a beautiful little girl was standing on the edge of an empty chest, and leaning over the iron rail around the poop deck, watching a school of sharks that were hanging around the ship. Suddenly the child's feet slipped from under her, and to the horror of all, she rolled overboard.

In an instant Simon Gobble, who had been seizing a ratline in the mizzen rigging, threw overboard the chest and then leaped after it, fairly lighting among the sharks. With one arm and a long sharp knife he kept off the sharks, while with the other he placed the child in the empty chest, where no shark could harm her. He now gave all his attention to the hungry monsters that surrounded him, and, to the surprise of everyone, was picked up by a boat which was sent to his assistance, with only two slight wounds — one in the side and one in the arm. He wished to place the little girl he had saved so gallantly in her mother's arms himself, but nothing could induce the child to go near him, and she would shrink away with a frightened look if he attempted to approach her. This was a terrible blow to poor Gobble, and he said: "I might as well be dead, as living and what I am. There is a curse upon me, and I have never done anything to deserve a curse. It is too hard — too hard!"

From the moment he saved the little girl, Simon Gobble was a hero in the estimation of the officers; but the men ascribed his success to the interposition of the devil, and from that time believed him to be in regular communication with the evil one. They dreaded him, if anything, more than ever, and Simon Gobble was as much alone on the crowded decks of the *St. Lawrence* as he would have been in the midst of the desert of Sahara. In a week we sailed for Valparaiso, and four days afterwards were struggling for existence in the track of a hurricane.

One night Simon Gobble and Terence Malone were stationed at the life buoys. I was midshipman of the quarter-deck, and Terence came to me and said: "If Simon Gobble is to remain at one of the life buoys, sir, I respectfully ax to be relieved. I haven't got the pluck to stay, sir." I relieved Gobble and sent another man in his place. Shortly afterwards I walked forward to speak to the officer of the forecastle. On my way there I heard a veritable sob. The sob came from the aching heart of Simon Gobble. I told him to cheer up, and asked him to come aft and have a talk with me. He replied that he "felt too bad to talk with anybody, but that some other time he would like to tell me his history." Poor fellow, the next morning he was found black and dead in his hammock. The ship was rolling and pitching at such a terrible rate, that it was impossible for the surgeon to examine into the cause of his death; but he determined to wait a little while in hopes that the hurricane might abate. Night came in, but there was no change for the better. It was observed that the body of Gobble was turning white rapidly, but this did not excite any particular comment at the time.

The order was given to prepare the body for burial, and it was immediately sewed up in a hammock with a sixty-four pound shot at the feet. It was then placed between a couple of guns, where it was intended to let it remain until daylight. The men seemed to be gathered in groups all over the ship, and to be discussing some subject very earnestly. One of the officers happened to overhear them, and the impression left upon his mind was, that they would rather go down with the ship than go aloft with the body of Gobble on board. This was quietly reported to the captain, and he gave orders to bury the corpse without delay.

It was nine o'clock at night and pitchy dark. The wind howled and shrieked through the rigging as I never wish to hear it again. Occasionally a deafening crash of thunder would burst upon our ears, or a flash of lurid lightning would illumine the sea for miles around. The gallant old ship in her struggles with the waves pitched and rolled until every timber moaned and quivered. In the midst of all, everyone was startled by the order—"All hands bury the dead!"—passed by the boatswain in a full, clear voice. Then his mates stationed about the ship, one by one, took up the order and repeated: "All hands bury the dead!"

The corpse was carried up to the gangway and placed on a plank ready for launching. The men huddled together forward of the gangway, and the officers assembled just abaft it. When everything was ready, the chaplain commenced to read the burial service, but occasionally the thunder would be so loud and long that he would have to stop and wait until it was over, before he could be heard. Then again a lurid flash of lightning would blind him so completely, that he could not see to read until after the effect of the lightning had passed away. At such times the eyes of all were so strangely affected that everything assumed a weird, unnatural shape. The faces of the ship's people looked like faces of the dead. The corpse seemed to move and to glare at us through its canvas coffin, and the St. Lawrence herself looked like a phantom ship. One man touched another to attract his attention, but

-353-

he did not dare to look around to see what it was that touched him. Somebody's hat blew out of his hand, and it struck Larry McBlather in the face. Larry sank to the deck in a fainting condition, and none of the others dared to move. They pretended to know nothing about the misery of poor Larry. As the chaplain read—"Now, therefore, we commit the body of our deceased brother to the deep"—the corpse was launched. And as it was launched a shriek, so wild and terrible that it chilled the very marrow in our bones, burst upon our ears, and then the faint echo of another shriek that was hushed forever in the seething, roaring waters, rose upon the gale. Simon Gobble had been in a trance, and we had buried him alive!

The hurricane lasted seven days. On the morning of the seventh it commenced to abate, and toward evening it was almost calm. In the afternoon an immense shark was observed to follow the ship. The men all said it was the spirit of Simon Gobble. However, the shark followed the ship for three days and three nights, when the wind fell to a dead calm. One of the midshipmen decided to "fish for Gobble," as the shark was called, and in less than an hour he was triced up over a scuttle on board the *St. Lawrence* ready for dissection.

Larry McBlather, who felt ashamed of his conduct on the night of the burial, volunteered his services to the midshipman, who wanted the shark's backbone for a cane. Larry commenced by cutting the shark's belly open from the tip of his nose to the end of his tail, and then, as is customary on such occasions, reached into his stomach to find what was there. The men were all interested spectators, and were cracking all kinds of jokes at poor Gobble's expense. Larry sung out to trice up a little on the shark. As they did so, he pulled something out of the shark's stomach—that is, he pulled it partly out, and then with one wild look dropped his knife and both he and the men who were looking on, took to their heels. The men who were tricing up, let go the rope, and the shark went down through the scuttle into the sea. Larry McBlather had extracted from the stomach of the shark the horrible, hideous, half-digested head of Simon Gobble.

Epilogue

Well, we don't think we could have found a more macabre finale to our adventures with the Bohemians! Now that your journey with Bret Harte's *Overland* writers has ended, you may be interested to know something about the fate of the magazine after Harte's departure in 1871.

The publisher, John H. Carmany, found the replacement of Bret to be a difficult job, indeed. After a succession of inefficient editors, William Bartlett took over the magazine and did a fine job with it, as did Benjamin P. Avery, his successor and the last editor of the old *Overland*. In 1875, when Avery was appointed Minister to China, Carmany ended its publication, claiming that the venture had cost him thirty thousand dollars and, in his words, "I grew tired of throwing my money away." But he added, "I shall always look back to that period of my life as the brightest of my existence in connection and close association with the stars of California literature. And they have reason to remember me, for never have such prices been paid for poems, stories and articles as I paid to the writers of the old *Overland*."

The magazine was later resurrected and published well into the 20th century. But the real glory days of the *Overland* were gone with Bret Harte. And what became of Harte? When he left San Francisco he journeyed to Chicago where he had been offered his own magazine, to be known as *The Lakeside*. Harte failed to show up at the banquet held to finalize the deal, and his backers withdrew their offer. His absence was blamed on his wife, who some of Harte's friends recalled as a very domineering woman. Because she had not been invited to the dinner, they claimed, she did not allow Harte to attend.

Harte then moved on to Boston where he was offered a ten thousand dollar retainer by the *Atlantic Monthly*. Whatever was done to earn such a stipend has been hotly debated over the years, the most vocal claiming that Harte did not produce one word to earn his money. He worked in the East until 1878, when a Republican president appointed him consul at Crefeld, a small Rhenish city in Germany. Here, as in his position at the San Francisco mint, Bret enjoyed abundant leisure as well as a comfortable income. In 1880 he was transferred to Glasgow, Scotland. Finally, in 1885, Harte was discharged by a Democratic president, and he left for London where he made his home until his death in 1902.

Noah Brooks claimed that Harte was always impatient, even bored, with the crudeness and unfinished aspect of things American. He loved the leisure and comforts of England where he was welcomed into the homes of the most exclusive set of English nobility and gentry. He was as companionable and fascinating to them as he had ever been to the good fellows of San Francisco and New York.

A memorial issue honoring Harte was published in September, 1902 in the *Overland Monthly*. In this issue the survivors of the old *Overland* days recalled some of their Bret Harte memorabilia. It was Joaquin Miller who composed the following verse bidding a last farewell to Harte:

Good Bye, Bret Harte!
by Joaquin Miller

Yon yellow sun melts in the sea;
A somber ship sweeps silently
Past Alcatraz tow'rd Orient skies —
A mist is rising to the eyes —
   Good bye, Bret Harte, good night, good night!

Your sea bank booms far funeral guns! —
What secrets of His central suns,
Companion of the peak and pine,
What secrets of the spheres are thine?
   Good bye, Bret Harte, good night, good night!

You loved the lowly, laughed at pride,
We mocked, we mocked and pierced your side;
And yet for all harsh scoffings heard,
You answered not one unkind word,
   But went your way, as now: Good night!

How stately tall your ship, how vast,
With night nailed to your leaning mast
With mighty stars of hammered gold
And moon-wrought cordage manifold!
   Good bye, Bret Harte, good night, good night!

            — *Memorial Day, 1902*
               The Hights

INDEX

The Bohemians II

If the *Overland's* light was dimmed with Bret Harte's departure, it was still bright enough to attract contributions from a whole new generation of Western writers, including Jack London, Joaquin Miller, John Muir, Frances Fuller Victor, and a host of others. A second volume of *The Bohemians* is now in preparation and will include more fascinating tales taken from the *Overland* years of 1870 to 1875. If you enjoyed these stories, then prepare yourself for more exciting adventures in *The Bohemians II*.

Other Books

by Robert A. Bennett

Walla Walla
  Portrait of a Western Town, 1804-1899

Walla Walla
  A Town Built to be a City, 1900-1919

We'll All Go Home in the Spring
  Personal Accounts and Adventures as Told by the Pioneers of the West

A Small World of Our Own
  Authentic Pioneer Stories of the Pacific Northwest from the Old Settlers
  Contest of 1892

Pioneer Press Books
35 South Palouse
Walla Walla, WA 99362